The Structure of Discourse-Pragmatic Variation

Studies in Language Variation

The series aims to include empirical studies of linguistic variation as well as its description, explanation and interpretation in structural, social and cognitive terms. The series will cover any relevant subdiscipline: sociolinguistics, contact linguistics, dialectology, historical linguistics, anthropology/anthropological linguistics. The emphasis will be on linguistic aspects and on the interaction between linguistic and extralinguistic aspects — not on extralinguistic aspects (including language ideology, policy etc.) as such.

For an overview of all books published in this series, please see *http://benjamins.com/catalog/silv*

Editors

Volume 13

The Structure of Discourse-Pragmatic Variation
by Heike Pichler

The Structure of
Discourse-Pragmatic Variation

Heike Pichler
Newcastle University

John Benjamins Publishing Company

Amsterdam / Philadelphia

The paper used in this publication meets the minimum requirements of
the American National Standard for Information Sciences – Permanence
of Paper for Printed Library Materials, ANSI Z39.48-1984.

Library of Congress Cataloging-in-Publication Data

Pichler, Heike.
  The structure of discourse-pragmatic variation / Heike Pichler.
      p.   cm. (Studies in Language Variation, ISSN 1872-9592 ; v. 13)
  Includes bibliographical references and index.
  1. Pragmatics. 2. Discourse markers. 3. Linguistic change. I. Title.
  P99.4.P72P434   2013
  401ʼ.41--dc23   2012048981
  ISBN 978 90 272 3493 3   (Hb ; alk. paper)
  ISBN 978 90 272 7218 8   (Eb)

John Benjamins Publishing Co. · P.O. Box 36224 · 1020 ME Amsterdam · The Netherlands
John Benjamins North America · P.O. Box 27519 · Philadelphia PA 19118-0519 · USA

Table of contents

Part II

List of figures

List of tables

List of abbreviations
and typographical conventions

BNC	British National Corpus
BwE	Berwick English
CA	conversation analysis
COLT	Corpus of London Teenage Speech
CPP	Cognitive Prominence Principle
CTRP	complex Transition Relevance Place
LIC	Linguistics Innovator Corpus
NEG-TAGS	negative polarity question tags
OED	Oxford English Dictionary
p	proposition
SAP	Social Agreement Principle
TAM	tense-aspect-modality
TCU	turn-constructional unit
TQ	tag question
*	denotes grammatically incorrect sentences

SMALL CAPITALS denote the discourse-pragmatic variables analysed in Part II
the primary verbs BE, HAVE and DO as lexical items

lower case italics denote the formal variants of the discourse-pragmatic variables
analysed in Part II
discourse-pragmatic variables other than the ones
analysed in Part II
grammatical forms of the primary verbs BE, HAVE and DO

Key to transcription conventions

[ ], [[ ]]	overlap
==	latching
=	turn continuation
-	false start, truncation
" "	quoted speech
(h), (.h)	inbreath, outbreath
@	laughter
+	tisking
%	sniffle
$	swallowing
<@ @>	produced with laughter
<£ £>	produced with smiley voice or suppressed laughter
< >	increased tempo
> <	reduced tempo
CAPITALS	louder than surrounding talk
underlining	emphatic stress
o o	soft speech
superscript font	higher than usual pitch
subscript font	lower than usual pitch
:, ::	syllable lengthening
(.), (..), (…)	short, medium, long pause
.	final intonation contour
,	continuing intonation contour
?	rising intonation contour
(text)	uncertain transcription
(?)	undecipherable words
((text))	extra-linguistic information
italics	used in examples to highlight the variable/variant discussed in the text

Glossary of dialect words

aggro	bother, inconvenience
auld	old
aye	yes
bog	toilet
cannae	can't
cannit	can't
Cockney	person from/dialect of London
dear	expensive
dinnae	don't
divn't	don't
doylem	idiot
fither	father
frae	from
gie	give
Geordie	person from/dialect of Newcastle/Tyneside
hae	have
hantle	head
heed	head
jougle	dog
kecks	trousers, underpants
ken	know
knaa	know
knacker	strenuous work
mind	remember
mingin	dirty, gross
-nae	-n't
nay	no
no	not
nowt	nothing
pet	love (endearment form)
skint	short of money
twang	language, dialect
wa	our
whae	who
wi	with
winnae	won't
youse	you

Acknowledgements

Writing this book has been both challenging and rewarding, and I count myself lucky to have learned from ongoing discussions with some of the very best: Jenny Cheshire, Alex D'Arcy, Stephen Levey, Sali Tagliamonte and Elizabeth Traugott. Many other fellow linguists have provided invaluable support and advice at various stages in the writing process: Alex Bellem, Oliver Bond, Lynn Clark, Karen Corrigan, Liesbeth Degand, Damien Hall, Daniel Ezra Johnson, Yuni Kim, Nick Roberts, Jane Setter, Dominic Watt and many others who, though not mentioned, have not been forgotten. Gisle Andersen, Elizabeth Traugott, Suzanne Evans Wagner and two anonymous reviewers have provided detailed and helpful comments on parts or the whole of earlier drafts of this book for which I am grateful. Of course, any remaining shortcomings of the book remain my own responsibility. Anne Sherwin came to the rescue when my stress levels failed to cope with EndNote, and Jeff Wilson helped with technical issues at the very end. I thank Paul Kerswill for inviting me to submit the manuscript to SiLV. At John Benjamins, the series editor Peter Auer, the acquisition editor Anke de Looper and the production coordinator Patricia Leplae have patiently provided guidance throughout the writing and production process.

To my family in Austria I must apologise for the numerous occasions where I was too busy to return their calls or thank them for their unconditional supply of chocolates. Thank you to Sue Fox, Erika Fulop, Iris Gruber-La Sala, Martha Marizzi, Martina Pfeiler, Annu Rist and Fran Sanchez for keeping me on-line company during insane hours and for providing encouragement when I needed it. Cheers to Olly Bond and Yuni Kim for entertainment and laughter. Andy Gordon has been my rock of love and support through all of this. Thank you for everything.

And, finally, thank you to the people of Berwick for supplying the discourse-pragmatic variables celebrated in this book.

PART I

CHAPTER 1

Introduction

1.1 Variationist sociolinguistics and discourse-pragmatic features

Variationist sociolinguistics emphasises the importance of analysing language in its social context and treats language *use* as the central object of study. The systematic focus on analysing actual language use has produced an ever-growing body of empirical evidence to support three principal tenets: (1) that language use is highly variable, and that this variability evinces "structured heterogeneity" (Weinreich et al. 1968: 99–100) along multiple extra- and intra-linguistic factors; (2) that language use is in a constant state of flux, and that these fluctuations are regular, rule-governed and observable in synchronic language variation; (3) that language use conveys social meanings, and that these social indexicalities are reflected in structured patterns of linguistic variation and change. Support for these tenets has been provided mainly by analyses of phonological and, to a somewhat lesser degree, morpho-syntactic features. Although the use of discourse-pragmatic features, i.e., polyfunctional linguistic items and constructions such as *oh, just, so, I mean, mind you, stuff like that*, is also variable, changeable and accessible for creating social indices, the number of studies which have systematically correlated their use with contextual predictors is comparatively modest. This has led Macaulay (2002a: 298) to lament that "the study of discourse variation is still at an elementary stage" (see also Pichler 2010: 582).

The present investigation supports Macaulay's (2002a, 2005) call for a fuller integration of discourse-pragmatic features into the variationist research agenda. It develops an innovative, multidimensional methodology which accommodates the full complexity of variation and change in the use of the conventionalised polyfunctional elements introduced above. It applies this methodology to exploring patterns of variation and change in the use of three selected variables, each of whose variants are derived from the same source construction but differ in terms of their morpho-phonological encoding: I DON'T KNOW, I DON'T THINK and negative polarity question tags (henceforth NEG-TAGS). Principled and accountable analyses of these variables in a corpus of interview data collected in Berwick upon Tweed, north-east England, reveal important new insights into: the creation and organisation of discourse-pragmatic variability; the role of discourse-pragmatic variables in shaping synchronic language variation; and the way in which discourse-pragmatic variants acquire their social indexicality. By way of uncovering new findings which enrich and illuminate current models of language variation and change, this study demonstrates the importance of discourse variation analysis for testing and developing current theories of language.

This chapter provides an introduction to the variationist analysis of discourse-pragmatic features more generally and to the present investigation more specifically. Section 1.2 outlines how the class of discourse-pragmatic features and the boundaries of discourse variation analysis have been delimited for the purpose of this investigation. It demonstrates how the term 'discourse-pragmatic features' is used here in a non-traditional way to refer to the category of items and constructions that elsewhere tend to be subsumed under the labels 'discourse markers' or 'pragmatic particles,' and provides a rationale for the choice of terminology used. Section 1.3 explores the theoretical and methodological reasons for the neglect of discourse-pragmatic features in the variationist literature. The descriptive and theoretical value of extending the scope of variationist research to encompass discourse-pragmatic variables is detailed in Section 1.4. Finally, Sections 1.5 and 1.6 provide an overview of the aims and the structure of this book.

1.2 Discourse-pragmatic features: Definition of scope and terminology

As a result of their formal and functional heterogeneity and the fact that they have been studied within a diversity of analytical and theoretical frameworks (see, for example, Schiffrin 2001; Schourup 1999 for overviews), there is as yet no general consensus on such fundamental issues as the terminology applied to the category of linguistic elements referred to in this book as discourse-pragmatic features, the inventory of elements to be included in this category, or the linguistic properties uniting them as a category (see, for example, Brinton 1996: Chapter 2; Fischer 2006; Jucker & Ziv 1998; Schourup 1999 for overviews of relevant debates). Therefore, it is necessary to specify at the outset how this study defines the scope of the category and the terminology used.

Although this approach is not without its sceptics (see, for example, Fischer 2006: 5–7), the present study adopts the widespread practice to delineate the category of linguistic elements studied in this book on functional-pragmatic grounds. In this definition, discourse-pragmatic features constitute a formally heterogeneous category of syntactically optional elements which make little or no contribution to the truth-conditional meaning of their host units and – depending on their scope, linguistic co-text as well as sequential, situational and cognitive context – perform one or more of the following macro-functions: to express speaker stance; to guide utterance interpretation; and to structure discourse. In recognising the potential for discourse-pragmatic features to have variable scope and to perform multiple pragmatic and/or procedural functions, sometimes simultaneously, the current definition of the category is much broader than the seminal definitions provided by Blakemore (1987: 125, "expressions used to indicate how the relevance of one discourse segment is dependent on another"), Fraser (1999: 931, items that "signal a relationship between the interpretation of the segment they introduce, S2, and the prior segment, S1"), Östman (1981: 5, items that "'implicitly anchor' the utterance in which they function, to the speaker's attitudes towards aspects of the on-going interaction"), Schiffrin (1987: 31, "sequentially dependent elements which bracket units of talk"), or Schourup (1999: 234, items "used to relate [an] utterance to the immediately preceding utterance"). The breadth of the current definition and the preference for the label 'discourse-pragmatic features' as an umbrella term for the linguistic elements discussed in this book challenge the terminological and typological distinction made by Fraser (1990) between 'discourse markers,' which perform a structural role, and 'pragmatic particles,' which express speaker stance. Fraser's distinction is untenable in light of the evidence provided in Chapters 4 to 6 which shows that individual discourse-pragmatic features rarely perform only one of these broad functions. Regular use in this book of the alternative labels 'discourse-pragmatic variables' or 'formulaic constructions' reflects the methodological and conceptual approach it takes to the analysis of what are more neutrally called discourse-pragmatic features. The term 'construction' is used in a pre-theoretical way to refer to syntagmatic strings, and does not reflect a Construction Grammar view of the data (Goldberg 1995; Kay & Fillmore 1999); 'formulaic' is used in opposition to 'productive' to emphasise the conventionalised and non-compositional nature of discourse-pragmatic features (Wray 2002).

The current definition of discourse-pragmatic features further diverges from those presented elsewhere for the category of conventionalised polyfunctional elements described above in that it does not recognise as a unifying property of its members formal-syntactic specifications such as shortness, phonetic reduction, lack of stress and sentence-initial or -external positioning (see, for example, Brinton 1996: 33–34; Jucker & Ziv 1998: 3; Schiffrin 1987: 328). Strong adherence to these criteria would entail excluding from the category of discourse-pragmatic features comment clauses such as *I (don't) know, I (don't) think, as you know, what's more* and clause-final tags such as *don't you, isn't that so, you know what I mean, or something like that* because they do not consistently meet all of the phonological, prosodic and syntactic properties stipulated in the literature cited above. Considering, however, their strong resemblance to more prototypical discourse-pragmatic features in terms of their functional versatility and diachronic development (see further Brinton 2006, 2008; Hoffmann 2006), the exclusion of comment clauses and clause-final tags from the category of discourse-pragmatic features is theoretically unjustified and counter-productive to developing a comprehensive theory of linguistic elements that function primarily in the non-referential domains of language use.

The scope of discourse variation analysis in this book is delimited to the quantitative analysis of patterns of variation and change in the use of discourse-pragmatic features as defined above. Unlike other scholars (e.g. Jucker & Taavitsainen 2012; Macaulay 2002a; Schneider & Barron 2008), I do not include in my discussion and analysis of discourse-pragmatic variation and change the variable realisation or functionality of: pragmatic units such as speech acts; interactional strategies such as turn-exchange, topic-selection and back-channelling; or sequence structures such as greeting and leave-taking rituals. As shown *inter alia* by Barron (2008), Coupland (1983) and Johnstone (1990), these phenomena are also variable and mutable, and their variationist analysis is very valuable. The exclusion of these phenomena from the present investigation is dictated purely by considerations of scope.

1.3   Reasons for the neglect of discourse-pragmatic features in variationist research

At least two reasons can be identified why to date discourse-pragmatic features have not figured as prominently on the variationist research agenda as phonological or morpho-syntactic features. First, because their status in the linguistic system is different from that of other linguistic elements, discourse-pragmatic features are often described in negative terms and marginalised in traditional frameworks of grammar and linguistic analysis. Second, due to their unique semiotic, syntactic and functional characteristics, discourse-pragmatic features present a number of methodological challenges for variationist analysis which are not easily overcome. This section explores in more detail the theoretical and methodological reasons for the relative neglect of discourse-pragmatic features in (variationist) linguistic research, and examines recent shifts in how they are theorised and quantified.

Discourse-pragmatic features derive from diverse syntactic sources (including, amongst others, subject-verb combinations, adverbials, conjunctions and interjections), and they do not occupy a fixed syntactic position. Therefore, they cannot be described as constituting a homogeneous word class whose members share a set of morpho-syntactic properties. In addition to defying syntactic classification, discourse-pragmatic features eschew lexical definition. They do not generally communicate referential content but function to encode pragmatic and procedural meanings which are not easy to specify in lexical terms. Their indeterminate grammatical status and general lack of truth-conditional meaning have routinely been adduced as evidence that discourse-pragmatic features are extra- or a-grammatical elements of language which are not part of sentence grammar (Goldberg 1980; Stein 1985:99) and which can be marginalised as meaningless verbal fillers and superfluous hesitation markers (Brown 1977; Lakoff 1973). As such, they have been regularly dismissed as pseudo-linguistic devices not warranting scholarly investigation.[1]

Evidence from speech perception experiments (e.g. Parton et al. 2002; Russell et al. 2008), the media (e.g. Petersen 2004; the quotes in Levey 2003) as well as websites created by self-proclaimed communication experts (e.g. Berkley 2002) suggests that although speakers may be aware of the specific pragmatic meanings associated with individual features (Fox Tree 2007), negative perceptions and pre-scriptive stigmatisations of discourse-pragmatic features similar to those outlined above continue to be widespread among non-linguists, even those who make fre-quent use of such features themselves (Watts 1989). Amongst linguists, by contrast, a dramatic re-orientation in the evaluation and theorisation of discourse-pragmatic features has taken place since the 1980s. With the growing interest in "language above the sentence or above the clause" (Stubbs 1983:1) and in "the purpose or functions which [linguistic] forms are designed to serve in human affairs" (Brown & Yule 1983:1), scholars have begun to investigate the role of discourse-pragmatic features in the production, comprehension and interpretation of discourse. The seminal works on discourse-pragmatic features published in the 1980s (Blakemore 1987; Erman 1987; Östman 1981; Schiffrin 1987; Schourup 1985) as well as the subsequent proliferation of qualitative studies investigating the distribution and functionality of individual features have demonstrated that widespread assump-tions about their extra-grammatical status and superfluous nature are erroneous.

Scholars investigating the syntactic distribution, linguistic properties and multi-functionality of discourse-pragmatic features have convincingly demon-strated that they are not overt manifestations of verbal dysfluencies and inarticu-lateness, and that they indubitably constitute integral and indispensable elements of the core linguistic system. For example, Levey (2006:431–432) argues that dis-course *like* is not symptomatic of production problems or poor syntactic plan-ning because its rate of occurrence with aborted utterances or false starts is fairly low. Traugott (2003a; see also Traugott & Dasher 2002:158–159) postulates that discourse-pragmatic features occupy highly constrained sequential and syntactic positions. Recent variationist studies provide quantitative evidence in support of

---

1. Not all frameworks relegate discourse-pragmatic features to the periphery. Construction grammar, for example, does not distinguish between 'core' and 'peripheral' phenomena of gram-mar (Gisborne & Trousdale 2008). (See also further below on Kaltenböck et al.'s (2011) thetical grammar approach to theorising discourse-pragmatic features.)

this premise, demonstrating that the syntagmatic order of discourse-pragmatic features and other clausal constituents is far from random (Andersen 2001: 272–286; D'Arcy 2007: 480–482; Tagliamonte 2005). Observations such as these show that "in constituent structure terms [discourse-pragmatic features] are [core elements] of the structure of a sentence" (Traugott 2003a: 643) which cannot be disregarded in linguistic analysis on the basis of being marginal or peripheral to sentence grammar. Additional support for viewing discourse-pragmatic features as legitimate grammatical phenomena is provided by proponents of non-traditional conceptions of grammar. Kaltenböck et al. (2011) draw on the distinct linguistic properties of what they call 'theticals' (e.g. their prosodic and syntactic independence, positional mobility, non-restrictive meaning) to argue that they belong to thetical grammar, a domain of discourse grammar that is structurally independent from but not subordinate to sentence grammar. Other scholars, including Brinton (2006), Diewald (2006), Traugott (2003a) and the contributors in Degand & Simon-Vandenbergen (2011), argue in favour of extending the traditional notion of grammar beyond the level of the clause so that grammatical function is understood as an open category which comprises not just syntactic functions such as subject, object, complement, etc. but also pragmatic and procedural functions such as stance expression and discourse organisation. On this basis, discourse-pragmatic features are conceptualised as performing "genuine grammatical functions" (Diewald 2006: 424) which may be optional in terms of constituent structure but which are obligatory in terms of their pragmatic and interactional contribution to discourse.

Although some linguists continue to cite the syntactic flexibility and optionality as well as the lack of referential meaning of discourse-pragmatic features as evidence for their peripheral status in the linguistic system (see, for example, Eckardt 2012), the general consensus today is that discourse-pragmatic features are core elements of grammar which constitute *bona fide* objects of linguistic enquiry. As implied above, variationist sociolinguistics has the potential to corroborate claims about the grammatical status of discourse-pragmatic features through provision of quantitative empirical evidence of their usage and distribution in discourse. However, attempts to provide such evidence have been complicated by methodological issues.

The variationist paradigm was originally developed by Labov (1963, 1966) for the analysis of phonological variation and has been successfully applied to the analysis of morpho-syntactic variation. Yet because of fundamental differences in the nature and use of lower- and higher-level linguistic features, scholars have questioned the feasibility of extending the Labovian paradigm to the analysis of variation and change in discourse (and syntax) (see *inter alia* Cheshire 1987; Lavandera 1978; Romaine 1984; Winford 1984). Discourse-pragmatic features do not easily satisfy the criteria set out by Labov (1972) for the linguistic variable, the

principal methodological tool in variationist analysis. Firstly, the operation of semantic-pragmatic and interactional-situational constraints on the use of discourse-
pragmatic features regularly affects the frequency critical for quantitative analysis
(Labov 1972: 8). Secondly, their unique semiotic nature, intrinsic multifunctionality and great context-sensitivity prohibit most discourse-pragmatic variants from
being identified on the basis of semantic equivalence (Labov 1972: 271). Thirdly,
the syntactic mobility of discourse-pragmatic features as well as their multi-faceted
meanings and functional overlap with features from other components of language
cause difficulty in defining the scope of analyses. This hampers attempts to quantify
discourse-pragmatic variation in an accountable manner (Labov 1972: 71–72). As
a result of the aforementioned factors, discourse-pragmatic features have been
shunned in the early decades of variationist research.

In more recent decades, though, some progress has been made in addressing
the methodological challenges outlined above and bringing discourse-pragmatic
features more firmly under the remit of variationist linguistics. Dines (1980)
and Lavandera (1978) proposed to resolve issues in conceptualising discourse-
pragmatic features as linguistic variables by substituting the condition of semantic equivalence with one of functional comparability between variants (see also
Sankoff & Thibault 1981). Others argued that information about the social or
stylistic distribution of discourse-pragmatic features could be garnered from normalised frequency tabulations, usually given as the number of tokens per 1,000 or
10,000 words (Stubbe & Holmes 1995). Holmes (1986, 1987) devised methods for
providing accounts of discourse-pragmatic variation which consider the variable
functionality of discourse-pragmatic features in signalling social group membership. Finally, D'Arcy (2005) circumscribed the variable context of discourse *like* on
the basis of syntactic criteria in order to yield insights into its linguistic-structural
conditioning. While none of these studies have succeeded in fully resolving the
range of methodological challenges outlined earlier (see further Pichler 2010 and
Chapter 2.3), they nevertheless represent important milestones in the development
of discourse variation analysis.

As a result of the growing recognition that there is no theoretical reason for
exempting discourse-pragmatic features from variationist analysis and that their
quantitative analysis, albeit challenging and complex, is in fact feasible, recent
decades have witnessed a moderate expansion in discourse variation studies. The
next section will outline the value of variationist discourse analysis for different
subfields of linguistics.

1.4 Arguments in favour of the quantitative analysis of discourse-pragmatic features

Some qualitative scholars downplay the value of quantitative discourse studies, suggesting, for example, that a focus on distributional frequencies may yield skewed descriptions of the functionality of discourse-pragmatic features (Hansen 2006: 21–22) or that quantitative studies are simply futile (see Tottie 1992: 121). While it is true that quantification entails an inevitable degree of abstraction, observations such as these underestimate the methodological rigour of quantitative discourse studies as well as their descriptive and explanatory value within and beyond variationist linguistics. Variationist discourse studies are critical to providing comprehensive and accurate descriptions of social and geographical dialect variation and to formulating a holistic theory of language variation and change which, by definition, must be based on systematic analyses of all components of language, including discourse-pragmatics. Further, they are instrumental in enriching the empirical basis required to develop accurate descriptions and coherent theories of the characteristic linguistic properties and typical evolutionary trajectories of discourse-pragmatic features.

The variationist discourse studies carried out to date consistently highlight the fact that discourse-pragmatic features, like features at other levels of the linguistic system, evince orderly heterogeneity and undergo regular rule-governed change. In terms of variability, they have shown that correlations between linguistic variation patterns and socio-demographic categories, amply documented for variables in phonology and morpho-syntax, also emerge at the level of discourse-pragmatics (Macaulay 2005; Stubbe & Holmes 1995). Despite their comparative infrequency, discourse-pragmatic variables may even demonstrate a greater amount of socially stratified variation than phonological variables (Woods 1991). Third-wave variation studies indicate that discourse-pragmatic variables resemble other variables in constituting an important means for indexing social identities: variation in their use and design contributes to the negotiation of group-specific styles (Bakht 2010; Drager 2011; Moore & Podesva 2009). Additional evidence for the social salience of discourse-pragmatic features in the minds of speakers and hearers has been furnished by experimental studies. For example, Andersen et al.'s (1999) research into first language acquisition reveals that children as young as four years old are sensitive to the social meanings conveyed by discourse-pragmatic features: preschool children engaged in role-play used different sets of discourse-pragmatic features depending on whether they were impersonating lower-status or higher-status characters. Dines's (1980: 19–20) small-scale experiment in which middle-class speakers attributed a text to a working-class author on the basis that it contained general extenders, i.e., phrase- or clause-final constructions such as *and that, or something (like that)*, suggests that discourse-pragmatic features are productive resources for social stereotyping (see also Watts 1989).[2]

In terms of change, variationist discourse studies have shown that discourse-pragmatic features are an important source of linguistic innovations (Tagliamonte 2005, 2008). As is the case with innovative variants at other levels of the grammar, innovative variants in discourse-pragmatics spread by social and geographical diffusion (Buchstaller 2008; Buchstaller & D'Arcy 2009; Cheshire et al. 2005), and exhibit an adolescent peak in apparent-time change in progress, in line with Labov's (2001) logistic incrementation model (Tagliamonte & D'Arcy 2009). Moreover, discourse variation studies have demonstrated that changes in discourse-pragmatics affect both the function and the form of variables. Erman's (2001) study of *you know* in age-stratified datasets of London English reveals that young speakers use *you know* largely as a metalinguistic device, whereas adults use it largely as a textual device. Barbieri's (2008) exploration of language variation across the lifespan uncovers striking age-based differences in speakers' choice of discourse-pragmatic features to signal stance (see also Brinton [2001: 150–151] who argues that pragmatic functions endure while their form is continuously renewed). Finally, it has been shown that age-appropriate use of discourse-pragmatic features is part of speakers' sociolinguistic competence (Roth-Gordon 2007).

Yet despite the fact that they broadly conform to fundamental tenets of variationist sociolinguistics, it must not be assumed that discourse-pragmatic variables consistently exhibit patterns of sociolinguistic variation and change identical to those widely attested for phonological and lower-level morpho-syntactic variables. Cheshire et al.'s (2005) investigation of dialect convergence in contemporary British

---

2. Written social attitude questionnaires, matched-guise tests and other speech evaluation experiments have revealed that speakers harbour strong covert attitudes to discourse-pragmatic features. Their use is generally positively evaluated along social attractiveness/solidarity dimensions and negatively evaluated along status/competence dimensions (Buchstaller 2006b; Dailey-O'Cain 2000), so much so that frequent users of discourse-pragmatic features may be disadvantaged in the job hiring process (Parton et al. 2002; Russell et al. 2008). However, because experimental methods in discourse-pragmatics remain relatively unsophisticated in comparison to those recently developed in phonology, it is not clear which of the many (variable) properties of discourse-pragmatic features it is that trigger listeners' strong reactions to their use and users: their frequency; their role in constructing interactional styles; the way they seemingly disrupt the flow of discourse and the syntactic structure of utterances; or their regular occurrence in prosodically and pragmatically prominent positions. These are serious shortcomings, for, as pointed out by Kristiansen (2011: 277), our understanding of language variation and change depends, at least in part, on our understanding of "whether and how different aspects of language [use] may be differently available to awareness and/or social evaluation." To fully understand the social indexicality of discourse-pragmatic variation, it will be necessary to complement survey studies with well-designed experimental studies.

English reveals that whereas the social distribution of the tag variant *innit* parallels that of non-standard morpho-syntactic variants undergoing convergence, discourse *like* does not differentiate socio-economic groups in the same way as phonological innovations such as TH-fronting. Tagliamonte & D'Arcy's (2009) study of linguistic innovations in Toronto English also uncovers disparities between patterns of change in phonology and discourse-pragmatics. Although the patterns of BE *like*, *like* and *so* variation are analogous with those documented for phonological variables in exhibiting a peak in frequency during adolescence (see above), they do not mirror the patterns reported by Labov (2001) whereby males lag behind females in apparent-time incremental change in phonology. Instead, all three discourse-pragmatic variables (as well as a range of morpho-syntactic variables analysed) exhibit a lack of gender contrast in the apparent-time trajectory of change (see also D'Arcy 2005; Denis 2011). I will argue below that due to the unique semiotic properties of discourse-pragmatic features, their specific role in social interaction, and the multi-layered nature of their diachronic development, the findings summarised above may point towards more widespread differences in the distribution of discourse-pragmatic variables as opposed to other linguistic variables.

Phonological variables have no intrinsic referential meaning. Consequently, we can safely assume that their variants are identical in truth value and that patterns of variation in their rates of use reflect social group membership. Lower-level morpho-syntactic variants are regularly shown to parallel phonological variants in deriving their social meaning from their quantitative distribution across social cohorts (see, however, Levinson 1988: 166). Conversely, even though many discourse variation studies have drawn conclusions about the social indexicality of discourse-pragmatic variables on the basis of quantifying their frequency across independent social variables (Dailey-O'Cain 2000; Dines 1980; Dubois & Crouch 1975; Stubbe & Holmes 1995; Tagliamonte 2005), discourse-pragmatic variables are unlikely to differentiate social groups in purely quantitative terms. In contrast to phonological variables, discourse-pragmatic variables have by definition a meaning, for their use is motivated by their functionality. What scholars who quantify the use of discourse-pragmatic variables without studying them in their interactional context ignore is the fact that these meanings are multi-layered: individual variables encode multiple pragmatic meanings, often simultaneously. This property of discourse-pragmatic variables is crucial for indexing social group membership. Speakers exploit the multifunctionality of discourse-pragmatic variables to meet the specific interactional goals associated with particular speaker roles (Redeker 1990), to display and enhance their distinctiveness from members of other social groups (Cheshire 1981; Meyerhoff 1994; Moore & Podesva 2009; Starks et al. 2008), and to create or reinforce group-specific interactional styles (Barbieri 2008; Coates 2004: 88–92; Holmes 1986, 1995: 78–101; Macaulay 2002c).

It follows that the social embedding of discourse-pragmatic variation differs from that of phonological and lower-level morpho-syntactic variation in that it hinges on functionality at least as much as on frequency.

Variationist studies of sound change have plotted variants on a linear age-scale in order to establish the direction and social embedding of potential changes. The consistency of sex-differentiated patterns of change uncovered in these studies led Labov (1998) to formulate general principles of sound change which highlight the role of women as linguistic innovators: women lead in the importation of new prestige forms from outside the speech community, the elimination of forms that have become stigmatised, and changes that operate within the speech community (see, however, Labov 1963; Milroy & Milroy 1998). Foulkes & Docherty (1999:16) and Milroy et al. (1994) also draw attention to sex-differentiated patterns in the spread of sound change, proposing the following generalisations: women are instrumental in the spread of supra-local phonological variants, i.e., those that have a wide geographical distribution, while men favour the use of localised phonological variants, i.e., those that are characteristic of given localities. Due to deep-rooted differences in the linguistic conditioning of changes across lower- and higher-level linguistic variables, the above generalisations may not extend to discourse-pragmatic change in any straightforward way. Discourse-pragmatic features are generally understood to result from grammaticalisation which involves multiple changes affecting multiple levels of language use: phonetic reduction, decategorialisation, semantic-pragmatic shift (see further Chapter 2.4.1). These changes, although together constituting grammaticalisation, are separate processes which may not always co-evolve synchronously (Bisang 2004; Bybee 2010; Romaine 1995). Consequently, different processes of change may be advanced by different social groups at different points in time (see also Zilles 2005). Further, since the development of discourse-pragmatic features is not by necessity unidirectional or unidimensional (see, for example, Buchstaller [2004] who conceptualises the multifunctional uses of discourse *like* as a radial functional network), different social groups may initiate and advance different functional developments of individual variables (see D'Arcy 2005:222–224). Finally, because of the open-ended nature of the functional categories underpinning the conceptualisation of discourse-pragmatic features as linguistic variables (see further Chapter 2.3.2), different social groups may simultaneously propel the diffusion of different newcomer variants (see Tagliamonte 2008). It follows that, unlike the case in sound change, in discourse-pragmatic change it may not be possible to attribute the role of innovators to a single social group.

Beyond sharing with phonological and morpho-syntactic variables a capacity for diachronic change and social variation, discourse-pragmatic variables resemble other variables in being subject to geographical dialect variation. Recent discourse variation studies have revealed the following findings. Firstly, the occurrence of discourse-pragmatic variants may be geographically restricted (see, for example, Macaulay [2009] on the use of BE *all* as a quotative complementiser in Glasgow English; Sowa [2009] on the use of ADJECTIVE + *as* as an intensifier in Australian and New Zealand English). Secondly, their relative frequency and sociolinguistic distribution may vary across geographical space (see, for example, Cheshire et al. [2005] on the use of *innit* across three English towns; Denis [MS] on the use of *and stuff* in the English town of York and the Canadian city of Toronto). Thirdly, and relatedly, variants may be more socially diffused and more grammaticalised in some varieties than others (see, for example, Buchstaller & D'Arcy [2009] on quotative BE *like* in British, American and New Zealand English). Nonetheless, systematic accounts of dialect variation in discourse-pragmatics are virtually non-existent. For example, recently published overviews of British English dialect variation, including Hughes et al. (2012) as well as the contributions in Britain (2007) and Kortmann et al. (2004), focus almost exclusively on phonological and morpho-syntactic variation. Discourse-pragmatic variation is mentioned only in passing, if at all, thus leaving a large proportion of speakers' linguistic repertoires virtually unaccounted for.[3] The cause for this neglect does not lie with the authors or the editors of these volumes. Systematic analyses of discourse-pragmatic variation are in such short supply that attempts to reconcile the findings from individual studies into a coherent overview of geographical dialect variation reveal little else but glaring gaps in the canon of variables as well as localities that have been investigated. The problem is exacerbated by the fact that meaningful accounts of dialect variation in discourse-pragmatics cannot be produced based on cross-variety comparisons of variables' or variants' frequency rates. In order for such accounts to be of any descriptive or theoretical value at all, they require systematic comparison of the variable grammar underlying variables' or variants' use. Only if this information is readily available can scholars establish whether variables and their variants have the same social and functional meanings across varieties and whether they have been grammaticalising along identical paths, at identical speeds and to identical degrees. Alas, even where a sufficient number of studies are available that investigate discourse-pragmatic features' variable grammars, their results are not easily comparable due to a lack of uniform methodologies (see further Pichler 2010). It follows that the current dearth of systematic and accountable quantitative discourse studies is a serious shortcoming in descriptive sociolinguistics.

---

3. Fischer (2000: 11) and Rudolph (1991: 208) estimate that discourse-pragmatic features constitute between ten to 24 per cent of all words spoken in informal interactions.

In addition to being indispensable for establishing the precise nature and full extent of geographical dialect variation and for probing the robustness of long-standing principles of language variation and change that are based largely on the analysis of phonological and morpho-syntactic variables, discourse variation studies are of great value for advancing theories and descriptions of discourse-pragmatic features themselves. In stark contrast to their finite coverage in variationist linguistics, discourse-pragmatic features have figured very prominently in qualitative research paradigms. Qualitative discourse studies have investigated the linguistic attributes, functional versatility, context-boundedness and diachronic evolution of discourse-pragmatic features as well as, to a more limited extent, their cross-linguistic resemblance, use in bilingual interactions, and acquisition by children and second language learners (see, for example, Aijmer & Simon-Vandenbergen 2011; Brinton 1996: Chapter 2; Fischer 2006; Fox Tree 2010; Schiffrin 2001; Schourup 1999 for overviews). I will argue below that the patterns and regularities discovered in quantitative discourse studies can bear on a number of these issues, serving in particular to verify current and construct new descriptions of the usage, distribution and evolution of discourse-pragmatic features.

Through adherence to the "principle of accountability" (Labov 1972: 72), quantitative discourse studies exhaustively report all occurrences of a targeted variable in a given dataset. (Where it is possible to determine all potential environments for its occurrence, non-occurrences are also reported.) Because this approach generates accounts of discourse-pragmatic variables which are firmly grounded in the complete set of available data, it constitutes a valuable check on any descriptions provided by qualitative studies that are based on (either randomly or carefully) selected subsets of available tokens. For example, Andersen's (2001: 227–271) accountable analysis of the discourse-pragmatic variable *like* in the *Bergen Corpus of London Teenage Language* (henceforth COLT) established that discourse *like* performs a wide range of subjective, textual and quotative functions, with the former far outnumbering the latter. Andersen's findings thus challenge the comprehensiveness and adequateness of the descriptions yielded by Jucker & Smith's (1998), Miller & Weinert's (1995) and Romaine & Lange's (1991) qualitative studies which have foregrounded individual functions of *like* at the neglect of others. Moreover, quantitative methods make possible reliable comparison of the functional profile and proportional or relative frequency of discourse-pragmatic features across diverse social and interactional-situational contexts. As shown *inter alia* by Fuller (2003) and Schleef (2008), such comparisons have the potential to provide numerical evidence for claims made in the qualitative literature about the sensitivity of discourse-pragmatic features to external constraints.

Further insights which are relevant to modelling regularities in the usage and distribution of discourse-pragmatic features can be gleaned from the stepwise multiple-regression procedure incorporated in the variable rule programme (see further Chapter 2.3.3). By determining the relative importance of multiple contextual predictors on the distribution of variants when all predictors are considered simultaneously, this procedure yields fine-grained and reliable descriptions of the social, discourse-functional and linguistic-structural properties of discourse-pragmatic variables and their variants. For example, Pichler & Levey's (2011) multivariate analyses of general extenders in Berwick English discredit previous claims in the literature that general extenders function first and foremost to implicate a more general set (Dines 1980: 22–23), or that short variants occur by definition in extended morpho-syntactic contexts (Aijmer 2002: 249). When carried out on socially stratified real- or apparent-time data, multivariate analyses can also uncover subtle shifts over time in the sociolinguistic conditioning of discourse-pragmatic features which may serve to verify claims from the qualitative literature about features' diachronic development. For example, D'Arcy's (2005) multivariate analysis of discourse *like* in Toronto English models the gradual and systematic diffusion of *like* across syntactic contexts. The results challenge developmental trajectories of *like* depicted as preposition/conjunction > discourse marker (Meehan 1991) and contest claims that *like* underwent abrupt scope expansion (Romaine & Lange 1991). They postulate instead that *like* developed as a sentential adverb before it developed as a discourse marker. Moreover, variationist discourse studies of the kind described above can shed light on the social forces driving discourse-pragmatic developments. As shown *inter alia* by Andersen (2001) and Tagliamonte & D'Arcy (2007), these studies thus complement more traditional grammaticalisation research which focuses on the structural dimension and language-internal motivation of language change phenomena (see, for example, Brinton 1996, 2008).

The preceding discussion in no way negates the intrinsic value of qualitative discourse studies. Qualitative studies reveal patterns that may remain hidden in quantification, such as the clustering or scattering of discourse-pragmatic features at certain points of an interaction (Bell & Johnson 1997). Importantly, the distributional properties of discourse-pragmatic features cannot be interpreted accurately without qualitative investigation of their functionality (see further Chapter 2.5). The fact remains, though, that in addition to providing the empirical evidence required to advance current knowledge of language variation and change mechanisms, systematic, exhaustive and accountable quantitative analyses have the potential to test, validate and refine current models of discourse-pragmatic features.

1.5   Aims and focus of the book

This book reports the results of an in-depth investigation into patterns of variation and change in the morpho-phonological encoding of three discourse-pragmatic variables in the variety of English spoken in Berwick upon Tweed, a small market town in the far north-east of England. The variables chosen for analysis are the negative polarity constructions I DON'T KNOW, I DON'T THINK and NEG-TAGS. They are construed as linguistic variables by virtue of the fact that their respective variants (differentiated by the variable realisation of the negative auxiliary and/or the optional fusion of adjacent morphemes) are derivations of the same linear string of components (see further Chapter 2.3.2). Research investigating these variables in other varieties has shown that their formal variability is closely constrained by extra- and intra-linguistic predictors (Andersen 2001; Bybee & Scheibman 1999; Cheshire 1981). The principal objective of the current investigation is to establish whether similar constraints on variant choice are also operative in the present dataset of Berwick English (henceforth BwE) where non-localised variants co-exist alongside supra-local and localised variants in the pool of available variants. By establishing the sociolinguistic mechanisms that give rise to observed patterns of variability in the form, frequency and strategic use of the selected variables, this project uncovers important new insights into the creation and organisation of synchronic language variation. It thereby demonstrates the important contribution discourse variation analysis can make to current theories of language.

To achieve the objectives set out above and capture the complex nature of discourse-pragmatic variation and change without sacrificing accountability, the study develops an innovative methodology which combines the theoretical insights and empirical methods from variationist sociolinguistics, grammaticalisation studies and conversation analysis. Close integration of these approaches combined with new ways of conceptualising discourse-pragmatic variables, closing the envelope of variation, and quantifying multifunctionality ensure reliable and intersubjective results as well as accountable and theoretically relevant explanations of these results. Through full articulation and detailed illustration of the methodology, the study provides a framework in which future studies can be planned and executed.

The viability of the approach is demonstrated by the empirical and theoretical insights it affords. The results of the analysis demonstrate that the availability of a range of formal variants to encode discourse-pragmatic variables is strategically exploited by speakers: the variation between non-localised variants of I DON'T KNOW and I DON'T THINK signals important meaning differences; the use of localised/supra-local variants of I DON'T KNOW, I DON'T THINK and NEG-TAGS indexes social identities which are closely linked to variables' and/or variants' functional compartmentalisation in the variety. These correlations highlight the centrality of discourse-functional constraints in accounting for formal and social variation patterns in discourse-pragmatics, and demonstrate the complex and potentially isomorphic nature of discourse-pragmatic variability. Moreover, the analysis uncovers that the different realisations of negative periphrastic DO in BwE do not have the same social and functional meanings across the formulaic and productive constructions investigated in this book. These differences highlight the prominent role of formulaic constructions in shaping linguistic variation, and demonstrate that the diachronic processes creating synchronic variation affect constructions heterogeneously. Close inspection of variant distributions affords far-reaching hypotheses about the social and interactional causes of this heterogeneity. In sum, the investigation shows that systematic and accountable analyses of discourse-pragmatic features are crucial to advancing current understanding of the sociolinguistic embedding of language variation as well as the sociolinguistic mechanisms creating it.

1.6 Organisation of the book

Part I consists of three chapters which provide the context for the empirical analysis of the selected discourse-pragmatic variables in Part II. Chapter 1 has reviewed the current state of discourse variation analysis and has outlined reasons for the fuller integration of discourse-pragmatic features in variationist research. Chapter 2 introduces the corpus data on which this analysis is based and articulates the innovative methodology developed for this project to uncover patterns of variation and change in the formal encoding of I DON'T KNOW, I DON'T THINK and NEG-TAGS. To contextualise patterns of variation and change in the use of these variables, Chapter 3 introduces the verb negation system of BwE and explores its variability in productive constructions. This chapter also introduces in more detail the discourse-pragmatic variables chosen for in-depth analysis in Part II.

Part II constitutes the analytical heart of the book. It is divided into three chapters, one for each of the selected variables. The three chapters are organised uniformly to facilitate comparison of the analyses and results. Each chapter begins with a short general introduction and a thorough review of previous studies investigating the targeted variable. There follows an outline of how the variable was circumscribed and how the data were coded for quantitative analysis. A concise description of the multiple functions performed by each variable in the BwE data precedes the quantitative analysis which tests the combined impact on the observed variation of multiple contextual factors. In the discussion section, the findings obtained from the quantitative analysis are compared with those obtained in related studies, and the mechanisms giving rise to the variable's synchronic distribution patterns are examined. This is necessary to understand the nature and origin of the formal and functional variation in the data, and to appreciate the complex mechanisms underlying discourse-pragmatic variability which are explored further in Part III. Although Chapters 4 to 6 build on each other to cumulatively demonstrate the complex nature of discourse-pragmatic variation and change as well as the central role of discourse-pragmatic variables in the linguistic system, the chapters are organised in such a way that they can act as self-contained standalone studies. Inevitably, this leads to some repetition of methodological information across the three chapters.

Part III assesses the methodological and theoretical implications of the results obtained in Part II as well as the future of the field. Chapter 7 synthesises the results produced in Part II with a view to: (1) demonstrating their far-reaching methodological and theoretical implications for grammaticalisation studies and variationist sociolinguistics; (2) illuminating why discourse-pragmatic variables do not correspond fully to patterns of variation and change reported for other levels of the linguistic system; and (3) illustrating the fully grammatical status of discourse-pragmatic variables in the linguistic system. Finally, Chapter 8 identifies and explores some of the challenges discourse variation analysis still faces in its attempt to provide comprehensive accounts of discourse-pragmatic variation and change. Some suggestions are provided as to how these challenges might be overcome and how the field might be advanced beyond its current state.

Data, methodology
and theoretical framework

2.1 Introduction

The present investigation explores the sociolinguistic mechanisms underlying patterns of variation and change in the morpho-phonological encoding of the discourse-pragmatic variables I DON'T KNOW, I DON'T THINK and NEG-TAGS with a view to providing new insights into the structure of discourse-pragmatic variation and demonstrating the descriptive, explanatory and theoretical value of discourse variation analysis. Achievement of these objectives is contingent on a methodology which computes discourse-pragmatic variation and change in a principled and accountable manner. Alas, this criterion is not easily met, for discourse-pragmatic features eschew easy definition as linguistic variables. Identifying all contexts in which a discourse-pragmatic feature can occur and closing off the set of competing variants are far from straightforward tasks. Matters are complicated by the fact that discourse-pragmatic features are variable and changeable on multiple, closely interlinked levels: their frequency, form and functionality as well as their distribution across morpho-syntactic contexts, interactional-situational settings and social groups. What is needed, then, to provide a comprehensive and illuminative account of discourse-pragmatic variation and change is a multidimensional methodology which accommodates the full complexity of synchronic discourse-pragmatic variation.

The innovative methodology developed for the present investigation and outlined in part in Pichler (2010) meets this criterion. It combines the empirical methods and theoretical insights from variationist sociolinguistics, grammaticalisation studies and conversation analysis (henceforth CA) in order to uncover and account for patterns of formal discourse variation and change in synchronic dialect data. Insights from variationist sociolinguistics inform the sampling decisions and data collection methods; the quantitative methods associated with the variationist paradigm are employed to determine the joint effect of contextual factors on observed patterns of variation. The grammaticalisation framework provides hypotheses about the nature and trajectory of linguistic changes; these hypotheses inform the coding decisions as well as the interpretation of the synchronic distribution patterns of discourse-pragmatic variants. Finally, CA theories and methods are drawn on in the qualitative data analysis to establish the functional repertoires of the selected variables and allocate each token of the variables to a functional category; these categories constitute factors of the factor group functionality which is included in the quantitative data analyses to determine its impact on variant choice. The analyses in Part II will demonstrate that a multidimensional approach like the one introduced here is a methodological necessity if our aims are: to capture the complex nature of discourse-pragmatic variation and change, and to fully understand its underlying mechanisms.

The remainder of this chapter introduces in more detail the theoretical and analytical framework that underpins the present investigation as well as the data on which the investigation is based. Section 2.2 describes the corpus and provides details about the design of the speaker sample. It includes a critical assessment of the strengths and limitations of interview data for variationist discourse studies as well as a rationale for the choice of extra-linguistic variables used. The theories and methods associated with variationist sociolinguistics, the grammaticalisation framework and CA are introduced in Sections 2.3 to 2.5. Section 2.3 is a detailed outline of the quantitative methods used. It explores the applicability of the variationist paradigm and the linguistic variable to higher-level linguistic analysis, and discusses the technicalities and practicalities of multivariate statistical analysis with Rbrul. The grammaticalisation framework is introduced in Section 2.4. It outlines the processes of change constituting grammaticalisation, explores the applicability of the framework to the analysis of discourse-pragmatic features and synchronic data, and presents the methods used for identifying and tracing ongoing grammaticalisation in synchronic cross-generational data. Finally, Section 2.5 introduces the principal concepts of CA which guide the functional data analysis. It also sets out the functional domains in which discourse-pragmatic features operate, discusses how this study operationalises multifunctionality for quantitative analysis, and summarises the methods employed for validating the qualitative analyses in Chapters 4 to 6.

2.2 Data

2.2.1 Corpus

Successful variation studies require access to language as it is actually used by speakers: empirical data constitute the basis for testing hypotheses, performing analyses and formulating theories. To meet this requirement, the present investigation into discourse-pragmatic variation and change is based on a corpus of some 260,000 words of transcribed speech which I collected between 2003 and 2005 in

Berwick upon Tweed. Berwick is a small market town of some 13,040 inhabitants located in the far north-east of England, only three miles (five kilometres) south of the Scottish-English border (see Figure 2.1).[4]

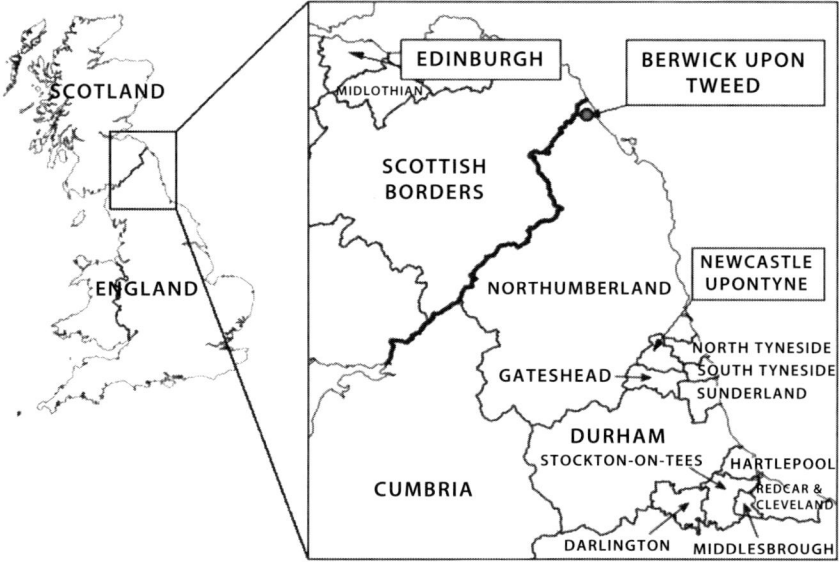

Figure 2.1 Location of Berwick upon Tweed, Northumberland*

* ©Crown copyright 2013. All rights reserved. Reproduced with permission from Watt & Ingham (2000).

The data were gathered using the interview protocol designed for the Survey of Regional English to solicit information about informants' use of local dialect words and attitudes towards their locality and dialect (Llamas 2007a). Scholars have expressed reservations not only about the efficacy of sociolinguistic interviews to overcome the Observer's Paradox and elicit informants' vernacular style "in which the minimum attention is given to the monitoring of speech" (Labov 1972:208) but also about the ability of non-community members and non-native speakers to tap into the vernacular (see in particular Douglas-Cowie 1978; Hazen 2000; Wolfson 1976). I do not deny the possibility that any potential effects of the recording situation on the nature of the data elicited may have been exacerbated by my status as a non-native speaking outsider to the community. Yet the quality of the data suggests that such effects were successfully attenuated through the use of

---

4. The word count includes false starts, truncations, filled pauses and minimal response particles, but excludes the interviewer's contributions. It equals some 35 hours of recorded speech.

various fieldwork techniques including conducting interviews with self-selected pairs in informants' homes. As demonstrated in Examples (1)–(7) below, the data manifest vernacular structures and inherent variability characteristic of casual and unmonitored speech styles (Labov 1972: 85–99).[5]

(1)   And you know for a fact where they are, what they're up to, and other people*s* looking out for them because everybody knows everybody else. It's *no* like living in a city where you *divn't* know who lives next door to you, *you know*. We might *no* know their name but we know what they look like.

(2)   I *divn't knaa*. I can*nae mind*.

(3)   Well, I don't know whether you realise it or *no*, but it's *dear*er to live in Scotland *than what* it is to live in England. *See*, we're on a thing called stay-warm for the heating. Between *wa* gas and electric. We pay every, I pay every month for my stay-warm. *Now*, if I lived up in Scotland, I'd be paying at least another fifteen or seventeen *pound* a month more *than what* I do by living in England.

(4)   I *ken* his dad, *you know*.

(5)   It depends on *whae* you *was* talking to. If I was talking to him. He's a Spittaler and, but if we *was* talking to someone that's not from Berwick, I would just say we're Berwickers.

(6)   I have*n't* got *nowt* down for that. I can't think of anything.

(7)   I *seen* a bit of a programme last year Ø was on about Berwick. Something to do *wi*, I think, something to do with the parking all the cars *and that*. Some people reckon they've ruined it putting these things down. The shopkeepers *is* losing money *and that* now. And obviously cars *isn't* allowed to park on the street. And *well*, they're *no* going into the shops. The street's nice-looking but th- th-, *you know*, at one time there *was* all cars up there. And people would go into Boots and Woolworths but they can*nae* do that now.

These examples also illustrate the hybrid nature of BwE, which exhibits characteristics of both Northumbrian and Lowland Scottish dialects (see further Llamas et al. 2009; Watt & Ingham 2000; Watt et al. 2012). For example, in Extracts (1)–(2), speakers use negative auxiliary variants that are typically associated with Northumbrian varieties (*divn't* for 'don't') alongside ones that are typically associated with Scottish varieties (*cannae, 's no, might no* for 'can't, 's not, might not'). In Extracts (2)–(6), they use lexical items that are usually associated with Scottish varieties such as *mind* ('remember'), *ken* ('know') and *whae* ('who') as well as lexical items that are usually associated with Northumbrian and Tyneside varieties such as *knaa* ('know'), *dear* ('expensive') and *wa* ('our'). This linguistic hybridity

---

5.   Page XIX provides a glossary of all the non-standard dialect words that are contained in the *verbatim* data extracts given here and elsewhere in the book.

is due to the town's border location, its turbulent history as a place which was repeatedly sacked and recaptured by Scottish and English kings, its continued importance as a communication point between England and Scotland as well as BwE's shared history with dialects spoken on both sides of today's border (Murray 1873: 5–6; Wales 2006: 49).

An important advantage offered by sociolinguistic interviews is that the data obtained are comparable in content and context: the same topics are discussed in the same setting with all speakers. This reduces the likelihood that any intra- and inter-group differences in the frequency and functionality of I DON'T KNOW, I DON'T THINK and NEG-TAGS reported in Chapters 4 to 6 are an artefact of interactional-situational constraints on their use (see Pichler 2010: 584–586). However, due to the strong context-dependency of discourse-pragmatic features, any conclusions drawn in this book about the targeted variables' functional profiles and typical rates of occurrence may not generalise to other speech events (Fuller 2003; Lam 2009). This is not to distract from the value of the present investigation which offers important new insights into the functional versatility of I DON'T KNOW, I DON'T THINK and NEG-TAGS and thereby improves currently available descriptions of their use.

2.2.2 Speaker sample

Table 2.1 gives a breakdown of the speaker sample constructed for this study. It includes 36 speakers who are equally stratified across speaker sex and age, and who represent a socially homogeneous group of working-class speakers, as determined via a combination of traditional social class indicators (housing, education, occupation) and informants' own assessment of their social class membership.

Table 2.1 Speaker sample

young (17–23)		middle (27–48)		old (60–81)	
male	female	male	female	male	female
6	6	6	6	6	6

The stratification of speaker samples across pre-fabricated social categories has recently come under criticism. It has been argued that social identities are not monolithic speaker attributes but dynamic products of social interaction which are locally situated and emerge "from practice, from what people *do* rather than what they intrinsically are" (Cameron 2005: 488–489, italics in the original) (see also Eckert 1997; Eckert & McConnell-Ginet 1992). The present investigation is not concerned with the performative nature of social identities or with how individuals exploit sociolinguistic resources to construct social identities. Its objective is to explore the sociolinguistic embedding of variation and change in discourse-pragmatics. It therefore utilises sex and age as broad methodological and exploratory tools to test the combined effect of extra- and intra-linguistic factors on discourse-pragmatic variation and change (Milroy & Milroy 1997:53). This enables us to draw comparisons with studies of phonological (and morpho-syntactic) variables which have associated men with the use of non-standard or localised variants, and credited women with community-internal changes, the elimination of stigmatised variants as well as the spread of prestige and supra-local variants (Labov 1998; Milroy et al. 1994).[6]

In order to identify the existence and direction of any ongoing changes in the data, I draw on the apparent-time framework as a surrogate for real-time data (Bailey 2002). The apparent-time construct hinges on the notion that the speech patterns recorded for different age groups at a single synchronic point in time represent different diachronic stages in language change. Age-based differences in synchronic speech patterns can therefore be interpreted as evidence of ongoing, real-time linguistic change. Inferences about change in progress that are drawn on the basis of apparent-time data rely on the basic hypothesis that individuals do not fundamentally alter their speech patterns as they grow older. The empirical validity of such inferences – and of the apparent-time construct more generally – has been confirmed by real-time panel studies attesting the stability of vernaculars throughout adult life (Sankoff & Blondeau 2007) as well as by real-time trend studies verifying the hypotheses inferred from synchronic data with diachronic evidence (Pope et al. 2007). To operationalise apparent time and add explanatory value to age as a dynamic social variable (Eckert 1997), the sample for this study was stratified across three emically-defined age cohorts reflecting shared life stages: teenagers and young adults in short-term unsalaried employment or full-time education and co-habiting with their parents (ages 17 to 23); adults in full-time salaried employment with dependent children and their own household (ages 27 to 48); retired people with no dependent children (ages 60 to 81).

---

6. No attempt has been made in this study to include in the analysis social-psychological variables such as local loyalty or identity. This is not to deny the possibility that speakers' frequent use of localised variants such as *I divn't knaa* or *I divn't think* may reflect their locally oriented (as opposed to outwardly oriented) identities. The exclusion of such variables from the analysis was motivated by the aim of the study: to provide an account of the synchronic structure of discourse-pragmatic variation which can be compared and contrasted with existing accounts of the synchronic structure of phonological (and morpho-syntactic) variation. Since the latter are generally based on inclusion of broad demographic variables such as speaker sex and age, it is important for the purpose of comparison and generalisability that extra-linguistic factors are kept constant.

2.2.3 Summary

Access to a corpus of BwE makes it possible to investigate discourse-pragmatic variation and change in a transitional and peripheral variety of British English, and it also complements previous discourse variation studies which have tended to focus on more mainstream varieties. The stratification of the speaker sample along two broad social dimensions, sex and age, affords us the opportunity to establish whether the sex effect in discourse-pragmatic variation and change is comparable to that in phonological or morpho-syntactic variation and change, and to trace the progress of any ongoing discourse-pragmatic changes in apparent time.

2.3 Variationist sociolinguistics

As stated in Chapter 1, a central aspect of the current investigation is to uncover which contextual factors contribute to the choice process between formal variants of the variables I DON'T KNOW, I DON'T THINK and NEG-TAGS, and to determine whether the sociolinguistic conditioning of variant choice is changing in apparent time. To this end, quantitative methods of variationist sociolinguistics are adopted. This section outlines the main theoretical principles of the variationist paradigm, argues in favour of its extension to the analysis of discourse-pragmatic features provided that the original definition of the linguistic variable is modified accordingly, and describes how the choice process can be reliably modelled with Rbrul.

2.3.1 Premises of variationist sociolinguistics

The quantitative variationist paradigm originates in the work conducted by Labov (1963, 1966, 1972) on the American east coast in the 1960s and 1970s. It is based on two fundamental premises. Firstly, that the choice process between variable linguistic forms is systematically constrained by multiple contextual factors, including "the phonological environment, the syntactic context, the discursive function of the utterance, topic style, situation and personal and/or socio-demographic characteristics of the speaker and other participants" (Sankoff 1988: 151). Secondly, that ongoing linguistic changes may be inferred from fluid patterns in the sociolinguistic conditioning of variant choice across different age groups in a community (Labov 1994) (see Section 2.2 above). Support for these premises is provided through quantitative analysis, which involves examining patterns in the distribution of a linguistic form across contextual factors and expressing in quantitative terms the strength of co-occurrence between them ("principle of quantitative modelling," Bayley 2002: 118). Co-occurrence patterns are taken to represent the social and grammatical structure giving rise to the observed variability which, viewed in apparent time, may yield insights into the embedding and trajectories of ongoing changes.

2.3.2 Discourse-pragmatic variables

The key theoretical construct of the variationist framework is the linguistic variable, which was initially developed by Labov (1963, 1966) for the analysis of phonological variation. In its most basic sense, a variable is a linguistic feature with two or more identifiable realisations, i.e., variants, which differ in their social and stylistic distribution but are equivalent in referential meaning ("saying 'the same thing' in several different ways," Labov 1972: 271). In order to fully understand the mechanisms underlying the choice process, it is necessary to isolate the whole set of possible variants and calculate each variant's occurrence out of all possible contexts of occurrence, i.e., those where it *did* occur and those where it could have occurred but did *not* ("principle of accountability," Labov 1972: 72). Because discourse-pragmatic features have unique semiotic and distributional properties, it is not easy to apply the parameters outlined above to their conceptualisation as variables or to their quantitative analysis. Firstly, discourse-pragmatic features are typically semantically bleached and therefore cannot be defined in terms of semantic equivalence between variants. Secondly, they are typically both referentially and syntactically optional, and thus eschew straightforward reporting as non-occurrences (see, however, D'Arcy 2005). Consequently, it is not immediately obvious on what basis to identify co-variants of a discourse-pragmatic variable and how to produce accountable results.

Due to these difficulties, scholars have often resorted to analysing discourse-pragmatic variation and change without reference to the linguistic variable. The most common approach has been to generate (normalised) frequency tabulations for individual discourse-pragmatic features without any consideration of their potential co-variants. Through comparison of these frequencies across individuals, social groups and/or communities, scholars strove to gauge variables' social indexicalities and test their robustness in and across communities (e.g. Macaulay 2002c; Stubbe & Holmes 1995; Tagliamonte 2005). However, this approach ignores the fact that discourse-pragmatic features may derive their social indexicality not just from frequency alternations but also from: variation in their form (see, for example, Cheshire [2007] who found that although working-class and middle-class adolescents use the general extender variable with comparable frequency, they favour different general extender variants); variation in their strategic usage (see, for example, Erman [1992] who found that women use *you know, you see, I mean* to link consecutive arguments while men use these features to draw attention or signal repair); and variation in their syntactic-semantic distribution (see, for example, Andersen [2001] who found that ethnic groups are not differentiated by their use of the tag variant *innit per se* but by their use of *innit* in non-third person singular contexts with BE). Furthermore, the approach described above treats discourse-pragmatic features as if they operated in a systemic vacuum. This is highly problematic since the overall structure of variation and change cannot be detected if variable features are analysed in complete isolation from their potential co-variants (Winford 1996: 189). An alternative but equally problematic approach has been to quantitatively model the distribution and conditioning of alternative forms without conceptualising them as co-variants of a linguistic variable (e.g. Cheshire 2007; Ferrara 1997; Macaulay 1995). Unless the forms included in an analysis are identified under the umbrella of a variable, it may prove difficult to establish how these forms are related to each other, what the theoretical basis is for including them in the same analysis, and what forms are, in fact, subjected to quantitative analysis. As a result, it may be difficult to replicate these studies or discern how scholars arrived at their results.

It is clear, then, that the extension of the linguistic variable to the level of discourse-pragmatics is a methodological necessity for producing reliable, intersubjective and accountable results. Yet despite Sankoff's (1973: 44,58) reassurance that the extension of the linguistic variable to levels "above and beyond phonology [is] not a conceptually difficult jump," suggestions to do so fuelled a heated controversy which continued throughout the 1970s and 1980s. Dines (1980) and Lavandera (1978), for example, questioned the methodological and theoretical soundness of scholars' wholesale transfer of the linguistic variable to the analysis of variable non-phonological features because referential meaning cannot be employed to establish equivalence relationships between higher-level variants (see above). Dines's and Lavandera's proposals to modify the defining criterion of the linguistic variable for the analysis of discourse-pragmatic (and syntactic) features were criticised by Cheshire (1987) and Romaine (1984) for being made without consideration of the theoretical assumptions underlying the variable's original conception. Yet it is hard to conceive how the mechanisms underlying discourse-pragmatic variation can be satisfactorily explained without modifying the definition of the linguistic variable in accordance with the unique semiotic and distributional properties of discourse-pragmatic features or without catering for the differential motivation for their use.

Dines (1980) and Lavandera (1978) therefore proposed to abandon the criterion of semantic equivalence for defining discourse-pragmatic (and syntactic) variables and to substitute it for one of functional comparability. For example, general extenders, i.e., clause- or phrase-final constructions such as *and that, and stuff like that, or something,* were argued to constitute a variable on the basis that all of its variants perform the common function of "cue[ing] the listener to interpret the preceding element as an illustrative example of some more general case" (Dines 1980:22). The function-based conceptualisation of discourse-pragmatic variables has proven very successful and has been widely adopted in studies of quotatives ("all strategies used to introduce reported speech, sounds, gesture and thought by self or other," Buchstaller 2006a:5; see also Macaulay 2001; Tagliamonte and Hudson 1999) and intensifiers ("every option speakers have at their disposition to reinforce or boost the property denoted by the head they modify," Rickford et al. 2007:7; see also Ito and Tagliamonte 2003; Macaulay 2006). The appeal of Dines's (1980) and Lavandera's (1978) definition is that it allows scholars to treat the general extender, quotative and intensifier systems as closed sets of variants and model the distribution of variants within a standard variationist framework. Moreover, Terkourafi (2011) has recently capitalised on the notion of procedural meaning as expounded in relevance theory (Sperber & Wilson 1995) in order to provide a theoretical justification for the function-based conceptualisation of discourse-pragmatic variables. Discourse-pragmatic features encode procedural meanings which "constrain the inferential phase of comprehension by indicating the type of inference process the hearer is expected to go through" (Wilson & Sperber 1993:11; see also Blakemore 1987). Thus, Terkourafi (2011:363) argues, quotatives instruct hearers to "interpret the speech that follows as attributed to a speaker other than the speaker's current self;" and intensifiers instruct them to "interpret the property denoted by the head as one that the speaker wishes to fore-ground or reinforce." The stable inference processes constitute a unifying criterion for establishing equivalence relationships between quotative variants on the one hand and intensifier variants on the other hand.

Yet as discussed in detail in Pichler (2010:587–591), the function- or inference-based conceptualisation of discourse-pragmatic variables is not universally applicable. Because function is an open category, some functions such as hedging may be signalled by a vast number of linguistic features from different levels of the linguistic system. Not only might it then be beyond the remit of individual analyses to close off the set of variants and report each variant's actual and potential occurrences, but including a range of elements from different components of the grammar "in the same analytic unit [...] is surely stretching the concept of the variable beyond all credibility" (Cheshire et al. 2005:164). Moreover, postulating discourse-pragmatic variables on the basis of shared functions or inference processes disregards the synchronic polyvalence of form-function relationships stemming from grammati-calisation. Older and newer layers of language use regularly co-exist synchronically either as variation in form, whereby different forms are used side-by-side for similar or identical functions (see above), or as variation in function, whereby a single item or construction serves a diversity of functions (see Chapters 4 to 6). Function- or inference-based approaches to defining discourse-pragmatic variables are not easily reconcilable with the latter layering effect.[7] What is needed to quantify variation in the use of multifunctional discourse-pragmatic features is a definition of discourse-pragmatic variables which accommodates their polysemic layering in synchronic data while still ensuring that *"the variants are in some way the same,* have something in common" (Dines 1980: 18; italics in the original).

A definition which fulfils these criteria and which is adopted for the present investigation is one based on variants' derivational equivalence (see also Pichler 2010). In this definition, I DON'T KNOW and I DON'T THINK constitute variables by virtue of the fact that their respective variants are derived from the same linear string of components schematised as: (first person singular pronominal subject) + (negative periphrastic DO) + (predicate *know*)/(predicate *think*). NEG-TAGS constitute a variable by virtue of the fact that its variants are derived from the same linear string of components schematised as: (auxiliary) + (negator) + (pronoun) or (auxiliary) + (pronoun) + (negator). As detailed in Chapters 4 to 6, the variants of these variables differ from each other in terms of their morpho-phonological encoding which primarily affects the realisation of the negative auxiliary as well as the fusion of adjacent morphemes.[8] This derivation-based definition of discourse-pragmatic variables makes it possible to: delimit the analysis to a finite set of variants that are derived from the same source construction; and conduct an accountable investigation into patterns of discourse-pragmatic variation and change. Importantly, because function is not the unifying denominator, this definition makes it possible

---

7.   Terkourafi (2011) argues that her inference-based postulation of pragmatic variables caters for both layering effects outlined above: variation in form (e.g. marking discourse-new entities) and variation in function/procedural meaning (e.g. quotative and intensifier uses of *all*). As stated above, Terkourafi (2011: 363) defines quotatives as hearer instructions to "interpret the speech that follows as attributed to a speaker other than the speaker's current self;" and intensifiers as instructions to "interpret the property denoted by the head as one that the speaker wishes to foreground or reinforce." With quotative and intensifier meanings thus defined, it is not clear to me how an inference-based postulation of pragmatic variables can unite both the quotative and intensifier use of the form *all* under the umbrella of a single variable. *All* signals different procedural meanings and alternates with a different set of co-variants depending on its role as a quotative or intensifier. Unless quotative and intensifier uses of *all* were argued to be united by virtue of signalling procedural rather than conceptual meaning, which would not in fact successfully delimit the variable context to the form *all*, I cannot see how Terkourafi's postulation of pragmatic variables can be applied to quantifying variation in function.

8.   The derivation-based conceptualisation of discourse-pragmatic variables has also been adopted in recent studies of general extenders. Recognising that function is not a diachronically stable denominator and that general extenders do not in fact constitute a unitary functional category, as originally postulated by Dines (1980), Pichler & Levey (2011: 448) define general extenders "as semi-fixed constructions which prototypically share the following schematic pattern: (connector) (modifier) (generic noun/pro-form) (similative) (deictic)."

to operationalise function as an independent variable and test its effect on observed patterns of formal variability.[9]

2.3.3 Quantitative methods

With the variable contexts thus defined, all variants of the selected variables are isolated to determine the conditioning of variability in the data and identify any ongoing changes in the distribution of variants. For each of the variables analysed, the frequency of individual variants is reported as the proportion of the total number of instantiations of the variable. The overall distribution patterns to emerge from these tabulations establish the proportional composition and robustness of the variable systems investigated in Chapters 4 to 6. They make it possible to situate the results obtained for individual variables in relation to previous research, and allow us to compare the relative frequency of variants (e.g. localised vs. non-localised) across variables.

However, overall distributions do not reveal the mechanisms producing the alternation between competing variants within the variable context. To uncover these mechanisms, I follow for each of the variables investigated in Part II a set of standard variationist procedures: operationalising as independent variables, *aka* extra- and intra-linguistic factor groups (or predictors), any hypotheses derived from the literature about variant choice (e.g. gender; preceding subject); coding each instantiation of the variable for one of the categories, *aka* factors, which together constitute the set of possible or reasonable divisions of factor groups (e.g. male vs. female; person, number and type of preceding subject); and examining in detail the quantitative distribution of variants across the factors of each factor group (Bayley 2002; Guy 1993). Because the choice process is generally conditioned by multiple extra- and intra-linguistic variables ("principle of multiple causes," Young & Bayley 1996: 253) and because the data under investigation are unbalanced (see Chapters 4.5.1, 5.5.1 and 6.5.1), multivariate analyses are conducted with Rbrul (Johnson 2009). Like GoldVarb (Sankoff et al. 2005), Rbrul uses

---

9. Torres Cacoullos & Walker (2009) demonstrate that functional differences between morphosyntactic variants can be identified even where the variable context is delimited in terms of function. They delimited their research area by postulating that *will, going to*, the Present and the Present Progressive constitute variants of one variable on the basis that they function to refer to events or states that occur after speech time. They then investigated the linguistic conditioning of variants to refine their analysis, and established that the variation between *will* and *going to* is not determined by each variant having an invariant semantic reading. Rather, each variant occupies different lexical, syntactic and pragmatic niches. Future research will establish whether this approach can be extended to the analysis of discourse-pragmatic variables.

a stepwise multiple-regression procedure to assess the contribution of each factor group included in the analysis to the observed variation when all factor groups are considered simultaneously. However, unlike GoldVarb, Rbrul incorporates mixed-effects modelling which takes into account inter-speaker and intra-group variation. It is thus able to account for the fact that individual speakers may contribute different amounts of data, and that they may favour or disfavour individual variants as well as particular factor levels to a greater or lesser degree than a fixed model would predict. This reduces the risk that a single speaker will bias the results for external and internal predictors, and thus produces more accurate results (Baayen 2008: Chapter 7).

The multivariate analyses in Chapters 4 to 6 yield a number of different results that help us interpret the data. Firstly, they give the input value which indicates the overall probability of variant occurrence regardless of contextual constraints. Secondly, they give log-odds, i.e., raw co-efficients which range from negative infinity to positive infinity: the larger the number, the bigger the effect size; the smaller the number, the more moderate the effect size. To facilitate comparison with results obtained from analyses with GoldVarb, Rbrul converts log-odds to centred factor weights, with values between 0 and 1. Like log-odds, they indicate the likelihood of variant occurrence with each factor of a factor group. Values >.5 signal favouring effects; values <.5 signal disfavouring effects. To make the results accessible to a wide audience, this study reports both log-odds and factor weights when reporting the outcome of multivariate analyses. In addition to providing input values and log-odds/factor weights, the multivariate analyses provide three lines of evidence that help us uncover the structure of variability in the data (Poplack & Tagliamonte 2001: 93–94): (1) statistical significance at the 0.05 level, which reveals which of the factor groups included in a data run make a significant contribution to the choice of a variant (non-significance of factor groups is indicated by enclosing their log-odds and factor weights in square brackets); (2) the range, or magnitude of effect, which indicates the relative strength of factor groups included in a run and situates factor groups with respect to each other (the greater the range, the greater the effect of the factor group on variant choice); and (3) the constraint hierarchy, which is the ordering of factors within a factor group and represents the grammar underlying the surface variability. Comparison of the relative strength of identical factor groups and constraint rankings of individual factors across the variables analysed in Part II makes possible comparison of their underlying grammars. Where variables occur with sufficient token numbers, apparent-time analyses are conducted of the data. Comparison of the significance, strength and especially the ordering of constraints across the age groups represented in the corpus makes it possible to identify the existence and direction of any ongoing changes to the structure of variation.

The fact that the discourse-pragmatic variables analysed in Part II do not occur with very high frequency may affect the robustness of the results obtained. Statistical significance of weaker conditioning effects is less easily achieved with small samples because they tend to involve greater levels of random fluctuation in the distribution of variants than larger samples (Young & Bayley 1996: 258–259). Following Poplack & Tagliamonte (2001: 93), the constraint hierarchies yielded through variable rule analysis are therefore construed as a window on the underlying structure of variability even when factor groups are not selected as statistically significant. To enable readers to evaluate for themselves the robustness of the results, all graphs and tables in Part II provide the raw token numbers on which the results are based. Where tokens occur in quantities insufficient to permit variable rule analysis, i.e., lower than ten to 30 (Guy 1980: 20), no statistical tests are conducted and results are reported on the basis of percentages and raw token numbers only. While such results can only yield tentative hypotheses about the conditioning of linguistic variability, the discussion in Chapter 7 demonstrates that they nevertheless have important implications for current theories of language variation and change.

Despite their acknowledged limitations (see Section 2.3.2), normalised frequency tabulations are generated to supplement the quantitative analyses described above and establish the inter- and intra-group robustness of the selected variables in the BwE data. Normalised frequencies are gauged by adopting the approach propagated by Macaulay (2005): the raw number of occurrences of a discourse-pragmatic feature is divided by the total number of words produced by a speaker or social group; this figure is then multiplied by 10,000 to provide a normalising measure for comparing frequencies.[10] I acknowledge that the overall frequency of I DON'T THINK and NEG-TAGS could be reported as proportions of the total number of clauses. Unlike with I DON'T KNOW, the syntactic positioning of these variants is fairly fixed and predictable. I refrain from taking this approach for two reasons. Firstly, because speech is replete with dysfluencies, discerning what constitutes a clause is a complex and potentially subjective task. Secondly, by consistently quantifying the frequency of all discourse-pragmatic variables per 10,000 words, scholars are in a much better position to draw reliable comparisons of their frequencies across individuals, social groups and varieties.

---

10. As stated earlier, false starts, truncations, minimal response particles and filled pauses are included in the word counts. Readers are referred to Pichler (2010: 594) for a justification of this approach.

2.3.4 Summary

This study conceptualises the discourse-pragmatic features chosen for analysis (I DON'T KNOW, I DON'T THINK, NEG-TAGS) as linguistic variables on the basis that their variants are derived from the same source construction. This allows inclusion of function as a factor group in the multiple regression analyses conducted with Rbrul. Rbrul tests the combined effect of multiple predictors on variant choice and includes speaker as a random effect in the analysis. It thus provides a reliable mirror on the grammar underlying observed patterns of formal variability in the use of the targeted variables. Viewed in apparent time, the output of the variable rule analyses helps uncover any ongoing changes in the use of the selected variables.

2.4 Grammaticalisation

Synchronic language structures arise from historical developments (Bybee 2010: Chapter 6). Consequently, synchronic patterns of variation in the morpho-phonological encoding, morpho-syntactic distribution and functional versatility of I DON'T KNOW, I DON'T THINK and NEG-TAGS may find a natural explanation in grammaticalisation, a diachronic process of change which generally affects multiple levels of the linguistic system (phonetics, morpho-syntax, semantics-pragmatics). This section introduces the set of changes that constitute grammaticalisation, and explores the applicability of the grammaticalisation framework to accounting for the evolution of discourse-pragmatic features. In addition to briefly addressing the status of grammaticalisation as a distinct process and coherent theory of language change, it outlines how the progression or product of grammaticalisation can be systematically observed in synchronic data.

2.4.1 Mechanisms of change in grammaticalisation

Grammaticalisation has been defined as "the change whereby lexical items and constructions come in certain linguistic contexts to serve grammatical functions and, once grammaticalised, continue to develop new grammatical functions" (Hopper & Traugott 2003: 18), or as "the process by which a frequently used sequence of words or morphemes becomes automated as a single processing unit" (Bybee 2003: 603). In what follows I will unpack these definitions and draw on illustrative examples from the literature to introduce the effects of grammaticalisation on language use and structure.

Although the language change processes associated with grammaticalisation have been widely discussed in the eighteenth and nineteenth centuries, Meillet

(1912) is generally credited with the first use of the term 'grammaticalisation'. Meillet conceived of grammaticalisation in two ways: (a) the change whereby free or pragmatically motivated word orders (e.g. in Latin) develop into fixed or more restricted word orders (e.g. in French); (b) the change whereby independent lexical items (e.g. nouns, verbs, adjectives) develop into grammatical function words (e.g. prepositions, adverbs, auxiliaries) which may then grammaticalise further into affixes. The evolution of grammatical elements from major lexical to minor grammatical categories is sketched by Hopper & Traugott (2003:7) as a "cline of grammaticality" of the following type:

(8)   content item > grammatical item > clitic > inflectional affix

From a diachronic point of view, a cline such as (8) depicts a path along which lexical items or content words progress as they develop functional roles. The developments are generally understood to be: (i) continuous: the labels on the cline refer to cluster and focal points along the trajectory of change; (ii) unidirectional: items tend to shift from the lexical to the grammatical end of the cline but not generally *vice versa* (Hopper & Traugott 2003:99–139); (iii) gradual: innovative uses co-exist alongside older uses during intermediate stages of development (see Hopper's [1991] notion of layering).[11] The developmental clines depicted in (8)–(10) are also called "grammaticalisation chains" (Heine 1993) and "paths" or "pathways" of grammaticalisation (Brinton 2006). From a synchronic point of view, they can be understood as continua: fuller, lexical items and constructions cluster towards the left end of a continuum and reduced, grammatical items and constructions towards its right end (Hopper & Traugott 2003:6).

Initially, the focus of grammaticalisation studies was largely on morpho-syntactic changes (see in particular Lehmann 1995 [1982]). With Traugott (1982), the focus of interest shifted to semantic-pragmatic aspects of grammaticalisation. Traugott argued that pragmatic meanings develop from referential (or propositional) meanings, a hypothesis that she conceptualised as the unidirectional cline in (9). More recently, Traugott & Dasher (2002) have postulated a more complex unidirectional model of semantic-pragmatic change whereby linguistic material becomes increasingly pragmatic, procedural and meta-textual as it progresses along the multiple developmental paths depicted in (10).

---

11. Kaltenböck et al. (2011) propose that what they call 'theticals' arise at first through instantaneous co-optation of units taken from sentence grammar and only later undergo gradual formulaicisation. This view is not supported by variationist studies that have tracked the progression of grammaticalising discourse variables in apparent time (see, for example, Romaine & Lange 1991).

(9)   propositional (> textual) > expressive[12]

(Traugott 1982:256)

(10)   truth-conditional > non-truth-conditional
       content > content/procedural > procedural
       nonsubjective > subjective > intersubjective

(Traugott & Dasher 2002:40)

As implied above, the grammaticalisation of linguistic material involves a com-plex set of interrelated mechanisms which affect all levels of the linguistic system. According to Heine (2003:579), these mechanisms include: desemanticisation, extension, decategorialisation and erosion. Desemanticisation, or semantic bleaching, refers to the loss of referential content. Typically, bleaching tends to occur only in later stages of grammaticalisation as items develop more pragmatic meanings to replace their original content meaning (Traugott & König 1991). Extension, or generalisation, obtains when items, as a result of the conventionali-sation of conversational inferences and the associated increase in their polysem-ies, progressively come to be used in new contexts where they were not used before. Decategorialisation refers to the process whereby a lexical or grammatical form loses the morpho-syntactic properties that are characteristic of its source category. Finally, erosion, or phonological attrition, refers to the reduction in the phonological representation of a form and/or fusion of adjacent words/mor-phemes. It is caused by the fact that as their inferences conventionalise and their uses generalise, frequently occurring items and constructions gradually weaken their prosodic emphasis and their referential contribution to utterance meaning (Bybee 2003, 2006).

Bybee (2003, 2006) argues that the changes outlined above are driven by the high token frequency of items and constructions undergoing grammaticalisation. With increased frequency and repetition, co-occurring morphemes or lexemes lose their internal structure and compositionality, and come to be stored and proc-essed as single units. As a result, they grow autonomous from their composite morphemes and their non-grammaticalised sources. However, frequency is not just a trigger but also a result of grammaticalisation. As grammaticalising items and constructions undergo context expansion and acquire more polysemies, they dramatically increase their frequency (see the notion of extension above).

The above outline demonstrates that the individual processes constitut-ing grammaticalisation (desemanticisation, extension, decategorialisation, ero-sion) are closely interrelated by virtue of the fact that they are all triggered by

---

12. 'Textual' here refers to meanings that signal intra-clausal truth-conditional cohesion (Traugott 2003a:633).

frequency and that they interact with each other in regular and predictable ways. Grammaticalisation scholars draw on these observations to refute criticisms expressed *inter alia* by Campbell (2001) and Janda (2001): that grammaticalisation is not a distinct process of change but an epiphenomenon of changes that elsewhere operate independently of one another. Haspelmath (2004: 26), for example, rejects these criticisms by arguing that grammaticalisation "is a macro-level phenomenon which cannot be reduced to the properties of corresponding micro-level phenomena" because its constituting processes are strongly correlated. Heine (2003: 583) posits that the different components of grammaticalisation together constitute an explanatory framework for elucidating the origins and development of grammatical forms, thereby rebutting suggestions that grammaticalisation cannot be considered a theory in its own right (see in particular Newmeyer 1998). Heine's (2003) view is supported by Bybee (2009: 353) who argues that grammaticalisation is "a diachronic theory of language." It describes how grammar arises and develops through language use, and furnishes strong hypotheses about synchronic language structure. Grammaticalisation thus constitutes a useful framework for variationist studies which explore the factors conditioning variation in synchronic language use.

2.4.2   Grammaticalisation and discourse-pragmatic features

A growing number of studies demonstrate that many of the processes defining grammaticalisation account for the diachronic development and synchronic properties not just of morpho-syntactic but also of discourse-pragmatic variables (see *inter alia* Brinton 1996, 2006, 2008 for diachronic studies; Andersen 2001; D'Arcy 2005; Ferrara & Bell 1995; Tagliamonte & Hudson 1999; Thompson & Mulac 1991b for synchronic studies). Close inspection of the relevant literature reveals that grammaticalising discourse-pragmatic features commonly undergo the following morpho-syntactic changes:

-   decategorialisation, i.e., the loss of morpho-syntactic properties characteristic of the original form (see Section 2.4.1): for example, the inability of *I mean* to be modified by adverbials or to take phrasal and clausal complements (Brinton 2007);
-   change from major (open) to minor (closed) word class (Lehmann 1995 [1982]): for example, the change of *I think* from a complement-taking matrix-clause to an epistemic adverb (Thompson & Mulac 1991a);
-   freezing or ossification of the feature in one grammatical construction or form (Lehmann 1995 [1982]): for example, its fossilisation in the imperative when *say* occurs before numerical expressions to mean 'about, approximately' (Brinton 2005).

In addition, there is evidence that grammaticalising discourse-pragmatic features commonly undergo the following semantic-pragmatic changes:

- desemanticisation or semantic bleaching, whereby items lose their full meaning and assume less concrete meanings (see Section 2.4.1): for example, their loss of concrete visual perception meaning when *you see* and *see* come to express speakers' subjective emotion (Brinton 2008: Chapter 6);
- shift from referential to non-referential meaning (see clines (9) and (10) above): for example, the use of *well* as part of an agreement signal (Macaulay 2005: 60);
- conventionalisation of conversational implicatures (Traugott & König 1991): for example, the use of the temporal adverb *now* as an emphatic topic-changer (Aijmer 2002: Chapter 2);
- subjectification, i.e., the process whereby lexical items increasingly signal speaker beliefs and attitudes (Traugott 1995, 2003b): for example, the use of *like* as a focusing device and quotative introducer (Romaine & Lange 1991).

However, previous studies also show that the evolution of discourse-pragmatic features may diverge from canonical cases of grammaticalisation, especially with regard to Lehmann's (1995 [1982]) parameters of grammaticalisation. Firstly, discourse-pragmatic features do not generally undergo coalescence whereby items lose their independent word status through affixation or morphological fusion (see, however, Traugott [2003a: 642] on the morphological bonding of *in* + *deed* and *any* + *way*). Secondly, instead of being subject to condensation or scope reduction, the grammaticalisation of discourse-pragmatic features generally involves a unidirectional expansion of scope (scope within a proposition > scope over a proposition > scope over discourse). Finally, not all discourse-pragmatic features manifest fixation. For example, while *oh* always occurs in turn- or utterance-initial position (Macaulay 2005: 60), *I think* has acquired increased syntactic mobility as a result of its grammaticalisation from a complement-introducing matrix clause to an epistemic adverbial. It consequently occurs not just utterance-initially but also utterance-medially and -finally (Thompson & Mulac 1991b).[13]

---

13. Traugott (2010) differentiates two models: 'grammaticalisation as reduction' and 'grammaticalisation as expansion.' In the former prototype model, grammaticalisation is conceived as involving reduction, freezing and obligatorification and as pertaining to the inflectional encoding of tense, aspect, mode, case, number, etc. In the latter extended model, grammaticalisation is conceived as involving structural expansion of various kinds (see Himmelmann 2004) and as pertaining to discourse-pragmatic features. According to Traugott, the two approaches are complementary because they address different questions, i.e., the development of morpho-syntactic forms through grammaticalisation vs. the types of functional changes involved in grammaticalisation.

Although some evolutionary differences are to be expected between features that develop differential grammatical roles (Traugott 2003a: 643), the fact that discourse-pragmatic features do not unequivocally fulfil all of Lehmann's (1995 [1982]) grammaticalisation criteria has led to some disagreement over whether grammaticalisation is indeed an appropriate theoretical framework for explaining and elucidating these features' diachronic evolution and synchronic distribution. The uncertainty over the status of discourse-pragmatic features in a theory of grammaticalisation has been augmented by claims that the diachronic processes observed in their evolution yield pragmatic rather than grammatical items and constructions which have not traditionally been considered part of grammar (see Chapter 1.3). Despite the implicit suggestion in Meillet (1912) to apply the term 'grammaticalisation' broadly (see Section 2.4.1), some scholars propose that the emergence of discourse-pragmatic features be conceptualised as constituting a separate process from grammaticalisation: pragmaticalisation (Aijmer 1997; Erman & Kotsinas 1993). Pragmaticalisation separates the domains of grammar and pragmatics, and accommodates in its definition the linguistic developments specific to the emergence of pragmatic features such as lack of bonding, scope expansion and syntactic mobility (see above). However, the proposal to distinguish the emergence of pragmatic elements from that of grammatical elements has not been universally accepted (see in particular the papers in Degand & Simon-Vandenbergen 2011). Several arguments can be identified for its almost unanimous rejection. First, it must be acknowledged that Meillet's (1912) conception of grammaticalisation includes the syntacticisation of word order (see Section 2.4.1 above), which is relevant to the fixing and freezing of multi-unit discourse-pragmatic variables. Second, the outline at the beginning of this section demonstrates that the emergence of discourse-pragmatic and morpho-syntactic features shares far more similarities than differences, leading Günthner (2000: 439) to argue that there is in fact no real difference between pragmaticalisation (the emergence of pragmatic functions) and grammaticalisation (the emergence of grammatical functions). Finally, some scholars have advocated a comprehensive notion of grammar which encompasses pragmatic meanings and recognises the status of discourse-pragmatic features as legitimate and integral elements of grammar (see Chapter 1.3). In light of these arguments, I adopt a broad conception of grammar inclusive of pragmatic meanings, and frame my account of the diachronic evolution and synchronic properties of discourse-pragmatic features in terms of grammaticalisation.

2.4.3   Grammaticalisation in synchronic data

Grammaticalisation is a diachronic process of change. Nonetheless, it is highly relevant to studying discourse-pragmatic variation in synchronic data. For a start, grammaticalisation studies provide testable hypotheses about the nature and trajectory of changes giving rise to synchronic language structure which can be operationalised as independent linguistic variables conditioning synchronic variation (Poplack 2011; Torres Cacoullos 2011). Moreover, because grammaticalisation typically occurs as a series of micro-steps, it can be observed in fluid patterns of synchronic language variation (Hopper & Traugott 2003; Traugott & Trousdale 2010). Key to tracking grammaticalisation in synchronic data is correlating the form undergoing change with independent linguistic predictors and comparing the results of independent multivariate analyses across age groups. The existence and directionality of any ongoing grammaticalisation changes can then be gleaned from apparent-time shifts in constraint hierarchies within factor groups (see Section 2.3.3 above). As shown in Chapters 4 to 6, evidence for the grammaticalised status of discourse-pragmatic variables can be deduced from the distribution of variants across intra-linguistic constraints even where no apparent-time shifts in the distribution of variants are observable or where apparent-time analyses are not possible due to insufficient data.

2.4.4   Summary

This investigation draws on the framework of grammaticalisation to explore the synchronic distribution of the selected discourse-pragmatic variables. The framework provides important hypotheses about the distribution of variants in synchronic data, thus guiding the analysis of the data as well as the interpretation of the results.

2.5   Conversation analysis (CA)

Among the hypotheses generated by the grammaticalisation framework is that grammaticalising material undergoes phonetic attrition and desemanticisation. To establish whether formal variation patterns in the use of the targeted variables (I DON'T KNOW, I DON'T THINK, NEG-TAGS) can be correlated with their differential positioning on a cline or continuum of semantic-pragmatic change, it is necessary to include function as a factor group in the quantitative analysis and establish for each of the targeted variables the factors that constitute this factor group. This section introduces the key concepts of conversation analysis (CA) which inform the functional data analysis. It also presents the functional domains in which discourse-pragmatic variables operate, and describes the measures employed for reducing the subjective dimension of the analysis and validating its results. First, however, it provides the rationale for the choice of CA.

2.5.1   Choice of CA

While coding data for independent linguistic-structural and broad extra-linguistic variables is relatively straightforward, there are no universally agreed methods for coding independent discourse-functional variables. In the literature, the semantic-pragmatic functions performed by discourse-pragmatic features have been studied within a wide range of theoretical and methodological frameworks including, amongst others, coherence theory (e.g. Lenk 1998; Schiffrin 1987), politeness theory (e.g. Algeo 1988, 1990; Holmes 1995) and relevance theory (e.g. Andersen 2001; Blakemore 1988; Jucker 1993). Studies conducted within these frameworks have yielded important insights into the role of discourse-pragmatic features in signalling coherence relations between discourse units, affecting social rapport between interlocutors, and guiding utterance interpretation. Top-down approaches such as these have the advantage of providing unified and thus easily comparable accounts of the functionality of discourse-pragmatic features. Yet, there is a high risk that the focus on a single theoretical explanation for their use might yield incomplete descriptions of features' functional versatility. An inductive bottom-up approach which is not tied to a single theoretical framework and which is sensitive to features' strong context-dependency might be better suited to yielding comprehensive functional taxonomies which reflect the fact that a single discourse-pragmatic variable is likely to perform multiple and highly diverse functions, sometimes even simultaneously. The present investigation therefore adopts a conversation analytic approach and examines the chosen discourse-pragmatic variables in their full interactional, sequential and linguistic contexts of occurrence. This will yield comprehensive descriptions of the variables' functional spectra in the BwE data.

2.5.2   Key concepts of CA

CA is an empirical field of investigation which conceptualises talk as an organised and ordered social activity, and provides insights into the interactional structure and sequential organisation of talk-in-interaction (see further Hutchby & Wooffitt

1998; Schegloff 2007). Chapters 4 to 6 draw on the following principal tenets of CA to establish broad functional taxonomies for the selected discourse-pragmatic variables:

–   recipient design: Talk-in-interaction is designed in a way that displays speakers' orientation and sensitivity to their co-participants in interaction (Sacks et al. 1974: 727).
–   preference organisation: In talk-in-interaction alternative but non-equivalent actions are available to speakers. One action is preferred or expected to be chosen (e.g. agreement, acceptance); the other is dispreferred (e.g. disagreement, refusal). Preferred next actions are generally performed directly and without delay ("preferred-action turn shape"); dispreferred next actions are generally performed indirectly and in a qualified manner, and are generally delayed between and within turns ("dispreferred-action turn shape") (Pomerantz 1984: 64).
–   turn-exchange mechanisms[14]: Turn-exchange is administered by participants in interaction to proceed smoothly. Usually only one speaker talks at a time, and transitions are finely co-ordinated to minimise gaps and overlaps. Speaker exchange is accomplished on a turn-by-turn basis through one of the following turn-allocation techniques: (i) the current speaker selects a next speaker; (ii) a next speaker self-selects themselves; or (iii) the current speaker continues to speak (Sacks et al. 1974).
–   topic-proffering sequences: By proffering a topic, speakers make available to co-conversationalists a particular topic which they expect their co-conversationalists to embrace or reject. Preferred responses to topic-proffers engender expansion of the topic; dispreferred responses engender topic-closure (Schegloff 2007: 169–180).

Knowledge of these tenets is important for functional data analysis because they provide some general indication of the interactional work discourse-pragmatic features do: conveying speaker and hearer attitudes; determining the preference status of actions; and signalling turn-exchange as well as topic-closure. In order to fine-tune the analysis and allocate each token of the targeted variables to specific functional categories, the qualitative analyses in Part II also exploit the following key concepts associated with CA:

---

14. Turns at talk have been defined in a variety of ways (see Edelsky [1993] for a critical appraisal of the literature). In this book, 'turn' refers to an interactional unit whose boundaries are marked by speaker exchange.

- sequential implicativeness: Utterances are "context-shaped" and "context-renewing" (Heritage 1984: 242), i.e., they occur in response or reaction to some prior utterance and project a relevant next utterance.
- adjacency pairs: Talk is sequentially organised into adjacency pairs. In their most basic form, adjacency pairs are (i) composed of two turns; (ii) produced by different speakers; (iii) adjacently positioned; (iv) ordered, i.e., consisting of a first pair part which initiates an exchange, and a second pair part which responds to the prior turn; and (v) pair-type related, i.e., the production of the first pair part requires the production of a second pair part that is from the same pair type as the first utterance (e.g. question-answer, offer-acceptance/ refusal, assessment-assessment) (Schegloff & Sacks 1973: 295–296).
- next-turn proof procedure: Because utterances are understood as directed to prior talk (see above), a current turn's talk displays a speaker's analysis and understanding of the immediately preceding turn's talk (Heritage & Atkinson 1984: 9–11).

These concepts postulate that the meaning of an utterance is activated by its sequential positioning and participation in adjacency pairs. Hence, the data interpretation in Part II is founded on a close reading of the larger and immediate sequential context in which the variables of interest are used as well as close examination of the structure and type of adjacency pairs in which they occur. Also, next-turn talk is carefully examined because it may display how the use of an utterance containing or constituted by a discourse-pragmatic variable was understood by co-participants in the interaction, thus serving as an important resource for guiding the allocation of discourse-pragmatic variables to functional categories.

In addition to the tenets and concepts outlined above, the qualitative data analysis is based on some observations from CA which have not been formulated as theories but which, due to their interactional importance, impact on utterance interpretation nevertheless:

- temporal development of interactions: Features such as overlaps and interruptions convey important information about speaker-hearer alignment (Du Bois et al. 1993: 52).
- false starts, repetitions and filled pauses (*em, er, um*): False starts and repetitions aid speakers in the planning of discourse (Cameron 2001: 34), and filled pauses perform a range of pragmatic functions similar to more prototypical discourse-pragmatic features (Kjellmer 2003; Stenström 1990).
- acknowledgment tokens (*mhm, uh-huh, yeah*): Depending on their strategic placement in discourse, these tokens function to signal hearers' continued interest and attention to the speaker, or to express agreement and acceptance (Schegloff 1982).

– prosodic and paralinguistic features (speech rate, stress, pauses, volume, duration, pitch movement, intonation contour, voice quality): These features contribute to the communicative meaning of utterances (Du Bois et al. 1993:61–73; Psathas & Anderson 1990:81–89), and are of great importance for disambiguating the functions performed by discourse-pragmatic variables (Wichmann 2011; Yang 2006).

Prosodic and paralinguistic features are dealt with in very broad terms. The differentiation between low, high and regular pitch is made impressionistically, and intonation contours are described in terms of a rough three-way distinction: continuing, final or rising. (Future work will elucidate the role of prosodic features in disambiguating the meanings encoded in the variables analysed in Part II.) In addition to the features listed above, close attention is paid to co-occurring discourse-pragmatic features and adverbs. While co-occurring elements may function in isolation of each other with each performing a different function (Fleischman 1999), more often than not they mutually reinforce each other (Aijmer 2002: Chapter 2; Fetzer 2011; Stubbe & Holmes 1995:83). Attention to the adjacent linguistic context thus constitutes an additional means for differentiating subtle nuances of meaning.

Finally, the qualitative data analysis draws on Brown & Levinson's (1987) politeness model. This model builds on Goffman's (1967) notion of face, which Brown & Levinson (1987:61) define as "the public self-image that every member [of a society] wants to claim for himself [sic]." Face consists of two related aspects: *positive face*, i.e., members' desire to be liked and have their actions and opinions approved of by others; and *negative face*, i.e., members' desire to have their actions unimpeded by others. Because of the mutual vulnerability of face, participants in interaction routinely employ a series of strategies that function to redress face-threatening acts, i.e., acts that run counter members' face wants. As shown in Part II, discourse-pragmatic features play a central role in mitigating potential face-threats.

2.5.3 Functional domains

Existing taxonomies of discourse functionality differ in terms of the number and types of domains or modes they identify. For example, Fischer (2000) and Schiffrin (1987) identify five domains on which discourse-pragmatic features operate, Bazzanella (2006) and Erman (2001) only three. This investigation follows Brinton (1996, 2008) in basing the functional classification of features on Halliday's (1979) three functional components of language: ideational, interpersonal, textual. This model offers the advantage that scholars can draw as many divisions within the broad functional components as are necessary for detailed and accurate descriptions of features' functional versatility. Yet at the same time it makes possible viable statistical analyses because it allows scholars to collate micro-functions along the broad components of language use outlined above. With other models, scholars might end up with too few tokens in each domain to warrant statistical testing, and collation of individual domains might seem functionally arbitrary.

Some items and constructions that commonly perform discourse-pragmatic functions may also operate in the ideational mode which is concerned with the representation of referential content. This is due to the diachronic origin of most discourse-pragmatic variables in referential material and the functional layering effect of old and new meanings in synchronic data (see Section 2.4). Where applicable, the ideational mode is included in the functional taxonomies and quantitative analyses in Part II of the book.

The interpersonal mode is concerned with the expression of speaker attitudes and the coordination of speaker-hearer alignment and relationships. Following Traugott (2003b), I distinguish in the interpersonal domain subjective from intersubjective functions, although the distinction between the two is not always clear-cut. Variables with a subjective function serve to indicate speakers' relation and attitude towards their propositions. They may signal speakers' subjective stance towards propositions (e.g. *I believe*) and/or speakers' assessment of the reliability of their propositions (e.g. *possibly, I'm convinced that, Absolutely!*). Variables with an intersubjective function make explicit speakers' attention to and awareness of their interlocutors. They may serve to request confirmation of assumptions presumed to be shared by speakers and hearers (e.g. *isn't that so?*) as well as to signal shared assumptions (e.g. *Indeed!*). Also, intersubjective tokens may contribute to creating a mitigating effect in conversation by reducing the anticipated unwelcome effect or illocutionary force of potential face-threats (Fraser 1980; Holmes 1984b). Although discourse-pragmatic features with interpersonal functions frequently serve to redress potential face-threats and to mitigate interactional conflict, politeness concerns are not a prerequisite for their use.

The textual mode relates to the text-structuring function of language. Discourse-pragmatic features operating in this domain signal the relation between sequentially arranged discourse units, including propositions, turns and topics (e.g. *and, however, as a result*). Textual tokens are also instrumental in the overall development and organisation of discourse. For example, they function to initiate and close discourse (e.g. *listen!, right*), to mark topic-shifts (e.g. *now, anyway*) or to indicate new and old information (e.g. *actually, in fact, as I said before*). In the textual mode, then, discourse-pragmatic features contribute to coherence and textuality in discourse. In this investigation, the textual domain is divided into the sub-domains repair marking, turn-exchange, topic-development, transition marking.

2.5.4 Quantifying multifunctionality

The model outlined above is used in this investigation to describe the functional versatility of the selected variables and to prepare the inclusion of function as an independent variable in the quantitative data analyses. However, endeavours to allocate tokens to functional categories are complicated by the intrinsic multi-functionality of discourse-pragmatic features: not only do they perform different functions in different contexts of use but a single instantiation of a feature can operate across discourse domains and perform multiple functions simultaneously (Schiffrin 1987). Holmes (1984a) argues that researchers can differentiate on the basis of the contextual cues discussed in Section 2.5.2 the primary from the secondary function of multifunctional discourse-pragmatic features and quantify functionality accordingly. This approach may be useful if the aim of the analysis is to explore the functional range of variables and to probe the overall salience of these functions in a given corpus (see Andersen 2001). Yet despite its popularity, this procedure is problematic. Not only does it add an unnecessary layer of arbitrariness and subjectivity to the analysis but it also yields misleading results. Conversationalists may exploit the multifunctionality of discourse-pragmatic features at strategic points in interaction (Coates 1987: 130), and it is features' multifunctional, not their unifunctional, uses that are unmarked (Cameron et al. 1988: 77). Holmes's (1984a) approach fails to reflect this.

The method adopted in the present investigation addresses these shortcomings by incorporating multifunctionality as a parameter in the analysis (see Pichler 2010: 597–598). When tokens perform multiple functions simultaneously (e.g. initiating or terminating a turn whilst also qualifying its content), these tokens are categorised as multifunctional tokens performing both functions concurrently. This approach is preferable to Holmes's (1984a) since it allows researchers to reflect in quantitative terms the multifunctional nature of discourse-pragmatic variables. Also, it is less subjective than Holmes's method since it does not rely on researchers' intuitive judgments as to which of the multiple functions is more important in a given context.

2.5.5   Validating qualitative analyses

In addition to accommodating multifunctionality in the functional taxonomy, this investigation adopted the following measures to reduce the subjectivity of the functional data analysis and validate its results. After an initial coding system had been devised for each variable through the interrogation of existing taxonomies, the functional categories and the coding of random tokens were cross-checked with two native speakers of British English. This resulted in some modifications being made to the initial coding schema. In the case of I DON'T KNOW, categories were also tested with the help of community members who may possess intuitive knowledge of the prototypical meanings and functions associated with discourse-pragmatic variables which are not accessible to an outsider (Fox Tree 2007). As part of a school project, sixth-formers at Berwick Community High School were introduced to the variable I DON'T KNOW and the functions I had identified for it, and asked to verify the functional categories by questioning their intuitions about the construction's use and observing its usage amongst family and friends over a two-week period. The students' intuitions and observations confirmed the accuracy of the initial taxonomic framework. For each variable, three independent and blind analyses were then conducted at two-month intervals. Tokens that had not been consistently allocated to the same functional category in all three passes were discussed with two independent coders. These discussions resulted in minor modifications to the taxonomy. In the end, the dynamic coding process established a detailed coding system to capture the function of all tokens of the selected variables in the data. To ensure the transparency of the analysis and facilitate its replication, Chapters 4 to 6 discuss illustrative examples of the variables' functions in some detail and outline precisely which contextual factors gave rise to the functional interpretations offered.

2.5.6   Summary

This investigation adopts a dynamic, bottom-up approach to functional data analysis. Application of CA theories and methods ensures the empirical discovery of the full functional range of the selected variables when they are examined in their interactional, sequential and linguistic context of occurrence. Multifunctionality is accounted for in the categorisation of tokens, and various methods are employed for validating the analysis.

2.6 Conclusion

The methodology developed for this project constitutes a great improvement on previously used methods. Firstly, it advocates a derivation-based conceptualisation of discourse-pragmatic variables which caters for the fact that discourse-pragmatic features are polysemic elements and that function is not by necessity a stable denominator. Secondly, although the investigation is resolutely variationist, it combines insights from various linguistic models to enhance current understanding of discourse-pragmatic variation and change. Thirdly, it goes beyond generating overall frequency counts and conducts multivariate analyses to target the grammatical system underlying the choice process between variants. Finally, the methodology advocated here includes multifunctionality as a parameter in the qualitative and quantitative data analysis to reflect the interactional and strategic motivations for the usage of discourse-pragmatic features. Together, these measures offer an enhanced method for studying discourse-pragmatic variation and change. By catering for the flexibility, multifunctionality and complexity of discourse-pragmatic features, they ensure a more accurate account of the mechanisms underlying discourse-pragmatic variation and change than would be possible by adopting a unidimensional approach. The full articulation of my innovative methodology in this chapter will serve as a model for future discourse variation studies.

## CHAPTER 3

The BwE verb negation system

3.1 Introduction

The focus of the present investigation is on exploring patterns of variation and change in the realisation of three discourse-pragmatic variables: I DON'T KNOW, I DON'T THINK and NEG-TAGS. In addition to operating at the discourse-pragmatic level and sharing similar developmental properties, the variables are related by virtue of containing negative auxiliaries. As shown in Example (1) below, negative auxiliaries are highly variable in the variety of English under scrutiny here.[15] In addition to Standard English variants such as *don't, shouldn't* or *doesn't*, the pool of available variants includes special forms such as *divn't* ('don't') in (1a) and (1b), negative auxiliaries formed with the isolate negator *no* such as *'m no* ("m not') in (1b), and negative auxiliaries formed with the enclitic negator *-nae* such as *would-nae* ('wouldn't'), *dinnae* ('don't') and *cannae* ('can't') in (1b)–(1d).

(1)   a.   Natalie: I *divn't* like being called a Berwicker.
            HP: No?
            Natalie: I *don't* like that.
      b.   Natalie: E:h, I *wouldnae* feel offended. I just say (.) "Well. I *divn't* have
                       a Geordie accent because (.) I'*m no* from Newcastle," you
                       know
      c.   Evelyn: Oh! I *shouldn't* say it but I *dinnae* like the Geordie twang.
      d.   Lori: She says she *cannae* understand youse at all. She says youse are
                       hard to understand. But she says she *doesn't* know if it's cos
                       you've got a low voice.

This chapter introduces in more detail the variants available in BwE for effecting verb negation, with the aim of setting the background for the analyses of the formulaic constructions I DON'T KNOW, I DON'T THINK and NEG-TAGS in Part II of the book, and establishing the robustness and distribution of negative auxiliary variants in productive constructions, i.e., constructions which have compositionally

---

15. Unless otherwise stated, examples are taken *verbatim* from the BwE corpus. All informant names are pseudonyms; HP is the interviewer. A key to the transcription conventions is provided on page XVII. A glossary of dialect words is provided on page XIX.

transparent meanings and are assembled on-line from an open category of components (Wray & Perkins 2000: 2). The chapter starts with a brief account of the history of verb negation in English and Scottish varieties in Section 3.2. Section 3.3 introduces the range of negative auxiliary variants found in BwE and discusses their geographical distribution in the English-speaking world. Before their extra- and intra-linguistic distribution in BwE is explored in Section 3.5, Section 3.4 reviews studies investigating their distribution in other UK varieties. Finally, Section 3.6 is the conclusion to this chapter and the transition to Part II of the book.

3.2   The evolution of verb negation and negative particles

In order to fully appreciate the nature and degree of variation in the form of negative auxiliaries in BwE, it is necessary to briefly examine the evolution of verb negation in English. Although scholars disagree on the precise causes and consequences of what is widely referred to as "Jespersen's Cycle" (see, for example, van der Auwera 2009; Wallage 2008 for outlines of different accounts), it is generally assumed that the development of verb negation involves the following stages: the use of the pre-verbal negative particle *ne* in Old English, as in (2); the addition of post-verbal negative particles such as *na* ('not a'), *nalles* ('not at all') or *noht* (< *nawiht, nowiht*) ('not a thing') in early Middle English, as in (3); the exclusive use of the negator *not* (< *noht*) due to the loss of the pre-verbal negative particle *ne* in late Middle English, as in (4).

(2)   ic **ne** secge.   (Jespersen 1917: 9, literally 'I not say')
(3)   I **ne** seye **not**.   (Jespersen 1917: 9, literally 'I not say not')
(4)   I say **not**.   (Jespersen 1917: 9)

Jespersen (1917: 9–11) adds as separate stages in the development the introduction of DO-support and placement of the negative marker before the verb in late Middle English, as exemplified in (5), as well as the subsequent weakening in this position of *not* to the clitic *-n't*, as exemplified in (6).[16] As a result of the developments sketched out in (2)–(6), modern Standard English has two clause negators: isolate *not* and clitic *-n't*. In declaratives, they are placed after the auxiliary and before the predication.

(5)   I **do not** say.   (Jespersen 1917: 11)
(6)   I **don't** say.   (Jespersen 1917: 11)

---

16. Following Quirk et al. (1985), small capitals are used throughout this book to refer to the primary verbs BE, HAVE and DO as lexical items. Lower case italics are used to refer to their grammatical forms (e.g. *was, is, has, had, did, does*) and to modal auxiliaries (e.g. *could, would, will*) which are invariable in their form.

In Scottish varieties, negation followed the same cycle of development as in Standard English, albeit later (Aitken 1979: 88).[17] Importantly, in addition to *not* and *-n't*, the following negative particles were preserved in Scotland: isolate *no* and clitic *-nae* or *-na*, with the alternative spellings of the clitic representing differences in the realisation of its vowel ([ne], [nɛ] and [nʌ]). The clitic *-na(e)* derives from Old English *nā* (= *ne*) (Craigie et al. 1937–2002), which was originally a competitor of *not* (Jespersen 1917: 17). While it was lost in Standard English early on, it still prevails in many Scottish varieties as a clitic that is attached to auxiliary verbs (Macafee 1992). Isolate *no* is a reduced form of Old English *noht* (Craigie et al. 1937–2002) and, like clitic *-na(e)*, is used in Scottish varieties to this day alongside the Standard English particles *not* and *-n't* (Macafee 1992).[18]

These developments are highly relevant to the present study. As pointed out in Chapter 2.2, Berwick upon Tweed shares close historical, demographic and linguistic links with neighbouring areas in Northumberland as well as south-east Scotland. These links are reflected in the BwE verb negation system.

3.3 Negative auxiliaries in BwE

3.3.1 Negative auxiliary variants in BwE

As in other varieties of English, we find in BwE verb forms that are negated with the negative markers *not* and *-n't*, as shown in (7) and (8).

(7)   It's *not* a community like it used to be, Spittal.
      He'll *not* use very much slang.
      We've *not* got any of these high-rise blocks, which is nice.
      I might *not* like the accent but at least it identifies who I am.

---

17. Modern Scottish speech is commonly described as a continuum with two extreme poles: (Broad) Scots on one end and (Scottish) Standard English on the other end (Aitken 1984: 519–527; Corbett et al. 2003: 1–3). The relationship between the two poles of the continuum is far from clear-cut and it is beyond the constraints of this book to explore it. To avoid implying that certain linguistic features are situated more towards one end of the continuum or the other, I will throughout this book refer to modern Scottish speech as 'Scottish varieties' or 'varieties of Scotland.' All I mean to imply when I talk about features being typical of Scottish varieties or varieties of Scotland is that they are commonly associated with Scotland as a geographical area. (There are, of course, non-Germanic language varieties spoken in Scotland which are not subsumed under my labels.)

18. There are regional differences in the form of the localised negative particles in Scotland. While isolate *no* and clitic *-nae* prevail in southern and western Scotland, their counterparts in north-eastern Scotland are isolate *nae* and clitic *-na* (Macafee 1992; Millar 2007: 76–77; Smith 2000: 239). In the northern northern varieties, a mixed pattern applies (Millar 2007: 132).

(8)   Berwick people aren't impressed very easily.
      They won't include you in the Borders.
      They haven't got a clue what I'm talking about.
      I don't like football.
      We wouldn't accept it being Scottish.

In addition, the BwE corpus contains verb forms that are negated with the independent negative particle *no* and the dependent negative particle *-na(e)*. The variable pronunciation of *-na(e)* (see Section 3.2 above) will not be pursued here, and the particle will henceforth be represented orthographically as *-nae*. The use of *no* and *-nae* is illustrated in (9) and (10).

(9)   I'm *no* a Scots, you know.
      You'll *no* get a much better place, you know.
      I've *no* finished mine.
(10) He is*nae* daft.
      They can*nae* even win now.
      We're a relaxed place to be but I would*nae* say we're a fashionable place to be.

When *do* and *will* are negated with the clitic *-nae*, they are phonetically modified, yielding the forms *dinnae* [dənə], [dənɪ] or [dɛnɪ] for 'don't' and *winnae* [wõnɪ] for 'won't', as shown in (11).

(11) a.   The people in Berwick *dinnae* like it when it's busy.
      b.   I'm sure you *winnae*.

In addition to the variants exemplified above, the BwE corpus contains two negative auxiliary variants that are formed with the negative particles *-n't* and *not* but which are not generally considered to be part of the repertoire of Standard English. These forms are *divn't* [dɪvənt] for 'don't' and *cannit* [ˈkʰanət] for 'can't.' In *divn't*, a KIT-vowel is preceded by a voiced alveolar plosive and followed by a labiodental fricative and the negative particle *-n't*. The unrounding and fronting of the vowel in DO may have arisen from Northern fronting in Early Middle English (Britton 2002). The form *cannit* differs from Standard English *cannot* in that the negative in *cannit* is not stressed. In contrast to *cannot*, *cannit* can therefore occur in unemphatic contexts. The use of *divn't* and *cannit* is illustrated in (12).

(12) a.   At the same time you *divn't* want the dialect and things to die out.
      b.   They *cannit* understand you.

In sum, the BwE data manifest a high degree of variability in the formal encoding of negative auxiliaries which reflects the historical development of verb negation in UK varieties as well as Berwick upon Tweed's location on the Scottish-English border. Below I will provide details about the geographical distribution of the variants introduced above.

3.3.2 Geographical distribution and categorisation of negative particle/negative auxiliary variants

The negative auxiliary variants introduced above differ in terms of their geographical distribution in England and the English-speaking world. Following Milroy et al. (1994), geographical distribution is used in this investigation as a basis for categorising variants.

As Standard English forms, the particles *-n't* and *not* are not confined to a specific locale but are widely used across England and the English-speaking world. They are therefore categorised as non-localised or non-localisable variants. Variants that are used in many varieties of English across the British Isles but are not generally associated with Standard English usage, such as the tag form *innit* discussed in Chapter 6, are subsumed under the category of supra-local variants.

The usage of the negative particles *-nae* and *no* is far more limited than that of *-n't* and *not*. According to the historical and contemporary literature, *-nae* and *no* are characteristic of Scottish varieties (Anderwald 2002: 53–58; Beal 1997: 370–371; Grant & Dixon 1921: 115–120; Grant & Murison 1931–1976; Miller & Brown 1982: 3–14; Miller 2003: 87–89; Murray 1873: 216–217; Wilson 1915: 126–127; Wright 1902). However, restricted use of *-nae* has also been reported for Ulster (Anderwald 2002: 50–52) and for the three northern-most counties of England: Cumbria, Northumberland and Durham (Anderwald 2002: 61; Glauser 1974; Orton & Halliday 1963; Upton et al. 1994; Wright 1902). In addition, isolated instances of the independent negator *no* have been reported for Northumberland (Orton & Halliday 1963). While the use of *-nae* and *no* is widespread in Scotland, their use in England is localised to varieties spoken close to the Scottish-English border. For this reason and because their sociolinguistic distribution in BwE is not identical to that in Scottish varieties (see Section 3.5 below), the negators *-nae* and *no* and auxiliaries negated with *-nae* and *no* are here and throughout categorised as localised variants. Yet due to their strong association with Scotland, these variants and their north-eastern Scottish equivalents (see footnote 18) are occasionally referred to as Scottish negators in Section 3.4.

Divn't and *cannit* are well-established features of northern/north-eastern England. Although searches of the *Scottish Corpus of Text and Speech* (Douglas 2003) yield isolated instances of *divn't* in negative polarity question tags in north-east Scotland, the historical and contemporary literature generally describes *divn't* as a characteristic feature of Tyneside/Northumberland and, to a lesser degree, Durham and Cumbria speech (Beal 1993: 192–193, 2004: 124; Beal & Corrigan 2005; Orton & Halliday 1963; Upton et al. 1994; Wright 1902). The use of *cannit* has so far been reported only for Tyneside/Northumberland (Beal 1993: 199, 2004: 123; Beal & Corrigan 2005). Seen within the context of England, then, *divn't* and *cannit* are localised to its most northern parts. They are therefore categorised here and throughout as localised variants.

Table 3.1 summarises the BwE inventory of negative particle and negative auxiliary variants in productive constructions, with an indication of their geographical spread in England.[19]

Table 3.1   Inventory of negative particle and negative auxiliary variants in BwE

non-localised negative particles	localised negative particles	localised negative auxiliaries
-n't	*-nae*	*divn't*
not	*no*	*cannit*

3.4 Previous research on negator and negative auxiliary variation

The extra- and intra-linguistic distribution of *-nae, no, divn't* and *cannit* has received only limited attention in the scholarly literature. To prepare the quantitative analysis of BwE negative auxiliary variation in Section 3.5, this section reviews the few extant studies of negative auxiliary variation in Scottish, Northumbrian and Ulster varieties. It focuses first on accounts of their external distribution before moving on to accounts of their internal distribution in these varieties.

3.4.1 Extra-linguistic distribution of variants

Based largely on their intuitions as native speakers of Edinburgh speech as well as data gathered through elicitation tasks and informal observations, Brown & Millar (1980: 111) and Miller (1993: 114–115) propose that the use of *-nae* for *-n't* in Edinburgh is stigmatised and avoided by educated speakers in formal contexts. Macaulay (1991: 50–57) provides empirical evidence for the social stratification of different negators in his study of socially differentiated language use in Ayrshire, south-west Scotland. He found that the middle-class speakers in his sample never used the variants *-nae* and *no*. By contrast, the lower-class speakers in his corpus generally preferred the use of *-nae* over *-n't* and displayed rates of *no* as high as 93%. Smith et al. (forthc.) report that 96% of all negative auxiliaries in adult-to-adult conversation in their data from Buckie, north-east Scotland, occurred with

---

19. The formulaic constructions I DON'T KNOW, I DON'T THINK and NEG-TAGS allow additional variants. These are introduced in Chapters 4 to 6.

the Scottish negators. In interactions between caregivers and their children in the same community, the rate of use of Scottish negators among caregivers dropped to 72%; children demonstrated a rate of Scottish negators of 47%, with older children displaying higher rates than younger children. Finally, Anderwald (2002: 47) reports that in Ulster, *-nae* has developed social significance as a symbol of Ulster Scots Protestant identity. In sum, these patterns suggest that the use of Scottish negators is relatively robust in Scottish varieties, and that their use in Scotland and Northern Ireland is constrained by the following social factors: socio-economic class, age, geography, ethnicity as well as identity or age of the interlocutor.

Little information is provided in the literature about the relative frequency and social distribution of the variants *divn't* and *cannit*. In Beal & Corrigan's (2005) small-scale study of negation in Tyneside, the use of the localised variant *cannit* was found to be marginal compared to that of the non-localised variant *can't* (20% and 80% respectively). No information is provided about the relative frequency of *don't* and *divn't*. The majority of tokens of *cannit* and all tokens of *divn't* were produced by three working-class men with minimal schooling and a negative attitude towards education. Beal & Corrigan (2005: 146–147) acknowledge that these speakers' use of *divn't* and *cannit* might be due to their having been less inhibited than other speakers by the recording situation. However, they also propose that these speakers may have been less influenced than other speakers by the prescriptive stigmatisation of *divn't*. While this might explain the non-occurrence of *divn't* amongst other speakers in their data, it does not explain why *cannit*, which according to Beal & Corrigan (2005: 148) is not overtly stigmatised, was used almost exclusively by working-class men. In sum, these findings indicate that the use of *divn't* and *cannit* in Tyneside is constrained by the following social factors: speaker sex and socio-economic class.

3.4.2 Intra-linguistic distribution of variants

In their description of auxiliary verbs in Edinburgh speech, Brown & Millar (1980: 102–120) point out that in declaratives the isolate negative particle *no* can only ever occur with cliticised auxiliaries (e.g. forms of BE), but never with non-cliticised auxiliaries such as DO. The particle *-nae* can cliticise onto all primary verbs and onto any modal auxiliary except for *might*. With the modal auxiliary *can*, the negative particle *-nae* is obligatory if it is the modal itself that is negated; if it is the following verb that is negated, *no* is used instead. Unlike *-n't*, *-nae* never inverts over the subject in interrogatives and tags; *no, not* or *-n't* are used instead. Irrespective of the auxiliary involved, it is not possible for both the auxiliary and the negative particle to undergo cliticisation. Similar patterns are reported in Miller

(2003: 87–88, 2004: 50–51) who points out that -*nae* is attached to all modal auxiliaries and to DO. *No*, he argues, is most frequent with *will* and forms of BE and HAVE. Isolate particles, i.e., *no* and *not*, are in fact the norm not just with *will*, BE and HAVE but also with interrogatives and question tags. By implication, the use of -*nae* is limited to declaratives and imperatives.

These accounts, which are largely based on informal observations, elicitations and the authors' native speaker intuitions, suggest that auxiliary type and clause type affect the distribution of Scottish negators in Scotland. A small number of quantitative corpus-based studies provide empirical corroboration of these accounts. Steele's (2003) study of caregiver and child speech in Buckie, north-east Scotland, reveals that DO has a lower rate of Scottish negators than other auxiliaries (see also Smith et al. forthc.). Also, *did* and *does* have higher rates than *do* of *nae* and -*na* (the Buckie equivalents of BwE *no* and -*nae*, see footnote 18 above) (94%, 89% and 62% respectively). With non-DO auxiliaries, forms of present tense BE show the highest and modal auxiliaries the lowest proportion of *nae* and -*na* (92% and 72% respectively). The effect of auxiliary type on the rate of Scottish negators is further corroborated by Anderwald's (2002: 50–51) investigation of verbal negatives in the *Northern Ireland Transcribed Corpus of Speech*. Anderwald reports that in Ulster the variation between Scottish and non-localised negators is restricted to a small number of auxiliaries: *no* and -*nae* never occur with *am, are, has, will* and only rarely with DO, *have, could* and past-tense BE. As regards clause type, Steele's (2003) analysis of Buckie reveals that forms of DO are more often negated with Scottish negators in imperatives than declaratives (77% and 46% respectively). With all the other auxiliaries, only declaratives are variable. Interrogatives are almost categorically formed with Scottish negators, while the reverse holds for question tags. Similar patterns are evident in Shetland, to the north-east coast of Scotland, where negative polarity tags are near-categorically formed with the negative particles -*n't* and *not* (Smith 2009).

The literature review, then, reveals that across the varieties that have been described or empirically investigated, the occurrence of Scottish negators is constrained by clause type and/or auxiliary type. However, comparison of the empirical studies also reveals some cross-variety differences in the frequency and distribution of negator variants. While Scottish negators occur with all auxiliaries in the varieties of Buckie and Shetland, they do not occur with *do* in recordings from Ayrshire. In Ulster, the variation between Scottish and non-localised negators is restricted to an even smaller number of auxiliaries. Also, where Scottish negative particles occur in Ulster, they do so at substantially lower rates than in the investigated Scottish varieties. In sum, the cross-corpora comparisons suggest that Scottish negative particles have a different language-internal distribution across varieties, and that they occur at lower rates outside of Scotland.

3.5 Quantitative analysis of negative particle and negative auxiliary variation

This section sets out to establish the robustness and distribution of negative particle and negative auxiliary variants in BwE productive constructions, i.e., in contexts other than I DON'T KNOW, I DON'T THINK and NEG-TAGS. It explores whether social factors, clause type and type of auxiliary contribute to the distribution of variants in BwE as they do in other varieties. Knowledge of the constraints on variation in productive constructions will allow us to contextualise the findings obtained in Part II of the book and establish the extent to which linguistic context affects the distribution of negative particle and negative auxiliary variants.

3.5.1 Distributional analysis

Figure 3.1 displays the overall distribution of the negator variants *-n't, not, -nae* and *no* as well as the localised negative auxiliary variants *divn't* and *cannit* in BwE productive constructions (N = 3,713). The distribution reveals a clear prevalence of non-localised over localised variants. Almost three quarters of negative auxiliaries in productive constructions are formed with *-n't* and *not*. The localised negators *-nae* and *no* combined constitute only one fifth of the data. The occurrence of *divn't* and *cannit* is not in fact as negligible as suggested in Figure 3.1. Table 3.2 shows that when their frequency is tabulated in the context of negative *do* and *can* only, *divn't* and *cannit* are far from marginal.

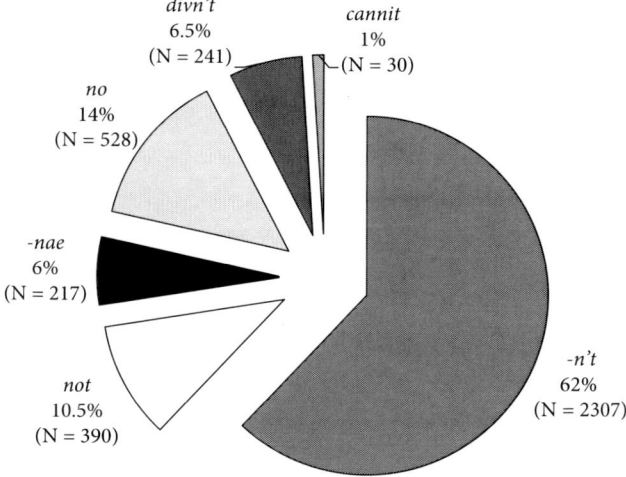

Figure 3.1 Overall distribution of negator and localised negative auxiliary variants in productive constructions (declaratives, interrogatives and imperatives)

Initial data runs reveal that speakers do not make full use of the formal variability available to them for effecting verb negation. Firstly, out of the 36 speakers in the sample, eight speakers near-categorically employ non-localised negative particle variants and non-localised negative auxiliary variants (> 95%). Five of these speakers are from the youngest age group; three are from the middle age group. To avoid obscuring constraints on variation, data produced by these speakers are removed from further analysis (N = 689). Secondly, variable speakers do not use localised negators with the full range of auxiliaries. Table 3.2 displays for each auxiliary form listed in the left-most column the proportion of negator and negative auxiliary variants listed in the top row of the table. The results show that the use of -*nae* is virtually limited to non-third person singular present tense forms of DO and the modal auxiliary *can*, while the use of *no* is virtually limited to present tense forms of BE, non-third person singular present tense auxiliary *have* and the modal *will*.[20] In the BwE corpus, the variation between non-localised and localised negator variants thus affects only a small number of auxiliaries. Moreover, the patterns outlined above suggest that the choice between negator variants is closely linked to contraction and cliticisation strategies: (1) the negator variant -*nae* is used with auxiliaries that cannot undergo contraction (*do, can*); the variant *no* is used with auxiliaries that regularly undergo contraction (present tense BE, auxiliary *have, will*); (2) with auxiliary *have* and modal *will*, there is a strong association between negator cliticisation and the use of the non-localised clitic negator -*n't* on the one hand, and between auxiliary contraction and the use of the localised non-clitic negator *no* on the other hand; (3) with present tense BE, variation between non-localised and localised negators is virtually restricted to isolate negators and contexts of auxiliary contraction.

As implied above, it is not just auxiliary type that exerts a strong conditioning effect on the occurrence of negator variants but also auxiliary form and function. The top rows in Table 3.2 show that negative periphrastic DO is one of the most variable auxiliaries in the data. However, the variation only affects *do*; negative *does* and negative *did* are virtually never realised as *divn't* and they only very rarely occur with *no*. Conversely, almost half of the instantiations of *do* amongst variable speakers are constituted by localised variants: *divn't, dinnae, do no* (listed in order

---

20. Following Quirk et al. (1985: 129–148), I distinguish the following auxiliary functions for HAVE: main verb uses (e.g. *I haven't a clue*) and auxiliary uses (e.g. *I haven't seen it*) (see Huddleston's [2002: 103] non-core and core uses). The former are henceforth referred to as main HAVE, the latter as auxiliary HAVE. Auxiliaries, then, refer to a syntactic class of verb forms that always occur in finite form in a fixed position in a sentence; auxiliary uses refer to the functions of auxiliaries in a sentence. Included in the latter category are instances of HAVE GOT (e.g. *I've no got nowt to hide*) (see Huddleston 2002: 112).

Table 3.2 Distribution of negator variants across auxiliaries (on the left) and distribution of localised negative auxiliary variants (on the right)

	-n't		not		-nae		no		divn't		cannit		
	%	N	%	N	%	N	%	N	%	N	%	N	TOTAL N
do	52.8	347	0.9	6	9.4	62	1.1	7	35.8	235	–	–	657
does	97	164	0.6	1	0	0	0.6	1	1.8	3	–	–	169
did	95.4	206	1.9	4	0	0	2.8	6	0	0	–	–	216
present BE	11	77	28.8	200	0.2	1	60	416	–	–	–	–	694
past BE	93.8	106	2.7	3	0	0	3.5	4	–	–	–	–	113
auxiliary have	57	90	5.7	9	0	0	37.3	59	–	–	–	–	158
auxiliary had	81.2	13	12.5	2	6.3	1	0	0	–	–	–	–	16
auxiliary has	57.7	15	34.6	9	0	0	7.7	2	–	–	–	–	26
main HAVE	100	13	0	0	0	0	0	0	–	–	–	–	13
can	31.5	82	0.8	2	55	143	1.9	5	–		10.8	28	260
will	40.5	15	8.1	3	5.4	2	45.9	17	–	–	–	–	37
could	99.2	119	0	0	0.8	1	0	0	–	–	–	–	120
would	98.2	508	0.4	2	1.2	6	0.2	1	–	–	–	–	517
might	14.3	1	42.9	3	0	0	42.9	3	–	–	–	–	7
should	89.5	17	0	0	5.3	1	5.3	1	–	–	–	–	19
may	0	0	0	0	0	0	100	1	–	–	–	–	1
must	100	1	0	0	0	0	0	0	–	–	–	–	1

of frequency). The patterns for BE and HAVE confirm the effect of tense and person on negative auxiliary variation. While present tense forms of BE display a high degree of variation, with the localised variant *no* constituting the preferred option amongst variable speakers for effecting present tense BE-negation, past tense forms are virtually categorically negated with the non-localised variants -*n't* and *not*. Although inferences must remain tentative due to low token numbers, a similar pattern can be observed with HAVE: all but one token of *had* are negated with -*n't* and *not*. Furthermore, HAVE resembles DO in terms of the effect of person: *have* is far more likely to be negated with localised negators than *has*. Finally, the pattern for HAVE reveals the effect of auxiliary function on negator variation. In contrast to auxiliary uses of HAVE, main verb uses of HAVE occur categorically with the non-localised negator -*n't*. Among the modal auxiliaries, *can* is the most variable. Roughly two thirds of all tokens of negative *can* among variable speakers take a localised form: *cannae, cannit, can no* (listed in order of frequency). This is in stark contrast to the modal auxiliaries *could* and *would* which are near-categorically negated with the non-localised particles -*n't* and *not*. The modal *will* demonstrates a tendency to be negated either with non-localised -*n't* or localised *no*. However, low token numbers mean that these patterns have to be interpreted with caution. The same holds for the modals *should, might, may* and *must* which occur too infrequently in the data to allow any conclusions to be drawn about their variability in negative contexts. In sum, the context of negative auxiliary variation in BwE is highly circumscribed by the type, function, tense and person of the auxiliary being negated. With primary verbs, use of localised variants is virtually restricted to *do* as well as auxiliary *have* and present tense BE when they are contracted. With modal auxiliaries, use of localised variants is virtually limited to *can* and *will*.

Table 3.3 compares the distribution of variants across clause type. The results reveal important parallels with those reported for Scottish varieties (see Section 3.4.2): the enclitic negator *-nae* never occurs in interrogatives; the isolate negator *no* never occurs in imperatives. *No* and *not* evince a propensity to occur in interrogatives. Together they account for more than 60% of all negative particles in interrogatives, thus demonstrating that interrogatives are more likely to be negated with isolate than enclitic negative particles. In contrast to *no* and *not*, *-nae* and the negative auxiliary variant *divn't* evince a propensity to occur in imperatives. Considering that negative imperatives are uniformly formed with DO, the results indicate that imperatives are the only clause type that is more likely to be negated with localised variants (*divn't, dinnae*) than with non-localised variants (*don't*) (61.7% vs. 38.3%). Like *no* and *-nae*, the occurrence of *divn't* and *cannit* is also affected by clause type: the former never occurs in interrogatives; the latter only ever occurs in declaratives. The only negator variant that occurs across the clause types investigated here is *-n't*. In sum, the patterns in Table 3.3 demonstrate that clause type is implicated in negative auxiliary variation. The use of localised variants is associated with interrogatives and imperatives.

Table 3.3 Distribution of negator and localised negative auxiliary variants across clause types

	-n't		*not*		*-nae*		*no*		*divn't*		*cannit*		
	%	N	%	N	%	N	%	N	%	N	%	N	TOTAL N
declaratives	59.5	1727	8	232	7.2	208	16.9	492	7.5	218	1	28	2905
interrogatives	38.9	28	16.7	12	0	0	44.4	32	0	0	0	0	72
imperatives	38.3	18	0	0	19.1	9	0	0	42.6	20	0	0	47

3.5.2 Multivariate analysis

Having established which auxiliaries are subject to variation in the BwE data and how variants are distributed across clause types, this section sets out to establish the joint contribution of intra- and extra-linguistic predictors to variant choice among the variable speakers in the sample. The analysis focuses first on the use of the negator variants *-nae* and *no*. It includes other negator variants as non-application values and is based only on those auxiliaries that have been shown to be variable in Table 3.2: *can, do*, present tense BE and, with *no*, auxiliary *have*. (*Will* is not included in the analysis due to low token numbers.) The analysis then focuses on the variant *divn't*. Since its co-variants are formed exclusively with third person singular present tense *do*, auxiliary is not included as a factor group in the analysis for this variant. The only variants included as non-application values in the run for this variant are therefore: *don't, do not, dinnae* and *do no*. Individual speaker is included as a random effect in all three multiple regressions in order to account for any effects of unbalanced data.

Table 3.4 presents the results of the independent multivariate analyses for *-nae, no* and *divn't*. The em-rule indicates that factors were not included in the analysis because variants never occur in these environments (see Table 3.3). (More information on how to read and interpret the results of multivariate analyses is provided in Chapter 2.3.3). As evident from the range values, auxiliary type makes the most important contribution to the occurrence of the non-localised negator variants *-nae* and *no*. The negator *-nae* is strongly favoured with *can* and *do* and strongly disfavoured with present tense forms of BE. Age exerts the second most important effect on the occurrence of *-nae*. It is favoured by speakers from the old and middle age groups and strongly disfavoured by speakers from the young age group, suggesting that its frequency and importance may be waning in apparent time. (See also the low input probability given at the top of the table which is indicative of the variant's marginal status in the BwE negation system). Speaker sex and clause type were not selected as making a significant contribution to the occurrence of *-nae*, even though this negator shows a tendency to occur more often in imperatives than declaratives. In stark contrast to *-nae*, which is favoured with auxiliaries that do not undergo contraction, the isolate negator *no* is strongly favoured with those auxiliaries that regularly undergo contraction: auxiliary *have* and present tense forms of BE. As far as auxiliary is concerned, then, *-nae* and *no* are in complementary distribution. The second most important constraint on the use of *no* is clause type. *No* is favoured in interrogatives and disfavoured in declaratives. Speaker sex and age do not make a significant contribution to the occurence of *no*, despite factor weights indicating apparent-time fluctuations in its use. Finally, the results

Table 3.4 Contribution of external and internal factors to the probability of -nae, no and divn't

	-nae				no				divn't			
	factor weights	%	N	log odds	factor weights	%	N	log odds	factor weights	%	N	log odds
input prob.	.025				.133				.365			
total N	1563				1723				644			
deviance	630.681				1087.787				707.363			
age	p = 0.0289				not significant				not significant			
old	[.711]	16.2	752	0.900	[.589]	29.8	842	[0.362]	[.455]	32.0	306	[−0.182]
middle	[.590]	15.0	440	0.364	[.643]	35.3	490	[0.591]	[.487]	33.8	142	[−0.050]
young	[.220]	4.9	371	−1.264	[.278]	16.1	391	[−0.952]	[.558]	54.4	196	[0.232]
range	.491				–				–			
sex	not significant				not significant				not significant			
male	[.500]	13.4	949	[−0.002]	[.522]	28.5	1026	[0.089]	[.451]	31.7	398	[−0.195]
female	[.500]	13.6	614	[0.002]	[.478]	28.0	697	[−0.089]	[.549]	44.3	246	[0.195]
range	–				–				–			
clause type	not significant				p = 0.00216				not significant			
declarative	[.380]	13.0	1517	[−0.488]	.346	27.9	1667	−0.638	[.507]	43.5	598	[0.028]
interrogative	–	–	–	–	.654	39.3	56	0.638	–	–	–	–
imperative	[.620]	19.6	46	[0.488]	–	–	–	–	[.493]	36.0	46	[−0.028]
range	–				.308				–			
auxiliary	p = 3.96e-109				p = 308e-179							
can	.977	57.0	251	3.737	.100	1.9	260	−2.200				
do	.619	9.6	944	0.487	.074	1.1	611	−2.528				
present BE	.014	1.0	668	−4.224	.953	59.9	694	3.001				
auxiliary have	–	–	–	–	.849	37.3	158	1.727				
range	.963				.879							
speaker	random st. dv 1.423				random st. dv 1.323				random st. dv 1.507			

for *divn't* show that none of the independent variables included in the analysis significantly constrains its use. The variant occurs with roughly equal probability across age groups, speaker sex and clause type.

3.5.3 Summary of results

The quantitative analysis of verb negation in BwE productive constructions corroborates the findings obtained in previous studies of negative auxiliary variation which have shown that the locus of variation is highly circumscribed by the type, person, tense and function of the auxiliary as well as by the clause type in which variants occur. Yet despite these broad similarities, the sociolinguistic distribution of variants is not identical across the investigated varieties. The variation between localised and non-localised negators is restricted to a smaller number of auxiliaries in BwE compared to the Scottish varieties discussed in Section 3.4. Also, where localised negators occur in BwE, they do so with markedly lower rates than in the Scottish varieties. Moreover, BwE differs from the Scottish varieties discussed earlier in that the occurrence of *-nae* is not robust. Yet with the exception of the effect of speaker age on *-nae*, social factors are not implicated in the choice of *-nae, no* and *divn't* amongst those speakers who used the variants during the recordings made for this study.

3.6 Conclusion

The analysis presented in Section 3.5 has shown that negative auxiliaries in BwE productive constructions are highly variable in their form and that this variation is for the most part not random but systematically constrained by language-internal and, to a much lesser degree, language-external factors. These observations are highly pertinent to the analysis of discourse-pragmatic variation and change in Part II of this book. Each of the three discourse-pragmatic variables selected for analysis contains a negative auxiliary. In I DON'T KNOW and I DON'T THINK, negative periphrastic DO occurs between the first person singular pronominal subject *I* and the cognitive verb *know* or *think*. Variants thus are derived from the same linear string of components: (first person singular pronominal subject) + (present tense negative DO) + (cognitive verb). However, they differ in the details of their morpho-phonology, including the realisation of negative *do* (see further Chapters 4 and 5). In NEG-TAGS, the negative auxiliary either precedes a pronoun/existential *there*, or the pronoun/existential *there* occurs between the auxiliary and the isolate negator. Variants thus are derived from the same linear string of components: (auxiliary) + (negator) + (pronoun) or (auxiliary) + (pronoun) + (negator). However, they differ in their realisation of the negative auxiliary and its adjacent elements (see further Chapter 6). By investigating whether different negator variants and different variants of negative periphrastic DO exhibit comparable frequencies, social indexicalities, linguistic distributions and/or discourse-pragmatic functionalities across the combined set of productive constructions investigated above and each of the three formulaic constructions investigated in Part II of the book, it is possible to establish the extent to which patterns of variation in the realisation of negative auxiliaries are contoured by linguistic context and usage constraints.

PART II

## CHAPTER 4

The construction I DON'T KNOW*

4.1 Introduction

Corpus linguists draw attention to the fact that I DON'T KNOW is the most frequent negative collocation in spoken corpora and as such constitutes one of the most common epistemic markers in English conversation (Baumgarten & House 2010: 1186; Kärkkäinen 2003: 51; Scheibman 2001: 70–71). A growing number of studies in the fields of discourse and conversation analysis corroborate these claims, representing as negligible the role of I DON'T KNOW in signalling a cognitive state and emphasising its interactional role within and beyond marking epistemicity (see further Section 4.2.1 below). In stark contrast to the attention it has received in qualitative paradigms, in the field of variationist sociolinguistics I DON'T KNOW has been largely ignored despite its frequency and highly variable functional and formal properties. Building on the few extant studies concerned with variation and change in the use of I DON'T KNOW, in particular Bybee & Scheibman (1999) and Scheibman (2000), this chapter sets out to address the current shortage of variationist studies of I DON'T KNOW, with the aim of accounting for the construction's variable realisation in BwE. The formal variability is illustrated in the extracts from the corpus in (1). It is depicted here and throughout by means of variation in orthography, with each orthographic form (*I don't know, I dono, I dunno, I divn't knaa, I dinnae ken*) representing a different variant whose phonetic, phonological and morphemic properties are described in detail in Section 4.3.2.

(1) a. Jerry: I *I dono* if if the percentage is maybe more one way than the other, *I don't know*.
     b. HP: Why not.
         Natalie: @ *I don't know*? (.) *I dunno*? I just don't like being called a Berwicker.

---

* An earlier analysis of a subsample of the data investigated here was presented in Pichler (2009). This chapter investigates a larger set of tokens of I DON'T KNOW, including those followed by a phrasal or clausal complement, and offers a more advanced analysis and interpretation of the data.

c. HP: Do you sometimes deliberately change the way you speak?
    Jerry: *(h)* I I
    Elizabeth: *I dunno* if em I change (.) deliberately would change the
               way I speak. Because (.) *(h)* like I say, (.) I I *don't know*
               whether it's very much of an age thing (.) and that?
d. Luke: *I dunno?* It's just something ab- *I dunno?* It's just only, I think
               only Berwick people can tell.   *I divn't knaa* what it is. Just
    HP: yeah
    Luke: = just as if you h-hear someone you say "Ah it's a Berwick per-
               son."   *I divn't knaa* how. Don't have a clue. It's weird. @
    HP: yeah yeah
e. Keith: Well, *I dinnae ken.*   I (.) maybe. (..) I mean, we know who
    HP: mhm
    Keith: = said it (..) first or the first person I heard (?). *I divn't knaa.*
               I mean, we know exactly who he's talking about but *I dunno*
               where it (.) where that is a (.)

Systematic analysis of the construction's usage and distribution in the socially
stratified BwE dataset provides important new insights into the social, linguistic and interactional mechanisms that give rise to the variation observed in (1).
The analysis uncovers a robust functional split between the most frequent non-
localised variants of I DON'T KNOW (*I don't know*, *I dunno*), which is similar to
that reported in Bybee & Scheibman (1999) and is argued to be a product of long-
standing grammaticalisation processes. Moreover, it reveals that social factors
have primacy over linguistic factors in conditioning the occurrence of the most
frequent localised variant (*I divn't knaa*) which, unlike the frequently occurring
non-localised variants, does not evince function-specific patterning. Together with
the analyses in other chapters, the analysis presented here addresses the broader
research aims of this project set out in Chapter 1 which include establishing the
structure of discourse-pragmatic variation and demonstrating the important role
of discourse-pragmatic variables in shaping synchronic language variation.

The chapter begins in Section 4.2 with a review of the literature that informs
the current analysis of I DON'T KNOW, followed by a more detailed outline of the
aims of this chapter. Section 4.3 describes the decisions regarding the circumscription of the variable context and the coding of the data. This section also details the
variants of I DON'T KNOW which have been identified in the BwE corpus. By providing a detailed outline of the variable's functional repertoire in the present dataset,
Section 4.4 demonstrates how the data were coded for pragmatic function. Section
4.5 presents the results of the quantitative analysis, outlining the synchronic structure and apparent-time robustness of the formal variation observed in the data. The
results are discussed in Section 4.6. Finally, Section 4.7 is the conclusion.

4.2 Previous research on I DON'T KNOW

I DON'T KNOW has received a fair amount of scholarly attention. This section reviews first qualitative studies concerned with the construction's pragmatic functions in discourse before reviewing quantitative studies concerned with patterns of variation and change in its use. There follows at the end of this section an outline of how the present study extends the scope of previous research by including multiple contextual factors in the quantification of all tokens of the variable in a socially stratified corpus of interview data.

4.2.1 Qualitative studies: Discourse-pragmatic functions of I DON'T KNOW[21]

Discourse and conversation analysts argue that the construction I DON'T KNOW has little importance as a verbal representation of a cognitive mental state, i.e., lack of knowledge. Instead, analysts who have studied I DON'T KNOW in its sequential and interactional context of occurrence concur in highlighting the construction's significance as a pragmatic device that performs multiple interpersonal and textual functions in discourse.

Potter (2004: 212) describes I DON'T KNOW as a "stake inoculation" device: it serves to avert potential contradictions from interlocutors and to protect speakers' positive face wants by denying the relevance of immediately following and/or preceding utterances and reducing the risk that these are interpreted unfavourably (see also Drew 1992). To exemplify this function of I DON'T KNOW, Potter draws on Martin Bashir's 1995 Panorama interview with Princess Diana. Potter argues that when the late Princess precedes and follows her assessment of why she had given consent to Andrew Morton's biography with 'dunno,' the construction serves to manage a potentially unsympathetic inference of her as "a spurned and vindictive ex-wife" (2004: 215). Wooffitt's (2005: 125) analysis supports a description of I DON'T KNOW as an interpersonal face-saving device which "attend[s] to sensitive or delicate matters generated in interaction." Wooffitt observes that when youth are asked in interviews whether they belong to a particular subculture (e.g. punks), they frequently preface their turns with I DON'T KNOW in attempts to distance themselves from subcultural categories and resist self-identification in these terms. One of the most comprehensive discussions of I DON'T KNOW's face-saving potential in everyday conversation is provided by Tsui (1991). She demonstrates that depending on the construction's placement in discourse, it may function to

---

21. Because the functional repertoire of I DON'T KNOW is illustrated in detail in Section 4.4, no examples are provided here of the functions identified for it in the literature.

qualify preceding or upcoming propositions; to soften the effect of disaligning or impolite remarks; or to withhold sequentially and interactionally dispreferred actions. Tsui thus draws attention to the fact that the functionality of I DON'T KNOW cannot be reduced to a single pragmatic meaning.

This view is supported by Beach & Metzger's (1997) analysis of casual conversations and courtroom interactions. They argue that in second pair parts of question-answer adjacency pairs I DON'T KNOW is strategically employed by interactants to achieve any of the following actions: to mark upcoming assessments as uncertain; to avoid requests for action by providing responsive yet noncommittal replies; to dismiss others' contributions in attempts to complete actions in progress or terminate problematic topics. They thus draw attention to the fact that I DON'T KNOW functions both in the interpersonal domain to express speaker stance and in the textual domain to structure discourse. The construction's textual functions have also been noted elsewhere. Ford & Thompson (1996: 169–170) suggest that claims of insufficient knowledge serve as topic-closing moves when speakers are reluctant to pursue a topic that is not of prime concern or interest to them. Hutchby (2002) argues that in counselling sessions children strategically use I DON'T KNOW to avoid answering unwelcome questions and resist discussing problematic topics. According to Hutchby, it is the construction's potential to be produced in response to virtually any question, including requests for elaboration following declarations of insufficient knowledge, which makes it such a powerful interactional tool. Beyond topic-control, I DON'T KNOW can also function in the textual domain as a turn-yielding and turn-initiating device (Östman 1981: 27; Schegloff 1996: 61–62).

Importantly, I DON'T KNOW can operate concurrently in the interpersonal and textual domains. Schegloff's (1996: 61–62) reference to turn-initial tokens of I DON'T KNOW as "prefatory epistemic disclaimer[s]" highlights these tokens' multifunctionality: they initiate a turn while at the same time hedging its content. This interpretation is confirmed by Weatherall's (2011) analysis of turn-initial tokens of I DON'T KNOW that constitute grammatically independent turn-constructional units. With the appropriate prosodic encoding, these tokens can signal epistemicity and turn continuation simultaneously. Weatherall also successfully demonstrates that the functionality of I DON'T KNOW is affected by the construction's prosodic encoding as well as by whether the next action follows a pause or contains an epistemic phrase. Diani's (2004) attempt to establish how the functionality of I DON'T KNOW is affected by its co-occurrence with other discourse-pragmatic features is only moderately successful. Not only is her analysis not consistently concerned with I DON'T KNOW as a pragmatic device, but her discussion is not firmly focused on the functionality of I DON'T KNOW (see, for example, Diani's [2004: 170] assessment that "in collocation with *I don't know*, *you know* seems to be used as an invitation to acknowledge a new piece of information").

The studies outlined above have analysed the functional versatility of I DON'T KNOW in different situational contexts, thereby demonstrating the construction's extensive functional range in discourse. However, because these studies have largely focused their analyses on the use of I DON'T KNOW in specific sequential contexts, notably second pair parts of (question-answer) adjacency pairs, we cannot be sure how comprehensive currently available descriptions of I DON'T KNOW are, or which of the functions introduced above are the most common in discourse. Moreover, while most studies have emphasised that the pragmatic meaning of a particular instance of I DON'T KNOW depends largely on its sequential context, few studies have successfully described the effect of the ambient linguistic context on the functions performed by I DON'T KNOW. The current study will address some of these limitations.

4.2.2 Quantitative studies: Variation and change in the use of I DON'T KNOW

As pointed out at the beginning of this chapter, quantitative studies of I DON'T KNOW are still in short supply. This shortage is regrettable, for the few extant studies demonstrate that quantitative analyses of I DON'T KNOW's functional versatility, syntactic positioning and formal encoding have the potential to enhance our understanding of the extra- and intra-linguistic mechanisms which create discourse-pragmatic variation.

Aijmer's (2009) analysis of I DON'T KNOW in a corpus of spoken learner English and a native speaker control corpus reveals the following differences between advanced learner and native speaker usage of I DON'T KNOW: learners prefer to use I DON'T KNOW in turn-final position as a speech-management signal (e.g. to curtail topics); native speakers prefer to use it in turn-initial position as a face-saving device (e.g. to avoid answering questions directly). Aijmer (2009: 166) attributes learners' frequent use of I DON'T KNOW for textual functions to the fact that they do not have at their disposal the same range of linguistic resources as native speakers to overcome planning difficulties in spoken interaction.

Similar acquisition-based differences in the use of I DON'T KNOW are reported in Baumgarten & House (2010). Their analysis reveals that in English as a lingua franca interactions I DON'T KNOW tends to be used mainly in simple-clause and matrix-complement constructions as an expression of insufficient knowledge; when used in extra-sentential position, it tends to function as a non-conventionalised signal of on-line planning difficulties. By contrast, in their recorded native speaker interactions, I DON'T KNOW is rarely used in clausal constructions and occurs mostly in extra-sentential positions with conventionalised interpersonal and textual functions such as stance-marking and turn-completion. Baumgarten & House (2010: 1197) attribute the differential distribution and use of I DON'T KNOW in learner and native discourses to inter-variety differences in the functional diversification of I DON'T KNOW which result from grammaticalisation processes only affecting native varieties of English.

The grammaticalisation of I DON'T KNOW and its effects on the construction's phonetic encoding, functional versatility and constituent structure are discussed in two studies drawing on the same data of American English: Bybee & Scheibman (1999) and Scheibman (2000). Depending on the realisation of the vowel in *don't* as either full, [o], or reduced, [ə], these scholars classified the 37 tokens of I DON'T KNOW in their data of naturally occurring conversations into two categories: full vowel variants and reduced vowel variants.[22] Distributional analyses showed that an overwhelming majority of tokens were produced with a reduced vowel (78%, N = 29). Further, the results revealed a strong correlation between phonetic realisation and discourse function: referential uses were realised with full variants as well as reduced variants (N = 7 and N = 12 respectively); tokens functioning as a mitigation device were overwhelmingly realised with reduced variants (N = 9 out of 10); and all turn-yielding tokens of the variable were realised with a reduced vowel in *don't* (N = 8). Scheibman (2000: 120) summarises the distribution of phonetic variants according to function as follows:

> [a]ll variants of *don't* in [I DON'T KNOW] convey the expression's lexical meaning of 'not knowing', but, with one exception, only reduced vowel forms occur in contexts of the collocation's interactive, face-saving functions. Moreover, only reduced vowel variants participate in what is arguably the most conventionalized, or ritualized, use of the expression – that of signalling a speaker change.

These results, then, reveal a distribution of variants along discourse-functional factors: full variants are associated with referential meanings and reduced variants with pragmatic meanings.

According to Bybee & Scheibman (1999), the underlying cause of the functional split between variants is high frequency of use and repetition. With increased use in interaction, I DON'T KNOW has become stored and processed as a single unit (chunking) and has gradually weakened its association with its composite parts

---

22. Bybee & Scheibman (1999: 579–580) initially also differentiated between full vowel variants that were produced with an initial stop or an initial reduced consonant (flap), and between reduced vowel variants that were produced with a reduced initial consonant or no initial consonant (see also Scheibman 2000: 107–109). They disregarded the consonantal differences in the quantification of the data.

(*I, don't, know*) (autonomy) (see also Bybee 2003:617–618, 2006:725–726). The loss of compositionality and analysability has triggered morpho-phonological and semantic-pragmatic changes which obscure the original internal structure and meaning of I DON'T KNOW. The association of the non-fused and non-reduced variant with referential uses on the one hand and of the fused and reduced variant with pragmatic uses on the other hand, then, is a result of the variable's grammaticalisation, i.e., "the process by which a frequently used sequence of words or morphemes becomes automated as a single processing unit" (Bybee 2003:603).

The studies outlined above demonstrate the structured nature of observed variation patterns in the usage and distribution of I DON'T KNOW, and highlight the importance of function in conditioning the variation. Function accounts for the construction's differential frequency and positional distribution in learner and native speaker interactions, and operates as a constraint on its formal variation in American English conversation. The limited size of Bybee & Scheibman's dataset (37 tokens from six speakers aged 27–52, two male and four female) precludes investigation of the social embedding of variation in the form of I DON'T KNOW and of the robustness of the functional split between its variants. Grant's (2010) analysis of the functional distribution of full and reduced variants of I DON'T KNOW across age, sex, region and conversation type in the spoken part of the *British National Corpus* (henceforth BNC) (one million words) fails to provide this information because it suffers from serious methodological flaws. Firstly, as Grant (2010:2290) readily admits, it is not known on what basis the transcribers of the BNC distinguished between full and reduced variants of I DON'T KNOW or how rigorously this distinction was adhered to in the transcription process. Secondly, and perhaps even more worryingly, Grant reports raw numbers of the variable and its variants instead of following standard variationist procedure, i.e., indexing frequency scores of the variable as proportions of total word counts and reporting the proportional frequency of variants out of the variable, as dictated by the principle of accountability (see Chapter 2.3.2). In the absence of reliable transcriptions and accountable quantifications, Grant's (2010) study can offer no insights into the formal variability of I DON'T KNOW in contemporary British English.[23] In contrast to Grant (2010), the following study of I DON'T KNOW is based on faithful transcriptions and accountable statistical analyses, thus affording reliable new insights into the variable's distribution in discourse.

---

23. The same criticisms apply to Grant's (2010) analysis of I DON'T KNOW in the *Wellington Spoken Corpus*. However, this part of the study does not investigate form variation in the construction's use and is therefore not of concern here.

4.2.3   Aims and contribution of this chapter

As mentioned at the beginning, this chapter investigates the high degree of variation in the realisation of I DON'T KNOW in a sizeable and socially stratified corpus of a variety of English spoken in north-east England. It differs from previous analyses of I DON'T KNOW by testing the effect on variation of social factors, conducting an apparent-time analysis of I DON'T KNOW variation, and studying the distribution of both non-localised and localised variants.

Inclusion of social factors alongside linguistic factors as independent variables in the analysis allows us to model the simultaneous effect of multiple contextual factors (age, sex, function, syntax) on the formal variation of I DON'T KNOW. Further, apparent-time analysis of a large number of tokens of the variable makes it possible to establish the robustness of variation in the data, and to identify the existence and trajectory of any ongoing changes to variants' intra- and extra-linguistic conditioning. Finally, investigation of a variety which features both non-localised and localised variants of I DON'T KNOW (see further Section 4.3.2) enables us to determine whether constraints on variant choice are identical across variants with differential geographical distribution. The current project thus has a much broader scope than previous studies which focused exclusively on the distribution of non-localised variants, left unaccounted for the role of extra-linguistic factors in the distribution of I DON'T KNOW variants, and did not probe the stability of form-meaning correlations in apparent time (see Section 4.2.2). The broad scope of the present analysis contributes new insights into the grammar underpinning the formal variation of I DON'T KNOW and thereby illuminates the sociolinguistic embedding of discourse-pragmatic variation and change.

In order to integrate function as an independent variable in the quantitative analysis and test previous claims about its impact on the formal variation of I DON'T KNOW, this study must necessarily establish the inventory of functions performed by I DON'T KNOW in the BwE corpus. The qualitative data analysis presented in Section 4.4 represents a development beyond the studies reviewed in Section 4.2.1 because it investigates all tokens of the variable in their range of utterance- and turn-positions, fully acknowledges the multifunctionality of individual tokens of the variable, and describes the effect of co-occurring linguistic material on the functionality of I DON'T KNOW. The analysis thus yields a comprehensive functional taxonomy of I DON'T KNOW which, albeit representative only of interview data, makes an important contribution to current descriptions of the construction's functional repertoire. Also, by quantifying the results of the qualitative data analysis, the study establishes the relative frequency and importance of the various functions performed by I DON'T KNOW in the interview data.

Prior to presenting the results of the qualitative and quantitative analyses, the next section sets out the procedures for circumscribing the variable context, allocating tokens of I DON'T KNOW to variant categories, and coding the data for extra- and intra-linguistic conditioning factors.

4.3 The variable context and data coding

4.3.1 The variable and the envelope of variation

The variable under investigation in this chapter is the construction I DON'T KNOW, as defined in Chapter 2.3.2. To yield principled and accountable results, every instance of a construction derived from the following linear string of components was extracted from the data: (*I*) + (present tense negative DO) + (*know*). This yielded tokens in different syntactic configurations: unbound tokens of I DON'T KNOW without overt complementation (2a); tokens with a dependent WH-word (2b); and bound tokens with phrasal or clausal complements in the form of noun phrases (2c), adverbial phrases (2d), prepositional phrases (2e), finite conditional clauses with *if* or *whether* (2f), or finite WH-interrogative clauses (2g).[24] This study departs from the practice in previous studies (e.g. Aijmer 2009) and includes in the variable context all tokens of I DON'T KNOW in all syntactic configurations. This decision was motivated by the preliminary observation that all instances of I DON'T KNOW in the BwE corpus are variable in form and function.

(2) a. *I dinnae ken*, Mary. I'm no sure.
         Americans just, *I dunno*, they have this thing about Scotland.
     b. And *I dunno* <u>why</u>, but people in Berwick have a stigma.
     c. But I feel sort of intimidated wi Muslims, cos *I divn't knaa* <u>their religion</u>.
     d. *I dunno* <u>much</u> about it.
     e. Drunk? *I dunno* <u>about drunk</u> now. What would drunk be?

---

24. When I DON'T KNOW signals pragmatic meanings, we are not in fact dealing with a matrix-complement construction as is the case when it functions referentially. Instead, we are dealing with a mono-clausal construction that contains an epistemic frame (see further Section 4.6). For ease of reference, however, the labels 'matrix clause' and 'complement clause' are used throughout this chapter to identify the construction I DON'T KNOW and the clause over which it has scope, irrespective of their actual syntactic hierarchy or status in specific contexts of use (see also Boye & Harder 2007; van Bogaert 2010).

f.   And *I don't know* <u>if they have a Romany connection.</u>
     I don't know <u>whether it's very much of an age thing and that.</u>
g.   *I divn't knaa* <u>what else I would call the rain.</u>

Following standard variationist procedure, tokens of the variable whose form could not be determined and tokens which occurred in quoted speech were excluded from the database. A total of 600 tokens of the variable I DON'T KNOW were retained for in-depth analysis. Each of these tokens was coded for its form and a series of extra- and intra-linguistic factors which were hypothesised to have an effect on the construction's morpho-phonology. The following sections detail the coding decisions.

4.3.2   The dependent variable: Variants of I DON'T KNOW in BwE

The extracts from the data given in (1) in Section 4.1 illustrate that the variable I DON'T KNOW manifests a high degree of formal variation in BwE. The variation affects the realisation of negative periphrastic DO, the morpheme boundary between negative DO and the cognition verb, as well as the choice of the negator and the lexical item signalling a cognitive state. Although allocation of tokens to discrete categories necessarily masks the full details of variation, close auditory analysis of all tokens of I DON'T KNOW in the BwE corpus indicates that, for quantitative purposes, tokens can be meaningfully divided into five variant categories. This section introduces the five formal variants identified in the data, and broadly groups them into localised and non-localised variants based on their geographical dispersion within England and the English-speaking world.

Tokens in the first three categories of variants differ from each other with regard to the morpheme boundary between *don't* and *know* (audible vs. non-audible) and/or the vowel quality in *don't* (full vs. reduced). The first category contains tokens such as [dɔnʔnɔː] or [dʊnʔ'nʊ]: the vowel in *don't* is realised as [ɔ] or [ʊ] and a conspicuous morpheme boundary occurs between the nasals of *don't* and *know*, usually in the form of [ʔ]. Due to their relative lack of reduction, these variants are labelled full variants and are orthographically represented as *I don't know*. The second category contains tokens such as [dʊ'nɔː]: the first vowel is produced with lip-rounding but in contrast to the full variants there is no morpheme boundary between the nasals of *don't* and *know*. Because they share properties with full variants (lip-rounded vowel) as well as reduced variants (inaudible morpheme boundary), these variants are labelled semi-reduced variants and are orthographically represented as *I dono*. The third category contains tokens such as [dənɔ] or [dənʊ]:

there is no audible morpheme boundary between the nasals of *don't* and *know*, and the vowel in *don't* is reduced to [ə]. Because of their high degree of articulatory reduction, these variants are labelled reduced variants and are orthographically represented as *I dunno*.

The full variant *I don't know* is the standard variant and as such is non-localisable. The semi-reduced variant *I dono* represents a stage in the development from non-reduced to reduced realisations (*don't know > dono > dunno*) which is likely to occur in any variety in which I DON'T KNOW is affected by gradual fusion and attrition due to frequency of use and repetition (see further Section 4.6). The vowel quality in the first syllable of *dono* will, however, differ across varieties. The reduced variant *I dunno* is cited in the *Oxford English Dictionary* (henceforth OED) (2010) without a geographical label. Although the precise nature of the variation is not always detailed, the co-occurrence of full and reduced variants of I DON'T KNOW has also been reported for other varieties in the UK and the US (Aijmer 2009; Baumgarten & House 2010; Bybee & Scheibman 1999; Grant 2010; Östman 1981; Scheibman 2000). Since it can be assumed that they are widely distributed throughout England and the English-speaking world, the variants *I don't know*, *I dono* and *I dunno* are categorised as non-localised variants.

Tokens in the fourth and fifth categories of variants differ from those above in that negative periphrastic DO is realised as *divn't* or *dinnae* (see Chapter 3.3) and the cognitive verb may in some instances take a form other than *know*. The category of variants orthographically represented as *I divn't knaa* contains tokens such as [dɪvn̩nãː] or [tɪfn̩ˈnɐ]: negative periphrastic DO contains a KIT-vowel and some degree of friction. Also, with this category of tokens, the lexical item *know* is usually, but not always, replaced with *knaa* [nɐ]. The category of variants orthographically represented as *I dinnae ken* contains tokens such as [dənɪ̈xen]: periphrastic DO is negated with the negative clitic -*nae*, yielding the negative auxiliary *dinnae* [dənɪ] or [dənə]. Also, with this category of tokens, *know* is usually, but not always, replaced with *ken* [ken].

As detailed in Chapter 3.3.2, the forms *divn't* and *dinnae* are not used throughout all of England or the English-speaking world. *Divn't* is strongly associated with the north(-east) of England; the same is true of *knaa* (Griffiths 2005). *Dinnae* is strongly linked with Scotland, although its use has been recorded in Northumberland; *ken* is a shibboleth of Scottish speech (Grant & Murison 1931). Because their distribution in England is largely restricted to the north(-east), the variants *I divn't knaa* and *I dinnae ken* are categorised here as localised variants.

Table 4.1 summarises the BwE inventory of variants for I DON'T KNOW, with an indication of their geographical distribution in England.

Table 4.1 Inventory of variants of the construction I DON'T KNOW in BwE

non-localised variants	localised variants
I don't know	I divn't knaa
I dono	I dinnae ken
I dunno	

4.3.3 Independent variables: Data coding

In addition to coding each occurrence of I DON'T KNOW for its variant form, every token of the variable was coded for the operation of extra- and intra-linguistic constraints hypothesised to have an effect on variant selection.

Previous research has demonstrated that the grammaticalisation processes leading to the synchronic co-existence of discourse-pragmatic variants are socially embedded, and that social factors, including sex, age, socio-economic class, education and locality, are strongly implicated in the synchronic distribution of formal variants in discourse-pragmatics (see, for example, Buchstaller & D'Arcy 2009; Cheshire 2007; Ferrara 1997; Ito & Tagliamonte 2003; Macaulay 2002b; Palander-Collin 1999; Pichler & Levey 2011; Tagliamonte & Hudson 1999). Moreover, the results reported in Chapter 3 have shown that in productive constructions the occurrence of negative auxiliaries formed with -nae is strongly constrained by age. Assuming, for now, that the formal variation illustrated in (1) and introduced in more detail in Section 4.3.2 reflects the layering effect associated with grammaticalisation and that conditioning factors remain constant across productive and formulaic constructions, we may hypothesise that social factors are implicated in the formal variation of I DON'T KNOW. To test this hypothesis and probe the social distribution of variants, each token of the variable was coded for speaker sex and age. Inclusion of the independent variable age in the coding protocol also allows us to evoke the apparent-time construct with a view to identifying any ongoing changes to the conditioning of variants, and locating the leaders of any such changes. All tokens were further coded for individual speaker. This allows us to control for individual speaker effects on the extra- and intra-linguistic distribution of variants in the multivariate analysis of the data (see Chapter 2.3.3).

Bybee & Scheibman (1999) and Scheibman (2000) have demonstrated that the variation between full and reduced variants of I DON'T KNOW in American English conversational data is conditioned by discourse-functional constraints. Similar conditioning effects arising from grammaticalisation have been reported for other discourse-pragmatic variables. For example, Lindemann & Mauranen (2001) and Stenström (1998) found that phonetically full forms of just and because correlated with older layers of meaning ('exactly' for *just*; grammatical subordination for *because*), while phonetically reduced forms correlated with newer, grammatical-ised layers of meaning (mitigation for *just*; continuation signalling for *because*) (see also Andersen 2001:213; Drager 2011 on lexical vs. discourse *like*). To test whether function is also implicated in the formal variation of I DON'T KNOW in BwE and whether it affects non-localised and localised variants alike, all tokens of the variable were coded for their function in the data. Viewing any emergent form-function correlations in apparent time will enable us to assess whether they are conventionalising and strengthening over time, as predicted by Bybee (2006:725–726). The results of the qualitative data analysis and the coding schema for discourse-functional constraints are outlined in Section 4.4.

4.4 Qualitative analysis of I DON'T KNOW

Applying the methods outlined in Chapter 2.5, this section identifies the functions performed by I DON'T KNOW in the BwE interview data. To demonstrate the valid-ity of the analysis, each function is illustrated with one or more examples from the data. The examples are presented in their sequential and interactional con-text of occurrence; typographical means are employed to replicate accompanying paralinguistic and prosodic features (see page XVII for a key to the transcription conventions). These features as well as lexical material in the ambient context, notably co-occurring discourse-pragmatic features, adverbs and filled pauses, are discussed below when they make a systematic contribution to data interpretation. Recurrent co-occurrence patterns are listed in Appendices 1–3 which summarise the results of the qualitative analysis. Where pertinent to the analysis, the larger discourse context and the situational context in which I DON'T KNOW occurs are attended to in the discussion of the data, and specific reference is made to any CA theories implicated in the interpretation of the data. Through providing a detailed description and illustration of the functionality of I DON'T KNOW in the BwE interview data, the analysis presented here yields a detailed coding protocol for the factor group functionality (see Table 4.2 in Section 4.4.4), suitable for replication and elaboration in future studies of the variable.

Because tokens in different syntactic configurations cover different functional spectra, the functionality of unbound tokens, bound tokens with a phrasal or clausal complement, and tokens with a dependent WH-word is discussed sepa-rately. I will start with unbound tokens since these are numerically the most fre-quent and functionally the most versatile. The discussion of other tokens will be less detailed, relying heavily on the insights gained from the preceding analysis of unbound tokens.

4.4.1 Functions performed by unbound I DON'T KNOW

Unbound tokens of I DON'T KNOW constitute structurally and intonationally independent units in discourse which can occur in a range of clause or utterance positions. As a result of their syntactic freedom and positional mobility, they perform a wide range of interpersonal and textual functions related to expressing speaker attitudes and coordinating speaker-hearer relations as well as creating structure and coherence in discourse.

In the interpersonal domain, I DON'T KNOW functions subjectively to signal speakers' doubts regarding the accuracy of their propositions. This use is illustrated in Extract (3) from the data, where Keith tells the interviewer HP and his interview partner Adam about a confrontation he had during a night out in Carlisle. Keith signals that his assessment of the origin of his interlocutors may not be reliable by retrospectively qualifying it with *I dunno*. The tentative effect of *I dunno* is produced and reinforced by its fall-rise intonation contour and its co-occurrence with other hedging devices (*probably, or something like that*). The qualification fulfils an important face-saving function because it allows Keith to avoid committing himself to his proposition.

(3)   Keith: When I was in the in the toilet, someone   well a a lad said
      HP: mhm
      Keith: = "What do you want a cigarette?"   And I said "No." And then
      HP: @
      Keith: = his pal came in. They were I-Irish. They were [probably] from up
      HP: [yeah]
      Keith: = the road. They were probably [gipsies] or something like that.
      HP: [mhm]
      Keith: = *I dunno*?   And they were (.) they said "O:h. Where are you
      HP: [mhm]
      Adam: [@]
      Keith: = from." You know, straight away.

I DON'T KNOW does not always occur outside the main constituents of an utterance, nor does it always have scope over entire propositions. This is illustrated in (4), where two teenage informants had been asked their opinion of the Labour party's regional government proposals for the north-east. Rebecca argues in favour of a devolved government and implies that whereas the present government is remote from Berwick and oblivious to its current affairs, a regional government in nearby Durham would be better informed about the town. The end of Rebecca's turn contains several linguistic features that are indicative of her difficulty in formulating a coherent justification for her support of regional devolution: a false start (*and it's just*), prosodic lengthening of sounds (*mo:re, s:ense*), unfilled pauses, and instances of I DON'T KNOW as turn-holding and epistemic repair devices. Near the end of the extract, we find another instance of *I dunno*. This token occurs internal to the syntactic structure between obligatory constituents of the clause: NP *I dunno* VP. By bringing not the entire proposition but merely the immediately following lexical items in its scope, *I dunno* signals that the following expression only loosely communicates Rebecca's thoughts and/or that she is unsure of her choice of wording. The attenuating effect of *I dunno* is achieved prosodically through its rising intonation contour and the slow production of the items in its scope.

(4) Alicia: I think it would make a difference. [I think] we'd be included a
     HP: [mhm]
     Alicia: = lot more [in things.]
     HP: [yeah]
     Rebecca: [Yeah.] *(h)* Because like (.) likes of the people down
                in London, they don't know >what's going on in Berwick
                [and things.]< *(h)* (..) And (.) they'd have to travel forever to get
     HP: [mhm]
     Rebecca: = here. *(h)* [Whereas if] <they're just at Durham,> (..) although
     HP: [mhm]
     Rebecca: = they're not gonna be here, (.) they're closer!   And it's just
     HP: mhm
     Rebecca: = (.) I dunno? It'll be mo:re (..) <@ I dunno really? It would be
                better. @> [They] just (..) *I dunno?* >have more s:ense< of
     HP: [mhm]
     Rebecca: = what's going on (.) really, if they were in the north-east.

In the interpersonal domain I DON'T KNOW can also function intersubjectively. It mitigates interactional conflict by reducing the anticipated unwelcome effect of disparaging remarks, contentious propositions or disagreements. This effect is implicit in Examples (3) and (4) above and is illustrated more clearly in the examples in (5) below. In (5a), Luke blames children's drug abuse on their parents' negligence. By prefacing his turn with *I divn't knaa* and terminating it in final rising pitch, Luke marks his assertion to appear uncertain and unreliable (see also his use of the hedges *I think* and *just*). If challenged, this allows him to distance himself from this potentially controversial assessment and to avert open conflict. In (5b), Lori disaligns herself from her father's positive evaluation of the Isle of Skye. Her diverging view is prefaced and delayed by *I dunno* which works towards accomplishing the disagreement in a mitigated way and to redress its potentially face-threatening effect (Pomerantz 1984:64–77) (see also Tsui 1991:610–612).

The fact that Lori starts her modified disagreement in a higher than usual pitch reinforces this effect.

(5)   a.   Luke: For the kids that are on drugs I blame the parents me. @
          HP: Why.
          Luke: *I divn't knaa?* I think they're just (?) Aye. They're no looking after their kids properly, or they just (.) just letting them get away wi it?
     b.   Godfrey: °Yeah,° it was it's a really nice place.
          HP: [°Yeah.°]
          Lori: [*I dunno*,] because I got
          Godfrey: == I had a <u>great</u> holiday up there.
          HP: Yeah?
          Lori: I got bored and sunburnt.

Besides using I DON'T KNOW to attenuate assessments, speakers sometimes claim insufficient knowledge in order to avoid making assessments (see also Beach & Metzger 1997: 575; Tsui 1991: 609–610). This is particularly true in situations such as (6) where provision of an assessment may lead to interactional conflict. In this example, Leah and Shannon discuss the fact that some Berwickers differentiate between the north and south parts of the town and regard the north side as the 'posh' side. Shannon, who lives on the south side of the town, is getting increasingly upset as the conversation proceeds on this issue (see the increase in volume and speech rate in the third line of the extract). When she asks Leah why her sister, Judith, disdains the south side of the town, Leah withholds the requested assessment. She uses *don't know* to avoid attending to an issue that seems highly sensitive to her friend.

(6)   Shannon: °What's wrong with (.) <u>not</u> north?° @
      Leah: Judith doesn't like (.) <u>not</u> north
      Shannon: <WHAT'S WRONG [WITH <u>NOT</u> NORTH?>]
      HP: [No. But] some people, you know, make the difference between north and south.
      Leah: Mhm.
      Shannon: See, I [>never ever<] WHY.
      Leah: [See, Judith does.]
                  Don't know.
      Shannon: But she lives in ORD!
      Leah: <£ Yeah, I know. But that's posh Ord. £>

In addition to the functions I DON'T KNOW performs in the interpersonal domain, it fulfils a range of functions relating to repair-marking, topic-development and turn-exchange in the textual domain. As shown in (7), I DON'T KNOW can be used to fill the gap between the repaired and the repairing segments in self-initiated turn-repairs "in which an emerging utterance is stopped in some way and is then aborted, recast, continued or redone" (Fox et al. 1996: 190). In (7a), Daniel recasts his utterance after a cut-off; in (7b), Charlene abandons her initial utterance. In both examples, the transition between the interrupted or abandoned utterance (*I s-, I think it's getting more*) and the beginning of the rephrased or recast utterance (*I keep saying* ..., *It's only an hour* ...) is bridged with *I dunno*. In (7b), *I dunno* is surrounded by filled and unfilled pauses and uttered with moderately higher but lowering pitch. This introduces an element of hesitation to the repair sequence.[25]

(7) a. Daniel: No, well, (.) I s- *I dunno*, I keep saying, (.) if if it's so good where you came from, why don't you go back? That's what I say, you know?

    b. Charlene: I think it's getting mo:re (..) e:m °*I dunno*.° (..) It's only an hour on the train to [Newcastle] or Edinburgh now, so I

        HP: [mhm]

        Charlene: = think (.) a few people sort of work [*(h)* (.)] you know,

        HP: [mhm]

        Charlene: = Edinburgh or Newcastle or (.) and they prefer to live (.) either Alnwick or (.) Berwick or somewhere similar than, you know, in the city.

In the textual domain, I DON'T KNOW can also be strategically employed by speakers to affect the topical development of interactions. This usage of I DON'T KNOW is particularly pertinent to interview situations. Because the topical agenda is generally set by the interviewer, successful topic-development requires interviewees' collaboration and access to proffered topics (see Geluykens 1993; Schegloff 2007: 169–180). What happens when these conditions are not met is illustrated in Extract (8) where HP, the interviewer, asks Gabriel, the interviewee, about age-based differences in non-standard language use. Gabriel replies to HP's follow-up (*Why do you think*) with the minimal response token *dunno*. This token serves

---

25. By virtue of bridging a gap in discourse, repair tokens of I DON'T KNOW also aid speakers in securing their hold on the floor. What distinguishes the tokens in (7) from the turn-holding tokens discussed in (12) below is their syntactic context of occurrence, i.e., the former's occurrence between repaired and repairing elements of utterances.

two functions. On the one hand, it attends to HP's face needs as an interviewer by providing a response to her question, albeit a minimal one. On the other hand, it serves to decline the proffered topic by disavowing access to it (see also Pomerantz 1984: 57–58; Schegloff 2007: 169–180). Although Gabriel's *dunno* does not have a marked descending intonation contour, it is strongly closure-implicative, not least because it cannot be challenged (e.g. with 'why not?'). This is attested by HP's subsequent behaviour. HP does not probe Gabriel's minimal response but acknowledges the complexity of her question (*It's hard to say*) and almost immediately moves on to the next item on the interview agenda.

(8)   HP: Would you say that younger people, older people use more
                 non-standard grammar than younger ones?
      Gabriel: Yeah.
      HP: Yeah? <u>Why</u> do you think.
      Gabriel: *Dunno*
      HP: It's hard to say.
      Gabriel: Mhm.
      HP: == Yeah. (..) Ok. *(h)* And do you think there's a difference
                 between girls and boys, or males and females?

As well as to decline topics, I DON'T KNOW serves to curtail topics (see also Beach & Metzger 1997: 571–575; Ford & Thompson 1996: 169–170). Example (9) illustrates this usage. Gregory and Julia initially embrace the topic proffered by HP's question regarding characteristic features of BwE. However, following a brief and unsuccessful attempt to provide a satisfactory response, Gregory curtails the topic by declaring insufficient knowledge to expand on the issue. Gregory's desire to bring the topic sequence to a close is reinforced by the following *just can*, with *just* indicating "a speaker's assumption that nothing more can or need be said about a proposition" (Wauchope 1993: 182).

(9)   HP: What gives it away as a Berwick accent.
      (..)
      Gregory: Couldn't really nail it down like, but
      Julia: No. You cannae, but it's just
      (..)
      Gregory: You can tell when someone's (.) frae Berwick. You can,
      Julia: You can.
      Gregory: = *don't know*   just can.
      HP: mhm

Finally, as far as topic-development functions are concerned, I DON'T KNOW is used by interviewees to discard successful interruptions by their interview partners (see also Beach & Metzger 1997: 571–575). This function is illustrated in (10) where Adam provides information about football in Berwick. When Adam uses a lengthened filled pause (*e::m*) mid-utterance, Keith successfully disrupts his hold on the floor to put forward a verification-seeking tag question. Adam's response, *I divn't knaa*, attends to Keith's face wants by providing the required second pair part of the adjacency pair. Yet at the same time, this response disclaims the knowledge required to respond to the question more fully (see (8) above). Talk on the issue raised by Keith cannot therefore be sustained and Adam is in a position to resume his account of football in Berwick, with *but* marking the return to the original topic (Schiffrin 1987: 177). The slight prosodic rise on *knaa* adds a tone of tentativeness to Adam's minimal response. It makes his reluctance to engage with Keith's question sound less abrupt and hostile, and thus presumably more acceptable to Keith.

(10) Adam: Well, Berwick Rangers they s::- (..) play in the Scottish league
      HP: mhm
      Adam: *(h) (h)* but then you have like $ [e::m *(.h)*]
      Keith: [They] <u>can</u> play in either or
             though, can't they?
      Adam: *I divn't knaa?* But
      Keith: == They used to be (?).
      Adam: You have like (.) *(h)* teams like em Highfields and (.) Spittal
      HP: mhm
      Adam: = and that. [And] they play wi like (.) in a league called the Nor-
      HP: [mhm]
      Adam: = thern Alliance.

However, the most frequent textual uses of I DON'T KNOW in the BwE corpus do not relate to repair-marking or topic-development but to turn-exchange. In combination with other linguistic material, the construction regularly serves to affect and prevent turn-transfer between interviewees. The extracts from the data in (11) serve to illustrate the use of I DON'T KNOW as a turn-taking device. In (11a), Godfrey launches his turn at the very moment Lori's turn reaches a complex transition relevance place (henceforth CTRP), i.e., a place where speaker change can occur because the current speaker's turn has reached syntactic, pragmatic and intonational completion (Ford & Thompson 1996). Godfrey's turn-initial instance of *I dunno* neither contributes to the propositional content of his turn, nor communicates an affective stance (reflected in the lack of noticeable pitch movement). Instead, it allows Godfrey to secure his hold on the floor while he is still in the process of planning his contribution. This interpretation is supported by the fact that Lori temporarily manages to regain the floor, that *I dunno* is produced with increased speech rate, and that other turn elements are present which are suggestive of Godfrey's lack of planning: a false start; a vague expression (*it all depends*); syllable lengthening on the continuation signal *because*. In (11b), Luke's turn-initial use of *I dunno* is not motivated by a competition for the floor (he is the sole interviewee), an attempt to stall for time (apart from *th-*, the beginning of his turn does not contain any elements suggestive of planning or hesitation), nor a desire to mitigate potential unwelcome effects of his utterance (he overtly expresses his dislike of Geordies). *I dunno* here functions as a take-off for further talk. It avoids impairing the projectability of Luke's turn, the start of which overlaps with the closure of HP's preceding turn (see Sacks et al. 1974:718–721). In fact, the lengthening on the final syllable of *dunno* might be motivated by Luke's attempt to delay the actual start of his proposition until HP's turn reaches a CTRP.

(11)	a.	HP:	Would you say that either old or young people are lazier or sloppier with their grammar?
		Lori:	Younger. @
		HP:	Yeah?
		Lori:	Younger but then again (I mean) old people, (h) they've been taught like, and miss words out.
		Godfrey:	== <*I dunno,*> it it all depends >becaus::e<,
		Lori:	== Things that they're saying.
		Godfrey:	>aulder people. (..) likes of (…) my father's generation.<
		HP:	mhm
		Godfrey:	= They was all (.) constructed in the army and all that <and they had to change their language.> To be under-
		HP:	yeah
		Godfrey:	= stood.
	b.	Luke:	I despise <@ Geordies. @>
		HP:	Why. Wh-what is [wrong with them.]
		Luke:	[*I dunno::,*] every time I go down to Newcastle th- all the Geordies are always really cheeky. You know, they'll say º"ah you fucking"º and gie you abuse all the time, [and] all the rest of it, and then I hate to be associated with
		HP:	[yeah]
		Luke:	= them. I just, I hate them. @
		HP:	yeah

In turn-medial position, when it does not occur between elements of a repair sequence, I DON'T KNOW often functions to secure speakers' hold on the floor. This function is illustrated in the examples in (12). In (12a), *I dunno* occurs between syntactically complete turn-constructional units (henceforth TCUs), i.e., the building blocks (clauses, phrases, words) which combine to constitute a turn or action (Sacks et al. 1974:702–703). *I dunno* is produced without noticeable pitch movement, thus projecting that there is more to come and working towards extending the turn past its possible completion point. The fact that *I dunno* and the following lexical elements are uttered in faster tempo than the surrounding discourse indicates that *I dunno* also works towards preventing other interactants from taking the floor and enabling Rebecca to build a multi-unit turn. The risk of losing one's hold on the floor is highest when speakers hesitate in their construction of an extended or forthcoming turn, as is the case in (12b). Keith's use of *and* following the TCU *And that was with her* signals his intention to extend his turn past a CTRP, for *and* regularly marks speaker continuation (Schiffrin 1987:141–150). The fact that the following *I dunno* is uttered without noticeable pitch movement and is followed by a clause containing *obviously* rule out an epistemic interpretation of this token. Rather, *I dunno*, together with the preceding filled pause *eh*, secures Keith's hold on the floor by signalling his communicative presence while he is preparing the continuation of his turn.

(12) a. Rebecca: They think nothing of it?   [It's just] a normal thing?
          HP: mhm
          Alicia: [yeah]
          Rebecca: = [<*I dunno*,] I think that's just> because it's such large
          HP: [mhm]
          Rebecca: = widespread country.
      b. Keith: And then eh (..) my girlfriend at the time, we broke up and
                    that [was who: (.)] I was gonna go away with and (.) I'd never
          HP: [mhm]
          Keith: = rea- I do- never <I'd only been away once before.>
          HP: mhm
          Keith: = >And that was< with her. [And] eh (..) *I dunno* (.) just like
          HP: [mhm]
          Keith: = obviously I wanted to go Australia [and that. I wanted] to go
          HP: [mhm mhm]
          Keith: = away, like, for a year.

Apart from turn-taking and turn-holding tokens, the corpus also contains tokens of I DON'T KNOW that function as turn-yielding cues. In (13), Rebecca answers HP's question about the positive aspects of life in Berwick upon Tweed posed shortly before Rebecca's interview partner, Alicia, rejoined the interview following a brief comfort break. Although Rebecca talks in response to HP's question for no less than 57 seconds (not all reproduced below), her answer fails to directly address it. After Alicia's return to the interview room and HP's informing her about the current topic of conversation, Rebecca immediately yields the floor to Alicia. This speaker shift is initiated in multiple ways: (i) the use of the turn-relinquishing and pre-closing discourse feature *so* (Schegloff & Sacks 1973:306; Schiffrin 1987:218); (ii) the use of *I dunno* as an appeal to Alicia to take over, with the falling intonation on *dunno* indicating a CTRP; (iii) Rebecca's question (*what do you think?*), which as the first pair part of an adjacency pair requires the provision of a relevant second pair part, i.e., an answer; and (iv) the contrastive stress on *I* in *I dunno* and on *you* in the following question. The combination of these features constitutes a rather forceful turn-yielder. However, the fact that Alicia begins her response before the completion of Rebecca's turn-yielding question suggests that the use of *so* and *I dunno* alone might have been quite sufficient in affecting turn-transfer.

(13)   Rebecca: I mean i- likes of (.) like, everyone says <"oh if you go to
                  Newcastle there's loads of things to do." But like what,> what
                  would you do,   if you lived in Newcastle?   People
       HP: mhm
       Alicia: mhm
       Rebecca: = there'll probably say all the time "Oh, there's nothing to do,
                  there's [nothing to do."]
       HP: [mhm mhm] mhm ((*to Alicia*)) We're talking about the
                  good things in [Berwick.] Yeah.
       Alicia: [Yeah.]
       Rebecca: [@]
                  °So I dunno. ((*to Alicia*)) What [do you think.°]
       Alicia: [I like (.)] the good things. I
                  like the friendliness of the people. Everyone gets on.

With some turn-final instances of I DON'T KNOW, such as those in (14), it is not entirely clear whether they function as turn-exchange or topic-development devices. When Adam's contribution in (14a) (*I don't even think you have to go as far as the border*) reaches a CTRP, it is not immediately followed by further talk or recipient uptake. It is only after an unfilled pause of 2.3 seconds that Adam resumes talk with *and*, a signal of speaker continuation (Schiffrin 1987: 150), followed by *I divn't knaa*. The descending intonation contour on *I divn't knaa* signals that the construction functions to re-occasion turn-completion. It is, however, not clear whether Adam's intention is to bring the topic sequence to a close or to yield the turn to Keith. The ambiguity is reflected in the ensuing non-talk: HP fails to provide the next topic-proffer and Keith does not immediately take up the floor. In (14b), Leah aborts her turn before it reaches a CTRP (*cos you never*). The following *I dunno* thus functions to signal turn-completion, with the high-rising intonation signalling an appeal for co-operation. Whether the appeal is directed at Leah's interview partner to provide an assessment or to HP to proffer the next topic is unclear. While the speakers' intention behind using I DON'T KNOW in (14) may be ambiguous between turn-yielding and topic-closing, the effect is clearly to close speaker turns.

(14) a. HP: So would you say the border is like a linguistic divide?
          Keith: E::h *(.h)*
          Adam: A::h (.) I don't even think you have to go as far as the border.
                  (..) And *I divn't knaa*. @
          (...)
          Keith: Um (..) Aye w-w-w-we're we're (..) we're definitely different.
      b. Leah: *(.h)* >Has no effect on Berwick cos you never,< (.) *I dunno*?

The examples above have shown that some tokens that perform a mitigating function also signal epistemicity and *vice versa*, and that some tokens which function as repair devices or turn-taking/holding devices simultaneously convey a strong element of hesitation. I DON'T KNOW can also be multifunctional in the sense of a single token operating simultaneously across the communicative domains, i.e., concurrently performing interpersonal and textual functions. In (15), for example, the turn-initial token of I DON'T KNOW is produced with rising pitch. It functions to launch Barbara's turn (similar to the tokens in (11) above) as well as to reduce her commitment to the following assessment regarding causes for generational differences in non-standard language use (see also her use of *maybe, just* and *e:h*).

(15) ((*Barbara has just asserted that older people use more non-standard grammar than younger people.*))
      HP: Why do you think that is.
      Barbara: *I dunno*? Maybe just just just e:h education at the schools.

In (16), I DON'T KNOW occurs turn-medially and functions as an epistemic or mitigating repair and turn-holding device. The token in (16a), by nature of its positioning between an abandoned and a recast utterance, bridges the gap between the repaired and repairing element. At the same time, though, it hedges Luke's commitment to his upcoming description of the Newcastle dialect, as evident from the rising contour on *I dunno*. The token in (16b) serves to link two syntactically complete utterances while simultaneously working towards toning down Albert's negative evaluation of a third party's opinion.

(16)   a.   Luke: But with like a proper Geordie from Newcastle they talk really,
                     (h) like like a proper Geordie, they're (.) mo:re *I dunno*? Their
                     words are more (.) <u>shorter</u>.   Frae like a Berwick person.
             HP: Yeah?
       b.   *((Albert just told HP about a man who, after emigrating to New Zealand,
             described New Zealand as the best place to live in the world.))*
             Albert: There was nothing that he (.) eh he described *(h)* in the place
                     he lived in New Zealand <£ that was any different frae here £>,
                     [you know.] *I don't know* I I I found that a little bit weird, you
             HP: [yeah yeah]
             Albert: = know.

Finally, the data contain multifunctional turn-final tokens of I DON'T KNOW. In (17), for example, Leah's *I dunno* is produced with a very moderate final fall and a decrease in volume. It thus serves to retrospectively qualify her description of her accent as well as to close her turn.

(17)   HP: What accent would you say you had and do you like it?
       (.)
       Leah: Em. It's a mixture of probably Scottish and Geordie. But °*I dunno*°.

The preceding discussion has demonstrated the functional versatility of unbound I DON'T KNOW in the BwE interview data. To conclude this section, the extracts in (18) illustrate referential uses of I DON'T KNOW which convey speakers' lack of knowledge. Although they do not constitute a discourse-pragmatic feature, these tokens have been included in the variable context in order to test whether pragmatic and referential uses of I DON'T KNOW favour different realisations.

(18)   a.   HP: And would you rather have a different accent or dialect?
             Ryan: *I don't know*? Never really thought about it.
       b.   Jane: Well, I was a telephonist for years and a lot of people thought,
                    you know frae further down the country thought I was Welsh.
             HP: Why?
             Jane: *I dunno*? We divn't knaa the connection?

The distinction between referential and pragmatic meanings of I DON'T KNOW is necessarily fluid and fuzzy, not least because pragmatic uses are not completely devoid of referential meanings (see Hopper's [1991] notion of persistence). Following previous claims that prosodic features help disambiguate referential from pragmatic meanings (see, for example, Dehé & Wichmann 2010; Hirschberg & Litman 1993), these features were identified as typifying referential rather than pragmatic uses of I DON'T KNOW: primary stress on *know*; lack of perceptible variation in speech rate, loudness and pitch range. (The rising intonation contour on *know* in the examples in (18) is moderate and serves to signal speakers' willingness to elaborate on their initial declaration of insufficient knowledge.) Moreover, in the present dataset referential tokens do not generally co-occur with other discourse-pragmatic features, filled or unfilled pauses, and when they occur as second pair parts of question-answer adjacency pairs, they are always followed by an account for the lack of knowledge, as in (18a) above (*Never really thought about it*), and never by the provision of the requested assessment, which is typical of epistemic uses, as in (15) (*Maybe just just just e:h education at the schools*).

Appendix 1 summarises the functional categories identified for unbound I DON'T KNOW in the BwE data, including short descriptions of their use, characteristic positions and co-occurring linguistic features.

4.4.2 Functions performed by bound I DON'T KNOW with phrasal or clausal complements

In contrast to the unbound tokens discussed above, bound tokens of I DON'T KNOW are followed by a phrasal or clausal complement with which they are prosodically integrated to form one tone unit. Due to their structural and prosodic integration, these tokens lack the positional mobility and functional versatility characteristic of unbound tokens of I DON'T KNOW. Their usage is limited to signalling insufficient knowledge and epistemicity.[26]

The use of bound I DON'T KNOW to signal its referential meaning of insufficient knowledge is exemplified in (19). In (19a) and (19b), I DON'T KNOW communicates the speakers' lack of familiarity with the referent in the phrasal complement. In both instances, I DON'T KNOW is accented and the complement carries a falling

---

26. The strong association between bound I DON'T KNOW and epistemicity confirms the validity of the labels attributed to I DON'T KNOW in the literature: "low modality item" (He 1993, quoted in Kärkkäinen 2003:24), "epistemic item/marker/phrase" or "subjective marker of epistemic stance" (Kärkkäinen 2003:25, 37), "formulaic stance marker" or "stance formula" (Thompson 2002:125, 139) or "epistemic clause" (Thompson & Hopper 2001:38).

intonation contour. These prosodic features, together with the emphasis on the negative polarity item *anybody* in the complement in (19b), signal the speakers' commitment to their assertions and rule out an epistemic reading of their utterances. Prosodic features also suggest a referential reading of I DON'T KNOW in (19c). Almost all elements of Joseph's utterance, including I DON'T KNOW and its clausal complement, are emphasised and produced in staccato articulation. What Joseph communicates here is not his uncertainty regarding the defining characteristics of a true Berwicker, but his cognitive inability to provide such characteristics.

(19) a. Daniel: <I've nothing against the blacks! I think the [blacks] are alright
          HP: [mhm]
          Daniel: = really.   But I feel sort of intimidated wi Muslims. Cos
          HP: mhm
          Daniel: = *I divn't knaa* their religion.
      b. HP: And do they sometimes when they come here, do they take on
                   a Spittal accent? [or]
          Joseph: [+ *(h)*] Well, very little, [very little.] No.
          HP: [very little]
                   <@ It's too hard. @>
          Joseph: I-it i- *I don't know* of <u>anybody</u> that's come s-, a stranger
                   coming in *(h)* and after a few years (started to speak Spittal).
      c. ((*Joseph has already indicated that he finds it difficult to provide defining
          criteria of a Berwicker.*))
          HP: Do you have to be born or bred here?
          Joseph: I cannae I >*don't know* what makes< a Berwicker.

While bound tokens with phrasal complements most commonly function referentially, as in (19a) and (19b) above, it would be misleading to assume that such tokens never function epistemically. In specific contexts, phrasal complements after negative *know* correspond semantically to WH-clauses (e.g. 'I don't know the reason for that.' = 'I don't know what the reason for that is.') (Quirk et al. 1985: 1052–1053). The potential for such tokens to express a non-referential meaning is illustrated in (20) where Helen uses *divn't knaa* to signal her uncertainty regarding Scottish pensioners' exemption from paying TV licence.

(20) ((*Talking about the financial benefits received by pensioners in Scotland.*))
      Helen: Well, [they] get free buses for a start.   *Divn't knaa*
      HP: [mhm]   mhm mhm
      Jane: mhm
      Helen: = about the TV licence?

With regard to constructions with overt WH-interrogative complements as in (19c), Quirk et al. (1985: 1051) argue that these "leave a gap of unknown information, represented by the WH-word." This is not to say, though, that I DON'T KNOW followed by a WH-interrogative clause only ever has referential meaning. In (21), for example, the WH-word does not signal what Glenn lacks knowledge of. Rather, it signals what it is he is uncertain about.

(21)   HP: So what would you say is the local football derby. Berwick Rangers playing who.
       Glenn: E:h (.) *Divn't knaa* who it would be? <There isn't one, is there.>

As predicted by Akatsuka (1985: 635–636), who places constructions containing negative *know* towards the irrealis pole of the epistemic scale, the degree of uncertainty expressed by I DON'T KNOW is generally very high, especially if the complement is uttered in continuously rising pitch, as in (21) above, or if the utterance containing the variable is softly spoken, as in (22) below.

(22)   Luke: If I if I won loads of money <u>now</u>, I'd still live in Berwick like.
       HP: Yeah?
       Luke: In Britain anyway. Aye, definitely. °*I divn't knaa* if I could live in a city°.

In (20)–(22) above, the epistemic scope of I DON'T KNOW is limited to its complement. This is not always the case. In certain contexts, such as those in (23) below, the epistemic scope of I DON'T KNOW can extend over the larger surrounding discourse. In (23a), Keith makes a guess at the transmission date of a television programme he had seen recently (*probably over a year*). This guess is hedged not just with the modal adverb *probably* but also by the preceding utterance containing I DON'T KNOW in which Keith raises his uncertainty regarding the time of the broadcast (*I divn't knaa how long ago it was*). Similarly, in (23b), Janet's epistemic stance relates not only to her being funny but, together with the rising intonation on the following *but*-clause, it also modifies her viewpoint expressed in this clause, i.e., that linguistic variation is socially conditioned.

(23)   a.   Keith: There's been a thing on the telly recen- well. I'm saying recently, it was (.) *I divn't knaa* how long ago it was. Probably over a year. It was to do wi Eyemouth.
       b.   *((Talking about the causes of inter-speaker linguistic variation.))*
            Janet: I d- I'm no <*I dunno* whether I'm being> (..) s- funny here or no, but it's more of a social thing?

The potential of bound I DON'T KNOW to have global scope is restricted to the following contexts: where the construction's complement explicitly raises the question answered in the following utterance, as in (23a); where it contains information that does not constitute the main argument of a speaker's turn, as in (23b); or where it constitutes what Brown & Levinson (1987: 168–171) call a "relevance hedge," as in (24). In this example, I DON'T KNOW *per se* has local scope over the following conditional clause (*if you're interested*). Yet the utterance containing I DON'T KNOW has more global scope. It constitutes a parenthetical discourse unit which comments on the rest of the turn and signals Daniel's uncertainty as to whether pictures of historic Berwick are in fact relevant to HP and the interview context. The subsidiary status of *I dunno if you're interested* is indicated by the heightened tempo with which it is spoken (see Couper-Kuhlen & Selting 1996: 28).

> (24)   Daniel: I've got em (..) old pictures of Berwick eh (..) I'll get a a picture of
> Berwick <*I dunno* if you're interested> of the <u>old</u> where it looks
> like in the old days.

For the sake of completeness, the examples in (25) are included here to illustrate that syntactic structures containing I DON'T KNOW can also serve textual functions in discourse, similar to those identified for unbound tokens. In (25a), Cody's assertion that he lacks the knowledge necessary to discuss the effects of Scottish devolution on the border serves to decline the proffered topic. In (25b), Shannon's assessment that she is uncertain whether the Scottish parliament has devolved powers other than the ones already discussed works towards terminating the topic under discussion. Finally, in (25c), Natalie's uncertainty regarding the geographical distribution of the dialect word *doylem* has a turn-yielding effect. In all examples, it is the positioning of the utterances containing I DON'T KNOW that triggers their textual effect.

> (25)   a.   (*(Following HP's question whether the significance of the Scottish-
> English border has changed in the aftermath of Scottish devolution.*))
> Glenn: <@ Can't remember. @>
> Cody: Neither do I. °*I dunno* much about it.°
>   b.   (*(At the end of a lengthy discussion about the devolved powers of the
> Scottish parliament.*))
> HP: Any other reasons why you would rather be governed by
> Scotland?
> Shannon: *I dunno* anything else that they do?

   c.   *((Discussing the dialect word 'doylem' for standard English 'idiot'.))*
        Natalie: Aye, but you occasionally Betty comes in, she says "Oh,
                       you're such a doylem, man." (.) Don't you?   Doylem's
        Charlene: yeah
        Natalie: = a it's *I dunno* if it's a a Berwick word.
        Charlene: °I don't think it is.°

Appendix 2 summarises the functional categories identified in the BwE data for bound I DON'T KNOW and those identified for utterances containing I DON'T KNOW. Note that the latter are not included in Section 4.5 as factors in the factor group function since the analysis is concerned with the construction I DON'T KNOW *per se*, not with utterances containing it. Depending on their meaning, tokens of bound I DON'T KNOW such as those in (25) were therefore recoded as referential or epistemic tokens for the quantitative analysis. As with unbound tokens, the boundary between referential and pragmatic uses of bound I DON'T KNOW is not sharp but fluid. One of the main cues differentiating the two meanings is whether I DON'T KNOW is accented and carries full stress.

4.4.3 Functions performed by I DON'T KNOW with dependent WH-words

Finally, tokens of I DON'T KNOW which are followed by a dependent WH-word constitute a syntactic, pragmatic and intonational unit. The data contain no tokens of I DON'T KNOW WH-word which function referentially. Epistemicity is their prime function in the BwE corpus. All tokens are encoded with high pitch and they signal either local epistemicity, as in (26a), or global epistemicity, as in (26b).

  (26) a.   Leah: <It's like, @ they think you're all psycho. @ *I don't know why*. Cos
                      most of them probably haven't even been to Berwick.
       b.   HP: Yeah, how does it how is it [portrayed.]
           Albert: [+ It al-] it always seems to come
                    across very well.   Em. *I don't know* why? Maybe cos cos
          HP: yeah
          Albert: = you live here and you relate to it, you know.

Like utterances containing unbound I DON'T KNOW, the whole unit of I DON'T KNOW WH-word can fulfil textual functions such as topic-decline (27a) and turn-closure (27b).

  (27) a.   HP: Would you say the way you speak is more Scots or more Geordie?
          Adam: Me, personally, I would say more Scots.
          HP: Yeah because of your (..)
          Adam: Just (.) *I divn't knaa* why. @

b.   Adam: Having said that, when (.) like the World Cup was on and that.
             (h) I was still supporting Ireland.
     HP: [mhm]
     Keith: [Oh!] (?)
     Adam: == [[@]]
     HP: == [[mhm]] mhm
     Adam: But no. (..) Wouldn't support Wales.   And *divn't knaa* why.
     HP: mhm

Appendix 3 summarises the functional categories identified for I DON'T KNOW
WH-word. Because the interest of this investigation is in the construction I DON'T
KNOW *per se* rather than the utterances containing it, tokens such as those in (27)
were coded as belonging to the epistemic category.

4.4.4 Summary of functions

The preceding sections have provided detailed overviews and illustrations of
the broad spectrum of uses I DON'T KNOW is put to in the BwE interview data.
Unbound I DON'T KNOW has been shown to perform a wide range of functions
beyond signalling insufficient knowledge. In the interpersonal domain, it serves
to signal speakers' epistemic stance vis-à-vis their propositions and word choice,
and works towards mitigating interactional conflict by attenuating the illocutionary force of speech acts and by allowing speakers to disengage from controversial
topics. It thus frequently serves a face-saving function in discourse. In the textual
domain, unbound I DON'T KNOW contributes to the smooth development and overall coherence of discourse. Apart from serving as a repair device that bridges the
gap between repaired and repairing elements, unbound I DON'T KNOW functions
as a topic-development device which allows speakers to exert some control over
the topical development of the interview. Also, I DON'T KNOW plays an important
role in turn-exchange, serving to launch, hold, yield and close turns. Lastly, some
instances of unbound I DON'T KNOW function across communicative domains as
textual devices with epistemic and mitigating effects. These uses illustrate well the
intrinsic multifunctionality of discourse-pragmatic features, thus providing empirical evidence for the view expressed in Chapter 1.2: that Fraser's (1990) typological
distinction between 'discourse markers' and 'pragmatic particles' is untenable (see
also Chapter 5.4). The functional range of bound I DON'T KNOW and I DON'T KNOW
WH-word is far more limited than that of unbound tokens of I DON'T KNOW. In the
current dataset, these tokens are used exclusively to express lack of knowledge and
to signal epistemicity.

Because the preceding analysis was based on data from one speech event (interviews) and one dialect (BwE), the functional inventory outlined above cannot claim to be comprehensive of all uses of I DON'T KNOW across all text types and all varieties of English. Discourse-pragmatic features regularly perform different functions across text types (e.g. Lam 2009) and varieties (e.g. Hoffmann et al. forthc.). Future studies will modify and elaborate the above account to incorporate any alternative or additional functions which I DON'T KNOW may perform in other speech events or varieties. Yet despite the aforementioned limitations, the analysis presented above constitutes an important contribution to current descriptions of I DON'T KNOW. It has incorporated in its remit all tokens of I DON'T KNOW in all sequential environments and syntactic configurations, thus providing the first full account of the construction's functionality in a corpus of British English interview data.

The main aim of the qualitative data analysis was to develop a coding schema which details the factors typifying the factor group function in the BwE interview data and enables us to include function as an independent variable in the quantitative data analysis. Table 4.2 outlines the coding schema which arose from the qualitative analysis outlined in Sections 4.4.1 to 4.4.3. Following this coding protocol, each token of the variable I DON'T KNOW in the data was allocated to the functional category which best described its use. As pointed out previously, the individual categories are not discretely distinct from each other. They should be conceptualised as a network of meanings which are related by virtue of retaining nuances of the construction's source meaning even in their most bleached functions.

Table 4.2 Coding schema for I DON'T KNOW functions

	unbound	bound	WH-word
ideational mode	referential marker of insufficient knowledge	referential marker of insufficient knowledge	
interpersonal mode	epistemic marker	epistemic marker	epistemic marker
	mitigation device		
textual mode	repair marker		
	topic-development device (decline, curtail, close, discard)		
	turn-exchange device (take, hold, yield, close)		
interpers.-text. mode	epistemic repair marker		
	epistemic/mitigating turn-exchange device		

4.5   Quantitative analysis of I DON'T KNOW

Having identified the variants of I DON'T KNOW, the factor groups that might affect their distribution as well as the factors that constitute these factor groups, this section presents the results of the quantitative analysis into the formal, functional and social variability of I DON'T KNOW usage in the BwE data. An outline of the overall distribution of variants in the corpus, across individuals and across social cohorts is followed by a short description of how the variable and its variants are distributed across functional categories and syntactic configurations. These distributions determine how the data are configured for the mixed-effects multiple regression analyses. They model the simultaneous effect of the independent variables on the observed patterns of formal variability in the data whilst accounting for individual levels of variance. Together with detailed investigation of the variable's and its variants' frequencies across individual speakers, close scrutiny of the results that emerge from the apparent-time regression analyses will reveal the organisation, robustness and stability of the variable grammar underlying the distribution of variants. This will afford important new insights into the distribution of non-localised and localised variants of I DON'T KNOW, the nature and strength of any form-function correlations in the data as well as the sociolinguistic mechanisms of discourse-pragmatic variation and change more generally.

4.5.1   Distributional analysis

The dataset available for analysis consists of 600 tokens of I DON'T KNOW which, following close auditory analysis, were categorised into five formal variants (see Section 4.3.2 above). The frequency of these variants is given in Figure 4.1. *I dunno* is proportionally dominant. All the other variants combined occur less often than *I dunno*. *I divn't knaa* is the second and *I don't know* the third most frequent variant in the data, constituting roughly a fifth and a sixth of all tokens respectively. *I dono* is comparatively infrequent, accounting for less than ten per cent of all occurrences of the variable. Even though it is no less functionally versatile than other variants, *I dinnae ken* is only negligibly instantiated in the data. Due to its paucity, this variant is excluded from further analysis.

Initial data runs reveal that the remaining variants are not evenly distributed across the 35 speakers in the sample who use the variable I DON'T KNOW. Firstly, one speaker categorically uses the variant *I dunno* (N = 5). Following standard variationist practice, data from this speaker are removed from the ensuing analysis. Secondly, while all of the 34 variable speakers employ non-localised variants of I DON'T KNOW, albeit with differential frequencies, only nineteen of these speakers

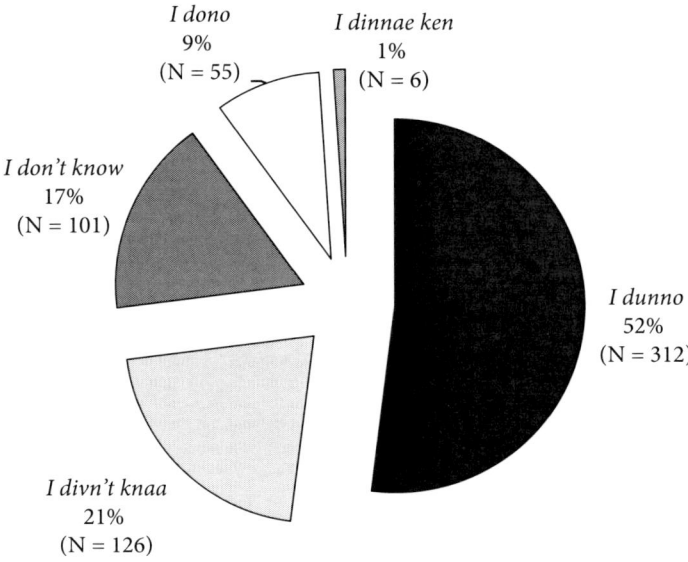

I dono
9%
(N = 55)

I dinnae ken
1%
(N = 6)

I don't know
17%
(N = 101)

I dunno
52%
(N = 312)

I divn't knaa
21%
(N = 126)

Figure 4.1 Overall distribution of the variants of I DON'T KNOW

employ the localised variant *I divn't knaa*. To avoid skewing the results and concealing important constraints on observed variation patterns, only speakers who employ *I divn't knaa* are included in the quantification of this variant across independent variables.[27] Thirdly, the social cohorts represented in the corpus data differ in the frequency with which they use non-localised and localised variants of I DON'T KNOW. The black bars along the y-axis in Figure 4.2 show that *I dunno* is the most frequent variant in most of the social cohorts listed along the x-axis. Older and younger males' lower than average rate of *I dunno* (black bars) is counterbalanced by their proportionally higher rates of *I don't know* (dark grey bars) and *I divn't knaa* (light grey bars) respectively. Speakers from the middle age group, in particular males, seem to boast the highest proportion of *I dono* (white bars). However, some of these distributions must be interpreted cautiously. As shown in Section 4.5.2 which explores in more detail the precise nature and statistical significance of social and linguistic constraints on variant choice, the overall association in Figure 4.2 of *I dono* with middle (male) speakers, of *I don't know* with

---

27. As a result, the percentages provided for *I divn't knaa* in Figures 4.2 and 4.3 below are derived from consideration of a subsample of the I DON'T KNOW token numbers given next to the factors listed along the x-axis.

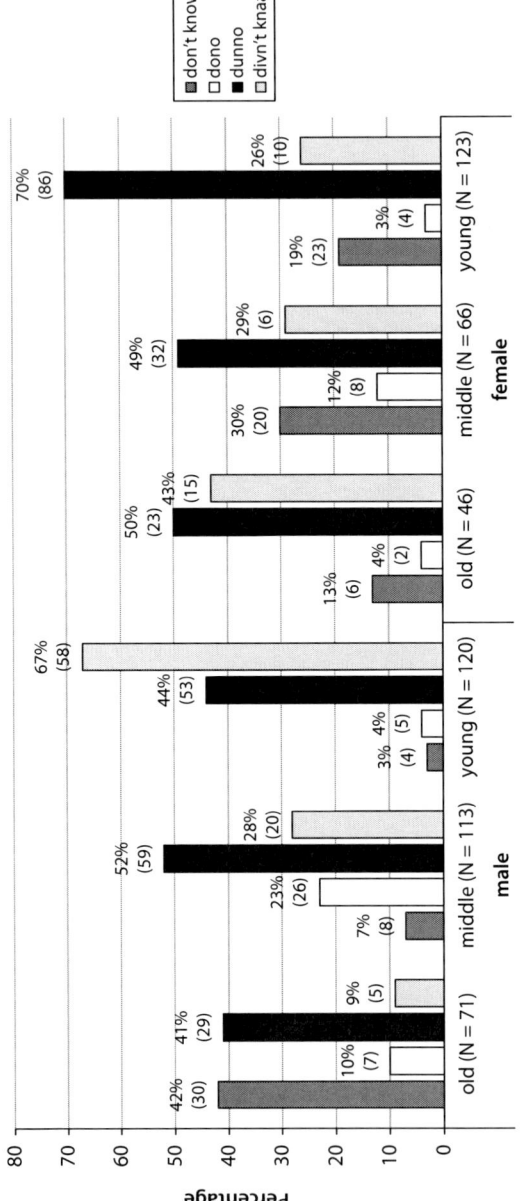

Figure 4.2 Distribution of variants of I DON'T KNOW across speaker sex and age (Figures in round brackets indicate raw token numbers. The results for *I divn't knaa* are derived from data produced by *divn't knaa*-users only [N = 305].)

middle female speakers and of *I dunno* with young female speakers is created by some individuals' disproportionate use of the variable or these variants. Even so, Figure 4.2 provides some preliminary evidence that the variation between variants of I DON'T KNOW is constrained by social factors.

The distributional analysis in Figure 4.2 is based on a reduced dataset of 539 tokens. It does not include tokens of *I dinnae ken* (N = 6), tokens produced by an invariable speaker (N = 5), tokens not coded for syntactic configuration and/or function due to insufficient context (inaudible turn continuation, interruption, truncation) (N = 20), and tokens followed by a dependent WH-word (N = 30).[28] As shown in Table 4.3, tokens of I DON'T KNOW with a dependent WH-word are liminal, accounting for only five per cent of all tokens of the variable in the data. Because of these tokens' marginal occurrence, socially skewed distribution (young speakers produced three quarters of tokens) and functional invariability (all tokens signal epistemicity), the quantitative analysis focuses on unbound and bound tokens of I DON'T KNOW. These are more frequently instantiated in the corpus, more evenly distributed across social cohorts, and more functionally versatile.[29]

Table 4.3 Distribution of I DON'T KNOW across syntactic configurations (not including tokens of *I dinnae ken*, tokens produced by an invariable speaker, and tokens not coded for syntactic configuration and/or function)

	%	N
unbound	65.4	372
bound	29.3	167
WH-word	5.3	30
		569

The analysis in Section 4.4 revealed that bound tokens of I DON'T KNOW perform a smaller range of functions than unbound tokens which, in addition to signalling insufficient knowledge and epistemicity, also function to structure and control discourse. The percentages for the functional categories along the x-axis in Figure 4.3 reveal that interpersonal uses account for the vast majority of instances of bound

---

28. Inclusion of the latter sets of tokens in the distributional analysis slightly alters some percentages but does not affect the overall pattern of variant distribution outlined in Figure 4.2. While Goldvarb has a slash-function which removes tokens not coded for one particular factor group from consideration in this factor group only, Rbrul does not offer this option. Consequently, tokens not coded for one factor group must be removed from consideration in all factor groups.

29. All of the 30 tokens of I DON'T KNOW with a dependent WH-word function epistemically. 43% of them were realised as *I dunno* and 23% as *I don't know*, suggesting that these tokens exhibit similar form-function correlations as bound and unbound tokens (see Figure 4.3).

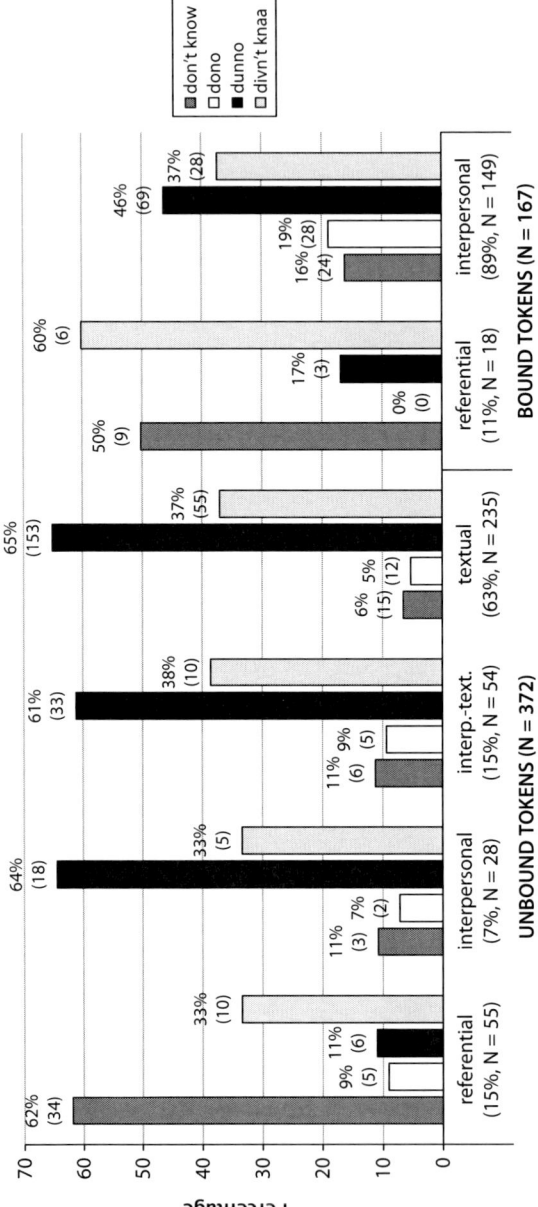

Figure 4.3 Distribution of variants of I DON'T KNOW across syntactic contexts and functional categories (Figures in round brackets indicate raw token numbers. The results for *I divn't knaa* are derived from data produced by *divn't knaa*-users [N = 305].)

I DON'T KNOW (on the right). This stands in stark contrast to unbound tokens (on the left) which exhibit a propensity for textual uses. Neither unbound nor bound tokens manifest a high concentration of referential uses.[30] These overall functional distributions are fairly consistently repeated across social cohorts, as shown in Tables 4.4 and 4.5. It is only the relative frequency of unbound non-textual tokens which differentiates social cohorts. Speakers from the oldest age group and female speakers from the middle age group have comparatively high rates of referential tokens; male speakers from the middle age group have higher rates than other cohorts of interpersonal tokens; and speakers from the youngest age group have higher rates of interpersonal-textual tokens than they do of referential or inter-personal tokens. These patterns are in line with previous reports of age- and sex-differentiated functional uses of discourse-pragmatic variables (e.g. Erman 1992; Stubbe & Holmes 1995).

Table 4.4 Frequency in per cent of unbound I DON'T KNOW across functional categories by age and sex (Figures in brackets indicate raw token numbers.)

	old		middle		young	
	male	female	male	female	male	female
referential	30 (11)	29 (8)	5 (4)	26 (11)	8 (8)	14 (13)
interpersonal	5 (2)	7 (2)	13 (9)	5 (2)	6 (6)	8 (7)
interp.-text.	16 (6)	14 (4)	5 (4)	14 (6)	20 (19)	16 (15)
textual	49 (18)	50 (14)	77 (57)	55 (23)	66 (65)	62 (58)
TOTAL N	37	28	74	42	98	93

Table 4.5 Frequency in per cent of bound I DON'T KNOW across functional categories by age and sex (Figures in brackets indicate raw token numbers.)

	old		middle		young	
	male	female	male	female	male	female
referential	12 (4)	6 (1)	8 (3)	12 (3)	5 (1)	20 (6)
interpersonal	88 (30)	94 (17)	92 (36)	87 (21)	96 (21)	80 (24)
TOTAL N	34	18	39	24	22	30

---

30. Of the unbound textual tokens, the majority signal turn-exchange. Topic-development is the second-most frequent textual function, followed by repair marking. Of the bound interpersonal tokens, the vast majority have local epistemic scope.

Returning to Figure 4.3, the bars along the y-axis indicate the frequency of formal variants across the functional categories and syntactic contexts listed along the x-axis.[31] The differential frequency of full and reduced variants across function in both unbound and bound contexts is strongly reminiscent of the results reported in Bybee & Scheibman (1999) and Scheibman (2000): *I don't know* (dark grey bars) is tightly linked to referential uses; *I dunno* (black bars) is consistently associated with pragmatic uses. In contrast to *I don't know* and *I dunno*, the semi-reduced variant *I dono* (white bars) and the localised variant *I divn't knaa* (light grey bars) are differently distributed across unbound and bound contexts. In the former, they occur with similar frequency across functional categories; in the latter, *I dono* is used exclusively to serve interpersonal functions while *I divn't knaa* shows a slight propensity to signal insufficient knowledge. Taken together, the patterns in Figure 4.3 demonstrate that in addition to the extra-linguistic variables discussed earlier, function and, to a lesser degree, syntax are implicated in the occurrence of different variants of I DON'T KNOW in BwE.

Prior to subjecting these observations to statistical testing, it is necessary to establish the degree of inter-speaker variation in the frequency of use of I DON'T KNOW. Figures 4.4 and 4.5 plot the frequency of referential and pragmatic uses of I DON'T KNOW across individual speakers in the sample. Individuals are arranged by age on the x-axis, from youngest on the left to oldest on the right. The bullets and squares along the y-axis show the normalised frequency per 10,000 words with which each of the 18 male speakers in the sample (black bullets) and each of the 18 female speakers in the sample (grey squares) use I DON'T KNOW for referential or pragmatic uses. (Pragmatic uses include all tokens that perform interpersonal, textual or a combination of these functions.) The closer a bullet or square is located to the x-axis, the lower a speaker's frequency of use of I DON'T KNOW; the more distant it is from the x-axis, the higher a speaker's frequency of use of I DON'T KNOW. Figure 4.4 shows that, with the exception of three female speakers who use referential I DON'T KNOW with a rate of 13–15 tokens per 10,000 words, the vast majority of speakers use referential I DON'T KNOW with a frequency of 0–4 tokens per 10,000 words. This is particularly true of male speakers. The linear

---

31. Within the broad functional categories displayed in Figure 4.3, variants are similarly distributed across the fine-grained functions identified for I DON'T KNOW in Section 4.4. This is not to imply that the detailed functional analysis in Section 4.4 was unneeded. Previous studies (e.g. Plug 2010) as well as the analysis of I DON'T THINK in Chapter 5 demonstrate that micro-level functional distinctions may be key to interpreting formal variation patterns in discourse-pragmatics. While this turns out not to be the case for I DON'T KNOW in BwE, the validity of the results reported in this chapter cannot be ascertained unless this possibility is ruled out at the outset.

trend-lines for males and females further indicate that despite individual levels of variance, the average frequency of use of referential I DON'T KNOW is fairly stable in apparent time. This is not the case with pragmatic I DON'T KNOW. The linear trend-lines in Figure 4.5 indicate a general tendency for rates of pragmatic I DON'T KNOW to rise in apparent time, both amongst males and females. While the vast majority of speakers, especially those in the middle and old age groups, use pragmatic I DON'T KNOW with rates lower than 30 tokens per 10,000 words, some young male speakers far exceed this rate. Consequently, individual rates of use of pragmatic I DON'T KNOW are highly variable, ranging from 0 up to 69 tokens per 10,000 words. To avoid skewing the results in Section 4.5.2 below, it is necessary to account for this high degree of inter-speaker variability in the multivariate analyses.

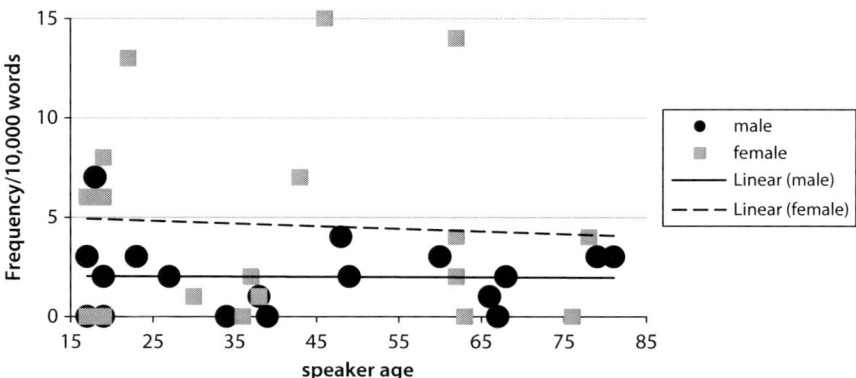

Figure 4.4 Normalised frequencies of referential uses of I DON'T KNOW across individuals

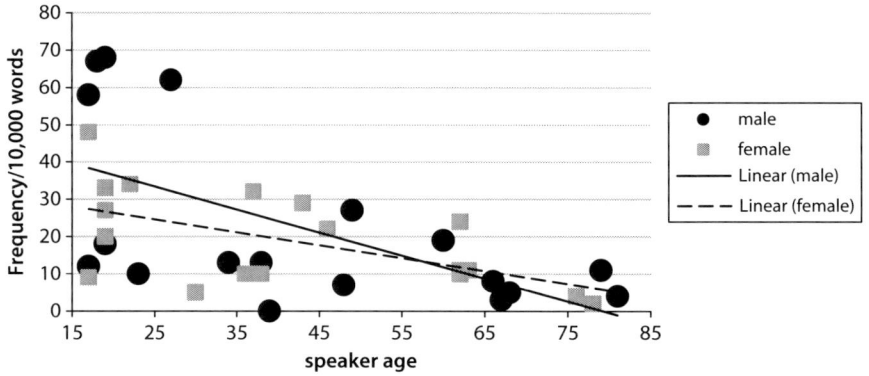

Figure 4.5 Normalised frequencies of pragmatic uses of I DON'T KNOW across individuals

4.5.2   Multivariate analysis

In this section, mixed-effects multiple regression analyses are conducted with Rbrul (see Chapter 2.3.3 for details on the technicalities and practicalities of Rbrul-based analyses). They will establish the relative contribution and combined impact of the independent variables discussed above to the occurrence of the variants of I DON'T KNOW while consistently accounting for the high levels of individual variance in I DON'T KNOW usage shown in Figures 4.4 and 4.5. For the more frequently instantiated variants in the corpus – *I don't know, I dunno, I divn't knaa* – independent multivariate analyses are carried out for each of the three age groups represented in the corpus. Identical apparent-time analyses for these variants and close inspection of the direction of effect, significance and relative contribution of predictors enable us to assess the stability of the variants' underlying grammars across age groups and to compare the organisation of variability across variants. Because *I dono* does not occur at sufficient frequency thresholds for viable apparent-time statistical modelling (see footnote 32 below), its distribution is examined across all age groups combined. While this procedure does not afford an apparent-time window on the variant's sociolinguistic conditioning, it still affords insights into the underlying grammar of *I dono* in the sample as a whole. Adverse effects associated with badly distributed data are mitigated by collapsing the three pragmatic factors identified for unbound tokens (interpersonal, interpersonal-textual, textual) into one factor pragmatic which together with the factor referential constitutes the factor group function. Also, unbound and bound tokens are included in the same runs, albeit differentiated as two factors constituting the factor group syntax. While these configurations may obscure the differential patterning of *I don't know* and *I dono* in non-referential uses across unbound and bound contexts (see Figure 4.3), they maximise cell sizes and thus improve the overall reliability of the results (Guy 1980). In addition, application of mixed-effects modelling and inclusion of individual speaker as a random effect in the regressions reduces the risk of providing inaccurate significance estimates of social factors in the unbalanced dataset under scrutiny here. Readers unfamiliar with the output of multivariate analyses are referred to Chapter 2.3.3, which provides a detailed explanation of how to interpret the quantitative results shown in Tables 4.6 to 4.9.

Table 4.6 displays the results of three independent multivariate analyses of the contribution of sex, function and syntax to the choice of *I don't know* for the three age groups in the corpus. The range values indicate that in all age groups it is function that makes the most important contribution to the occurrence of this variant. The associated factor values confirm that *I don't know* is strongly favoured for referential uses and strongly disfavoured for pragmatic

Table 4.6 Contribution of external and internal factors to the probability of *I don't know* (with *I dunno, I dono* and *I divn't knaa* as non-application values)

	OLD				MIDDLE				YOUNG			
	factor weights	%	N	log odds	factor weights	%	N	log odds	factor weights	%	N	log odds
input prob.	0.324				0.303				0.156			
total N	117				179				243			
deviance	102.519				108.352				119.997			
sex	p=0.0393				not significant				p=0.0397			
female	.232	13.0	46	-1.197	[.672]	30.3	66	[0.718]	.739	18.7	123	1.043
male	.768	42.3	71	1.197	[.328]	7.1	113	[-0.718]	.261	3.3	120	-1.043
range	.536								.478			
function	p=2.16e-05				p=1.74e-07				p=1.93e-08			
referential	.806	66.7	24	1.424	.837	66.7	21	1.639	.853	46.4	28	1.756
pragmatic	.194	21.5	93	-1.424	.163	8.9	158	-1.639	.147	6.5	215	-1.756
range	.612				.674				.706			
syntax	not significant				p=0.0191				not significant			
unbound	[.542]	33.8	65	[0.167]	.342	12.1	116	-0.656	[.541]	11.5	191	[0.163]
bound	[.458]	26.9	52	[-0.167]	.658	22.2	63	0.656	[.459]	9.6	52	[-0.163]
range					.316							
speaker	random st. dv 1.418				random st. dv 0.93				random st. dv 1.187			

uses.[32] These form-function correlations exhibit remarkable apparent-time stability, as indicated by the consistency across age groups in statistical significance and constraint hierarchies. In contrast to the relative stability in the functional conditioning of *I don't know*, its social conditioning is less stable. The input probabilities given at the top of the table demonstrate a slight decrease in the overall frequency of use of *I don't know* in the middle age group which is accelerated in the youngest age group. Moreover, the sex effect for *I don't know* reverses across age. While use of the variant is strongly favoured by male speakers in the oldest age cohort, in the youngest cohort its use is strongly favoured by female speakers. In the middle cohort, the contribution of sex to the occurrence of *I don't know* does not reach statistical significance despite much higher factor weights for females than males. (This is due to individual levels of variance and token imbalance among female speakers in this age group.) In contrast to speaker sex, which exerts a significant effect to the occurrence of *I don't know* in the old and young but not the middle cohort, syntax exerts a significant effect to the occurrence of *I don't know* in the middle but not in the old and young cohorts. Among the latter cohorts, *I don't know* is weakly preferred in unbound contexts; among the former cohort, it is favoured in bound contexts. Considering the consistently strong association of *I don't know* with referential uses, the syntactic distribution of *I don't know* across age suggests that speakers from the middle age group are more likely than speakers from other age groups to specify through overt complementation what it is they lack knowledge of.

The variable grammar underlying the occurrence of *I dunno* is remarkably constant in apparent time. The results of the three independent multivariate analyses for this variant in Table 4.7 show that both internal constraints operate in the same direction across all age groups: *I dunno* is consistently associated with pragmatic uses and unbound contexts. Parallel to *I don't know*, function is the most explanatory factor group for *I dunno* by far, as revealed by the high range values. The consistently high factor values for pragmatic uses confirm the functional asymmetry between *I don't know* and *I dunno* noted earlier: while the former is largely reserved for referential uses, the latter is largely reserved for pragmatic uses. The second strongest constraint on the occurrence of *I dunno* is syntax. Although this effect only reaches statistical significance in the middle and young age groups, unbound contexts consistently have higher rates of *I dunno* than bound contexts.

---

32. According to general statistical laws, the threshold for obtaining reliable results is 30 tokens per cell. However, Guy (1980) points out that acceptable levels of accuracy can be obtained with numbers in excess of ten tokens. Consequently, we can be reasonably confident that the results for the factor referential, which contains between 21 and 28 tokens in each age group, are not greatly skewed by random perturbations in the data.

Table 4.7 Contribution of external and internal factors to the probability of *I dunno* (with *I don't know, I dono* and *I divn't knaa* as non-application values)

	OLD				MIDDLE				YOUNG			
	factor weights	%	N	log odds	factor weights	%	N	log odds	factor weights	%	N	log odds
input prob.	0.174				0.173				0.308			
total N	117				179				243			
deviance	118.927				215.584				251.617			
sex	not significant				not significant				not significant			
female	[.538]	50.0	46	[0.153]	[.534]	48.5	66	[0.135]	[.605]	69.9	123	[0.425]
male	[.462]	40.8	71	[−0.153]	[.466]	52.2	113	[−0.135]	[.395]	44.2	120	[−0.425]
range												
function	p = 0.000402				p = 3.7e-07				p = 5.5e-08			
referential	.201	8.3	24	−1.381	.152	4.8	21	−1.718	.189	21.4	28	−1.459
pragmatic	.799	53.8	93	1.381	.848	57.0	158	1.718	.811	61.9	215	1.459
range	.598				.696				.622			
syntax	not significant				p = 0.0191				p = 0.0247			
unbound	[.562]	46.2	65	[0.248]	.619	57.8	116	0.484	.614	59.2	191	0.463
bound	[.438]	42.3	52	[−0.248]	.381	38.1	63	−0.484	.386	50.0	52	−0.463
range					.238				.228			
speaker	random st. dv 1.655				random st. dv 0				random st. dv 1.483			

Speaker sex does not make a significant contribution to the occurrence of *I dunno* in any of the age groups. In the old age group *I dunno* is weakly associated with female speakers; in the middle age group it is weakly associated with male speakers. (The interaction effect in the middle age group is caused by the fact that females in this age group never use *I dunno* referentially.) The appearance of a strong sex effect in the youngest age group (see the divergent factor values) is created by within-group variation. As indicated by the lack of statistical significance, however, there is in fact little evidence of a real sex effect in this age group. Lastly, the input probabilities at the top of Table 4.7 demonstrate a sudden increase in the use of *I dunno* in the youngest age group which, considering the strong association of *I dunno* with pragmatic uses, may be linked to the apparent-time rise of pragmatic uses of I DON'T KNOW noted in Figure 4.5.

Moving on to Table 4.8 which shows the contribution of contextual factors to the probability of the non-localised semi-reduced variant *I dono*, the results confirm that this variant occurs far less often in the data than either of the non-localised variants discussed above (see the low input probability given at the top of the table). Also, *I dono* is affected differently by function than *I don't know* and *I dunno*. Unlike the use of full and reduced variants, the use of the semi-reduced variant is not correlated with a functional category but occurs with roughly equal probability across referential and pragmatic uses. However, this distribution pattern arises from viewing the data in the aggregate. As shown earlier in Figure 4.3, *I dono* is never used referentially in bound contexts and has slightly higher rates of pragmatic compared to referential uses in unbound contexts (9% vs. 6%). External factors make no significant contribution to the occurrence of *I dono* either, despite relatively divergent factor weights especially for age. The appearance of social effects is produced by individual speaker variation. While age, sex and function have no or little effect on the use of *I dono* when individual variance is considered, syntax makes a significant contribution to the occurrence of this variant. Unlike the reduced variant *I dunno*, the semi-reduced variant *I dono* is favoured in bound contexts. Cross-tabulations with age (not shown here) demonstrate that this effect as well as that of function and speaker sex remain relatively constant across age groups, suggesting that *I dono* resembles the other non-localised variants in exhibiting relatively stable variation patterns.

Finally, Table 4.9 displays the results of three independent multivariate analyses for the localised variant *I divn't knaa* which, as outlined earlier, is only used by a subsample of speakers in the data. Unlike with any other variant of I DON'T KNOW in the BwE data, speaker sex has the strongest effect on the occurrence of *I divn't knaa*. However, the direction of effect is inconsistent in apparent time. In the oldest age group, the variant is strongly favoured by females. This correlation weakens in the middle age group to the extent that the female preference for *I*

Table 4.8 Contribution of external and internal factors to the probability of *I dono* (with *I don't know, I dunno* and *I divn't knaa* as non-application values)

	I dono			
input prob.	0.06			
total N	539			
deviance	298.66			
	factor weights	%	N	log odds
age	not significant			
old	[.450]	7.7	117	[−0.202]
middle	[.695]	19.0	179	[0.824]
young	[.349]	3.7	243	[−0.621]
range				
sex	not significant			
female	[.429]	6.0	235	[−0.284]
male	[.571]	12.5	304	[0.284]
range				
function	not significant			
referential	[.478]	6.8	73	[−0.087]
pragmatic	[.522]	10.1	466	[0.087]
range				
syntax	p=0.0357			
unbound	.412	6.5	372	−0.356
bound	.588	16.8	167	0.356
range	*.176*			
speaker	random st. dv 1.097			

divn't knaa is no longer significant. In the youngest age group, the sex effect is reversed and regains significance. Here it is males, not females, who exhibit a strong favouring effect for *I divn't knaa*. When the data are reconfigured to combine age and sex into one social factor group with six factors (old male, old female, middle male, middle female, young male, young female), analyses not shown here reveal that the favouring effect is stronger among young males than it is among older females (factor weights of .858 vs. .606). This result may account for the regular increase across age groups in the overall probability of *I divn't knaa*. The input probabilities show that the likelihood for *I divn't knaa* to occur in the BwE data more than doubles between the oldest and youngest generation. In stark contrast to the social constraints on the choice of *I divn't knaa*, the internal constraints do not generally fluctuate across age groups nor do they ever reach statistical significance. *I divn't knaa* shares with *I dono* a weak preference to occur in bound rather than

Table 4.9 Contribution of external and internal factors to the probability of *I divn't knaa* (with *I don't know*, *I dunno* and *I dono* as non-application values)

	OLD				MIDDLE				YOUNG			
	factor weights	%	N	log odds	factor weights	%	N	log odds	factor weights	%	N	log odds
input prob.	0.22				0.357				0.473			
total N	88				92				125			
deviance	79.56				104.926				151.036			
sex	p=0.0171				not significant				p=0.0147			
female	.739	42.9	35	1.042	[.523]	28.6	21	[0.093]	.296	25.6	39	-0.997
male	.261	9.4	53	-1.042	[.477]	28.2	71	[-0.093]	.731	67.4	86	0.997
range	.478								.435			
function	not significant				not significant				not significant			
referential	[.523]	29.4	17	[0.093]	[.505]	42.9	7	[0.020]	[.580]	50.0	16	[0.321]
pragmatic	[.477]	21.1	71	[-0.093]	[.495]	27.1	85	[-0.020]	[.420]	55.0	109	[-0.321]
range												
syntax	not significant				not significant				not significant			
unbound	[.411]	19.6	51	[-0.358]	[.401]	25.0	72	[-0.402]	[.409]	53.6	97	[-0.369]
bound	[.589]	27.0	37	[0.358]	[.599]	40.0	20	[0.402]	[.591]	57.1	28	[0.369]
range												
speaker	random st. dv 0.625				random st. dv 0.948				random st. dv 0.451			

unbound contexts as well as a tendency to occur with roughly equal probability across pragmatic and referential uses. While the low token numbers constituting the factor referential (see in particular the middle age group) warn that the results for function must be interpreted with caution (see footnote 32 above), an identical multivariate regression analysis of the data from all age groups combined confirms their robustness and reliability by producing factor weights of [.540] for referential and [.460] for pragmatic tokens. Yet, as reflected in the antithesis between the percentages and the factor weights for function in the youngest age group, the marginal preference for referential uses is not shared by all speakers in the young age cohort. Hidden cross-tabulations with gender reveal that young males exhibit a very slight propensity for pragmatic uses of *I divn't knaa*.

4.5.3 Summary of results

Identical analyses for *I don't know, I dunno* and *I divn't knaa* across the three age groups represented in the data and a corresponding analysis of *I dono* with all age groups combined make it possible to compare the mechanisms of variability across variants. The comparisons yield the following key insights into the formal variability of I DON'T KNOW in BwE:

–   *Different variants are exploited to signal different meanings*: The most frequent non-localised variants in the data, *I don't know* and *I dunno,* occupy asymmetrical functional niches in the system of I DON'T KNOW variants. The former is strongly associated with referential meanings; the latter is strongly associated with pragmatic meanings. In stark contrast, the marginally occurring non-localised variant *I dono* and the localised variant *I divn't knaa* are multi-purpose variants which are used in the BwE data to express insufficient knowledge just as much as to signal pragmatic meanings.
–   *The occurrence of non-localised and localised variants of I DON'T KNOW is conditioned by different parameters*: At least one internal factor always has primacy over social factors in constraining the occurrence of the non-localised variants, *I don't know, I dono* and *I dunno.* By contrast, external factors have primacy in conditioning the occurrence of the localised variant *I divn't knaa.*
–   *Internal and external conditioning factors do not operate in unison*: The internal conditioning of variant choice, in particular by function, exhibits remarkable apparent-time stability for all variants analysed above. Conversely, the social conditioning of some variants, notably of *I don't know* and *I divn't knaa* by speaker sex, is subject to rigorous change in the short time-span covered by the BwE corpus.

Inspection of social and individual patterns of variant distribution, inclusion of individual speaker as a random effect in the multivariate analyses, and tabulation of the frequency of I DON'T KNOW across and within social cohorts yield another key insight into the distribution of I DON'T KNOW in BwE:

–   *The frequency, usage and form of I DON'T KNOW exhibit a fair amount of inter-group and inter-speaker variability*: Social cohorts and individual speakers vary in the frequency with which they use the construction I DON'T KNOW, the functional uses to which they put it as well as their preference for individual variants.

4.6 Discussion

This chapter set out to account for the high degree of variation in the realisation of I DON'T KNOW in BwE, a peripheral variety of British English which features both non-localised and localised variants of the targeted variable. Systematic qualitative and quantitative data analyses in Sections 4.4 and 4.5 have provided a detailed overview of the construction's functionality in the BwE interview data and established the effect of extra- and intra-linguistic predictors on variant selection. This section discusses the key findings of the preceding analyses, situates them vis-á-vis previous studies of I DON'T KNOW in other contexts and varieties, and explores the diachronic and social mechanisms underlying observed patterns of synchronic variability.

The in-depth qualitative data analysis in Section 4.4 served to establish the functions performed by I DON'T KNOW in the BwE data with the aim of making possible inclusion of function as a factor group in the quantitative data analysis. By way of establishing the factors constituting the factor group function, the qualitative analysis has enhanced previous descriptions of the functional repertoire of I DON'T KNOW in several important ways. Firstly, by including in its scope all tokens of I DON'T KNOW in the data irrespective of their positioning within utterances, turns or sequences, this study has provided a comprehensive account of the complete functional inventory of I DON'T KNOW in the current dataset. It thus advances previous accounts which are largely based on subsets of tokens and yield potentially incomplete or biased descriptions of the construction's usage in social interaction. Secondly, by differentiating the syntactic configurations in which I DON'T KNOW occurs, this analysis has established that unbound tokens of I DON'T KNOW are more functionally versatile than bound tokens or tokens with a dependent WH-word whose usage is limited to signalling insufficient knowledge and epistemicity. It thus confirms that the functionality of discourse-pragmatic features is intricately linked to their syntactic integration and positional mobility (see Brinton 2006). Thirdly, by establishing the frequency with which different functions of I DON'T KNOW occur in the data, this analysis has provided numerical evidence for observations in the literature about the construction's great importance in qualifying propositions and structuring discourse and its negligible role in signalling a cognitive state. However, the overall predominance of textual over interpersonal uses revealed in Figure 4.2 may not generalise beyond the current data. Unlike in everyday casual conversations, in interviews speakers may be more concerned with exerting some control over the course and development of the interaction than with protecting their own and others' face needs. The preponderance in the current data of textual tokens of I DON'T KNOW may therefore reflect the specific constraints of the interview situation rather than more widespread functional preferences in the use of I DON'T KNOW. Notwithstanding this caveat, the functional data analysis in Section 4.4 provides important new insights into the usage of I DON'T KNOW in spoken interaction.

The quantitative data analysis in Section 4.5 served to establish the constraints operating on the formal variation in the data. To this end, multivariate analyses were run which tested the simultaneous effect of multiple contextual factors (age, sex, function, syntax) on the choice of formal variants of I DON'T KNOW. Where feasible, identical analyses were run for each of the three age groups represented in the corpus in order to establish the apparent-time stability of any constraints on variant choice. One of the overarching findings to emerge from these analyses is the complementary functional distribution of *I don't know* and *I dunno*, which confirms the results reported in Bybee & Scheibman (1999) and Scheibman (2000): the full variant is strongly favoured for referential uses; the reduced variant is strongly favoured for pragmatic uses. Beyond confirming that functional distribution patterns previously only documented for American English are also present in a peripheral variety of British English, the current analysis contributes important new insights into the robustness and stability of these form-function correlations (as well as others discussed below). Cross-tabulations (not shown here) of function with other predictors vindicate the regularities shown in Tables 4.6 and 4.7. The effect of function is consistent across unbound and bound contexts and although older male speakers are more likely than other speakers to use *I don't know* for pragmatic uses, the functional split between *I don't know* and *I dunno* is uniformly present in the speech of both sexes and virtually all individuals.[33] The results, then, demonstrate that the functional split between *I don't know* and

---

33. Where individuals appear not to participate in the form-function split outlined above, this is due to the fact that the emergence of any such patterns is impeded by these individuals' infrequent use of the variable overall or by their infrequent use of the variable for one of the two broad meanings (referential vs. pragmatic).

I dunno is firmly entrenched in the speaker sample and that it remains unaffected by inter-speaker and inter-group frequency fluctuations in the use of the variable or its non-localised variants.

Bybee & Scheibman (1999) and Scheibman (2000) posit that the functional split between full and reduced variants of I DON'T KNOW arises from the construction's gradual grammaticalisation and associated changes to its constituent structure. Due to high frequency of use and repetition, I DON'T KNOW has become conventionalised as a single storage and processing unit (chunking) and weakened its association with its composite parts (autonomy). Loss of compositionality and analysability has triggered morpho-phonological and semantic-pragmatic changes, i.e., vowel reduction of *don't* and its fusion with *know* as well as (inter-)subjectification of meaning. A grammaticalisation view of I DON'T KNOW is supported by Thompson (2002) who argues that I DON'T KNOW, together with other frequent subject-predicate constructions, has been reanalysed from a complement-taking matrix clause signalling insufficient knowledge (see, for example, Extract (19c) in Section 4.4.2) to a comment clause signalling an epistemic stance towards the content of the accompanying finite clause (see, for example, Extracts (21) and (22) in Section 4.4.2) (see also Kearns 2007; Keevallik 2006). According to these scholars, then, synchronic variation in the form, function and syntactic status of I DON'T KNOW reflects the co-existence of newer (i.e. phonetically reduced, non-compositional and decategorialised) uses of I DON'T KNOW alongside older (i.e. phonetically full, compositionally transparent and non-decategorialised) uses of I DON'T KNOW (see Hopper's [1991] principle of layering).

Apparent-time comparisons of the constraint hierarchies for functional factors in the current dataset do not furnish any evidence of grammaticalisation in progress (see in particular Tables 4.6 and 4.7). Also, observed changes in the significance and direction of effects of syntactic factors are inconsistent with any inferences of change in progress. Yet despite the absence of any statistical imprints of ongoing change in the linguistic conditioning of variants, the data do not invalidate hypotheses that the stable synchronic distribution of I DON'T KNOW in the BwE data is the product of grammaticalisation processes. Several observations from the BwE data support a grammaticalisation scenario.

Firstly, as is the case in Bybee & Scheibman's (1999) and Thompson's (2002) data, I DON'T KNOW is highly variable in BwE in terms of transparency, analysability and syntactic status. The data contain tokens of I DON'T KNOW which constitute fully compositional, referential matrix or independent clauses (see, for example, the extracts in (19c) and (18) in Section 4.4.2) as well as tokens which constitute non-compositional, conventionalised comment clauses or parentheticals (see, for example, the extracts in (21, 22) and (4, 7, 11, 12) in Section 4.4). As a compositional word sequence which is put together from three elements (*I, don't, know*), I DON'T KNOW retains its morpho-syntactic analysability. In the BwE data, this is reflected in the construction's regular modification through intervening adverbs such as *really* or *even*. Conversely, as a non-compositional formula I DON'T KNOW manifests several structural indices of unithood and freezing in BwE: its constituent structure is rendered opaque through phonetic reduction and fusion; and its modification through interpolation is virtually non-existent (0.4% with non-compositional uses compared to 12% with compositional uses). These patterns are indicative of the construction's decreased analysability and increased autonomy, thus supporting Bybee & Scheibman's (1999) view that I DON'T KNOW, when used non-referentially, tends to be accessed from memory as a single unit or chunk.

Secondly, the synchronic co-existence in the data of full and reduced variants of I DON'T KNOW with complementary functions and differential morpho-syntactic properties is compatible with current hypotheses about the unidirectionality and regularity of the changes constituting grammaticalisation. These hypotheses predict developments along the following clines:

(28) phonologically long > phonologically short   (see Bybee 2003:615–617)

(29) truth-conditional/content/non-subjective > non-truth-conditional/
      procedural/(inter-)subjective   (Traugott & Dasher 2002:40)

(30) major category > minor category   (Hopper & Traugott 2003:107)

The OED (2010) records the first attestation of the form *dunno* as dating from 1842. The first example of *dunno* in the OED that clearly conveys pragmatic rather than referential meanings dates from 1938 ("He'll begin to say to himself: 'Well, I dunno. P'raps I'm wrong.'"). These data suggest that the grammaticalisation changes creating the synchronic variability of I DON'T KNOW described above are not a recent development but have been operative for some time and have begun prior to the time-span covered by the BwE corpus. The synchronic stability of the form-meaning correlations affecting *I don't know* and *I dunno* in the BwE data may thus reflect the fact that the variants have become fossilised in their current distribution.

Thirdly, even though the linguistic conditioning of all variants in the BwE data is stable in apparent time and provides no evidence of ongoing grammaticalisation, the existence and distribution in the data of the variant *I dono* furnishes cogent evidence of synchronic gradience in the use of I DON'T KNOW. As detailed in Section 4.3.2, *I dono* shares the vowel quality in *don't* of full variants and the lack of a morpheme boundary between *don't* and *know* of reduced variants. Its form is therefore more opaque than that of *I don't know* and less opaque than that of *I dunno*. In terms of function, *I dono* differs from *I don't know* and *I dunno* in

that it does not occupy a functional niche but is used with roughly equal probability to signal compositional and non-compositional meanings. Thus, by the very
nature of its formal and functional properties in the data, *I dono* seems to occupy
an intermediate stage in the formal and semantic-pragmatic development from
I don't know to *I dunno*. Embracing Traugott & Trousdale's (2010:40) view that
"synchronic gradience is often the result of grammaticalisation" and that grammaticalisation typically involves a series of small-step changes, the synchronic
variation and gradience in the formal encoding and functional distribution of
non-localised variants of I DON'T KNOW can be argued to reflect: the gradualness of I DON'T KNOW's fusion, attrition and desemanticisation; and the gradual
establishment of form-function correlations over time. The relative infrequency
of *I dono* in the BwE data (see Figure 4.1) does not undermine the validity of this
argumentation since "not every position on a cline is likely to be equally elaborated
at any particular stage" (Hopper & Traugott 2003:109).

Like non-localised variants, the localised variant *I divn't knaa* has been affected
by the semantic-pragmatic meaning changes associated with the grammaticalisation of I DON'T KNOW. Unlike *I don't know* and *I dunno*, however, *I divn't knaa* has
not at present specialised to occupy a functional niche in the system of I DON'T
KNOW variants. Rather, it parallels *I dono* in being a multi-purpose variant which
occurs with roughly equal probability across referential and pragmatic uses. This
effect and that of syntax, which is also insignificant, is robust across age and sex,
confirming the apparent-time stability of linguistic constraints on variant choice
noted earlier. (Paucity of tokens precludes investigation of the variant's robust
linguistic conditioning across individuals.) Yet despite the lack of linguistic constraints, the occurrence of *I divn't knaa* in BwE is far from random. An important
finding to emerge from the inclusion in the variable context of non-localised and
localised variants is that their occurrence is conditioned by different parameters.
As shown in Tables 4.6 and 4.7, function is the most important conditioning factor
for the occurrence of the most frequent non-localised variants in the data, *I don't
know* and *I dunno*; social factors play only a secondary role in conditioning their
occurrence. Conversely, the localised variant *I divn't knaa* does not carry a functional load; as shown in Table 4.9, its occurrence is conditioned by social factors.
Thus, while frequent non-localised variants display function-specific patterning,
the localised variant analysed here parallels the behaviour of localised phonological
variants such as those investigated by Llamas (2007b) and Milroy et al. (1994) in
displaying systematic variation across social factors. *I divn't knaa* is thus a prime
candidate for marking social differentiation and indexing social group membership. Close inspection of variant distribution across individuals reveals that the
speakers who exhibit the strongest propensity for using the variant *I divn't knaa* are

the three young males with the highest rate of use of pragmatic I DON'T KNOW in the sample (see the top left corner of Figure 4.5 above). This pattern suggests that these young males cultivate the frequency and formal variability of I DON'T KNOW for its pragmatic and socially symbolic functions. The results also bolster evidence provided by recent studies of general extenders which have shown that the social indexicality of discourse-pragmatic features is not limited to their frequency and functionality but extends to their form (Cheshire 2007; Pichler & Levey 2011; Tagliamonte & Denis 2010).

A final key insight offered by careful consideration of both external and internal factors concerns their independence in discourse-pragmatic variation and change. As discussed above, the contribution of internal factors to variant choice is remarkably stable in apparent time. Yet the data exhibit strong evidence of instability in the social conditioning of variant selection. The analyses in Section 4.5.2 have shown that the variant *I dunno* almost doubles in frequency in the youngest age group, possibly as a result of the apparent-time increase in pragmatic uses of I DON'T KNOW with which this variant is closely associated (see Figure 4.5 above). Other variants undergo dramatic changes in terms of age as well as sex effects. *I don't know*, in addition to suddenly dipping in frequency in the youngest age group, loses its association with male speakers in the oldest age group to become strongly associated with female speakers in the youngest age group. *I divn't knaa*, in addition to exhibiting an incremental increase in frequency across age groups, loses its association with female speakers in the oldest age group to become strongly associated with male speakers in the youngest age group. These patterns reveal that social changes in variant choice occur despite the stable linguistic conditioning of variants discussed earlier (see also Pichler & Levey 2011). They thus demonstrate the methodological importance of including external factors in studies of language change and grammaticalisation, for exclusive focus on internal factors may yield inaccurate conclusions about the stability of variant selection (see also Labov 1982: 76).

In sum, the formal variability of I DON'T KNOW in BwE is characterised by external instability and internal stability. Despite high degrees of inter-group and inter-speaker variation in the frequency, function and form of I DON'T KNOW, all speakers in the sample, irrespective of age and sex, use individual variants for the same broad meanings. This reduces the cognitive load on utterance interpretation and promotes communicative efficiency. There might then be an interactional motivation for the stability in the functional conditioning of variant choice.

4.7 Conclusion

The preceding analysis of the construction I DON'T KNOW has shown that the distribution of its formal variants in BwE is not random but systematically constrained by age, sex, function and/or syntax. The results confirm the functional split between *I don't know* and *I dunno* previously reported for American English, and provide evidence for claims in the literature that the synchronic distribution of variants is an outcome of grammaticalisation (Baumgarten & House 2010; Bybee & Scheibman 1999; Scheibman 2000). Previously undocumented findings include the differential conditioning of non-localised and localised variants, the role of social factors in constraining patterns of formal variation in the use of I DON'T KNOW as well as the stability of internal and the instability of external predictors on variant selection.

Yet despite conducting an apparent-time analysis of the data configured to test the simultaneous effect on variant choice of internal as well as external predictors, this chapter has failed to illuminate the developmental trajectory of the variants of I DON'T KNOW or the social forces driving the grammaticalisation of I DON'T KNOW. This is due to the internal stability of linguistic variation in the dataset and the relatively shallow time-depth of the BwE corpus. Comparable diachronic and longitudinal data are required to: verify the grammaticalisation scenario postulated in Section 4.6; explore whether the sex-differentiated patterns in the usage and distribution of the variable and its variants noted in Sections 4.5.1 and 4.5.2 are indicative of male- or female-led innovations; and establish whether young males are in the process of assigning a specialised meaning to *I divn't knaa*, as suggested by the patterns discussed at the end of Section 4.5.2.

## CHAPTER 5

The construction I DON'T THINK*

5.1 Introduction

The construction I DON'T THINK has been studied quite extensively as a prototypical example of transferred negation or negative raising (Fillmore 1963; Fischer 1998; Horn 1978, 2001: 308–330; Nuyts 1990; Tovena 2001), whereby the negative particle adjacent to the predicate in the complement clause is transferred, or raised, to the predicate in the matrix clause, as illustrated in (1).[34]

(1) a. I think that he will *not* come.
     b. I do *not* think that he will come.   (Horn 2001: 315)

Although most of these studies have addressed the alleged synonymy between sentence (1a) and weak readings of sentence (1b) (see further Section 5.2.1), little is known about the interactional importance of I DON'T THINK except that it functions as an epistemic device that serves in casual conversation to hedge utterances and to mitigate interactional conflict (Bublitz 1992; Simon-Vandenbergen 1998). This chapter explores the functionality of I DON'T THINK in the BwE corpus with a view to establishing whether function, together with speaker sex, age and complement type, affects the construction's formal variability in the data. The variable form of I DON'T THINK is illustrated in the extracts from the corpus in (2). It is depicted here and throughout by means of variation in orthography, with each orthographic form (*I don't think, I doØ think, I divn't think, I dinnae think*) representing a different variant whose phonetic, phonological and morphemic properties are described in detail in Section 5.3.2.

(2) a. HP: When you're married.
         Ryan: *I don't think* I've got one for when you're married. *I doØ think* there is one sort of like.

---

* An earlier, less advanced analysis of the data investigated here was presented in Pichler (2009).

34. Although pragmatic uses of I DON'T THINK constitute epistemic phrases modifying their following host clauses (see further Section 5.6), the labels matrix clause and complement clause are employed throughout this chapter to differentiate the syntactic components of I DON'T THINK-*p* constructions (see further Chapter 4, footnote 24).

b.   HP: Would you call it the bog?
     Alicia: >Not really.<
     HP: No.
     Alicia: [*(h)* I think that doesn't] sound right, does it? [I'm going
     Rebecca: [*I don't think* I̲ would use it.]   [I've heard
     Alicia: = to the bog.]
     Rebecca: = people] say it, but *I do*Ø *think* I̲ would.
c.   HP: If you could, would you change where you came from?
     Godfrey: [*I don't*] *think* so.
     Lori: [No.]
                No.
     Godfrey: *I divn't think* so.
d.   HP   Do you think that ol- eh younger people also <u>talk</u> differently
                than older people?
     Evelyn: °No, *I dinnae think* so. No.°

Bybee & Scheibman's (1999) analysis of I DON'T THINK in a corpus of American
English conversational data revealed that the construction is not consistently
phonetically reduced even though it constitutes a compositionally unanalys-
able unit which functions exclusively in the interpersonal domain of discourse
to hedge or mitigate utterances and is never used referentially to express a lack
of cognitive activity. Systematic analysis of the construction's variable form and
function in the socially stratified BwE corpus uncovers similar patterns, and
demonstrates that the lack of consistent reduction of I DON'T THINK (*I don't
think* > *I do*Ø *think*) is, at least in part, interactionally motivated to signal fine-
grained nuances of pragmatic meaning. Moreover, the analysis shows that non-
localised and localised variants are conditioned by different parameters, with
the former carrying a functional and the latter a social load. Close analysis of
the construction's distribution and usage in the data also reveals that, despite its
lack of consistent attrition, I DON'T THINK constitutes a formulaic discourse unit
in BwE. The analysis presented here thus addresses the broader research aim of
this project set out in Chapter 1 which is to establish the mechanisms underlying discourse-pragmatic variation and change. Attainment of this objective is
warranted in large part by conducting an analysis of I DON'T THINK which is
comparable to that of I DON'T KNOW in the previous chapter.

For ease of cross-variable comparison, the organisation of this chapter parallels
that of Chapter 4. Section 5.2 reviews previous studies of I DON'T THINK which
inform the current analysis, and sets out in more detail the aims which guide the
analysis. Section 5.3 circumscribes the variable context, outlines the coding decisions, and details the variants of I DON'T THINK identified in the BwE corpus. This

is followed by Section 5.4 which introduces the range of functions performed by I DON'T THINK in the present dataset and thus isolates the factors constituting the factor group function. The effect of function and other predictors on the distribution of formal variants of I DON'T THINK is examined in Section 5.5 which presents the results of the quantitative analysis. The results are discussed in Section 5.6. Finally, Section 5.7 is the conclusion.

5.2 Previous research on I DON'T THINK

This section reviews the recent literature on I DON'T THINK. It discusses first studies which provide insights into the semantic-pragmatic uses of I DON'T THINK in spoken discourse. It then reviews previous studies of *don't*-reduction, including the only quantitative study carried out to date which has focused specifically on the formal variability of I DON'T THINK. The section ends with an outline of how the present study illuminates the conditioning of form variation in the use of I DON'T THINK by including non-localised and localised variants in the envelope of variation, isolating fine-grained pragmatic meanings of the construction's use, and including multiple contextual factors in the quantitative analysis of a socially stratified corpus of interview data.

5.2.1 Qualitative studies: Discourse-pragmatic functions of I DON'T THINK[35]

Accounts of the construction's semantic-pragmatic meanings have been largely concerned with exploring the differential readings of negative raising with I DON'T THINK, and with invalidating claims about the alleged synonymy between weak readings of I DON'T THINK and corresponding structures with the negative clitic in the complement clause.

   Scholars investigating I DON'T THINK as a phenomenon of transferred negation distinguish two readings for sentences of the type 'I don't think *p*,' as in (1b) above. In what is commonly referred to as their strong reading, these sentences are construed as negative propositions: transferred negation does not occur and the negative takes scope over *think* (Simon-Vandenbergen 1998: 313–315). Speakers use I DON'T THINK in this way to correct or deny a suggestion made in the preceding discourse that they hold the opinion expressed in the following complement

---

35. Section 5.4 describes in detail the functional repertoire of I DON'T THINK. Therefore, no examples are provided here of the functions identified for it in the literature.

(Nuyts 1990: 572). Simon-Vandenbergen (1998) refers to this reading as the construction's propositional or literal reading. In what is commonly referred to as their weak reading, sentences of the type 'I don't think *p*' are construed as negative modal expressions: the negative does not apply to *think* but, through negative transfer, applies to the predicate in the following complement clause (Simon-Vandenbergen 1998: 313–315). The transfer of the negative is possible because in the weak reading the clause boundary between the matrix clause and complement clause is transparent to the scope of negation (Bublitz 1992: 557–558).[36] This reading of (1b) is generally paraphrased as 'I think not-*p*.' Because it constitutes an epistemic modality marker that signals speakers' reduced commitment to their propositions (Bublitz 1992), Simon-Vandenbergen (1998) refers to this reading as the construction's non-propositional or modal reading.

Nuyts (1990) and Simon-Vandenbergen (1998) posit that the scalar distinction between the propositional and modal readings of I DON'T THINK is largely affected by the construction's ambient linguistic context. Tonic stress on the negative, an intonational break between the negative and *think*, and the construction's co-occurrence with lexical items that strengthen the illocutionary force of an utterance (e.g. *at all, really*) combine to trigger a strong or propositional reading of I DON'T THINK. By contrast, the co-occurrence of I DON'T THINK with weakening elements (e.g. the hedges *well, you know, a bit, sort of*), neutral prosody, i.e., lack of tonic stress on any of its elements, or tonic prominence on *think* when the construction is followed by *so* trigger a weak or modal reading of I DON'T THINK. What both readings seem to share, though, is that they refer to Persson's (1993) stative meaning of *think* in the sense of 'believe/find,' i.e., a cognitive state resulting from a cognitive process, rather than the verb's dynamic meaning in the sense of 'cogitate/conceptualise' (Simon-Vandenbergen 1998: 313–314; see also Bybee & Scheibman 1999: 587–588).

Scholars addressing the meaning relation between the weak reading of transferred negatives, (1b), and their corresponding structures with the negative in the complement clause, (1a), have argued that the two do not stand in total synonymy. The negative force of 'I don't think *p*' is said to be weaker than that of 'I think not-*p*' (Givón 1993: 201; Horn 1978: 131–136, 2001: 315; Tovena 2001: 333). This suggestion is supported by Bublitz's (1992) detailed exploration of the interactional

---

36. Transferred negation with weak reading is restricted to the semantic classes of predicates that denote opinion, perception, probability, intention/volition and judgment/weak obligation (Horn 1978: 187–208). With predicates that fall into other semantic classes, the clause boundary is also the boundary to the scope of negation, and the transfer of the negative from the complement to the matrix clause results in a change of propositional content (for further details, see Bublitz 1992; Tovena 2001).

motivation for negative raising with first person singular pronouns and opinion predicates in the *London-Lund Corpus* (Svartvik 1990). Bublitz argues that transferred negatives increase the tentativeness of positive polarity epistemic markers through: (i) the distance of the negative from the proposition that it negates (see also Horn 1978: 132–133, 2001: 315); (ii) the type of predicate that is negated; and (iii) the utterance-initial positioning of the negative. By raising the negative from the complement clause where it semantically belongs to the preceding matrix clause, the negative becomes dislocated from the constituent that it negates. This weakens the force of the negative. Further, the transferred negative weakens the force of the proposition by reinforcing the epistemic modality already inherent in opinion predicates such as *think* (Urmson 1952). Lastly, the dislocation of the negative from near-turn-final positioning, which is typical of new information, to utterance-initial positioning adjacent to *I* marks the following proposition as more subjective, and softens the novelty and the potentially antagonistic effect of disaligning turns. Bublitz's (1992: 560) account of I DON'T THINK thus highlights the construction's interactional import as "an expression of epistemic modality, involvement and politeness [which is] used by the speaker to increase the degree of qualification and tentativeness of the underlying proposition" (see also Kärkkäinen 2003: 20, 36; Thompson 2002).

Based on her analysis of casual conversations and political genres, Simon-Vandenbergen (1998) provides an overview of I DON'T THINK's most frequent contexts of occurrence. They include: disagreement sequences; contexts which require polite rejections or refusals; contexts where speakers aim to distinguish their own point of view from that of others; and contexts where speakers strive to signal from the start their attitude towards an upcoming proposition. In addition to performing interpersonal functions in these contexts, I DON'T THINK has been argued to have a textual function related to the theme/rheme structure of discourse: transferred negatives are preferred to non-transferred negatives because they avoid focal prominence on the negation (Horn 1978; Nuyts 1990; Simon-Vandenbergen 1998).

The review of the literature demonstrates that I DON'T THINK is employed by speakers to qualify their commitment to their propositions or to forcefully deny suggestions that they entertain particular opinions. The distinction between these readings is largely affected by prosody. Without marked tonic prominence the construction tends to have an attenuating effect, whereas with tonic accent on one of its elements it tends to signal its propositional reading. There is reason to suspect, however, that currently available descriptions of the functionality of I DON'T THINK may be inadequate and incomplete. While it is conceivable that transferred negation with I DON'T THINK is motivated by concerns for textual coherence, as outlined immediately above, it seems equally plausible that this strategy may be motivated by concerns about face and attempts to reduce the negative force of interactionally dispreferred turns. Consequently, a straightforward classification of such uses as operating in the textual domain seems debatable. This is not to deny the possibility that I DON'T THINK may perform textual functions. Its positive counterpart, *I think*, performs a number of routine organisational tasks in addition to signalling various degrees of epistemic modality (see, for example, Kärkkäinen 2003). It is therefore plausible that the pragmatic usage of I DON'T THINK may not be restricted to the interpersonal domain, as suggested in previous studies. Similar to *I think*, I DON'T THINK may also play a discourse- and information-structuring role, albeit in negative contexts. Comparison with *I think* reveals another potential weakness of current functional accounts of I DON'T THINK. As demonstrated above, Bublitz (1992) argues that transferred negation increases the attenuating effect of *I think*. Yet *I think* functions not just as a hedge to signal reduced epistemicity; it also functions as a booster to strengthen speakers' commitment to their propositions (see, for example, Holmes 1990, 1995: 92–95). It is therefore plausible that, depending on their prosodic encoding, transferred negatives might reinforce not just the attenuating but also the strengthening effect of *I think*. The current study explores the various possibilities raised above.

5.2.2   Quantitative studies: Variation and change in the use of I DON'T THINK

Even rarer than qualitative studies are quantitative studies of I DON'T THINK, especially those exploring variation in the construction's morpho-phonology or phonetics. This shortage is deplorable. Together with detailed analysis of negative periphrastic DO variation in other constructions, systematic quantitative analysis of the formal variation of I DON'T THINK enhances current understanding of the nature and correlation of grammaticalisation processes which give rise to structured patterns of synchronic language variation.

Previous quantifications of the distribution of I DON'T THINK in spoken corpora have generally been concerned with comparing the relative frequency of I DON'T THINK with that of 'I think not-*p*'-constructions and with providing interactionally-based explanations for the marked preference for the former (see further Bublitz 1992; Simon-Vandenbergen 1998). To date, only one study has examined the formal and functional variation of I DON'T THINK. This study was conducted by Bybee & Scheibman (1999) on a small corpus of American English conversational data and was motivated by their contention that non-referential modal uses of I DON'T THINK, as described in Section 5.2.1 above, constitute a grammaticalised discourse unit. With increased frequency in discourse, I DON'T THINK has lost its internal structure, become automated as a processing unit (chunking) and weakened its association with its composite parts (*I, don't, think*)

(autonomy). As a result of these changes, I DON'T THINK has generalised its meaning and developed functions in the interpersonal domain of discourse. In Bybee &
Scheibman's data, all tokens of I DON'T THINK were used non-referentially to signal an epistemic stance or to soften disagreements. In order to establish whether
the construction's desemanticised status is reflected in its realisation as a reduced
form, as was the case in their data with I DON'T KNOW, Bybee & Scheibman coded
the 19 tokens of I DON'T THINK in their corpus for their phonetic form: full vowel
variants with [o] and reduced vowel variants with [ə] in *don't* (see further footnote 22 in Chapter 4.2.2). The fact that the majority of I DON'T THINK tokens
were non-reduced showed that the grammaticalised status of I DON'T THINK as a
formulaic construction with interpersonal functions is not congruent with phonetic reduction:

> though the meaning of [I DON'T THINK] is compositionally unanalyzable in con-
> versation – indicating a more grammaticized unit – there is no consistent formal
> reduction concomitant with this functional shift [...] (i.e., we find in the data both
> full and reduced variants of *don't* in [I DON'T THINK]).
>
> (Bybee & Scheibman 1999: 588)

These findings contrast sharply with the results obtained by Bybee & Scheibman
for I DON'T KNOW which suggested that formal reduction and semantic-pragmatic change operate in unison (see also Chapter 4 of this book). However,
the findings for I DON'T THINK correspond to Brinton's (2005: 293, 2006: 308)
observation that attrition may occur when discourse-pragmatic variables undergo grammaticalisation but that it is not a necessary concomitant of semantic-
pragmatic change.

Patterns of variation in the realisation of *don't* have also been explored in a
small number of studies of so-called 'secondary contraction' in Yorkshire varieties
of British English (Petyt 1978; Richards 2008; Whisker 2007; Whisker-Taylor in
prep.). These studies demonstrate that *don't*-reduction in northern British English
primarily affects the nasal and, to some extent, the plosive of the clitic particle in
don't, yielding variants such as [doːt], [dõt], [dot], [dõʔ] or [doʔ]. They also reveal
that the reduction of the nasal is conditioned by social and stylistic factors: the
frequency of reduction varies across the varieties investigated; where it occurs, it
is generally more frequent among younger speakers, among speakers from the
lower socio-economic classes and in informal contexts. However, these studies
have not isolated the construction I DON'T THINK from productive constructions
containing negative periphrastic DO. Consequently, they provide little insight into
the specific nature and conditioning of variability in the form of I DON'T THINK
in British English.

The lack of consistent reduction of pragmatic tokens of I DON'T THINK in Bybee & Scheibman's (1999) American English data suggests that the variation between full and reduced variants of I DON'T THINK is not conditioned by broad referential vs. pragmatic meaning distinctions. Because their study was concerned with constituent structure rather than the structure of discourse-pragmatic variation, Bybee & Scheibman made no attempt to uncover the impact of other factors on the alternation between full and reduced variants of I DON'T THINK. Even if they had attempted to test claims made elsewhere regarding for example the importance of social factors in conditioning *don't*-reduction, these would have been foiled by the limited size of their dataset (N = 19). The socially stratified BwE corpus contains a far larger number of I DON'T THINK tokens and thus makes possible testing these claims.

5.2.3   Aims and contribution of this chapter

The present investigation into form variation in the use of I DON'T THINK in the 260,000-word corpus of BwE develops previous quantitative and qualitative studies of this construction by: testing the contribution of both internal and external factors to observed patterns of form variation in the data; including both non-localised and localised variants in the envelope of variation; and investigating in finer detail the range of pragmatic functions performed by I DON'T THINK across all domains of discourse.

Examination in this study of the joint effect of intra- and extra-linguistic predictors (function, complement type, sex, age) on formal variation patterns in the data represents a development beyond Bybee & Scheibman's (1999) single factor analysis which allows us to fully uncover the organisation of variability in the realisation of I DON'T THINK in BwE. Consideration of social factors in the quantitative analysis also makes it possible to assess whether any apparent-time changes in the frequency of reduced variants of I DON'T THINK in the BwE corpus parallel those reported for secondary reduction in Yorkshire English (Richards 2008; Whisker 2007; Whisker-Taylor in prep.). Further, examination of the sociolinguistic distribution of variants with different geographical spreads (see further Section 5.3.2) broadens the scope of Bybee & Scheibman's (1999) analysis which focused on non-localised variants, and enables us to determine whether the differential patterning of non-localised and localised variants established for I DON'T KNOW in Chapter 4 extends to variants of I DON'T THINK. Finally, the thorough functional analysis of I DON'T THINK in Section 5.4 makes it possible to establish in Section 5.5 whether observed patterns of variation in the construction's form are conditioned by fine-grained pragmatic differences in its use. Also, close inspection of the construction's semantic-pragmatic meanings in all its sequential contexts of occurrence and across multiple discourse domains yields a more detailed and accurate description of the construction's functional repertoire than are currently available in the literature. The broad scope of the analysis thus affords important new insights into the constraints on the formal variation of I DON'T THINK and contributes to advancing our current understanding of the structure of discourse-pragmatic variation.

Because the results of any variationist analysis are determined in large part by the methodological procedures adopted for circumscribing the variable context, identifying the set of alternative variants and coding the data for contextual constraints, it is important to detail these procedures in Section 5.3.

5.3 The variable context and data coding

5.3.1 The variable and the envelope of variation

The variable selected for analysis in this chapter is the construction labelled I DON'T THINK, defined as any first person singular subject-negative-opinion predicate construction in the present tense (see Chapter 2.3.2).[37] Inclusion in the variable context of the range of opinion predicates instantiated in the corpus (*think, suppose, believe, feel*) enables us to establish the lexical formulaicity and internal, morphological

---

37. Van Bogaert (2010) notes that in the BNC subject(-negative)-opinion predicate constructions manifest a high degree of variation in terms of TAM (tense-aspect-modality) specifications which does not bar them from functioning as epistemic markers. The existence of tense and modality variation in the present dataset does not affect the circumscription of the variable context set out above. Although subject-negative-opinion predicate constructions in the past tense or with modal verbs can function pragmatically in the BwE data (e.g. *I didn't think they did but mum and Amber thought so. – I wouldn't think it was fashionable.*), they are not included in the envelope of variation. As shown in Chapter 3, past tense periphrastic DO and modal *would* are virtually categorically negated with non-localised negative particles, i.e., they are not subject to the same degree of variation as present tense negative DO. Furthermore, second and third person subject-negative-opinion predicate constructions (e.g. *Do you not think Geordie's a lot more common than Scottish? – They don't really think, like, the people who are intelligent have a life.*) were not included in the envelope of variation either. Constructions with second person subjects function pragmatically only in questions (Thompson & Mulac 1991a: 243), a context which is far less variable in BwE than declaratives (see Chapter 3). Constructions with third person subjects do not generally function non-referentially (Urmson 1952) (for exceptions, see Kearns 2007).

fixation of negative epistemic marking with opinion predicates.[38] With the variable thus defined, the initial stage in the creation of the data file involved extraction from the corpus of every instance of a construction derived from the linear string of components exemplified in (3): (*I*) + (present tense negative DO) + (opinion predicate). Unless otherwise stated, the label I DON'T THINK is used as the umbrella term for the diversity of constructions included in the variable context. Individual opinion predicates are differentiated only in the context of the quantitative analysis in Section 5.5 and in the discussion of the results in Section 5.6.

(3) a. *I doØ think* we've ever had another name for cat.
     b. *I don't suppose* I would be able to alter their opinion.

The extraction process described above yielded instances where *think, suppose, believe* and *feel* denote 'have a sensation' (4a), 'accept the claim that' (4b), 'regard as having a certain quality' (4c), or where they refer to a cognitive process (4d). When they denote these meanings, opinion predicates are followed by non-finite phrasal complements, and the matrix clauses of which they are a part do not constitute examples of transferred negation. They are thus not subject to the same functional versatility as tokens that denote 'believe, find' and are followed by a finite clausal complement or the pro-form *so* (see the examples in (3) above and (5) below). These tokens were therefore removed from the variable context of analysis.

(4) a. I don't *feel* <u>a Borderer</u>.
     b. I don't *believe* <u>it</u>.
     c. I dinnae *think* <u>of it</u> that way.
     d. Na. Don't really *think* <u>about the border</u>.
         I don't *think* <u>like that</u> so much now.

---

38. The semantic-pragmatic meanings of these predicates are addressed in the course of this chapter. Note that they have elsewhere been termed "modal verbs" (Coates 1987), "weak assertive predicates" (Hooper 1975), "epistemic verbs" (Kearns 2007), "psychological verbs" (Leech 1983), "private verbs" (Stubbs 1986), "parenthetical verbs" (Urmson 1952) or "mental predicates" (van Bogaert 2010, 2011). Positive polarity constructions of these predicates with *I* have been referred to in the literature as "(first person) epistemic parentheticals" (Brinton 1996: 211–212; Thompson & Mulac 1991a, b), "epistemic phrases" (Kärkkäinen 2003), "comment reduced parenthetical clauses" (Kaltenböck 2005), "comment clauses" or "content/parenthetical disjuncts" (Quirk et al. 1985: 1112). I refrain from using these terms because they imply that the predicates listed above (*think, believe, suppose, feel*) are always used to qualify an assertion. As shown in Section 5.4, however, this is not necessarily the case. 'Opinion predicates' is therefore used here as a neutral label. In contrast to the labels listed above, it also has the advantage of more precisely delimiting the range of predicates included in the analysis.

In the BwE data, tokens of I DON'T THINK that qualify as matrix clause constructions with transferred negation are followed either by complement
clauses introduced with *that* (5a), by complement clauses introduced with a
zero-complementiser (5b), or by the pro-form *so* (5c). The pro-form presup-
poses across sentence boundaries the element to which it is structurally related
(Halliday & Hasan 1976: 130–141; Quirk et al. 1985: 880–881). In other words,
I DON'T THINK *so* substitutes for a complement clause and denies or modifies
a preceding assertion by self or other without repeating it. It thus contributes
to the cohesion of discourse.[39] Unlike I DON'T THINK and its clausal complements, I DON'T THINK and *so* are always intonationally integrated with each
other. Tokens followed by clausal complements and tokens followed by *so* alike
are included in the analysis.

(5) a. Now they would still be from Berwick because *I don't think* <u>that you talk
          about people being from Tweedmouth or Spittal.</u>
     b. Because certainly Alan Beith, our MP, *I don't think* <u>Ø he has much power
          with the Labour government in London.</u>
     c. *I divn't think* <u>so.</u> They're all just grouped together.

In addition to containing tokens of I DON'T THINK which occur before the clause
that they are construed with in terms of negation, as in (5) above, the data contain tokens which occur after the clause over which they have scope, as shown
in (6) below. These tokens are referred to here as post-positioned or post-posed
tokens of the variable. Unlike pre-positioned tokens, which form an intonation
unit with the following complement, post-positioned tokens always constitute a
separate intonation unit and occur only if the associated clause is independently
negated. Both pre- and post-positioned tokens of I DON'T THINK are included in
the analysis.

(6) He wouldn't call him fither to his face, *I divn't think.*

After tokens whose form could not be determined had been removed, a total of 270
tokens of the variable I DON'T THINK remained in the database for in-depth analysis. To uncover the constraints on their distribution, these tokens were coded for
their form, as described in Section 5.3.2, as well as a series of potential contextual
constraints, as described in Section 5.3.3.

---

39. Its more formal equivalents *I don't think that* and *I think not* do not occur in the data.

5.3.2 The dependent variable: Variants of I DON'T THINK in BwE

The main focus of this analysis is on uncovering the constraints on the variable morpho-phonology of I DON'T THINK illustrated in the extracts in (2) in Section 5.1. As was the case with I DON'T KNOW in Chapter 4, the variation mainly affects the realisation of negative periphrastic DO and the choice of the negative clitic. Notwithstanding the drawbacks of allocating tokens to discrete categories (see Chapter 4.3.2), auditory analyses established that the 270 tokens of I DON'T THINK in the database could be meaningfully divided into four discrete variant categories. This section introduces these categories and assigns them the status of non-localised or localised variants depending on their geographical dispersion.

Tokens in the first two categories of variants differ from each other with regard to the realisation of the negative clitic particle -n't (full realisation vs. reduction/deletion) and optionally the vowel quality of do (full vs. nasalised/reduced). The first category contains tokens such as [dɒnʔθɪŋk] or [dʊnθɪŋk]: the nasal of the negative clitic particle -n't is fully realised, and the final plosive of the clitic is either realised as [ʔ] or omitted. Due to their relative lack of phonological reduction, these variants are labelled full variants and are orthographically represented as I don't think. The second category contains tokens such as [dɒʔθɪŋk], [dʊθɪŋk] or [dəθɪŋk]: the negative clitic particle -n't is either reduced to [ʔ] or deleted altogether, and do is optionally produced with vocalic nasality and/or reduced to [ə]; very occasionally, the initial fricative of think is realised as [f] or [ɦ] or is omitted altogether, resulting in forms like [dɒʔĩŋk] or [dəʔɪŋk]. Because of their phonological reduction, the variants with nasal deletion are labelled reduced variants and are orthographically represented as I doØ think.

The full variant I don't think is the standard variant and as such is non-localisable. The reduced variant I doØ think is reminiscent of secondary contraction reported for Yorkshire varieties of British English (see Section 5.2.1). Petyt (1978) argues that secondary contraction, i.e., the reduction or deletion of the clitic negative particle, is regionally restricted within Britain. However, this thesis is based on informal observations and is not confirmed by empirical studies of -n't-reduction across varieties of English. In her survey of negation strategies across UK varieties of English, Anderwald (2002: 66) reports secondary reduction for the Midlands. Bybee & Scheibman's (1999) American English data also contain tokens of I DON'T THINK without a nasal in don't. In light of these findings and the fact that it was the erosion of the negative particle that led to the introduction of DO-support in the first instance (Labov 1994), we may assume that the reduction of don't in I DON'T THINK is more widespread than implied in Petyt (1978) (see also Richards 2008: 124). Phonologically full and reduced variants of I DON'T THINK are therefore categorised as non-localised variants.

Tokens in the third and fourth categories of variants differ from those above in that negative periphrastic DO is realised as *divn't* or *dinnae* (see Chapter 3.3). The category of variants orthographically represented as *I divn't think* contains tokens such as [dɪvn̩θïŋk]: negative periphrastic DO contains a KIT-vowel and some degree of friction. The category of variants orthographically represented as *I dinnae think* contains tokens such as [dĕnïθïŋk]: periphrastic DO is negated with the negative clitic *-nae*, yielding the negative auxiliary *dinnae* [dənɪ] or [dənə] or [dɛnɪ]. As detailed in Chapter 3.3.2, the forms *divn't* and *dinnae* are not used throughout all of England or the English-speaking world. *Divn't* is strongly associated with the north(-east) of England. *Dinnae* is strongly linked with Scotland, although its use has been recorded in Northumberland. Because their distribution in England is largely restricted to the north(-east) of England, the variants *I divn't think* and *I dinnae think* are categorised as localised variants.

Table 5.1 summarises the BwE inventory of variants for I DON'T THINK, with an indication of their geographical distribution in England.

Table 5.1 Inventory of variants of the construction I DON'T THINK in BwE

non-localised variants	localised variants
I don't think	*I divn't think*
I doØ think	*I dinnae think*

5.3.3 Independent variables: Data coding

In addition to coding each occurrence of I DON'T THINK for its variant form, a coding schema was devised for those extra- and intra-linguistic constraints which were hypothesised to affect the formal variation in the data.

If Bybee & Scheibman's (1999) premise concerning the grammaticalised status of I DON'T THINK in their American English data applies more generally to BwE, we may assume that social factors impact on the formal variation introduced in Section 5.3.2 above. Grammaticalisation processes are generally socially embedded, and the synchronic distribution of grammaticalised variants tends to be socially conditioned (see Chapter 4.3.3 for relevant references). The hypothesis that social factors impact on the formal variation patterns in the data is supported by studies of northern English dialects which have demonstrated the effect of speaker sex and age on the frequency of *don't*-reduction (see Section 5.2.2 above) as well as the results reported in Chapters 3 and 4 which have shown the operation of social factors on the occurrence of negative auxiliaries with *-nae* in productive constructions and on the occurrence of *divn't* in formulaic constructions. In order to probe the social distribution of variants and control for the effect of individual speaker on formal distribution patterns in the data, each token of the variable was coded for speaker sex, age and individual speaker.

Furthermore, it is possible that complement type constrains the distribution of full and reduced variants of I DON'T THINK. Simon-Vandenbergen (1998) argues that when I DON'T THINK occurs in reply to a polar question and is followed by the pro-form *so*, the only new information provided is the modality and negation encoded in I DON'T THINK. The pro-form replaces a preceding proposition and as a result its role is cohesive rather than referential (see Section 5.3.1). We may therefore hypothesise that because it is the negative in I DON'T THINK *so* that introduces the new referential information, I DON'T THINK is less likely to be reduced when it occurs with the pro-form than when it occurs with a clausal complement which introduces new referential information. To test this hypothesis, all tokens of the variable were coded for complement type: finite clause vs. pro-form.

Finally, even though there is no close correlation between formal reduction and pragmatic meaning in Bybee & Scheibman's (1999) set of I DON'T THINK tokens, there is reason to believe that function may be implicated in the formal variation of I DON'T THINK. Kärkkäinen's (2003: 121–129) analysis of naturally-occurring American English data has shown that when *I think* does not signal an epistemic stance but instead does some routinised organisational work such as acting as a frame or marking boundaries in discourse, it is generally realised in reduced form. Plug's (2010) analysis of a set of formulaic constructions in spoken Dutch has revealed that these constructions have different phonetic realisations depending on their particular pragmatic functions and contexts of occurrence. These findings furnish hypotheses that macro- and/or micro-level intra-pragmatic distinctions may account for formal variation patterns in the use of I DON'T THINK in the BwE corpus. To test these hypotheses, each token of I DON'T THINK in the data was subjected to a painstaking functional analysis aimed at establishing its specific pragmatic function in its specific context of use. Section 5.4 details the results of the qualitative data analysis and introduces the coding schema for the factor group function.

5.4   Qualitative analysis of I DON'T THINK

The multiple functions performed by I DON'T THINK in the BwE interview data were isolated by following the procedures described in Chapter 2.5 and successfully applied in Chapter 4.4. To make the analysis transparent and replicable, each function is illustrated with examples from the data and described with reference to its interactional, sequential and ambient linguistic context (see page XVII for a key to the conventions used for replicating prosodic features). Because many of the functions detailed below have not previously been documented in the literature and because fine-grained functional differentiations in the use of I DON'T THINK are crucial for explaining the formal variation patterns described in Section 5.5, the analysis is presented in minute detail. The detailed coding protocol to emerge from it is summarised in Table 5.2 at the end of this section.

5.4.1 Functions performed by I DON'T THINK

The labels attributed to I DON'T THINK in the literature include "epistemic modification" (Halliday 1985: 333–340), "epistemic marker/clause" (Bublitz 1992; Kärkkäinen 2003: 20, 36; Thompson & Hopper 2001: 25), and "epistemic formulaic fragment" (Thompson 2002). They highlight the construction's interactional importance in the interpersonal domain to signal speakers' assessment of the reliability of their propositions. The usage of I DON'T THINK to hedge utterances is highly persuasive in the present data and is illustrated in the extracts in (7). By prefacing their assessments with I DON'T THINK, (7a) and (7b), and by choosing to replace or follow the negative response particle *no* with I DON'T THINK, (7c) and (7d), the speakers in (7) signal their uncertainty vis-à-vis the validity of the assessments and denials which they provide in response to the preceding opinion questions. The construction's attenuating effect in the examples in (7) is produced and/or reinforced by its prosodic encoding with lowered volume, reduced tempo, high pitch or a combination of these. The above examples, in particular (7a) with its marked emphasis on *I*, also demonstrate that I DON'T THINK is a marker of subjective epistemic modality, i.e., "a conclusion drawn by the speaker from [their] own knowledge of the state of the world at the time of speaking" (Watts 1984: 131). Examples (7c) and (7d) further illustrate that I DON'T THINK *so* constitutes a grammaticalised response particle.

(7) a. HP: What about males and females. Are there differences?
         Leah: *(.h)*
         Shannon: °*I don't think* there are [really.]°
         Leah: [Not] really. Not [(eh)]
         Shannon: °[*I don't*] *think* it's
                    male and female.°
     b. HP: Are you only temporarily skint or can you be skint and be in
                    serious debt?
         Jane: >°*I divn't think* you would say skint for serious debts.°< I
                    wouldn't say skint for serious debts.

    c.   HP: Is jougle a bit derogatory?
        (…)
        Charlene: *Um, I doØ think so*.

    d.   HP: Do you sometimes go broader Berwick than you would usually speak?
        (..)
        Rebecca: *No, I doØ think so*

Beyond modalising (near-)turn-initial assessments produced in response to polar or alternative questions, I DON'T THINK has the potential for signalling low degrees of certainty when it occurs towards the end of multi-unit turns, as in (8a), or when it occurs in extended opinion sequences involving one or more speakers, as in (8b). The tokens in (8) are produced without prosodic variation, thereby communicating a lower degree of uncertainty than those produced with contrastive prosody in (7) above.

(8) a. HP: And do you like the way you speak?
       Elizabeth: I (.) *(h)* never sort of gave it much thought, really, to be honest with you. *(h)* Only like em sort of like because em (.) with me going away up to university now, [and] up in
       HP: [mhm]
       Elizabeth: = Edinburgh,   and like (.) em when I'm speaking to
       HP: mhm
       Elizabeth: = people, they (.) they like em (.) sometimes they say to me, "E? Sometimes you sound really Scottish and [other
       HP: [mhm]
       Elizabeth: = times] you sound really Geordie."   You know? And
       HP: uh-huh
       Elizabeth: = it's just like (.) but (.) like I'm not like sort of (.) I do I don't mind, *I doØ think*, cos I've never thought about it that much.

      b. Elsie: They've got a lovely maternity hospital. [But] if anything if
       Ronald: [There's a (?)]
       Elsie: there's anything em (.) +
       Ronald: Slightest complication, [they're gone.]
       Elsie: [They're] they're they're whipped away,   [[aren't they?]] You know?
       HP: mhm   mhm
       Ronald: [[mhm]]
                I don't think there's a big percentage of first babies ever born in Berwick.

Although the literature describes I DON'T THINK solely in terms of reduced epistemicity, the BwE data contain tokens of I DON'T THINK which serve to signal
personal commitment and conviction. Immediately prior to the dissent-turn
sequence reproduced in (9), Matthew's view that it is possible to recognise the
Berwick accent on the television had been challenged by his interview partner
Gerald. As Kotthoff (1993: 213) points out, "giving up a position that has already
been argued for can [...] be face-threatening [to the speaker's own face], because it could be interpreted as submissiveness." While the conditional clause
in Matthew's first turn in (9) slightly qualifies his earlier view, several linguistic
features signal his commitment to his original position: stress on *don't*, tonic stress
on the negative polarity items in the complement (*any, at all*), the utterance-final
descending intonation contour, and the emphasis in the first turn on *any difficulty
at all* through reduced tempo.

(9)   Matthew: If they were speaking eh if they were speaking broad enough, *I
                 don't think* there's >any [difficulty at all.<]
      Gerald: [Th-they'd have to be speaking] very
                 broad.
      HP: Mhm.
      Matthew: *I don't think* there's any difficulty in spotting them at all.

Emphatic tokens of I DON'T THINK can also occur in second pair parts of question-
answer adjacency pairs. Extract (10) forms part of a discussion about the north-
east referendum of November 2004, in which an overwhelming majority voted
against the setting up of a regional assembly in the north-east. After Alfred had
explained to HP why he had voted against the assembly, HP asks if he did not think
a regional assembly would have benefited Berwick. Alfred forcefully disputes the
proposition implicit in HP's question. The strength of his denial is produced by
the lexical and prosodic encoding of the first TCU: the use and slow delivery of
I DON'T THINK, the stress on *don't think*, and the utterance-final falling intonation
contour. The animated tone and divergent content of the following TCUs, which
provide an alternative assessment to HP's, add further weight to the incongruity
between HP's and Alfred's turns.

(10)   HP: But would you (.) do you think it would have made it any bet-
                  ter if they [had the:]
       Alfred: [>*I don't think*] so<, to be [very honest wi you.] We
       HP: [if you were governed]
       Alfred: = could hae been worse off!   We could hae ended up being
       HP: Yeah?
       Alfred: = worse off!

In turn-initial thematic position, emphatic I DON'T THINK points backwards and forwards, signalling that the upcoming turn will bring a new or different perspective to the previous turn. This is not the case with post-positioned boosters which always only point backwards in discourse, as illustrated in (11):

(11) HP: So, would you eh would you rather be governed by Scotland
                 than by England?
      Theodore: Oh, it wouldn't make any difference, pet, *I don't think*.

Whether subjective tokens of I DON'T THINK function as hedges or boosters is determined primarily by the ambient linguistic context. As a hedge, I DON'T THINK is generally produced with reduced volume, high pitch and lack of tonic stress; where stress occurs, it is placed either on *I* to emphasise the subjectivity of the following assessment, or on *think* when the variable is followed by the pro-form *so*. As a booster, I DON'T THINK is generally produced with emphatic stress on *don't (think)*; decreased speech rate, increased volume and falling or final intonation contours also tend to signal high degrees of certainty and commitment. Moreover, hedges generally co-occur with low modality items (e.g. *sort of, maybe, would, may*) in the complement clause, while boosters tend to co-occur with assertiveness markers (e.g. *really, at all*). These co-occurrences intensify the degree of epistemic commitment expressed (Fetzer 2011: 265) and create macro-modalities of (un-)certainty (Simon-Vandenbergen 2000: 56).

The boosting function of I DON'T THINK must not be confused with the construction's literal meaning (see Section 5.2.1). In (9) to (11) above, I DON'T THINK does not serve to deny the suggestion that the speakers hold the opinion expressed in the complement: 'I do not believe that *p*' (propositional reading). Instead, it serves to forcefully deny the proposition expressed in the complement: '*p* is not the case' (modal reading). My reading of these tokens as modal rather than propositional tokens is guided by the construction's prosodic encoding and sequential context of occurrence as well as a set of criteria laid down to disambiguate modifier uses of first person opinion predicates from their main verb uses (Kearns 2007: 483, 496): the fact that I DON'T THINK can be omitted from these utterances without changing their propositional content ('There's no difficulty in spotting them at all.', 'No.', 'It wouldn't make any difference at all, pet.'); the fact that I DON'T THINK can be paraphrased with epistemic adverbials ('There's *absolutely* no difficulty in spotting them at all.', '*Certainly* not.', 'It wouldn't make any difference at all, pet, *no way*.'); and the fact that I DON'T THINK is not transparent to tag questions (*'I don't think there's any difficulty at all, *do I*?').

In the interpersonal domain I DON'T THINK functions not only subjectively to modify propositions but also intersubjectively to redress potential face-threats and to signal affiliation and involvement. In (12), Luke responds to HP's question regarding his potential desire to speak another accent than Berwick. The low-volume production of I DON'T THINK-*p* and the use of the irrealis *would* combine to mitigate what would otherwise be an overt and potentially offensive negation of Luke's desire to speak Cockney or Scouse. The strategic use of these features thus serves to protect both the speaker's and his hearers' face needs by reducing Luke's commitment to his proposition and forestalling his hearers' potential antagonism.

(12)   Luke: Aye if I spo- if I was Manchester spoken I'd be alright. But (.) I
                wouldn't like to sound like a Cockney or [(h)] a liver- (.) like you
       HP: [Yeah.]
       Luke: = know Liverpool, like a Scouser.   °*Divn't think* I'd like to
       HP: Yeah.
       Luke: = sound like them.° @

What makes I DON'T THINK such a useful interactional device is the fact that it combines several techniques commonly employed to weaken the negative effect of disagreements (see Pomerantz 1984:64–77; Schegloff 2007:64–73): it defers the proposition that is being negated by pushing it further into the turn while simultaneously marking it as uncertain (see also Bublitz 1992:572; Simon-Vandenbergen 1998:321). As illustrated in (13), this makes unemphatic tokens of I DON'T THINK particularly well-suited for softening the presentation of disaligning second pair parts of assessment sequences. In (13a), Glenn responds uncertainly to HP's question (see the slow tempo), indicating that he might accommodate to the speech of non-Berwickers *a little bit*. Cody disaffiliates from Glenn's response when he says *I don't think I would*. While the stress on *I* in the complement clearly indicates a divergent opinion, the slowly articulated, unaccented construction I DON'T THINK mitigates the potentially face-damaging effect of Cody's disaligning proposition and adds a tone of tentativeness to it. In (13b), Charlene softens her disagreement with HP's suggestion that she might have a telephone voice by delaying it with a follow-up question (*Have I?*) and prefacing it with I DON'T THINK. The mitigating effect of the turn sequence is heightened by its high-pitched encoding, demonstrating that speakers often draw on several linguistic devices to soften the unwelcome interactional effect of disaligning turns.

(13)   a.   HP: And do you think (.) for instance if you talked to a Scottish
                   person that you would go a bit more Scottish and a bit more
                   Geordie when speaking to a Geordie person?
            Cody: U::m?

	Glenn:	>A little bit.<
	HP:	°Yeah?°
	Cody:	I do- >*I doØ think* I would<, cos (..) I wouldn't go more Scottish cos (.) you know (.) we sound a little bit Scottish as it is
		[so,] and I wouldn't really go towards the Geordie
	HP:	[mhm] (.) mhm
	Glenn:	[mhm]
	Cody:	= side either cos, (..) I'd probably s:peak the same actually.
	HP:	°mhm°
b.	Charlene:	I would just stay the same. I use the phone a lot at work,
		[so we] sort of (..)
	HP:	[mhm]
		You have your [you've] a telephone voice. Yeah.
	Charlene:	[But I]
		I do- have I? *I doØ think* I've got a telephone voice.

The face-saving effect of I DON'T THINK is also evident in the examples in (14) where the construction serves to mitigate or avoid the bluntness and abruptness of negative assessments made in response to opinion questions (see also Simon-Vandenbergen 1998: 321). In (14a), Godfrey's turn consists of two TCUs: an emphatic negative response particle which rejects outright the proposition inherent in HP's question regarding the trendiness of Berwick upon Tweed; and *I don't think so somehow* which functions to attenuate the bluntness and abruptness of the preceding flat denial *no*. I DON'T THINK thus works towards maintaining a friendly and non-hostile atmosphere in the interview situation. In (14b), the utterances following Barbara's initial *I doØ think so* indicate that she is committed to her negative stance towards a devolved government in the north-east. Although the predicate in I DON'T THINK does not actually refer to a cognitive activity (see Section 5.2.1), its association with a mental process implies that Barbara is not rejecting HP's preceding proposition outright but has given it some thought before denying its validity. The denial is thereby not only made less blunt but also more acceptable. Unlike hedging uses of I DON'T THINK which are usually produced with prosodic variation, attenuating uses of I DON'T THINK like those in (14) are consistently produced with marked falling intonation contours and without variation in tempo or volume.

(14)	a.	HP:	Do you think Berwick is a fashionable place to be?
		@	
		Godfrey:	<@ No::. @ *I don't think* so somehow. @>

b. HP: But do you think you might be better off, because right
                now you're quite far away from London. But then if you
                were governed by Newcastle, do you think you might be
                better off?
    Barbara: [*I doØ think* so.] Th-they make a mess of everything. They
    Paula: [No, no, no.]
    Barbara: = cannae do anything right.
    Paula: No.

Presumably because of their association with contradictions, disagreements and
rejections, negatives are often described as dispreferred and unwelcome moves in
discourse (Givón 1993: 188, 193; Pomerantz 1984). However, in certain sequential
contexts, negatives are interactionally preferred moves signalling confirmation and
agreement, acceptance and support, or affiliation and sympathy (Heinemann 2005;
Jefferson 2002). The negative polarity construction I DON'T THINK is a case in point.
Following negatively framed assessments or verification questions, it can serve as an
intersubjective affiliation marker and positive politeness device, as shown in (15).
After discussing Berwick's peripheral status vis-à-vis England and Scotland preceding the extract in (15a), Jane comes to the conclusion that Berwickers are unwanted
mongrels. The final high rise on the following *you know* requests corroboration,
reassurance or validation of this assessment from Jane's interview partner. Helen's
assertive-sounding reaction *No. I divn't think so* (see the lower than usual pitch and
falling intonation contour) provides the requested confirmation and signals Helen's
affiliation with Jane's assessment as well as her involvement in the interaction (see
also Bublitz 1992). In (15b), HP requests some corroboration from Ronald of her
inference from what he had said about gendered language differences prior to the
extract given below. By mirroring the polarity of HP's negatively framed question
and producing *don't* (and the following *no*) with moderately raised pitch, Ronald's
response turn implements a tentative agreement and confirmation of HP's inference. In contrast to those contexts where I DON'T THINK is used in response to
positively framed utterances to implement disagreement, as in (13) above, affili-
ative instances of I DON'T THINK are not usually followed by an elaboration, as is
characteristic of preferred response types more generally (Ford 2001).

(15) a. Jane: Aye we're mongrels. I divn't think er- anybody really wants wa.
                  You know?
          HP: Yeah.
          Helen: No. *I divn't think* so.
      b. HP: So you wouldn't say that men are broader than women?
          Ronald: No, I *I don't think* so. No.

Contra reports in the literature, the use of I DON'T THINK is not motivated solely by speakers' desire to be tentative or assertive, or their motivation to create and maintain positive rapport with co-conversationalists. While at all times conveying speakers' subjective stance towards their propositions, strategically placed instances of I DON'T THINK may also function in the textual domain. Similar to some of the discourse-pragmatic features discussed in Redeker (1991) and Schiffrin (1980, 1987), I DON'T THINK can act as a frame which serves to mark a range of transitions and boundaries in discourse. The examples given below illustrate that it is in fact the construction's association with (inter-)subjectivity that makes it such a useful tool for structuring and organising information and texts.

In (16), Theodore introduces Scottish nationalism into the discussion about Berwick's status vis-à-vis England and Scotland. Following a longish stretch of discourse in which he relates to HP Scottish nationalists' past attempts to bring Berwick back under Scottish control, Theodore provides his own point of view on the subject: *But I doØ think it'll ever happen like, you know.* The connective *but* preceding *I doØ think* signals that the upcoming discourse unit stands in contrast to the preceding unit (Schiffrin 1987: 164–177). Drawing on its inherent subjectivity, I DON'T THINK (in neutral prosody) cues the co-participants in the interaction as to the kind of contrast and transition that is underway: that between the provision of factual information and the provision of a subjective assessment of these facts.

(16)   Theodore: You see, at one time th- (.) they reckon it they didn't want it to go back to England. *(h)* You'll know, you have heard of Wendy Wood?   She's the Scottish nationalist, and after the war
      HP: mhm
      Theodore: = she come down   with the pipers. (.) And they'd (.) kilts
      HP: mhm
      Theodore: = on, and they marched across the new bridge, you know the [Royal Tweed Bridge], [half way] across. And she took a chalk
      Guy: [mhm]
      HP: [mhm]
      Theodore: = and she marked it. They [wanted] Home Rule for [Ber-
      HP: [mhm]   [mhm]
      Theodore: = wick], for Scotland, Berwick for [Scotland]. They was trying
      HP: [mhm]
      Theodore: = to get it into Scotland for donkey's years.   (..) But
      Guy: mhm
      HP: mhm
      Theodore: = *I doØ think* it'll ever happen like, you know.

In addition to marking transitions between factual and evaluative propositions, I DON'T THINK serves to mark the transition to a conclusion that is based on speakers' preceding subjective reasoning behind it. This use of I DON'T THINK is illustrated in (17), where Ryan and Dawn are requested to share their views on local football and on the perceived importance of the post-devolution border. At the beginning of their turns, Ryan and Dawn reflect on HP's question and the appropriate answer to it. Towards the end of their turns, we find a combination of two discourse-pragmatic features, *so* and I DON'T THINK, followed by the requested opinion. The combination of *so* and I DON'T THINK signals: that what follows the validation sequence is the requested assessment; that this assessment is derived from the preceding subjective validation (see Schiffrin 1987: 204–207 on the functionality of *so*); and that the assessment provided is subjective and potentially unreliable (see the reduced volume in both examples as well as the turn-initial hedge *I dunno* and the turn-final proclaimer *certainly to me as a worker* in Dawn's turn). Elsewhere in the BwE data, I DON'T THINK also signals neutral or assertive conclusions, depending on its prosodic encoding and ambient linguistic context.

(17) a. HP: What do you consider the local football derby to be.
          (..)
          Ryan: Uh (..) Berwick's never really had one? Em (.) >it used to be
                    Meadowbank Thistle when they played in Edinburgh.<
          HP: mhm
          Ryan: = But they've moved to Livingston now, so °*I don't think* <Ber-
                    wick's really got one>°.
      b. HP: And do you think that the significance of the border has
                    changed since the since devolution?
          (..)
          Dawn: *(h)* °I dunno? E:m (..) we ge- cos we we still get (..) funding and
                    I still get to go on Scottish [training] courses. So *I don't think*
          HP: [mhm]
          Dawn: = it's made   that much difference.° Certainly to me as a
          HP: yeah
          Dawn: = worker.

The information-structuring role of I DON'T THINK is not limited to (near-)turn-final positioning. As shown in the second pair parts of the question-answer adjacency pairs in (18), I DON'T THINK also occurs near-turn-initially following clusters of hesitation signals or minimally coherent responses to mark the onset of longer opinion sequences. The beginning of Alfred's turn in (18a) contains several hesitation markers (*well*, unfilled pause, outbreath) and an overt indication of the speaker's uncertainty as to how to formulate the requested assessment (*How could I describe this?*). The following I DON'T THINK signals a subjective stance towards and marks the starting point of an extended opinion sequence presented in response to HP's question. In (18b), Luke launches his turn by emphatically denying the proposition inherent in HP's preceding question. The following I DON'T THINK marks the starting point of an elaboration which validates Luke's initial denial and serves to meet the interactional expectation that turn-initial denials be followed by accounts or corrections (Ford 2001). At the same time, I DON'T THINK signals that both the account and the initial denial represent a subjective opinion. Both instances of I DON'T THINK in (18) are produced without variation in prosody. They thus convey a neutral to assertive attitude.

(18)   a.   HP: And would you say that in Berwick that eh young people speak
                        different from older people?
             (...)
             Alfred: Well. (..) (.h) How could I describe this. (..) *I don't think* they've
                        got much other choice [to be very] frank wi you.   % Be-
             HP: [mhm]   mhm
             Alfred: = caus:e some of them (..) I mean (..) you'll have heard bad lan-
                        guage [and all the rest of it in the town,] and I mean a lot of the
             HP: [mhm mhm]
             Alfred: = young ones come out wi some terrible language!
       b.   HP: But would you, would you say an outsider had the <u>right</u> to (.)
                        [(?)]
             Luke: [No!] *I don't think* anybody has the right to come in and criti-
                        cise [somebody] else's town!   Like (.) No! I w- I like I would
             HP: [yeah]   yeah
             Luke: = never go to some- I would never go somewhere else and say,
                        "Oh, your town's shit."   Like that. Cos I think th-there's
             HP: yeah
             Luke: = nay need for that.

I DON'T THINK occasionally also marks slight shifts in the topical development of interactions. This use of the variable is illustrated in (19), where Elsie and Ronald discuss the fact that Berwick upon Tweed has few immigrants. Elsie conveys her contentment with this state of affairs because immigration has led to problems in southern England. When she puts a disclaimer on this proposition (*What you read in the paper, you know.*), Ronald suggests that Berwick lacks the infrastructure nec-essary to attract immigrants. This proposition is prefaced with unaccented I DON'T THINK which serves to introduce an unsolicited neutral opinion that is explored in the following discourse (not reproduced here). It thus marks a slight shift in the topical development of the interaction.

(19) Elsie: Aye, we're lucky. We've w-we're, you know, there's no immi-
                      grants here. [There's] *(h)* there's nothing like that. We haven't
      HP: [yeah]
      Elsie: = got anything like [(?)]
      HP: [yeah]
      Ronald: [There's] no sort of racial tension and
                      things like that, [you know.]
      HP: [yeah]
      Elsie: [Aye. We're] we're really lucky. I mean, if
                      you go down south, I mean,
      HP: yeah
      Ronald: Unfortunately, you know, [I mean], every country has an [aw-
      Elsie: [No.]   [But
      Ronald: = ful lot. But never mind.]
      Elsie: = mind,] I think we we wouldn't be a nice place if they did
                      come in.   I think we I we I think w- there would be a lot of
      HP: mhm
      Elsie: = (.) aggro, if immi- immigrants came here.   You know,
      HP: mhm
      Ronald: mhm
      Elsie: = e::h cos   that's what's happened down south, you know.
      Ronald: +
      Elsie: = [They g-], you know. [Well. What you read in the paper,
      HP: [mhm]
      Ronald: [It's (?), Elsie, I I think, but (.)]
      Elsie: = you know.]
      Ronald: = >*I doØ think* there's much (.) much here for them [really.<]
      HP: [mhm]
      Ronald: = [You know,] there's no heavy industry.
      Elsie: [No.]

A final information-structuring use of I DON'T THINK identified in the BwE corpus is exemplified in (20) where the construction contributes to structuring an
opinion sequence. Gabriel provides various points of view on the then England
football manager Sven Göran Eriksson, and his turn is interspersed with the
discourse-pragmatic features *I think* and I DON'T THINK which, as a result of their
lack of prosodic variation, do not signal a high degree of epistemicity. Instead,
they perform a routinised organisational task: that of bracketing the assessment
sequence and marking the contrast between what Gabriel does and does not
believe to be the case.

(20) HP: But do you think they should sack Sven (..) [Sven (.) Göran
      Gabriel: [E::h (.)]
      HP: Eriksson?]
      Gabriel: = I probably say yes. I think he's took the team as far as he can
                 go.   I think (.) he: picks his favourites. *I doØ think* he's one
      HP: yeah
      Gabriel: = of the managers that says, "Right, you're not playing well. In
                 bri- (.) we're gonna bring in youngsters."

When I DON'T THINK acts as a frame to mark boundaries and transitions in discourse, as described above, it frequently co-occurs with other discourse-pragmatic variables. These serve to signal precisely what kinds of transitions are under way (e.g. contrast, elaboration, or conclusion). In all instances, the degree of confidence conveyed by I DON'T THINK is dependent on its prosodic realisation. By nature of their positioning vis-à-vis the proposition they modify, post-positioned tokens of I DON'T THINK never mark transitions in discourse.

The data analysed here contain no tokens of I DON'T THINK signalling its propositional meaning: 'it is not the case that I hold the opinion.' Similar to other corpora previously investigated for I DON'T THINK usage (Bybee & Scheibman 1999), all tokens of I DON'T THINK in the BwE corpus have pragmatic meanings.

5.4.2 Summary of functions

The preceding description and illustration of the range of functions performed by I DON'T THINK in the BwE interview data demonstrates well the construction's intrinsic multifunctionality and interactional indispensability. In the interpersonal domain, I DON'T THINK serves to signal various degrees of confidence speakers attach to their propositions. Moreover, the construction's subjective epistemicity is frequently exploited in this domain to signal politeness and promote good social rapport. I DON'T THINK serves intersubjectively to redress potential face-threats, to soften the effect of disaligning turns, to attenuate or avoid blunt and abrupt denials or rejections, and to signal agreement and affiliation. Importantly, the preceding analysis has described for the first time the information- and discourse-structuring functions performed by I DON'T THINK in the interpersonal-textual domain. While always cuing hearers to interpret following propositions and assessments as inherently subjective, I DON'T THINK can simultaneously act as a frame to mark a range of discourse transitions (objective > subjective propositions; explications > provisions of assessments) and boundaries (onsets of opinion sequences; shifts in topical development; shifts in opinion sequences). Appendix 4 lists these functional categories together with short descriptions of their characteristic properties in order to illustrate more concisely that it is the construction's prosodic encoding, surrounding linguistic context, turn-positioning and immediate as well as larger sequential context of occurrence that determine which function it performs.

While the functional inventory of I DON'T THINK outlined above accounts for every token of the variable in the current dataset, it makes no claim to represent an exhaustive taxonomy of the functions performed by I DON'T THINK across varieties, speech events or genres. Additional functions may emerge from analyses of other dialects, casual conversations or even scripted talk. What this analysis has demonstrated, though, is that currently available descriptions of the construction's usage and functionality are inadequate and incomplete, and that more work needs to be done to identify the full range of textual functions performed by I DON'T THINK.

However, the main aim of the qualitative data analysis was not to criticise existing accounts of the use of I DON'T THINK. Rather, the aim was to make possible inclusion of the factor group function in the quantitative analysis by isolating the factors typifying it in the present dataset. Table 5.2 outlines the coding protocol which arose from this exercise and guided the preparation of the data for quantitative analysis.

Table 5.2 Coding schema for I DON'T THINK functions

	function	description
interpersonal domain	epistemic marker	signals tentativeness & uncertainty (hedge)
		signals assertiveness & commitment (booster)
	mitigator	redresses potential face-threats
		softens disalignments & disagreements
		attenuates denials & rejections
	affiliator	displays affiliation & agreement
interpersonal-textual domain	frame	marks transitions & boundaries in discourse
		structures opinion sequences

5.5 Quantitative analysis of I DON'T THINK

The previous sections have identified the variants of I DON'T THINK, the factor groups that may constrain their distribution as well as the factors that constitute these factor groups. This makes possible quantitative data analysis to uncover the sociolinguistic mechanisms underlying the formal variability of I DON'T THINK in the data. In order to facilitate comparison of results across variables, the analysis presented here parallels as far as possible that in Chapter 4. It begins with an outline of the overall distribution of variants and presentation of the marginal results which reveal how the variants are distributed across the following independent variables: individual speaker, speaker sex, age, opinion predicate, syntactic position, function and complement type. The marginal results determine the configuration of the mixed-effects multiple regression analysis which models the simultaneous effect of sex, age, function and complement on the variable realisation of I DON'T THINK whilst removing from the outcome individual levels of variance. Inspection of the results uncovered by the regression analysis is judiciously combined with careful examination of variant distribution across fine-grained functions to reveal the organisation of the variable grammar underlying the distribution of variants. The results yield important new insights into the distribution of non-localised and localised variants of I DON'T THINK as well as the role of extra- and intra-linguistic factors in discourse-pragmatic variation and change more generally.

5.5.1 Distributional analysis

Close auditory analysis of the data revealed that the 270 tokens of I DON'T THINK included in the variable context could be divided into four formal variants (see Section 5.3.2). Figure 5.1 below shows their relative frequency. Roughly half of all tokens of I DON'T THINK in the data are realised with the full variant, *I don't think*. The reduced variant, *I doØ think*, constitutes slightly less than one third of all instances of the variable. These results mirror those reported in Bybee & Scheibman (1999) for American English: the variable is not consistently reduced even though its meaning is categorically non-compositional (see Section 5.4.1). The localised variants, *I divn't think* and *I dinnae think*, are less frequent than the non-localised variants. *I divn't think* represents approximately one fifth of all tokens of the variable. *I dinnae think* occurs only twice and is only used by one older female speaker in the sample. Because of its negligible instantiation, this variant is removed from consideration in the ensuing analysis.

Inspection of the distribution of the more frequently attested variants in the data reveals high degrees of inter-speaker and inter-group variation in their use.

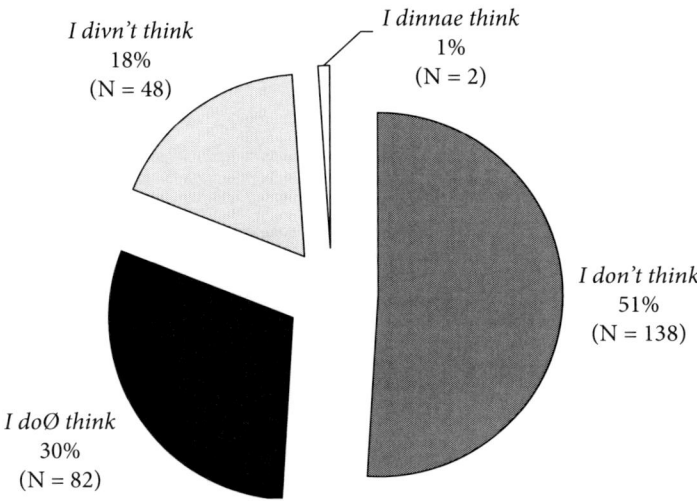

I divn't think
18%
(N = 48)

I dinnae think
1%
(N = 2)

I don't think
51%
(N = 138)

I doØ think
30%
(N = 82)

Figure 5.1 Overall distribution of the variants of I DON'T THINK

Firstly, not all speakers in the sample employ all of the variants that have been isolated in the BwE corpus. One speaker categorically uses the variant *I doØ think*. Only 10 speakers make use of the variant *I divn't think*. To account for these skewed distributions and avoid obscuring important constraints on the formal variation patterns in the data, the ensuing analysis proceeds as follows: the data contributed by the categorical *I doØ think*-user (N = 3) are removed from consideration in any quantifications of the data; only the ten speakers who employ *I divn't think* in the recorded data are included in quantifications of this variant across independent variables.[40] Secondly, not all variants are evenly distributed across social groups. While social groups differ only minimally in the frequency with which they use the reduced variant *I doØ think*, they differ more markedly in their frequency of use of the full variant *I don't think* and the localised variant *I divn't think*. The bars along the y-axis in Figure 5.2 show that the overall predominance of *I don't think* (dark grey bars) over *I doØ think* (black bars) noted in Figure 5.1 above is present across sexes and age groups but is more marked amongst male speakers and speakers from the middle age group. The frequency of *I divn't think* (light grey bars) also differs across social groups, especially across males and females. The latter have markedly higher rates of *I divn't think* than the former. However, the

---

40. As a result, the percentages provided for *I divn't think* in Figures 5.2, 5.3 and 5.4 are derived from consideration of a subsample of the I DON'T THINK token numbers given next to the factors listed along the x-axis.

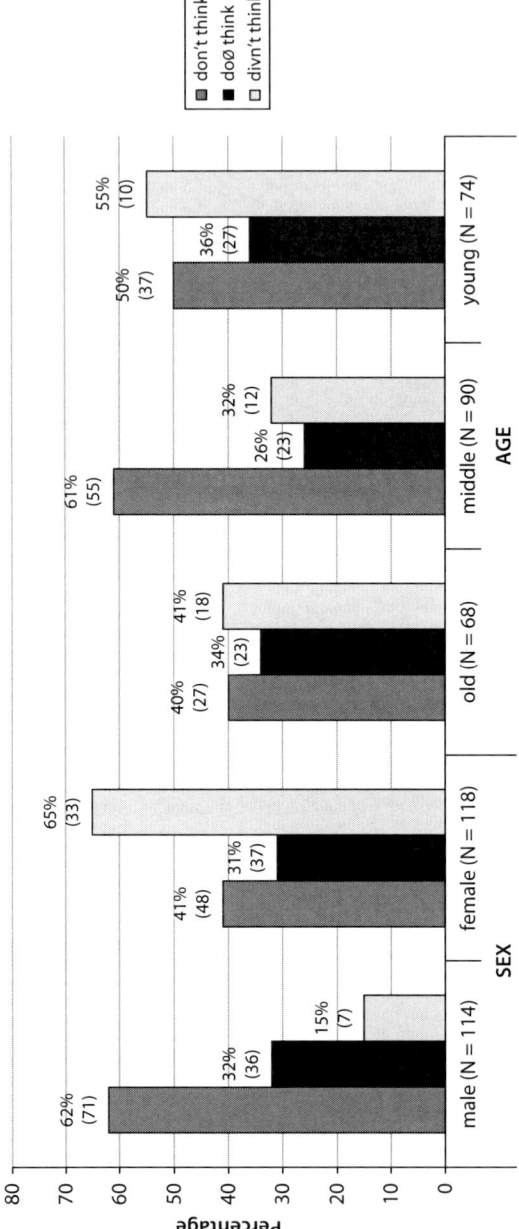

Figure 5.2 Distribution of variants of I DON'T THINK across speaker sex and age (Figures in round brackets indicate raw token numbers. The results for *I divn't think* are derived from data produced by *divn't think*-users only [N = 99].)

social distribution patterns displayed in Figure 5.2 must be interpreted with care. The figures ignore intra-group differences in the use of the variable and all of its variants; the figures for *I divn't think* are based on a restricted and socially skewed subsample of speakers. Nevertheless, Figure 5.2 suggests that provision of accurate accounts of form variation in the use of I DON'T THINK requires inclusion of social factors in the multiple regression analysis.

The distributional results in Figure 5.2 are based on a reduced dataset of 232 tokens. It does not include tokens of *I dinnae think* (N = 2), tokens produced by an invariable speaker (N = 3), tokens not coded for complement type and/or functionality due to insufficient context (inaudible turn continuation, interruption, truncation) (N = 21), tokens with the predicate *suppose* (N = 3), and tokens which occur in post-posed position (N = 9).[41] Tokens with *suppose* were removed from the analysis due to their relative lack of formal variability (the dataset contain no tokens of the reduced variant *I doØ suppose*) as well as their limited productivity which makes impossible systematic and reliable analysis of the effect of predicate type on variant selection. Post-posed tokens of I DON'T THINK were removed from the analysis due to their limited functional versatility (see Section 5.4.1) which might skew form-function correlations in the data, and due to their negligible occurrence which makes impossible systematic and reliable analysis of formal variation patterns across pre- and post-posed tokens of I DON'T THINK. The implications of the rarity of *suppose*-tokens and post-posed tokens for the construction's unithood and syntactic status are explored in the discussion of the results in Section 5.6.

In contrast to post-posed tokens of I DON'T THINK which invariably perform interpersonal functions and invariably modify a clause, pre-positioned tokens of I DON'T THINK perform interpersonal as well as interpersonal-textual functions (see Section 5.4.1) and occur with clausal complements as well as the pro-form *so* (see Section 5.3.1). The figures provided below the x-axis in Figure 5.3 demonstrate that pre-positioned tokens of I DON'T THINK are more than twice as likely to perform interpersonal functions (epistemic marking, mitigation, affiliation) than they are to perform interpersonal-textual functions (framing with a subjective stance). They also demonstrate the overall predominance of clausal complements over pro-form complements. The complete lack of pro-form complements with interpersonal-textual tokens reflects these tokens' role in marking transitions to new information units, i.e., to discourse units that have not previously been mentioned or cannot be inferred from the surrounding context. The bars along the

---

41. Exclusion of the latter sets of tokens from the distributional analysis slightly alters some percentages but does not affect the overall pattern of variant distribution outlined in Figures 5.2 and 5.3. The reasons for excluding these tokens from all quantitative analyses are outlined in Chapter 4, footnote 28.

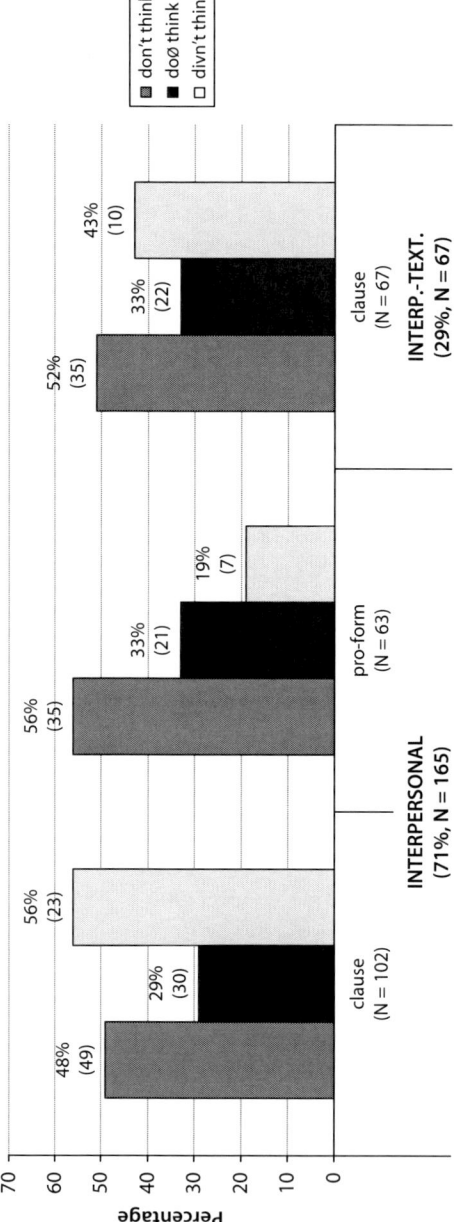

Figure 5.3 Distribution of variants of I DON'T THINK across functional domains and complement types (Figures in round brackets indicate raw token numbers. The results for I *divn't think* are derived from data produced by *divn't think*-users only [N = 99].)

y-axis in Figure 5.3 show the frequency of variants across functional domains and complement types. Neither function nor complement affect the distribution of the non-localised variants, *I don't think* (dark grey bars) and *I doØ think* (black bars), to any great extent: full variants always outweigh reduced variants. Conversely, the localised variant, *I divn't think* (light grey bars), manifests a stronger tendency to occur with clausal complements than with the pro-form. The multiple regression analysis in Section 5.5.2 will establish whether the effect of complement type on the occurrence of *I divn't think* is statistically significant.

Before proceeding to the multiple regression analyses, we must establish the necessity of treating individual speaker as a random effect. This is accomplished by way of comparing individuals' normalised frequencies of I DON'T THINK plotted along the y-axis in Figure 5.4. Each black bullet represents one of the 18 male speakers in the sample; each grey square represents one of the 18 female speakers in the sample. Comparison of the 36 data points reveals dramatic differences in the frequency of I DON'T THINK usage both within and across age groups (arranged from young to old along the x-axis). They range from zero to 25 tokens per 10,000 words in the youngest age group (on the left), from one to 34 in the middle age group (in the centre), and from two to 19 in the oldest age group (on the right). That highly divergent frequencies are particularly pervasive in the female data is demonstrated in the fact that two thirds of the male data but only one third of the female data are compressed into the range of zero to eight tokens per 10,000 words, and the fact that only four males but seven females have rates of I DON'T THINK higher than 15 per 10,000 words. The highly differential frequencies dictate that the effect of individual speaker be accounted for in the multiple regression analyses in Section 5.5.2. They may otherwise yield inaccurate results which over- or under-estimate the effect of social factors on variant choice (see Chapter 2.3.3).

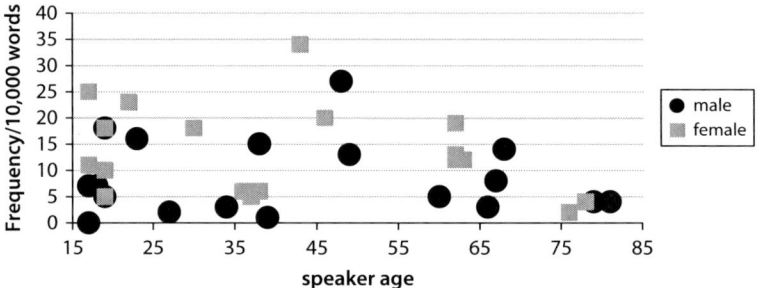

Figure 5.4 Normalised frequencies of I DON'T THINK across individuals

5.5.2 Multivariate analysis

To establish the joint contribution of independent variables to the probability of individual variants of I DON'T THINK while accounting for the high levels of inter-speaker variability discussed immediately above, mixed-effects multiple regression analyses are conducted with Rbrul (see Chapter 2.3.3 for details about Rbrul-based statistical analyses). Identical independent analyses for the three most frequently instantiated variants (*I don't think, I doØ think, I divn't think*) and close inspection of the direction of effect, statistical significance and relative contribution of predictors across variants enable us to compare the mechanisms of variability across variants and establish whether their occurrence is conditioned by the same parameters. (Detailed explanations on how to interpret the results yielded by the multivariate analyses in Table 5.3 are provided in Chapter 2.3.3). Restricted token numbers preclude apparent-time analyses of the data which are needed to identify any ongoing changes to the linguistic conditioning of variant selection. However, inclusion of age as a factor group in the analyses enables us to ascertain whether the probability of variant occurrence is changing in apparent time. In addition to age and sex, the analyses include two internal factor groups: function and complement. The factor group function is constituted by the factors interpersonal and interpersonal-textual. Running the regression analyses across broad functional categories is necessitated by low token numbers and motivated by the hypotheses about form-function correlations outlined in Section 5.3.3. The factor group complement is constituted by the factors clause and pro-form. In order to avoid empty cells, the former conflates tokens of I DON'T THINK followed by *zero*-complementisers and tokens followed by *that*-complementisers. The rare occurrence of *that*-complementisers (N = 2) is discussed in Section 5.6. Finally, application of mixed-effects modelling and inclusion of speaker as a random effect in the regressions removes from the outcome of the analyses individual levels of variance.

Table 5.3 displays the results of three independent multivariate analyses of the contribution of age, sex, function and complement to the choice of *I don't think, I doØ think* and *I divn't think* in the BwE interview data. The variant listed at the top of a column was the one chosen as the application value for this particular run, with the other two variants included in the run as non-application values. All variable speakers in the sample were included in the runs for *I don't think* and *I doØ think*; only the ten speakers who use *I divn't think* in the recordings were included in the run for this variant. Because interpersonal-textual tokens only ever occur with clausal complements (see Figure 5.3 above), these tokens were excluded from consideration in the runs for complement. (This explains the lower token numbers in this factor group.)

Table 5.3 Contribution of external and internal factors to the probability of *I don't think*, *I do∅ think* and *I divn't think* (The application value at the top of each column is modelled in opposition to all tokens of the other variants.)

	I don't think				I do∅ think				I divn't think			
input prob.	0.513				0.315				0.297			
total N	232				232				99			
deviance	259.574				253.744				97.332			
	factor weights	%	N	log odds	factor weights	%	N	log odds	factor weights	%	N	log odds
sex	not significant				not significant				p=0.00196			
female	[.453]	40.7	118	[-0.190]	[.410]	31.4	118	[-0.365]	.769	64.7	51	1.201
male	[.547]	62.3	114	[0.190]	[.590]	31.6	114	[0.365]	.231	14.6	48	-1.201
range									.538			
age	not significant				not significant				not significant			
old	[.321]	39.7	68	[-0.751]	[.536]	33.8	68	[0.146]	[.490]	40.9	44	[-0.039]
middle	[.678]	61.1	90	[0.754]	[.347]	25.6	90	[-0.632]	[.456]	31.6	38	[-0.176]
young	[.501]	50.0	74	[-0.006]	[.619]	36.5	74	[0.468]	[.553]	55.3	17	[0.214]
range												
function	not significant				not significant				not significant			
interpersonal	[.525]	50.9	165	[0.99]	[.442]	31.2	165	[-0.232]	[.547]	43.5	69	[0.190]
interp.-text.	[.475]	52.2	67	[-0.99]	[.558]	32.0	67	[0.232]	[.453]	33.3	30	[-0.190]
range												
complement	not significant				not significant				p=0.0105			
clause	[.488]	48.0	102	[-0.049]	[.395]	29.4	102	[-0.428]	.732	56.1	41	[1.006]
pro-form	[.512]	55.6	63	[0.049]	[.605]	33.3	63	[0.428]	.268	19.4	36	[-1.006]
range									.464			
speaker	random st. dv 1.741				random st. dv 1.57				random st. dv 0.238			

Despite the patterns depicted in Figure 5.2 and the divergent factor weights given in Table 5.3 which associate *I don't think* with male speakers and speakers from the middle age group, the results of the regression analysis reveal that social factors do not make a statistically significant contribution to the occurrence of the full variant. (The appearance of social effects is created by unbalanced data.) As predicted by the distributional analyses in Section 5.5.1, internal factors are not implicated in the distribution of *I don't think* either. The variant occurs with similar probabilities across broad functional categories and both complement types. (The interaction effect in the factor group function is due to high degrees of individual variation in the distribution of *I don't think* across functional categories. These differences are likely to be a fabrication of low token numbers in the data.) The results shown in Table 5.3 thus reject the hypothesis formulated in Section 5.3.3 that tokens followed by the pro-form *so* are less likely to be formally reduced by virtue of the negative constituting the new information contained in I DON'T THINK *so*. In sum, none of the factor groups included in the analysis for *I don't think* have been selected as making a significant contribution to its occurrence.

The same obtains for *I doØ think*. The results of the regression analysis shown in Table 5.3 are in line with the patterns depicted in Figures 5.2 and 5.3. Neither external nor internal factors significantly affect the distribution of the reduced variant. The specious favouring effects for male and young speakers are not real when all predictors are considered together and within-group differences in variant choice and token frequency are accounted for. The factor weights for age fluctuate but they are inconsistent with any inferences of change in progress. Due to a combination of limited data and intra-speaker variation, complement type does not affect the occurrence of *I doØ think* despite divergent factor weights. Finally, the result that *I doØ think* occurs with roughly similar probabilities across interpersonal and interpersonal-textual functions rejects the hypothesis formulated in Section 5.3.3: that tokens which function across discourse domains to act simultaneously as epistemic markers and discourse frames are more likely to occur with *don't*-reduction than tokens which function in the interpersonal domain only.

In the case of the localised variant, *I divn't think*, the multivariate results in Table 5.3 provide robust confirmation of the marginal results shown in Figures 5.2 and 5.3. Its occurrence is more constrained than that of the non-localised variants. As indicated by the range values, speaker sex makes the most important contribution to the occurrence of *I divn't think*, with the six female users of this variant in the data exhibiting a favouring effect over the four male users. Thus, while two thirds of the female speakers interviewed for this project never employ the variant *I divn't think* in the recordings, those who do employ it do so with remarkable frequency. Complement type is the second strongest constraint on the use of *I divn't think*. Clausal complements strongly favour its use while the pro-form disfavours it. Age and discourse-pragmatic function do not make a significant contribution to the occurrence of *I divn't think*. Its usage is not associated with a particular age group in the speaker sample and it occurs with similar probabilities across broad functional categories.

The results discussed above suggest that in contrast to the localised variant, *I divn't think*, the occurrence of the non-localised variants, *I don't think* and *I doØ think*, is largely unconstrained by the factor groups included in the multivariate analyses. They have refuted hypotheses about the impact of social factors on the choice of full and reduced variants as well as hypotheses that full variants may be favoured with the pro-form and reduced variants with interpersonal-textual functions (see Section 5.3.3). However, we have not yet tested the hypothesis that the distribution of variants may be conditioned by more fine-grained functional differences in their use (see Section 5.3.3). Figure 5.5 explores this possibility. It lists along the x-axis the range of micro-functions established for I DON'T THINK in Section 5.4: hedges (tokens attenuating propositions), boosters (tokens strengthening propositions), affiliators (tokens displaying affiliation or agreement), mitigators (tokens redressing face-threats, signalling disalignments, or attenuating denials/ rejections), and frames (tokens marking transitions/boundaries or structuring opinion sequences). The frequency with which each variant occurs across these functions is indicated by the bars along the y-axis.

Although low token numbers preclude firm conclusions to be drawn, the results suggest that the occurrence of *I divn't think* (light grey bars) is not greatly constrained by micro-functional distinctions. Disregarding its absence from the category of boosters, the variant is fairly evenly distributed across the categories listed on the x-axis, though it is somewhat less frequent in framing functions. By contrast, *I don't think* (dark grey bars) and *I doØ think* (black bars) display some function-specific patterning in line with Yaeger-Dror's (1985, 1997) Cognitive Prominence Principle (henceforth CPP) and Social Agreement Principle (henceforth SAP). These principles predict that negatives in interactional registers are: (1) uncontracted and prominent in terms of pitch, amplitude and/or duration when they carry important focal information (CPP) or show support of interlocutors (SAP); (2) contracted and non-prominent in terms of prosodic emphasis when they are non-supportive of co-conversationalists (SAP). Evidence for the operation of these principles on the realisation of I DON'T THINK is provided by the three categories in the middle of Figure 5.5. As predicted by the CPP, the negative particle in boosters is always fully enunciated because it is the bearer of important focal information, i.e., that something is *not* the case. As predicted by the SAP, the clitic in affiliators tends to be fully enunciated because the negative is supportive of interlocutors; conversely, the negative clitic in mitigators tends to be reduced to soften the unwelcome effect of disagreements or overt rejections. My

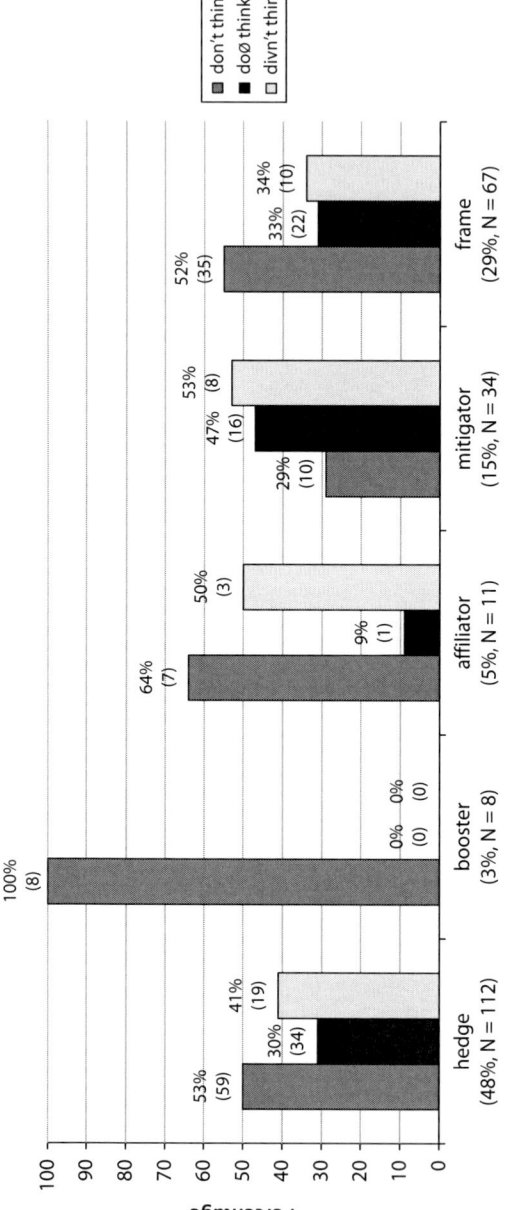

Figure 5.5 Distribution of variants of I DON'T THINK across micro-functions
(Figures in brackets indicate raw token numbers. The results for *I divn't think* are derived from data produced by *divn't think*-users only [N = 99].)

suggestion that the variation between full and reduced variants of I DON'T THINK is conditioned by Yaeger-Dror's (1985, 1997) CPP and SAP is necessarily tentative due to restricted data precluding statistical testing. Nonetheless, the results indicate that the non-localised variants of I DON'T THINK display some function-specific patterning at the micro-level of analysis.

The operation in the data of the CPP and SAP also helps explain why tokens acting as frames in discourse are not consistently reduced, as initially hypothesised. When these tokens mark transitions in discourse, they can convey either a neutral, tentative or assertive subjective stance towards the discourse unit they frame (see Examples (16), (17) and (18b) above in that order). Alternatively, they can also mitigate the proposition they frame (see Example (19) in Section 5.4.1). Re-inspection of these tokens demonstrates that interactional frames that unambiguously signal an assertive stance tend to be non-reduced while those that simultaneously perform some mitigating task tend to be reduced. These patterns demonstrate that even with multifunctional tokens that operate across discourse domains, it is the function I DON'T THINK performs in the interpersonal domain that tends to determine these tokens' realisation.

Finally, re-inspection of the hedging tokens of I DON'T THINK suggests that prosodic factors may be implicated in the formal variation of non-localised variants as well. Bybee (2003:616–617) points out that automatisation and meaning changes affect the prosody of grammaticalising words and constructions. Together with the decrease in the referential load of the grammaticalising items, the cognitive representation of multi-word constructions as fused storage and processing units leads to prosodic reduction. In frequent NP-negative DO-V collocations such as I DON'T THINK, loss of stress affects the medial syllable, i.e., negative periphrastic DO, which in turn leads to reduction of this syllable, as observed above (see also Bybee & Scheibman 1999:581–582). However, some non-boosting tokens of I DON'T THINK in the data carry pitch prominence on *don't* (see, for example, Extract (15b) in Section 5.4.1). Raised pitch on negative DO functions to signal high degrees of uncertainty. It could therefore be argued that the signalling of fine-grained nuances of meaning through prosody affects the formal variation in the data and contributes to the lack of consistent attrition of I DON'T THINK. A more thorough investigation of I DON'T THINK's prosodic realisation and of the degrees of uncertainty conveyed by the variable than was possible within the constraints of this project will confirm the extent of this effect on formal variability in discourse-pragmatics.

5.5.3   Summary of results

The key insights to emerge from the quantitative analysis into the formal variability of I DON'T THINK include the following:

- *Despite its non-compositional status in the data, I DON'T THINK is not consist-ently reduced*: Full variants of I DON'T THINK far outweigh reduced variants, even where the construction is used to perform routinised organisational tasks.
- *The variation between full and reduced variants of I DON'T THINK is exploited to signal micro-level functional distinctions*: The reduced variant *I doØ think* is associated with uses where the negative is non-supportive of interlocu-tors. The full variant *I don't think* is associated with uses where the nega-tive signals support of interlocutors or carries important focal information. Reduction is also impeded by pitch prominence on *don't* to signal high de-grees of tentativeness.
- *Variants with different geographical distributions do not share the same variable grammar*: While non-localised variants evince some function-specific pattern-ing in the data, the localised variant *I divn't think* largely eschews association with functional categories. Its use is strongly constrained by those predictors that have no effect on the occurrence of *I don't think* and *I doØ think*, namely speaker sex and complement type.

Inspection of variant distribution across individual speakers and cohorts of speak-ers, inclusion of individual speaker as a random effect in the multivariate analyses, and comparison of the frequency of I DON'T THINK across and within social cohorts yield another key insight into the distribution of I DON'T THINK in BwE:

- *The frequency and form of I DON'T THINK exhibit a considerable amount of inter-group and inter-speaker variability*: Social cohorts and individual speakers differ in the frequency with which they use the construction I DON'T THINK as well as their preference for individual variants. This is particularly true of the variant *I divn't think* which is only used by a subsample of ten speakers recorded for this project.

5.6   Discussion

This chapter set out to uncover the sociolinguistic mechanisms giving rise to the formal variability of I DON'T THINK in BwE, a peripheral variety of British English which features both non-localised and localised variants of the targeted variable. Principled and accountable analyses of the construction's usage and distribution in the data have provided important new insights into its functional versatility as well as the constraints on its formal variability. This section discusses these insights, compares them to those obtained in previous studies of I DON'T THINK-variation and *don't*-reduction in other varieties, and explores several indices of unithood to support claims that I DON'T THINK constitutes a routinised discourse formula.

The painstaking qualitative data analysis in Section 5.4 has established the functions performed by I DON'T THINK in the BwE data in order to make possible testing hypotheses that function might be implicated in the distribution of the construction's formal variants. Rigorous attempts to account for the usage of every token of the variable in the data revealed that I DON'T THINK performs a wider range of functions than previously described in the literature. Beyond signalling reduced epistemicity and mitigating the illocutionary force of dispreferred interactional moves, I DON'T THINK functions in the BwE data to boost the degree of commitment expressed, to implement interactionally preferred responses, and to mark transitions and boundaries in discourse. The distributional analyses in Section 5.5 showed the interactional importance of these previously undocumented functions. Although the majority of tokens of I DON'T THINK in the BwE corpus function to hedge propositions, more than a quarter of tokens also perform some routinised work in the organisation of discourse. Future studies will demonstrate whether the usage of I DON'T THINK as a textual frame is indicative of its ongoing grammaticalisation whereby the construction becomes increasingly desemanticised, and its epistemic and mitigating meanings gradually fade away (see, for example, Narrog [2012] who argues that textual functions can constitute endpoints of semantic-pragmatic change). In the present data, the subjective epistemicity conventionally associated with I DON'T THINK is very much part of its framing uses and there is no indication that its use as a hedging or mitigating device is decreasing and its use as a framing signal is increasing in apparent time. However, this may be due to the nature of the data on which the present analysis is based. The construction's epistemic meanings may be less prevalent in recording contexts that focus on the communication of referential information or the construction of coherent narratives than those that focus on the elicitation of personal opinions and subjective evaluations.

In addition to highlighting the shortcomings of existing functional taxonomies of I DON'T THINK usage, isolating fine-grained and previously undocumented functions of I DON'T THINK has proved crucial to accounting for the distribution of its non-localised variants. As was the case in Bybee & Scheibman's (1999) American English data, in the BwE data, I DON'T THINK is not consistently reduced either, even though the construction is exclusively used to signal non-compositional meanings. Close investigation of the distribution of full and reduced variants of I DON'T THINK across the fine-grained functions isolated in this study revealed that far from being randomly distributed in discourse, *I don't think* and *I doØ think* evince some function-specific patterning on a micro-level of analysis which tallies with Yaeger-Dror's (1985, 1997) CPP and SAP. Full variants are associated with contexts where the negative is the bearer of important focal information (boosters) or where it is interactionally preferred (aligning turns); reduced variants are associated with contexts in which the negative is interactionally dispreferred (face-threats, disaligning turns, outright rejections/denials). These constraints also affect the distribution of those tokens which in addition to signalling epistemicity act as frames at transitions or boundaries in discourse. Rather than being determined by their status as conventionalised discourse frames (see Section 5.3.3), the realisation of these tokens is at least to some extent dependent on whether they hedge, boost or mitigate the proposition they frame. These findings demonstrate the complex nature of form-meaning relations in discourse and counsel scholars against assuming a straightforward connection between discourse function and phonological substance. This view is supported by the observation that *don't*-reduction in I DON'T THINK is sometimes hampered by the construction's prosodic encoding with raised pitch on *don't* which signals high degrees of tentativeness. While the patterns outlined above may not explain the full extent of formal variation observed in the data, they demonstrate that the lack of consistent reduction of non-compositional I DON'T THINK tokens is at least to some extent interactionally motivated.

Inclusion of speaker sex and age in the multivariate analyses in Section 5.5 revealed that use of the non-localised variants of I DON'T THINK is not socially indexical. Although the frequency of full and reduced variants fluctuates slightly across speakers of different sexes and ages, the differences do not reach statistical significance and are not compatible with inferences of change in progress. These results contrast with those reported for secondary contraction in Yorkshire English where the deletion or reduction of the negative clitic particle *-n't* after vowels (e.g. *don't, can't, won't*) is favoured by females and is increasing in apparent time (Petyt 1978; Richards 2008; Whisker 2007; Whisker-Taylor in prep.). The differential results are likely due either to regional dialect variation or to methodological differences. The studies into secondary contraction listed above did not differentiate between individual auxiliary types or between high- and low-frequency constructions containing negative DO. The fact that there is no indication of any apparent-time monotonic increase or decrease of full and reduced variants of I DON'T THINK in the BwE data suggests that the discourse-functional distribution of variants outlined above is an inherent part of the linguistic system of this dialect rather than a reflection of an unstable and transitional state between a system of primarily full variants and a system of primarily reduced variants.

The results in Section 5.5 further reveal that the occurrence of the localised variant *I divn't think* is conditioned by different parameters than the occurrence of the non-localised variants. Amongst the subsample of speakers employing the localised variant in the BwE corpus, it is females who strongly favour its use. The female predominance in the use of the localised variant contradicts the pattern widely reported for localised phonological variants which are generally favoured by men (see, for example, Llamas 2007b; Milroy et al. 1994). Potential causes for this unexpected social pattern as well as for the low number of speakers using the variant are explored in Chapter 7. Whatever the nature of the underlying causes, *I divn't think* is a clear candidate for marking social differentiation in the BwE data. Another pattern that differentiates the localised variant from the non-localised variants is the fact that the occurrence of *I divn't think* is not conditioned by functionality *sensu stricto*. Bearing in mind the low token numbers, *I divn't think* is roughly evenly distributed across broad and narrow functional categories. However, after gender, the second strongest constraint on the use of *I divn't think* is complement type. As shown in Table 5.3 above, *I divn't think* is favoured with clausal complements and disfavoured with the pro-form *so*. Considering the cohesive function of the pro-form (see Section 5.3.1), these patterns suggest that *I divn't think* is not primarily used to negate or reject previously stated or inferred propositions but is used more often to negate discourse-new information. In a sense, then, the occurrence of *I divn't think* is also constrained by interactional factors.

The finding that the occurrence of variants with different geographical distributions is conditioned by different parameters is supported by closer comparison of their underlying grammars in Table 5.3 above. Because small datasets such as the one analysed here are less likely to yield statistically significant results than bigger datasets, the hierarchy of constraints constituting non-significant factor groups can nevertheless be construed as representing the grammar underlying the surface variability, and thus form the basis for comparing the underlying grammar of individual variants (Poplack & Tagliamonte 2001: 93). The comparison reveals that non-localised and localised variants of I DON'T THINK stand in almost complementary social and linguistic distribution. While *I don't think* and *I doØ think* are slightly more likely to occur in male speech, in interpersonal-textual uses and with the pro-form *so*, *I divn't think* is slightly more likely to occur in female speech, in interpersonal uses and with clausal complements. This demonstrates that discourse-pragmatic variants with differential geographical distributions may carry different social and linguistic loads and may therefore not be freely interchangeable.

Whatever the form selected for encoding I DON'T THINK in BwE, the data provide compelling evidence that I DON'T THINK constitutes a conventionalised discourse formula with a fairly fixed internal linguistic structure and a fairly robust unithood status. As pointed out in Section 5.5.1, *I*-negative DO-opinion predicate constructions are virtually categorically formed with *think* (99%, N = 267).

Constructions with *suppose* are exceptionally rare in the data (1%, N = 3); constructions with other opinion predicates (e.g. *believe, find*) are non-existent. Skewed distributions of lexical items are characteristic of frequent constructions and have been reported for negative and positive epistemic stance constructions elsewhere (Fetzer 2011; Kärkkäinen 2003, 2007). Together with the fact that in the current dataset I DON'T THINK is never modified by intervening adverbs, these patterns demonstrate the lexical formulaicity and internal fixation of negative epistemic marking with subject-negative-opinion predicate constructions in BwE.

The evidence provided above can be taken as indicative of the non-compositional status of I DON'T THINK, a claim that is supported by the 21:1 ratio of I DON'T THINK to 'I think not-*p*' constructions in the data (N = 270 vs. N = 13). Bublitz (1992) reports similar results and argues that the preference for negative raising with opinion predicates reflects its usefulness as an attenuation and mitigation strategy in contexts where speakers strive to develop and maintain good social relationships. Contra Bublitz, I would argue that the marked preponderance of I DON'T THINK over 'I think not-*p*' reflects a cognitively rather than interactionally motivated preference. When speakers wish to signal a subjective epistemic stance towards negative propositions, they access I DON'T THINK as a whole from memory rather than constructing a negative subjective stance from individual lexical items at the moment of speaking. Rare instances in the data of 'I think not-*p*' can be accounted for by interactional factors hampering negative raising. Firstly, 'I think not-*p*' tends to occur as a result of planning difficulties. In (21) below, the unfilled pause after *I think it was* and the following recast of the proposition in negative terms suggest that the speaker did not know at the outset that what would follow was a negative proposition (*it wasn't done properly*). Consequently, the negative could not be raised to the preceding matrix clause but instead had to occur with the proposition that it was construed with.

(21)   But to me, I think it was (..) it wasn't done properly.

Secondly, the occurrence of 'I think not-*p*' in the data can be explained on the grounds that it allows the addition of more layers of modification than is possible with I DON'T THINK, as illustrated in (22):

(22)   a.   *I think* I <u>probably</u> wouldn't change the way I talk.
       b.   **I don't think* I <u>probably</u> would change the way I talk.

The preceding discussion demonstrates that despite the huge variety of available linguistic resources, negative epistemic stance marking in BwE is highly regularised and routinised in terms of the linguistic forms and syntactic structures used. The high degree of internal fixation differentiates I DON'T THINK from positive polarity epistemic stance markers which are far more variable in terms of the opinion predicates used (Kärkkäinen 2003:37) and also allow a much higher degree of TAM variation than we encounter with negative epistemic stance markers in BwE (see van Bogaert 2011). Moreover, I DON'T THINK enjoys less syntactic freedom and positional mobility than positive polarity constructions such as *I think, I guess*, etc. While *I think* and its variants variably occur utterance-initially, -medially or -finally (see, for example, Thompson & Mulac 1991b), I DON'T THINK never occurs utterance-medially and only rarely utterance-finally (see Section 5.5.1). The strong preference for utterance-initial pre-positioning is largely interactionally motivated to secure alignment early on and guide hearers' interpretation of what follows. Also, post-positioned modification with I DON'T THINK is only possible if the qualified proposition has been independently negated, as in (23a). Simply transporting I DON'T THINK from one utterance position to another would result in grammatically incorrect utterances (23b) or meaning changes (23c).

(23) a. *I don't think* I mind it.   →   I <u>don't</u> mind it, *I don't think.*
      b. *I don't think* I mind it.   ↛   *I mind it, *I don't think.*
      c. I don't mind it, *I don't think.* ≠   *I don't think* I don't mind it.

What I DON'T THINK-*p* constructions share with *I think-p* constructions, though, is their near-consistent absence of *that*-complementisers (see Section 5.5.2). In the literature, *that* is generally described as demarcating the boundary between two clauses with referential content, while *zero* occurs when information-carrying finite clauses are preceded by an epistemic frame (Kearns 2007; Thompson & Mulac 1991a, b; Torres Cacoullos & Walker 2011:234). The near-categorical use of *zero*-complementisers in the current data can thus be interpreted as reflecting the syntactic and informational status of I DON'T THINK-*p* constructions. When I DON'T THINK performs its conventionalised role as a discourse-pragmatic variable, it constitutes an epistemic frame with scope over the following information-carrying finite clause rather than a matrix clause introducing a subordinate complement clause (see Thompson 2002). The fact that the negative in I DON'T THINK, through transferred negation, takes scope over the following proposition lends additional support to the non-existence of a clause boundary.

The preceding discussion was based on the assumption that the construction's modal usage derived through semantic bleaching and conventionalisation of implicatures from its propositional reading 'I do not hold the opinion that.' In other words, the modal or pragmatic meaning of I DON'T THINK was taken to be a grammaticalised, weak reading of negative raising (Horn 1978). While some scholars would argue that formal reduction is a necessary concomitant of grammaticalisation (e.g. Frank-Job 2006), the discussion above has identified several structural indices of unithood to demonstrate that I DON'T THINK qualifies as a non-compositional, routinised discourse formula despite its lack of consistent reduction of *don't*. While the data do not furnish any evidence of ongoing grammaticalisation, the synchronic distribution of variants shows all the signs of a grammaticalisation outcome: the synchronic co-existence of full and reduced variants; the construction's non-compositional usage and polysemic layering; and its syntactically reanalysed status as an epistemic frame rather than a complement-taking matrix clause.

5.7 Conclusion

The analysis presented in this chapter has confirmed the grammaticalised status of negative raising with opinion predicates (see Horn 1978) and the lack of consistent *don't*-reduction in the pragmatic usage of I DON'T THINK (see Bybee & Scheibman 1999). Systematic qualitative and quantitative analyses of the data have revealed several previously undocumented findings: that I DON'T THINK constitutes a highly conventionalised discourse formula with a wide range of functions in the interpersonal and textual domains of discourse; that the variation between its full and reduced variants is conditioned by fine-grained functional differences in the construction's use as well as by prosodic factors; and that the occurrence of its localised variant is socially indexical.

Because of limited data, no apparent-time analyses could be conducted to reveal how stable the organisation of the variable grammar is. Larger datasets and comparable longitudinal data from this and other varieties are needed to determine how stable the fine-grained functional patterning of full and reduced variants described in Section 5.5.2 is, how widespread the formal variation patterns outlined in Section 5.5.2 are, and whether the lexical formulaicity and internal fixation of I DON'T THINK documented in Section 5.6 is characteristic of (northern) (British) English more generally.

CHAPTER 6

Negative polarity question tags (NEG-TAGS)*

6.1 Introduction

A considerable amount of scholarly attention has been devoted to the investigation of English tag questions (henceforth TQs), which typically consist of an anchor clause to which an interrogative tag is appended. Scholars generally distinguish two types of tags: (i) invariant tags such as *right?, eh?, isn't that so?, don't you think?* which can be attached to any anchor irrespective of its grammatical features; and (ii) canonical tags such as *isn't it?, can't you?, won't we?* which generally bear a form-dependency on the preceding anchor (see further Section 6.3.2). Beyond providing detailed accounts of their syntactic-semantic properties (Cattell 1973; Hudson 1975; McGregor 1995) and thorough descriptions of their functional versatility (Algeo 1988, 1990; Andersen 2001; Coates 1996: 191–200; Erman 1998; Holmes 1982, 1984a, 1987, 1995: 79–86; Kimps 2007; Millar & Brown 1979), previous research on English TQs has yielded important insights into the extent to which the frequency and/or function of question tags varies across speaker sex, age, communities of practice, speaker role or power, and geographical space (Cameron et al. 1988; Cheshire 1981; Coates 1987; Dubois & Crouch 1975; Fishman 1983; Harris 1984; Hoffmann et al. forthc.; Holmes 1984a, 1987, 1995; Meyerhoff 1994; Moore & Podesva 2009; Tottie & Hoffmann 2006). To complete the present investigation into the formal variation of negative polarity discourse-pragmatic variables, this chapter builds on the small number of studies concerned with variation in the form of canonical and canonically-derived tag variants (Cheshire 1981; Moore & Podesva 2009) as well as those concerned with the origin, spread and grammaticalisation of the innovating tag variant *innit* (Andersen 2001; Cheshire et al. 2005: 155–159; Erman 1998; Krug 1998). It thus aims to: uncover the factors conditioning the formal variation in the BwE NEG-TAG system illustrated in (1) and introduced in more detail in Section 6.3.2; establish the entrenchment in the BwE data of the innovating variant *innit*; and assess the extent to which the BwE NEG-TAG system is affected by ongoing grammaticalisation.

---

* Throughout this chapter, the label 'tag question' is applied to the combination of anchor clause (e.g. *It's nice*) and question tag (e.g. *isn't it*). The label '(question) tag' is used to refer to the question tag element of TQ constructions only.

(1) a. Jane: I mean really, we could have a conversation, *(h)* if somebody
                     came in frae London (.) *(h)* o:r no even as far [south as Lon-
         Helen: [excuse me]
         Jane: = don.] And we could baffle them.   *Couldn't we.*
         HP: mhm mhm
         Jane: = [They wouldn't know what we was]
         Helen: [Oh aye. Wouldn't know what] we was talking about.
         Jane: *(h)* They [wouldn't know] what we was talking about.
         HP: [mhm mhm]
                     Yeah. Uh-huh. *(h)* And do you think that's a pity if i- <u>why</u> why
                     would it be such a pity if if it died out.
         Jane: *(h)* Because I think it's one of the em (..) no (a perk). *(h)* But
                     it's one of the Berwick (.) parts of the Berwick culture.
         HP: mhm
         Jane: And history.   [*In't it.*]
         HP: yeah

     b. Luke: Aye, it's no as bad as Eyemouth, though. [I mean,] you get
         HP: [yeah]
         Luke: = drugs every^where, [*divn't you*.] But it's no as bad as Eyemouth,
         HP: [yeah] yeah
         Luke: = like.

     c. Jane: Aye, but I think, for the younger ones they call their under-
                     pants kecks. But we called them trousers, *did we no*?

     d. Daniel: And Britain e:h (.) had to had to declare war. That was the
                     thing.   It's absolutely crazy, *innit.* If he had stopped at (..) I
         HP: yeah
         Daniel: = mean, after the First World War th- they didn't give Germa-
                     ny enough. They should have given the land back. And Britain
                     was for that.   E::h (..) but for the   Germans, <when they
         HP: mhm   yeah
         Daniel: = when they got stronger they wanted to take back their own
                     lands.> (h) And that's understandable, [th-] we would have
         HP: [yeah]
         Daniel: = been the same. But th- he went further than that, *didn't he*?

     e. Gregory: And he speaks completely different to me, *din he*.
         June: [Mhm. He does. Aye.] Uh-huh.
         HP: [Mhm. Mhm.]
         Gregory: And he was my best man at my wedding and [you'd] (.)
         June: [Aye.]
         Gregory: = think we was poles apart, *wouldn't you*.

Systematic analysis of the BwE NEG-TAG system reveals a dramatic social and functional split between canonical tag variants (e.g. *isn't it*, *couldn't we*, *didn't he*) and the canonically-derived tag variant *innit*. The results also show that while *innit* is more grammaticalised than canonical tags in terms of functionality, this is not the case with regard to analogical levelling. Neither *innit* nor its co-variant *isn't it* are regularly used outside their original context of use. Comparison of these results with those reported for *innit* in contemporary London English (Andersen 2001) provides important new insights into the social, geographical and linguistic diffusion of innovating discourse-pragmatic variants which complement and extend the insights uncovered in Chapters 4 and 5 into the sociolinguistic mechanisms of discourse-pragmatic variation and change.

This chapter is organised in the same way as Chapters 4 and 5. Section 6.2 offers a review of the literature which has provided the impetus for the current analysis of NEG-TAGS, and outlines in more detail the aims of this chapter. Section 6.3 sets out how the variable context was circumscribed. This section and Section 6.4 also describe how the dependent and independent variables were coded. Section 6.5 presents the results of the quantitative analysis and reveals the factors constraining observed patterns of variability in the choice of tag variants. The results are discussed in Section 6.6. Finally, Section 6.7 is the conclusion.

6.2 Previous research on question tags

As pointed out above, English TQs have received a fair amount of scholarly attention. This section reviews the literature on TQs that is directly relevant to the present investigation. The focus is on studies that have described question tags' functional properties, tag variants' distributional characteristics, and the tag system's increasing grammaticalisation. There follows at the end of this section an outline of how the present investigation constitutes a development beyond previous research by studying the NEG-TAG system as a whole and including social, functional as well as syntactic-semantic factors in the quantitative analysis of both canonical and canonically-derived tag variants.

6.2.1   Qualitative studies: Discourse-pragmatic functions of question tags[42]

Because they have been studied within a range of theoretical frameworks, a multitude of functional taxonomies have been proposed for English question tags (for the most comprehensive ones, see Holmes 1982; Kimps 2007). The following section is limited largely to reviewing those accounts which have impacted directly on establishing the functions performed by NEG-TAGS in the BwE data in Section 6.4 as well as those which are relevant to the discussion of the results in Section 6.6.

Academic interest in the functionality of question tags was triggered by Lakoff's (1973) intuitive account of TQs which distinguished between legitimate and illegitimate uses of tags. The former seek confirmation or verification of propositions in which speakers lack confidence; the latter are attached to propositions of which speakers are sure, thus signalling lack of assertiveness rather than lack of knowledge. Holmes's (1982, 1984a, 1987) in-depth analysis of TQs in a corpus of tape-recorded speech data challenges Lakoff's taxonomy and demonstrates that Lakoff's illegitimate tags do in fact perform important interpersonal functions in discourse. They express solidarity and function to encourage or make easier addressees' entry into or contribution to the discourse (facilitative tags); and they work towards mitigating the force of negatively affective speech acts such as directives, complaints or criticisms (softening tags). In her later work, Holmes (1995: 80–82) qualifies her earlier proposal that tags always serve as hedges attenuating the illocutionary force of preceding propositions, and shows that tags can also be confrontational and serve to boost the force of potential face-threats (challenging tags).

The view that tags constitute politeness as well as impoliteness devices is supported by others. The tag functions described by Algeo (1988, 1990) fall into three broad categories distinguished by their (im)politeness impact: tags seeking verification or corroboration are polite; punctuational tags serving to highlight speakers' propositions are neutral; and peremptory or aggressive tags signalling hostility are impolite. Cheshire (1981: 375–376) also identifies tags which serve to convey a hostile, aggressive or sarcastic overtone. Algeo and Cheshire concur that what distinguishes hostile or impolite tags from polite tags is the fact that the former are not response-eliciting. In (2) below, Jenny was not in a position to know that Cathy was going on holiday, and Cathy knew that Jenny did not know. The sincerity conditions on interrogatives ("The speaker believes that the hearer knows at least as well as the speaker does whether the proposition is true or false," Hudson 1975: 12)

---

42. Because the functional repertoire of NEG-TAGS is illustrated in detail in Section 6.4, few examples are provided here of the functions identified for it in the literature.

do not apply to this tag and it is non-conducive as a result. Only a TQ such as that in (3), which meets the sincerity conditions of both interrogatives (see above) and declaratives ("The speaker believes that the proposition is true," Hudson 1975:24), solicits a response from interlocutors.

(2) Jacky: We're going to Southsea on the seventeenth of next month. And
                 on Sunday they …
     Cathy: Yeah, and I can't bloody go.
     Jenny: Why not?
     Cathy: Cos I'm going on fucking holiday, *in I?*   (Cheshire 1981:375)
(3) Matthew: I was all brought up to say please and thank you.   *Wasn't I?*
     HP: mhm
     Gerald: Ah, you're ok there.

Andersen (2001:118–138) demonstrates that in COLT the tag variant *innit* performs a wide range of functions identical or similar to those described above. However, he analyses the functionality of *innit* within a relevance-theoretic framework which postulates that utterances are contextualised on the basis of existing beliefs so as to produce the greatest cognitive effect for minimal processing effort (see further Blakemore 1988; Sperber & Wilson 1995). Consequently, he describes the functions performed by *innit* not in terms of politeness or conduciveness but in terms of contextual alignment. Depending on its prosodic encoding, *innit* functions either to establish or to signal speakers' presumptions of common ground with their interlocutors.

The overview provided above is necessarily brief and does not do justice to the volume of literature investigating the functionality of TQs. Yet it successfully demonstrates that scholars' categorisations of tag functions largely overlap. The main differences pertain to the labels attached to individual functions and the number of functions identified. These differences are due at least in part to the differential methodological and theoretical frameworks employed and to the contrasting research goals pursued across studies. They should not distract from the fact that interrogative tags are consistently reported to perform important interpersonal functions in discourse. Yet because existing accounts of their functionality are largely based on the analysis of casual conversations, they may not capture tags' functional spectrum in other speech events or genres. The analysis in Section 6.4 explores this possibility and establishes the functions performed by interrogative tags in interview data.

6.2.2 Quantitative studies: Variation and change in the use of question tags

Contrary to other discourse-pragmatic variables, including those analysed in Chapters 4 and 5, question tags have a long history in quantitative variationist research. Scholars have investigated their variable frequency, function and/or form across a range of varieties in attempts to uncover the contextual constraints on their use. The following review of relevant studies provides important hypotheses about the conditioning of tag variation in the current data and suggests that an analysis which tests the combined effect of multiple contextual factors on variant choice may be urgently needed to further current understanding of TQ variation and change.

The initial impetus for quantifying the use of TQs was provided by Lakoff's (1973) account mentioned in Section 6.2.1 above, in particular by her intuitive observation that women's frequent tag usage reflects their lack of assertiveness and their desire for confirmation and approval. Empirically based studies of TQ usage challenged this claim by demonstrating that tags cannot be straightforwardly associated with women's language (Cameron et al. 1988; Dubois & Crouch 1975), and that men are in fact more likely to use tags for signalling reduced epistemicity than women who tend to use tags primarily to signal solidarity with co-conversationalists (Holmes 1984a, 1995). The social indexicality of canonical tags has been repeatedly confirmed over the last few decades, most recently in Moore & Podesva's (2009) ethnographic study of female adolescents in north-west England. Their in-depth analysis of 778 tags produced by members of four communities of practice demonstrates that tags derive their social meaning not just from their frequency of occurrence but first and foremost from a combination of their discourse properties (whether they solicit agreement in turn-medial position), their formal properties (whether the plosive in the negative clitic is released, glottalised or deleted), and their grammatical properties (whether the tag is produced with standard or non-standard morpho-syntax). Moore & Podesva (2009) argue that it is members' divergence across these three properties which enables them to construct distinct group styles.

The social meaning potential of tags' formal and grammatical variability has also been explored elsewhere, notably in the context of NEG-TAG variants that derive through morpho-phonological changes from the canonical tag *isn't it*: *ain't it, in't it* and *innit* (see further Section 6.3.2). Krug's (1998) analysis of these variants in the spoken subpart of the BNC, a ten million word corpus of spoken British English collected in 1991–1994, reveals that their proportional frequency varies dramatically across social groups and in apparent time. In stark contrast to *isn't it*, the canonically-derived variants *ain't it, in't it* and *innit* occur most frequently among speakers from the lower socio-economic classes and, in the case of *innit*,

among speakers with shorter periods in full-time education. In addition to a propensity for *innit* to occur in female speech, Krug also notes an apparent-time
increase in the rate of *innit* and a concomitant decrease in the rate of *isn't it*. He
argues that *innit* is gradually replacing *isn't it* as well as *ain't it* and *in't it* which are
already marginal. The association of *innit* with working-class, female and young
speakers is confirmed in Andersen's (2001) in-depth analysis of the distribution of
323 tokens of the tag variant *innit* in COLT (recorded in 1993) and the distribution of 96 tokens of *innit* in a specifically designed subset of the spoken part of the
BNC/London. Importantly, Andersen's (2001) analysis reveals that it is not just
the frequency of occurrence of *innit* that is socially indexical but also its syntactic-
semantic distribution.

Through analogical levelling the canonical tag *isn't it* and its derivational co-
variants *ain't it*, *in't it* and *innit* have begun to spread across the inflectional paradigm to non-third person singular neuter contexts of BE (see further Andersen
2001: 98; Cheshire 1982: 62; Krug 1998).[43] Evidence for this process is provided
by what Andersen (2001: 104–105) calls 'non-paradigmatic' uses of the above
variants: where they occur in contexts which according to Standard English tag
formation rules require an auxiliary-pronoun combination other than *is* + *it* (see
further Section 6.3.1). In Andersen's data, non-paradigmatic uses of *innit* are
limited to speakers under the age of 30 as well as speakers in inner- and outer-
London, and are more frequent amongst speakers from lower socio-economic
backgrounds and female speakers. The most marked differences in the use of
non-paradigmatic *innit*, though, are found across ethnic groups. Andersen demonstrates that ethnic minority speakers in London have markedly higher rates of
non-paradigmatic *innit* than white speakers. Based on these results and previous
research which showed that tags not matching the syntactic-semantic properties
of their anchor tend to thrive in multilingual environments (see *inter alia* Hewitt
1986; Todd & Hancock 1986; Trudgill & Hannah 1982), Andersen (2001: 112–114,
190–192) argues that the social forces driving the analogical levelling of *innit* are
ethnic minority speakers. Elsewhere, the spread of *isn't it*, *ain't it*, *in't it* and *innit*
across the inflectional paradigm has been attributed to their frequency in discourse (Cheshire 1982: 62; Krug 1998). In historical and contemporary data, third
person singular neuter tokens with present tense BE are proportionally the most

---

43. Andersen (2001: 98) uses the term 'invariabilisation' to refer to "the process of reanalysis
by which a form which was originally restricted to a particular syntactic environment comes
to be used in all syntactic environments across the inflectional paradigm." This terminology is
not adopted here as it is essentially co-referential with the more widespread and familiar term
'analogical levelling.'

dominant auxiliary-pronoun combination in NEG-TAGS (Hoffmann 2006: 42–43; Krug 1998:152–153; Tottie & Hoffmann 2006: 296).

Yet the fact that *innit* as well as *isn't it, ain't it* and *in't it* are levelling across the paradigm does not entail that their syntactic-semantic distribution is random. In keeping with Hopper's (1991: 28–30) principle of persistence, which predicts that the distribution of grammaticalising features is constrained by their origin, these tags have the highest rate of occurrence in those contexts that are syntactically and semantically closest to their original environment: after anchors with *it/that* and *is*. In COLT, *innit* is favoured in contexts that require a tag with negative polarity, the pronoun *it*, BE-verbs, present tense verbs, and *you*-subjects (Andersen 2001: 162–179). *In't*-tags are preferred in contexts that require a tag with BE in Scottish varieties (Macafee 1992), and contexts that require a tag with either BE or HAVE in Cheshire's (1981) Reading data. These results demonstrate that although the distribution of tags consisting of or derived from *is* + *-n't* + *it* is not limited to what is assumed to be their original context of use, it is nevertheless systematically constrained by the syntactic-semantic properties of the preceding anchor clause. Also, the observation that these variants are most frequent in those environments that bear the closest resemblance to their original environment suggests that their spread across the paradigm is gradual and ongoing (see Krug [1998: 171–172] for predictions about the variants' future syntactic-semantic trajectories of change).

In Andersen's (2001) teenage data from London, *innit* is used by all socio-economic groups. In Cheshire et al.'s (2005: 155–159) teenage data from Reading, Milton Keynes and Hull, by contrast, it is used only by working-class speakers. This suggests that the precise social meaning of *innit* might differ across varieties. A possible explanation for this is the variant's longer history and more advanced status of grammaticalisation in London compared to elsewhere (Cheshire et al. 2005: 156). This hypothesis is supported by the following observations: that *innit* occurs with a higher frequency in southern than northern UK varieties (Krug 1998); that paradigmatic and especially non-paradigmatic *innit* rarely occur in Hertfordshire, Reading, Hull and Milton Keynes (Andersen 2001; Cheshire et al. 2005: 155–159). The fact that all but one token of *innit* in the highest social classes and in Hertfordshire were produced by male speakers leads Andersen (2001) to argue that although females have a consistently higher rate of *innit* usage than males, it is males and not females who lead its social and geographical diffusion.

Beyond social and linguistic-structural factors, discourse-functional factors may also be implicated in question tag variability. Numerous studies have shown that social groups differ in the strategic use to which they put tags (see the references in Section 6.1 above). Of importance to the present investigation is Cheshire's (1981) study exploring the variation between [eɪnt]- and [ɪnt]-tags among working-class adolescents in Reading. Cheshire distinguishes between tags that function to seek confirmation from addressees and tags that convey overtones of aggression, assertion and hostility towards addressees (see Section 6.2.1). Her quantitative analysis reveals that the occurrence of [eɪnt]-tags is unconstrained by function, while the occurrence of [ɪnt]-tags is limited to signalling hostility and aggression. Because of its strong association with hostility and aggression, the tag form [ɪnt] is interpreted by Cheshire (1981) as a marker of the adolescents' vernacular culture which is dominated by violence. Beyond signalling functional meanings, the variant thus also communicates social meanings. Elsewhere, Cheshire (1982:61) reports that her Reading corpus (collected in the late 1970s) contains a few examples of the tag form that she represents as *in it* (*She's too good for you, in it? She makes her laugh, in it?*). Cheshire implies that, similar to the *in't*-tags discussed above, these tags are non-conducive and serve to signal hostility and aggression. We may tentatively deduce from this that it is both *in't*-tags and *in it* that are functionally differentiated from other tag forms in Cheshire's data. Cheshire's association of *in it* with hostility and aggression corroborates Krug's (1998:151–152) suggestion that disyllabic tags (e.g. *innit*) are favoured for peremptory and aggressive tag uses.

The results outlined above demonstrate the effect of language-external, linguistic-structural and discourse-functional constraints on the frequency and formal variability of tag usage in contemporary British English. Beyond furnishing important hypotheses for the present analysis into formal NEG-TAG variation in BwE, they call into question the validity of the results produced by Torgersen et al.'s (2011) recent analysis of *innit* in sub-corpora of COLT (recorded in inner- and outer-city London and Hertfordshire in 1993) and LIC (*Linguistics Innovator Corpus*, recorded in inner- and outer-city London in the period 2005–2006). Their cross-corpora comparison of the normalised frequency of *innit* shows that *innit* occurs with similar frequencies in both corpora (1,676 per million words in COLT; 1,569 per million words in LIC) and across most social groups. This leads Torgersen et al. (2011:107) to conclude that *innit* is an established and stable feature of London teenage English and that "the extent of use of *innit* is no longer characteristic of a particular group of speakers." Because this analysis ignores any language-internal constraints on the occurrence of *innit* and any potential changes to these constraints in the period 1993–2006, its results may yield a potentially misleading measure of language variation and change in contemporary London English. In contrast to Torgersen et al.'s (2011) investigation, this study includes external and internal predictors in the quantitative analysis of NEG-TAGS in BwE. It thus affords valid insights into the organisation and robustness of NEG-TAG variation in BwE.

6.2.3 Aims and contribution of this chapter

As pointed out at the beginning, this chapter investigates formal variation patterns in the use of NEG-TAGS in the BwE corpus. It represents a development beyond previous quantitative and qualitative studies of (negative polarity) TQs by: investigating their use in a peripheral variety of English; testing the combined effect of internal as well as external factors on variant selection; including in the envelope of variation the entire system of NEG-TAG variants; and investigating the functions performed by NEG-TAGS in interview data.

Investigation of NEG-TAG variation in BwE, a variety of British English remote from the alleged source of innovating tag uses in London and distinct from other varieties previously subjected to tag variation analysis, allows us to test two hypotheses advanced above: that *innit* might be less grammaticalised in northern than southern varieties of British English; and that some tag variants might have different social meanings across different varieties. Further, by conducting a multivariate analysis of NEG-TAGS, the present study overcomes the limitations of previous studies of question tag variation which have plotted the distribution of tag variants across multiple external and/or internal factors without testing the relative effect of multiple predictors when they are considered simultaneously (Andersen 2001; Krug 1998). This study thus enables us to provide a more reliable and precise description of the sociolinguistic conditioning of tag variation than previous studies. Moreover, inclusion in the variable context of all NEG-TAG variants found in the data makes it possible to determine how many and which variants are affected by analogical levelling and to assess how the grammaticalisation of some variants affects the frequency and sociolinguistic distribution of other variants. Finally, thorough functional analysis of NEG-TAGS in the current corpus of interview data allows us to establish the functional inventory of NEG-TAGS in this speech event and assess the comprehensiveness of functional taxonomies based on the analysis of conversational data. In sum, the analysis presented in this chapter extends and develops previous qualitative and quantitative studies of (negative polarity) TQs in order to advance current insights into their usage, distribution and development.

The next section identifies the contexts in which tag variants may alternate, introduces the variants isolated for NEG-TAGS in the current dataset, and explains the operationalisation of hypotheses about dependent variables that might condition the variation.

6.3 The variable context and data coding

6.3.1 The variable and the envelope of variation

The variable under investigation in this chapter is the BwE NEG-TAG system, i.e., the canon of reduced negative polarity interrogatives which are appended to a clausal or non-clausal anchor and are derived from the following linear string of components: (auxiliary) + (negative clitic) + (pronominal subject) or (auxiliary) + (pronominal subject) + (isolate negator) (see Chapter 2.3.2 and Section 6.3.2). To yield principled and accountable results, every instance of a NEG-TAG was extracted from the corpus. Because the focus of this project is on discourse-pragmatic variables with negative polarity, positive polarity tags, as in (4), were not included in the analysis. Invariant interrogative tags, as in (5), and invariant lexical tags, as in (6), were not included in the variable context either. These tags are diachronically and structurally unrelated to canonical or canonically-derived NEG-TAGS. Therefore, their inclusion in the variable context would not improve our understanding of the factors triggering the grammaticalisation of NEG-TAGS as I have defined them here. Omission from the analysis of the tags exemplified in (4)–(6) may affect the comprehensiveness of the qualitative analysis in Section 6.4 as well as intra- and inter-speaker frequency rates of TQ usage. However, their omission does not affect the conditioning of formal NEG-TAG variation.[44]

(4)   You have heard that, *have you*?
      It doesn't sound very good, *does it*?
(5)   Why can't they do something for them and then it would be so much better, *do you know what I mean*?
      But I also think if Berwick was in the English league, they wouldn't be as good, *you know what I mean*?
(6)   Would just be ugly if you're unattractive, *e*?
      I've said it for like five years, *right*?

The extraction process described above yielded instances of NEG-TAGS occurring in different syntactic-semantic contexts previously described by Andersen (2001: 104–105) as paradigmatic and non-paradigmatic. Paradigmatic NEG-TAGS, as exemplified in (7), match the syntactic-semantic properties of their anchor

---

44. For a comprehensive overview of positive polarity TQs, see Kimps (2007). For a discussion of invariant interrogative tags, see Torgersen et al. (2011). For a detailed account of invariant lexical tags, see Stenström et al. (2002: 165–191).

and thus follow the dependency rules of Standard English question tag formation outlined in Section 6.3.2 below. Non-paradigmatic NEG-TAGS, as exemplified in (8), do not match the syntactic-semantic properties of their anchor and violate the dependency rules of Standard English question tag formation.[45] Moreover, the data contain tokens of tag variants that are only partially paradigmatic. As shown in (9), these tags replicate the subject pronoun of their anchor but do not mirror the person and/or number of the auxiliary in the anchor, (9a), or the type of auxiliary used in the anchor, (9b) (*in't/in* derive from the third person singular form *isn't*, see further Section 6.3.2 below). I will therefore categorise these tokens as occurring in semi-paradigmatic contexts. Finally, the present dataset contains NEG-TAGS that occur with non-clausal anchors, i.e., anchors that do not contain an overt subject and finite verb, as in (10). However, the missing subject and verb of these NEG-TAGS can be straightforwardly inferred from the context (e.g. *It's an imaginary line, isn't it? – It's just the way they talk, innit? – I think it was last year, wasn't it?*). Therefore, they can be treated like tags following clausal anchors and be categorised according to paradigmaticity (see above). All instances of NEG-TAGS – paradigmatic, non-paradigmatic, semi-paradigmatic and those following a non-clausal anchor – are included in the variable context. This decision is dictated by the principle of accountability (see Chapter 2.3.2) and is further motivated by one of the aims of this chapter which is to assess the degree of analogical levelling across the BwE NEG-TAG system.

(7)   It's a different world when you go along there, *isn't it?*
      I suppose it's just the same, *in't it?*
      It's easier to get to and get parked, *innit?*

(8)   Newcastle and that, they call you a Jock, *isn't it,* Paula?
      Oh, I've answered this one before last time, *innit?*

---

45. In analogy to Holmes's (1982) distinction between canonical tags (e.g. *don't you, can't we, hasn't he*) and invariant tags (e.g. *eh, right*), Andersen (2001: 98, 104) applies the label 'invariant' to tag variants such as *innit* which frequently occur not just in paradigmatic but also in non-paradigmatic contexts. This terminology is not adopted here. In contrast to invariant lexical tags such as *eh, right* etc. and invariant interrogative tags such as *(do) you know what I mean,* the use of innovating tags such as *innit* is not entirely unconstrained by linguistic-structural factors. The diffusion of *innit* from its original context of use after anchors with third person singular subjects and present tense forms of BE is gradual and ongoing (Andersen 2001: 173–183; see also Section 6.5 below). I therefore reserve the label 'invariant' to refer to lexical or interrogative tags like those listed in (5) and (6) above, which – to the best of my knowledge – are not diffusing from an original context of use. I will refer to tokens such as those in (8) as non-paradigmatic instances of canonical or canonically-derived tag variants.

(9) a. You're quite near Hungary then, *in you?*
        Aye, we're Northumberland *in't we?*
        They're wise, *in't they?*
   b. They've got less pool to draw their players, *in't they?*
        We got a little visitor centre, *in't we?*
(10) An imaginary line really, *isn't it?*
      Just the way they talk and that, *innit?*
      I think last year, *wasn't it?*

Initial data observations further reveal that all NEG-TAGS in the data occur after declaratives. The vast majority of these follow an affirmative anchor clause, i.e., they form part of a reverse negative polarity TQ. Only one NEG-TAG in the data occurs after a negative polarity anchor, thus forming part of a constant negative polarity TQ, as illustrated in (11). Evelyn's proposition *the young ones don't want to go* echoes HP's preceding utterance regarding young Berwickers' reluctance to leave Berwick. The appended tag *do they no?* serves to signal Evelyn's surprise at the information offered by HP. This function, which has in the past also been identified for constant positive polarity tags (Kimps 2007: 282–283), is not performed by any of the reverse polarity NEG-TAGS in the data (see Section 6.4 below). In view of its rarity and functional anomalousness compared to reverse polarity NEG-TAGS, the token in (11) is not included in the envelope of variation.[46]

(11) HP: I've interviewed a lot of young people who said, "No. Maybe
               I have to go away for a job, [but I don't] [really want to."]
      Mary: [mhm]
      Evelyn: [Th-the] young ones
               don't want to go, *do they no?*

As in the preceding chapters, the following types of tokens were also excluded from the database: tokens of the variable whose form could not be determined; and tokens which occurred in quoted speech and thus could not be confidently assigned to the quoter's linguistic repertoire. In preparation for the quantitative analysis in Section 6.5, each of the 316 tokens of NEG-TAGS retained in the database was coded for its form and a number of predictors hypothesised to constrain NEG-TAG variation. The next sections set out the coding procedures.

---

46. The fact that only one NEG-TAG in the data follows a negative polarity anchor clause confirms the rarity of this construction noted elsewhere (Algeo 1988: 178; Hoffmann 2006: 35, 43; Kimps 2007: 271; McGregor 1995: 99; Quirk et al. 1985: 813; Tottie & Hoffmann 2006: 284, 289).

6.3.2 The dependent variable: NEG-TAG variants in BwE

The extracts from the data in (1) in Section 6.1 illustrate that BwE NEG-TAGS exhibit rich variation in their form. This is partly a result of the complex rules of tag formation in Standard English which affect the type, tense, number and person of the auxiliary as well as the person, number and gender of the pronoun in the tag. Yet it is also caused by the variable attrition, fusion and overall phonetic realisation of the construction's component parts. Moreover, in BwE NEG-TAGS it is not just the placement but also the form of the negative particle that is variable. To ensure consistent and accurate coding of what are often very similar realisations (e.g. *didn't he* vs. *din he, isn't it* vs. *in't it*), all NEG-TAG tokens were subjected to repeated auditory analysis, and the coding of a random sub-sample of tokens was verified by an independent coder. This section introduces the BwE NEG-TAG variants which have been identified through this procedure, and divides them according to their morpho-phonological encoding and geographical dispersion.

As pointed out in Section 6.1 above, canonical tags are grammatically dependent on their preceding anchor: the auxiliary in the tag is the same as the auxiliary in the anchor clause (12a); when the anchor contains no auxiliary, the tag is formed with DO-support, mirroring the tense, number and person of the finite verb in the anchor (12b); the pronoun in the tag repeats that from the anchor (12c), or agrees with the preceding nominal subject in number, person and gender (12d); the polarity of the anchor is usually reversed in the tag (12e). In contrast to the high degree of auxiliary-, pronoun- and polarity-variation, the tag-internal order of elements is fixed: (auxiliary) + (enclitic negator) + (personal pronoun). (As discussed further in Section 6.5.1, the BwE data contain no NEG-TAGS with *not* which, like *no* in (14) below, has a different placement than *-n't*.) Because they are formed with the range of English auxiliaries and personal pronouns, the NEG-TAG variants exemplified in (12) do not strictly speaking constitute a uniform formal category. Nevertheless, they are allocated here to one variant category and differentiated from other variants on the basis of their relative lack of formal reduction, their adherence to Standard English rules of tag formation, and their use of non-localised negators and negative auxiliaries. By virtue of sharing these characteristics, the canonical tags exemplified in (12) are found across England and the English-speaking world and as such are non-localisable.

(12) a. It'<u>s</u> nice and quiet, <u>*isn't it*</u>?
            They'<u>re</u> lovely flyers, <u>*aren't they*</u>?
            They <u>will</u> go on, <u>*won't they*</u>?
            You <u>can</u> pick them up, <u>*can't you*</u>?

   b.   We even <u>used</u> the contacts from the post-office, *didn't we*?

          They <u>think</u> it is part of Scotland, *don't they*?

          But war <u>brings</u> out the worst in people, *doesn't it*?

   c.   <u>We</u> would say gear, *wouldn't <u>we</u>*?

          <u>They</u>'re like a home nation, *aren't <u>they</u>*?

   d.   <u>Lydia</u> was born here, *wasn't <u>she</u>*?

          <u>The young ones</u> have too much now, *haven't <u>they</u>*?

   e.   It <u>was</u> a knacker doing them herrings, *was<u>n't</u> it*?

          We div<u>n't</u> go under the border community, *<u>do</u> we*?

Rare instances of NEG-TAGS which violate the rules of subject-verb agreement, as in (13), are also included in the category of non-localised canonical tag variants introduced above. These tags adhere to the rules of Standard English tag formation summarised above by mirroring the properties of the auxiliary (and subject) in the preceding anchor, and they reflect a tendency towards *was*-levelling which occurs throughout the English-speaking world (Adger & Smith 2005: 155).

(13)   We <u>was</u> doing that, *was<u>n't</u> we*?

In addition to the variants introduced above, the BwE corpus contains canonical tags that follow the dependency rules of the non-localisable canonical tags illustrated in (12) but deviate from these in that they contain the negative auxiliary variant *divn't* (14), or are formed with the independent negator *no* (15). Rather than occurring between the auxiliary and the pronoun, *no* is positioned after the pronoun. Because of the strong association of *divn't* with the north(-east) of England and of *no* with Scotland (see Chapter 3.3.2), these variants are subsumed here under the label localised canonical tags.

(14)   I mean, you get drugs everywhere, *divn't you*?

        They like the words, *divn't they*?

(15)   I think kecks really is underpants, is it *no*?

        But we called them trousers, did we *no*?

Finally, we find in the BwE corpus variants that derive from (non-localised) canonical tag variants through phonetic attrition. The variant *din* [dɪn] + (pronoun) in (16) is a reduced form of either *don't* (fronting of the vowel and loss of [t]) or of *divn't* (loss of [v] and [t]). The variants *in't* [ɪnt] or [ɪnʔ] + (pronoun) and *in* [ɪn] + (pronoun) in (17) and (18) derive through regular sound change from *isn't it* (loss of [z] and [t]) (Andersen 2001: 196–200; Cheshire 1981: 366–367). Following Cheshire (1981), *int/in*-variants are conflated in the remainder of this chapter to constitute one variant of *in't*-tags.

(16)   He speaks completely different to me, *din* he?
(17)   Well, it's proper cooking, *in't* it?
        They're wise, *in't* they?
(18)   Oh yeah, there's a whole heap of them, *in* there?

Another variant that derives through phonetic reduction and, in this case, structural reanalysis from non-localised canonical tags is *innit* in (19). The developmental pathway of *innit*, pronounced [ɪnɪt] or [ɪnɪʔ], is somewhat less certain than that of the variants in (16)–(18). Andersen (2001: 196–201) puts forward two alternative hypotheses which are sketched out in (20) and (21). The cline in (20) suggests that *innit* derives through phonetic attrition from *isn't it*, with loss of [t] preceding loss of [z]; the two formerly independent morphemes, [ɪn] and [ɪt], are subsequently reanalysed (or rebracketed) as a single unit, [ɪnɪt]. The cline in (21) suggests that *innit* derives through phonetic attrition from *ain't it* (raising of the initial vowel of the diphthong > monophthongisation > loss of final [t]). Andersen's (2001) data support the pathway in (20). He argues that if *innit* derived from *ain't it*, which in turn derived by regular sound change from negative present tense forms of BE and HAVE (Cheshire 1981: 366), it would be used for *hasn't it* in the initial stages of its spread. However, this is not borne out in his data, where *innit* first spreads in third person singular neuter contexts of BE before spreading to other contexts, including *hasn't it*. Also, he argues, the forms *in't* and *in* occur too infrequently in his data to be considered stepping stones on the path to *innit*.

(19)   Well, it's only an hour away from Edinburgh and Newcastle, *innit*?
(20)   *isn't it* [ɪznt ɪt] > *isn't it* [ɪzn ɪt] > *in it* [ɪn ɪt]   (Andersen 2001: 197)
(21)   *ain't it* [eɪnt ɪt] > *int it* [ɪnt ɪt] > *in it* [ɪn ɪt]   (Andersen 2001: 197)

The variants introduced in (16)–(18) are found across many varieties of British English. *Din* has been attested in Cambridgeshire (Peitsara & Vatso 2002) and northern England (Llamas 2001: 127, fn. 8: Moore & Podesva 2009). *In't*-tags have been reported for southern England (Andersen 2001; Cheshire 1981), northern England (Cheshire et al. 2005: 157; Moore & Podesva 2009), and south-eastern Scotland (Brown & Millar 1980: 118). Their widespread, albeit numerically variable, use across Britain is also confirmed in Krug (1998: 193–194). The use of *innit* in (19) is often associated with London and the south of England (Krug 1998: 193–195; Stenström et al. 2002: 168), but it has also been reported for varieties beyond London and the England-Scotland border (Cheshire 1982: 61; Cheshire et al. 2005: 155–158; Llamas 2001: 127, fn. 8; Moore & Podesva 2009). Because they are used in many varieties of English throughout the British Isles but are not generally associated with Standard English usage, the canonically-derived tag variants illustrated in (16)–(19) are subsumed here under the label supra-local variants.

Table 6.1 summarises the BwE inventory of NEG-TAG variants. It allocates variants to one of three categories which are differentiated on the basis of variants' morpho-phonological properties and geographical spread: non-localised canonical tags, localised canonical tags, and supra-local canonically-derived tags. Where appropriate, Sections 6.5 and 6.6 will make more fine-grained distinctions within these categories in order to draw attention to and account for the details of variants' composition and realisation.

Table 6.1 Inventory of NEG-TAG variants in BwE

non-localised canonical tags	localised canonical tags	supra-local canonically-derived tags
auxiliary + -*n't* + pronoun	auxiliary + pronoun + *no* *divn't* + pronoun	*din* + pronoun *in't* + pronoun *innit*

6.3.3 Independent variables: Data coding

Following the coding of each NEG-TAG token for its form (both in terms of variant category and constituent elements), the next step in the analysis was to create a coding system for the independent variables believed to be implicated in the conditioning of formal NEG-TAG variation in BwE.

The research on TQs reviewed in Section 6.2 has demonstrated that the morpho-phonological encoding of tag variants is strongly constrained by a range of social factors. It has also shown that the spread of *innit* across the inflectional paradigm is socially embedded. To test the hypothesis that social factors are also implicated in the formal variability of NEG-TAGS in BwE and to probe the social indexicality of the variants in the data, every token of the variable was coded for speaker sex and age. If the NEG-TAG system in BwE is undergoing grammaticalisation, as is the case in London English (see Section 6.2.2), inclusion of speaker sex and age as independent predictors also allows us to identify the innovators and leaders of any such changes, and assess whether innovating variants such as *innit* have identical social meanings across varieties. In order to avoid producing results that are distorted by high degrees of intra-group variation, all tokens were further coded for individual speaker. This makes possible application of mixed-effects modelling to accurately identify the rules governing variant selection.

The literature on TQs also highlights that the syntactic-semantic characteristics of the anchor clause have a bearing on the form of the appended tag, even when tag variants are levelling to contexts where their occurrence is not sanctioned by the rules of Standard English tag formation. To establish whether BwE NEG-TAGS are at all affected by levelling processes and whether these are gradual in nature, all tokens of the variable in the data were coded firstly for their syntactic-semantic context, i.e., paradigmatic, non-paradigmatic and semi-paradigmatic, as defined and illustrated in Section 6.3.1 and Extracts (7)–(10) above; and secondly for the syntactic-semantic properties of their anchors, i.e., person, number and gender of the subject as well as type, tense, person and number of the finite verb. Beyond establishing whether BwE NEG-TAGS are undergoing grammaticalisation, this may allow us to identify any trajectories of tags' spread across the inflectional paradigm. Moreover, if multiple NEG-TAG variants are undergoing levelling processes simul-taneoulsy, consistent coding for the semantic-syntactic properties of the anchor of all NEG-TAG tokens enables us to assess whether different variants are competing for the same syntactic-semantic contexts.

Finally, the results reported in Cheshire (1981) for *ain't*- and *in't*-tags demon-strate that variation in the formal realisation of NEG-TAGS may signal important functional differences in their use. To test whether function is implicated in the formal variability of NEG-TAGS in BwE, Section 6.4 develops a functional taxonomy for BwE NEG-TAGS. This taxonomy serves as a coding schema for the factor group function and makes it possible to test the effect of function on variant choice in Section 6.5.

6.4 Qualitative analysis of NEG-TAGS

The functions performed by NEG-TAGS in the BwE interview data are uncovered through development of the functional taxonomies available in the literature and application of the methods outlined in Chapter 2.5. Crucial to this endeavour is the close reading of tags in their larger sequential and interactional contexts of oc-currence, especially with regard to listeners' next-turn responses. They constitute a guide towards the interpretation of tags on-line in interaction and often suggest a particular reading of the data (see Chapter 2.5.2). Furthermore, meticulous at-tention is paid in utterance interpretation to the ambient linguistic material in the anchor and the tag. This material is faithfully reproduced in the data extracts provided below (see page XVII for a key to the orthographic conventions used for replicating non-verbal materials). The extracts serve to illustrate the range of functions isolated in the data and to demonstrate the validity of the analysis. The ultimate aim of the analysis is to operationalise function as a factor group for quantitative analysis.

6.4.1 Functions performed by NEG-TAGS

Although I embrace the general view that interrogative tags perform important interpersonal functions in social interaction, I depart from previous functional accounts which categorise tags in terms of modal vs. affective meanings (Holmes 1984a, 1987, 1995), polite vs. impolite functions (Algeo 1988, 1990), or conventional vs. non-conventional uses (Cheshire 1981). Instead, I broadly divide the interpersonal uses of NEG-TAGS into a subjective, speaker-oriented and an intersubjective, hearer-oriented category (see Chapter 2.5), recognising at all times that there is some overlap between the two.

The literature reviewed in Section 6.2.1 concurs in attributing an epistemic function to interrogative tags. The tag serves to reduce speakers' commitment to their propositions and to seek verification of these propositions from addressees. BwE NEG-TAGS regularly perform this function, as exemplified in (22) below. The tag *can't you* follows Charlene's proposition that she can be identified as being from Berwick despite not using many Berwick slang words. The opinion preceding the tag is expressed with confidence and assertiveness. Neither the anchor clause to which the tag is appended nor the preceding utterance contain any linguistic features that may be indicative of doubt or hesitancy, such as false starts, repetitions, epistemic markers, (un)filled pauses, high pitch, or rising intonation contours. The tag *can't you*, by contrast, is produced in higher than usual pitch and with a rising intonational contour. Both prosodic features convey a strong impression of tentativeness and doubt; the latter also serves to seek hearer validation. With this prosodic encoding, the tag serves a dual function. It retrospectively qualifies Charlene's commitment to her proposition, while at the same time seeking verification of this proposition from her co-interviewee.

(22) Charlene: I've lived in Berwick all my life but I don't use all the slang words. But you you can still tell I come from Berwick. *Can't you*?

In addition to attenuating the strength of assertive propositions, NEG-TAGS also function to reinforce the tentativeness already inherent in the turn elements over which they have scope. In (23a), Jane's halting deliberation about the denotations of *kecks*, a dialect word for 'trousers' or 'underpants,' is replete with linguistic features that signal reduced epistemic commitment: filled and unfilled pauses, the hedges *I divn't knaa* and *I think*, and the final rise on *underpants*. In (23b), high pitch signals which constituent of the elliptical anchor clause is the focal element of uncertainty: the month of the Riding of the Bounds, a long-standing annual ceremony which involves residents patrolling the boundaries of Berwick on horseback. In both examples, the NEG-TAG invites interlocutors to confirm or refute the assessments or facts presented as uncertain in the preceding discourse. As a result of their conduciveness, the tags also control turn-allocation.

(23) a. HP: Now, what's kecks. Is kecks [trousers or] underpants?
          Jane: [Trousers.]
                   No, trousers. (.) Eh now, I divn't knaa? (..) I think kecks really
                   is underpants, is it no?
      b. Evelyn: Have you heard about that story, the Riding [of the Bounds?]
          Mary: [Riding of the Bounds.]
          HP: [No.]
                   What's that?
          Evelyn: Well, (.) the first (.) of May? *Isn't it*, Mary.
          Mary: == It's the first of May.

As pointed out in the literature review, tags do not by definition signal reduced epistemicity or invoke a response from addressees. The extracts in (24) and (25) illustrate the interactional impact of non-tentative and non-conducive NEG-TAGS in the BwE corpus. In (24), Daniel, the sole interviewee, tells HP about an occasion on which he spoke to some Scottish people who had emigrated to the United States twenty years before his encounter with them. When Daniel reveals that the Scottish expatriates were pleased with his observation that they had retained their native accent, he follows this assessment with *innit*. HP was not present at the encounter that Daniel recounts and hence is not in a position to either confirm or refute Daniel's version of the events. The sincerity conditions on interrogatives are not met (see Section 6.2.1). Thus, rather than seeking confirmation and involvement, the tag serves to foreground Daniel's utterance and to reinforce a point he had been stressing throughout the interview: that Scottish people take great pride in their nationality. HP's acknowledgement tokens (*mhm, yeah, uh-huh*), which are produced in overlap with and in succession to Daniel's *innit*, do not preclude a non-conducive reading of *innit*. They do not constitute confirmatory responses but signal HP's continued interest in Daniel's narrative and encourage him to continue talking (Jefferson 2002; Schegloff 1982).

(24) Daniel: And they was still broa- I could tell, still tell they was Scots
      HP: mhm
      Daniel: = And I say, "Oh. You haven't (.) you haven't lost your accent."
               Oh, they was pleased as punch, [*innit*]   [They] always say,
      HP: [mhm] yeah [uh-huh]
      Daniel: = "We'll no do that." Because they live amongst Scots.

In (25), Keith presents a proposition that is generally accepted to be true: *home's always home*. The appended tag *innit* is non-conducive and functions to underline the obviousness of the preceding statement (see also Coates 1987: 117–118; Millar & Brown 1979: 34–35). Tag uses such as this often occur turn-finally at the end of an extended topic sequence. Because they do not invite addressees to contribute their view on the topic, they are generally followed by topic-change.

> (25) Keith: Home's always (..) home *innit*.

The extracts from the data in (24) and (25), then, illustrate that NEG-TAGS can function to emphasise speakers' attitudinal stance towards propositions to which they are fully committed. Following Tottie & Hoffmann (2006: 300–301), I label these tag uses attitudinal stance markers. They do not usually seek verification or confirmation from addressees, and are non-conducive as a result. Unlike the non-conducive tags described in Algeo (1988, 1990) and Cheshire (1981), however, they do not generally carry a hostile or antagonistic overtone.

In addition to the subjective functions outlined above (epistemic marking, attitudinal stance marking), NEG-TAGS also function intersubjectively. Tags functioning as mitigating devices exploit the tentativeness and corroboration-seeking effect associated with tags to soften the negative force of interactionally dispreferred moves (see also Andersen 2001: 124–128; Holmes 1982: 58–61). In (26a), Rebecca displays a negative stance towards HP's suggestion that incomers to Berwick might be requested to adopt the local dialect. Her turn-final utterance *cos that's just silly, isn't it* is produced with moderately reduced loudness. In addition, the lexical item *silly* and the tag *isn't it* are produced on a moderately high pitch level. With this pitch contour, the tag functions to soften the negative effect of Rebecca's potentially quite face-threatening dismissal. In (26b) and (26c), Germaine and Keith dispute the congruity and relevance of the dialect words suggested by HP and Adam. The rising contour on *in't it* in (26b) conveys that Germaine entertains some doubt regarding her correction. This reduces the face-threat constituted by her disaligning turn. In (26c), the slight fall on *divn't they* signals that the disagreement expressed in Keith's anchor is not an aggressive or hostile challenge but a matter-of-fact observation. The tag thus works towards averting interactional conflict. Finally, in (26d), Patrick ridicules HP's question regarding the fashionableness of Berwick upon Tweed. He offers fictional evidence for Berwick's trendiness so exaggerated as to indicate its lack of trendiness. By adding the tag *didn't we* he invites HP to pretend to agree with this proposition that he does not endorse himself. This attenuates the face-threat constituted by his sarcastic remark (see also Andersen 2001: 127–128). The examples discussed above demonstrate that tags used as softeners and mitigation devices can be conducive when they challenge addressees to justify the proposition the speaker disagrees with (26c), or non-conducive and topic-curtailing when they signal that the co-conversationalist's preceding proposition is in some way wrong or inappropriate (26a).

(26)   a.   HP: But would you say, if you want to live in Berwick, you have
                         to speak like us.
             (.)
             Rebecca: No:.
             HP: No.
             Alicia: Not really. [(h)]
             Rebecca: [There's] lots of different people live in Berwick
                          (.) [as it is (and)] and you never say, "Right. If you want to
             Alicia: [Yeah.]
             Rebecca: = live in Berwick you have to speak like a Berwicker." Cos
                          (..) °that's just ˢⁱˡˡʸ, *isn't it*.°
       b.   *((Discussing dialect words for standard English 'woman'.))*
             HP: Have you ever heard hantle [(.) for woman?]
             Germaine: [Hantle.] Em (..) is that's like
                          for your ʰᵉᵉᵈ, ⁱⁿ'ᵗ ⁱᵗ? °Hantle. [A hantle.]°
             HP: [Is it?] Uh-huh.
       c.   *((Discussing dialect words for 'attractive'.))*
             Adam: Eh fit.
             HP: °Mhm.°
             Keith: Fit's like any- e- (.) everywhere says fit though, [*divn't they.*]
             Adam: [Aye.] But it's
                          (.h) I was just trying to think of what I would say.
       d.   HP: Do you think Berwick is a fashionable place to be?
             (…)
             Patrick: We got a telephone <£ last week, *didn't we.* £>

Tokens that I refer to as involvement inducers (called facilitative or confirmatory tags in the literature, see Section 6.2.1) are always conducive. They draw listeners into the discourse by seeking their support or corroboration of a proposition. The tags in (27) are produced with a falling intonation contour that reflects speakers' confidence in the truth of their propositions. These do not therefore serve to modify the propositions expressed in the preceding anchor, but instead they invite addressees to express their agreement with these propositions. In (27a), Cody's invited contribution to the discourse amounts to no more than a minimal affirmation which serves to acknowledge Glenn's proposition but does not trigger turn-exchange. Cody thus performs a supportive rather than active role. In (27b), by contrast, Charlene's corroboration-seeking tag *isn't it* yields the turn to Natalie, allowing her to become an active and equal participant in the discussion of the topic. The corroboration-seeking interpretation of Charlene's tag is supported by the structure of Natalie's disaligning turn: it is delayed and hedged (*I'm not sure*), indicating that an affirmative response had in fact been invited. By inviting and encouraging co-interviewees' agreement and participation in talk, NEG-TAGS with a falling intonation contour serve to secure and maintain listeners' involvement in the interaction (hence the label) (see also Norrick 1995).

(27) a. Glenn: There's like (..) the young people (.) I know we're no old. *(h)*
                     But you know like the (.) thirteen- fourteen-year-olds,
          HP: mhm
          Glenn: = they're (.) even though they're from Berwick, they're more
                    Geordie *aren't they.*   [Cos] they walk around and they
          Cody: Oh yeah.
          HP: [Yeah?]
          Glenn: = talk Geordie, but you know, they (.) that's no Berwick what
                    they talk.

      b. *((Talking about different housing estates in Berwick.))*
          Charlene: Well, Highcliffe's on one side and Highcliffe's nice. But on
                     the other side is Eastcliffe,   which is a bit, I would
          HP: uh-huh
          Charlene: = say that's about the the [roughest] in the town. *Isn't it.*
          HP: [uh-huh]
          (.)
          Natalie: I'm not sure. Some parts of Highfields is quite
          Charlene: Highfields
          Natalie: =   run down.
          Charlene: = uh-huh

NEG-TAGS are not just a means by which speakers seek to ensure common ground with their listeners and a means of creating listeners' involvement in discourse. Like negation in general (Cheshire 1997, 1998), they can also be used by speakers to signal their alignment and involvement with prior speakers' talk. In the extract from the data in (28), HP expresses her fondness of the expletive *doylem*, a Berwick word for 'idiot'. Godfrey follows HP's statement with a tag-appended clause. The anchor in his turn (*that's a good one*) echoes HP's sentiment. The appended tag can therefore hardly be interpreted as seeking corroboration of this attitude. Rather, it serves to reinforce Godfrey's alignment with HP's turn that is already explicit in the anchor. By signalling Godfrey's alignment with and approval of HP's stance, the tag constitutes a positive politeness device.

(28)   Godfrey: Doylem. @ [@]
       HP: [<@ That's my one of my favourite ones. @>]
       Godfrey: <@ That's a good one *innit* @>

It was shown earlier that NEG-TAGS sometimes function to emphasise speakers' stance (see Example (24) above). In certain sequential contexts, assertive and emphatic tags can signal speakers' involvement with what is being said. When Lori in (29) tells HP about an occasion where her family deliberately attracted pigeons to her feet despite her fear of birds, Godfrey provides an unsolicited confirmation of the account: *yeah, we was doing that*. Godfrey terminates his confirmation with a non-conducive tag (*wasn't we*) that functions to signal his attitude towards the truth of Lori's turn and to manifest his interpersonal involvement in the interaction (see also Norrick 1995: 687). Godfrey's tag in (29) is similar to the token in (28) in that it signals involvement and alignment and is not response-eliciting.

(29)   Lori: *(h)* I said I divn't like birds. (..) And they all (shouted). You
                    know, we were walking along, and they threw bread and that at
                    my feet! <@ So that all swarmed on us. [I was petrified.] @>
       HP: [@]
       Godfrey: <@ Yeah. We was doing that, *wasn't we.* @>
       Lori: <@ Isn't that nasty? @>

The examples provided above highlight the interactional importance of NEG-TAGS in discourse. By signalling speakers' shared orientation to a topic and signalling involvement, they constitute a positive politeness device, contribute to the collaborative development of interaction, and work towards maintaining good rapport between interlocutors.

6.4.2   Summary of functions

The functional analysis of NEG-TAGS in the BwE interview data has shown that they perform important interpersonal functions in discourse. Subjectively, they function to signal speakers' degree of commitment and attitudinal stance towards their propositions. Intersubjectively, they serve to mitigate potential face-threats, to draw listeners into the discourse and maintain their active involvement, and to signal speakers' alignment with prior talk and active involvement in the interaction. The analysis thus confirms the interactional importance of tags and negation more generally, and provides supporting evidence for the non-conduciveness of some tag uses (see also Andersen 1998). There is, of course, some overlap between the functional categories established above, for tags – like other discourse-pragmatic variables – are intrinsically multifunctional (see also Coates 1987: 130). By describing NEG-TAGS not just in terms of the specific interpersonal functions they perform but also in terms of their conducive or non-conducive effects, the analysis demonstrates that individual instances of NEG-TAGS differ sufficiently to warrant allocation to distinct functional categories. A concise summary of the variable's functional inventory and recurring co-occurrence patterns is provided in Appendix 5.

The functional taxonomy of NEG-TAGS developed above accounts for every token of the variable in the current dataset. However, it must not be taken as representing an exhaustive list of the functions performed by question tags in everyday social interaction. Firstly, the analysis has focused exclusively on NEG-TAGS and has not considered the functional repertoires of positive polarity or invariant tags. These have been shown to perform functions not described above (Kimps 2007; Stenström et al. 2002: Chapter 7). Secondly, the analysis was based on interview data which may also have limited the scope of the analysis. What this analysis has demonstrated, though, is that with the exception of hostile or aggressive tags which have not been found to occur in the BwE corpus, the functionality of NEG-TAGS does not diverge to any great extent across the interview data analysed here and the more casual and spontaneous data previously analysed in the literature.

Table 6.2 below outlines the coding protocol which arose from the detailed functional analysis in Section 6.4.1. Following this protocol, each NEG-TAG in the data was allocated to the functional category which best described its use. This procedure makes it possible to test the contribution of function to variant choice.

Table 6.2 Coding schema for NEG-TAG functions

	conducive	non-conducive	either
subjective	epistemic marker	attitudinal stance m.	
intersubjective	involvement inducer	alignment signal	mitigation device

6.5 Quantitative analysis of NEG-TAGS

The preceding sections have served to prepare the data for quantitative analysis. They have isolated the variants available in the BwE pool of NEG-TAGS and operationalised hypotheses about their sociolinguistic distribution as factor groups for quantitative analysis. This section presents the results of the quantitative analysis. For ease of cross-variable comparison, its structure largely mirrors that of

preceding chapters. Section 6.5.1 begins with an outline of the overall distribution of variants in the corpus and an account of the highly uneven distribution
of variants within and across variant categories. There follows a short description
of how the variable and its most frequently instantiated variants are distributed
across social groups, syntactic-semantic contexts, functional categories and/or
individual speakers. These distributions affect the configuration of the mixed-
effects multiple regression analyses in Section 6.5.2 which model the simultaneous
effect of the independent variables on the observed patterns of formal variation
whilst at all times catering for the effect of intra-group variation. The multiple regression analyses will reveal the divergent distribution of non-localised canonical
and supra-local canonically-derived NEG-TAG variants in BwE. Close inspection
of these results affords important new insights into the usage and diffusion of
innovating tag variants as well as the structure of discourse-pragmatic variation
more generally.

6.5.1   Distributional analysis

In Section 6.3.2, each of the 316 NEG-TAG tokens in the data was allocated to one
of the three variant categories listed in the left-hand column of Table 6.3. The
table shows the numerical breakdown of individual variants across and within
the variant categories. Non-localised canonical tag variants of the form auxiliary
+ -n't + pronoun dominate the BwE NEG-TAG system. Constituting roughly two
thirds of all tokens of the variable, they dwarf the frequency of other variants,
especially those in the category of localised canonical tags where the negator takes
the form *no* or where negative periphrastic DO takes the form *divn't*. These two
variants account for less than 4% of all NEG-TAGS in the data. At 28.3%, the sum
of tokens in the category of supra-local canonically-derived variants occupies a
more prominent position in the NEG-TAG system. However, variants within this
category occur with unequal frequencies. *Din* + pronoun occurs only once in the
whole dataset. With 17 tokens, *in't* + pronoun is slightly more frequent but still
amounts to a mere 5% of all NEG-TAGS. The most frequent supra-local canonically-
derived variant by far is *innit*. It constitutes almost a quarter of the data and is the
second most frequent NEG-TAG variant in the BwE corpus overall. The distribution in Table 6.3, then, demonstrates that despite the range of options available to
BwE speakers for realising NEG-TAGS, a full 91% of NEG-TAGS are constituted by
just two variants: non-localised canonical tags and the supra-local canonically-
derived variant *innit*.

Table 6.3 Overall distribution of NEG-TAG variants

variant category	variant	N	%
non-localised canonical tags	auxiliary + -n't + pronoun	216	68
localised canonical tags	auxiliary + pronoun + *no*	2	0.7
	divn't + pronoun	9	3
supra-local canonically-derived tags	*din* + pronoun	1	0.3
	in't + pronoun	17	5
	innit	71	23

The observed paucity of tag variants with *no, divn't, din* and *in't* is largely a product of social, structural and functional constraints on their use. The negligible occurrence of tag variants with *no* (N = 2) and the complete absence of variants with *not* is consistent with the widely reported pattern whereby isolate negative particles are virtually missing from present-day English question tags (Beal & Corrigan 2005: 149; Hoffmann 2006: 46; Tagliamonte & Smith 2002: 263). The more general demise of the negator *no* in BwE (see Table 3.4 in Chapter 3.4) as well as the strong association of *no*-tags with the rather infrequently attested function of signalling epistemicity (see Figure 6.3 below) may exert additional inhibiting effects on the occurrence of *no*-tags. With *din-* and *divn't*-variants (N = 1 and N = 9 respectively), it is syntactic-semantic factors that limit their frequency in the BwE NEG-TAG system. Only 34 tokens of NEG-TAGS in the data are preceded by anchor clauses that require tags with present tense negative DO. When these constraints are considered, *divn't*-tags are not in fact all that marginal, accounting for 26% of all relevant tags. The rate of *in't it* (N = 6) is not restricted by the infrequency of anchors that require a negative tag with *is* and *it* (N = 136) but by the high productivity of its co-variants in this environment: *isn't it* and *innit* (see further below). Also, the inconspicuous occurrence of *in't*-tags overall (N = 17, including those with the pronoun *it* above) and among young speakers in particular parallels its marginality and social distribution in other corpora (Andersen 2001: 199; Anderwald 2002: 131; Krug 1998). It may therefore be symptomatic of the variant's more general paucity in contemporary British English. The distribution of tag variants with *no, divn't, din* and *in't* calls for further investigation in order to test the hypotheses proposed above. Due to low token numbers it cannot be pursued here. The following analysis will therefore focus on the distribution of the two most frequently attested variants in the BwE corpus: non-localised canonical tags and the supra-local canonically-derived tag *innit*.

Initial data runs reveal that these variants are not equally distributed across the 33 speakers in the sample who tag their propositions. Firstly, while all speakers use non-localised canonical tags, albeit with fluctuating frequencies, only 13 speakers in the sample use the supra-local canonically-derived tag variant *innit*. To ensure valid and reliable results, only data from the 13 speakers who use *innit* in the recordings are included in this variant's tabulation across independent variables (N = 145 NEG-TAG tokens). Secondly, the social cohorts represented in the corpus data differ in their frequency of use of *isn't it* and *innit*, two variants which by virtue of being composed of or derived from the same auxiliary-pronoun combination compete for the same syntactic-semantic environment. The grey bars along the y-axis in Figure 6.1 reveal a marked female predominance in the use of *isn't it*. They also show that the rate of *isn't it* is fairly constant across older and younger speakers but dips in the middle age group. By contrast, the black bars show a sharp increase in the rate of *innit* in the middle age group which stagnates in the young age group. Due to badly distributed data, the marginal results for *innit* across speaker sex are grossly misleading. Contrary to the patterns displayed in Figure 6.1 and those reported for COLT and the BNC (Andersen 2001: 184–186; Krug 1998: 186), *innit* is strongly associated with male speakers in the BwE data. Not only are eleven out of the 13 *innit*-users in the data male but their normalised frequency of *innit* is almost three times that of the two female *innit*-users' (7.5 vs. 2.6 per 10,000 words). These results and those depicted for *isn't it* suggest that social factors are implicated in the formal variability of the BwE NEG-TAG system.

The distributional analysis in Figure 6.1 is based on the quantification of the whole set of NEG-TAG tokens in the data. Infrequent variants, i.e., *no-*, *divn't-*, *din-* and *in't*-tags, are included in the quantification of the data in Figures 6.1 to 6.3 because they might affect the distribution of the more frequent variants. However, because any results obtained for these variants are potentially unreliable due to limited data (N = 29), they are not displayed in the figures summarising variant distributions. Non-localised canonical tags that do not contain the auxiliary *is* and the pronoun *it* (see Table 6.4 below) are also consistently included in the quantification of the data. The reason why their distribution across social groups is not displayed in Figure 6.1 is that it would provide little insight into the social mechanisms of formal tag variability. Rather, it would reflect social groups' differential tendencies to tag anchors that do not require tags with *is* and *it*, a phenomenon not pertinent to the aims of the present analysis.

Separating out *isn't it* from the other non-localised canonical tags in Figures 6.1 to 6.3 is motivated by the aims of the study as well as the results shown in Table 6.4 which examines the relative frequency of the 43 different auxiliary-pronoun combinations found in the BwE NEG-TAG system. As in other corpora (Hoffmann 2006: 42–43; Krug 1998: 152–153; Tottie & Hoffmann 2006: 296), *isn't it* is proportionally the most dominant auxiliary-pronoun combination in the category of non-localised canonical tag variants. It occurs five to six times more often than the

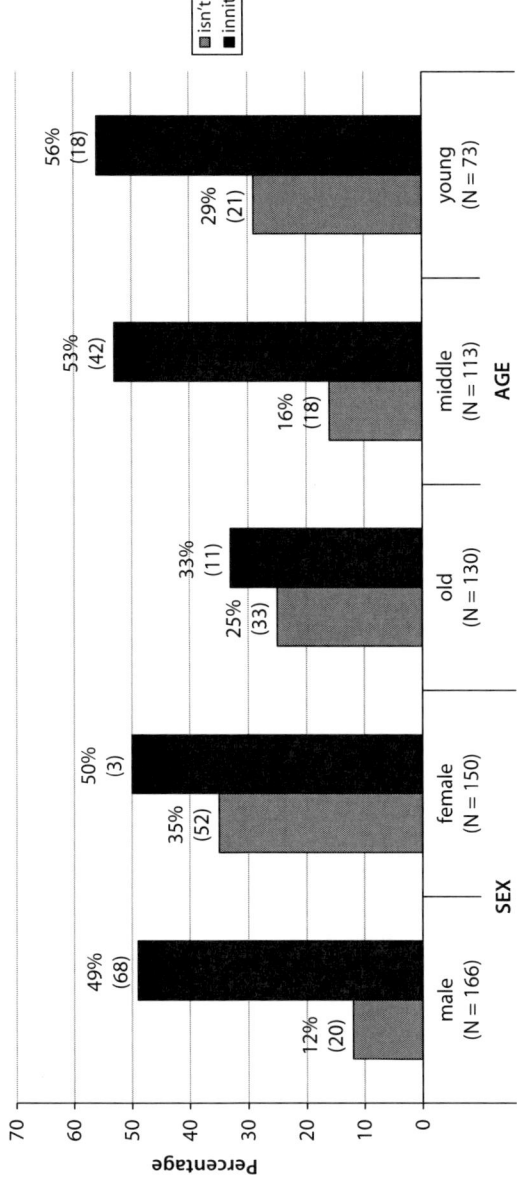

Figure 6.1 Distribution of NEG-TAG variants across speaker sex and age
(Figures in round brackets indicate raw token numbers, including all non-localised canonical and infrequent tag variants. The results for *innit* are derived from data produced by *innit*-users only [N = 145].)

next most frequent combinations: *aren't they, don't they* and *don't you*. The comparative frequency of *isn't it* goes some way towards explaining why this form has developed reduced variants (*in't it, innit*) and started to level across the inflectional paradigm (see Bybee [2003: 615–617, 2011: 66] on the role of frequency effects in phonological change and analogical levelling). Treating *isn't it* and the aggregate of other non-localised canonical tags as two separate variants enables us to: (i) explore whether the distribution of *isn't it* tallies with that of other canonical tags or with that of its reduced co-variant *innit*; and (ii) assess whether it is reduced as well as non-reduced variants of third person singular neuter tags with present tense BE that are levelling across the inflectional paradigm.

Table 6.4 Inventory and frequency of auxiliary-negative-pronoun combinations in non-localised canonical tags

	N	%		N	%		N	%
isn't it	72	33.3	aren't we	3	1.4	couldn't it	1	0.5
aren't they	14	6.5	didn't (s)he	3	1.4	couldn't we	1	0.5
don't they	13	6.0	didn't it	3	1.4	didn't they	1	0.5
don't you	12	5.6	haven't they	3	1.4	didn't you	1	0.5
didn't we	8	3.7	wasn't (s)he	3	1.4	doesn't (s)he	1	0.5
wasn't it	8	3.7	can't they	2	0.9	haven't we	1	0.5
isn't he	6	2.8	doesn't it	2	0.9	shouldn't I	1	0.5
wouldn't you	6	2.8	don't we	2	0.9	wasn't I	1	0.5
can't you	5	2.3	hasn't (s)he	2	0.9	wasn't they	1	0.5
aren't you	4	1.8	haven't you	2	0.9	weren't it	1	0.5
couldn't you	4	1.8	shouldn't you	2	0.9	weren't they	1	0.5
isn't there	4	1.8	wasn't we	2	0.9	won't it	1	0.5
wouldn't it	4	1.8	weren't you	2	0.9	won't they	1	0.5
wouldn't they	4	1.8	won't you	2	0.9			
hasn't it	4	1.8	wouldn't we	2	0.9	**TOTAL**	216	

The figures provided below the x-axis in Figure 6.2 reveal very little evidence of analogical levelling in the BwE NEG-TAG system. 91% of all NEG-TAG tokens included in the tabulation occur in paradigmatic contexts. The fact that only 9% of all NEG-TAG tokens occur in non-paradigmatic contexts suggests the following. The overall predominance in the data of NEG-TAGS with *is* and *it* (47%, N = 149, including *isn't it, innit, in't it*) is not diagnostic of the NEG-TAG system's advanced stage of analogical levelling. Rather, it is indicative of a more general trend whereby speakers are more likely to tag propositions containing third person singular neuter subjects and present tense BE than they are to tag those with other subject-verb combinations. When the overall frequency of non-paradigmatic tag usage is tabulated separately for individual variants, they turn out slightly higher for *innit*

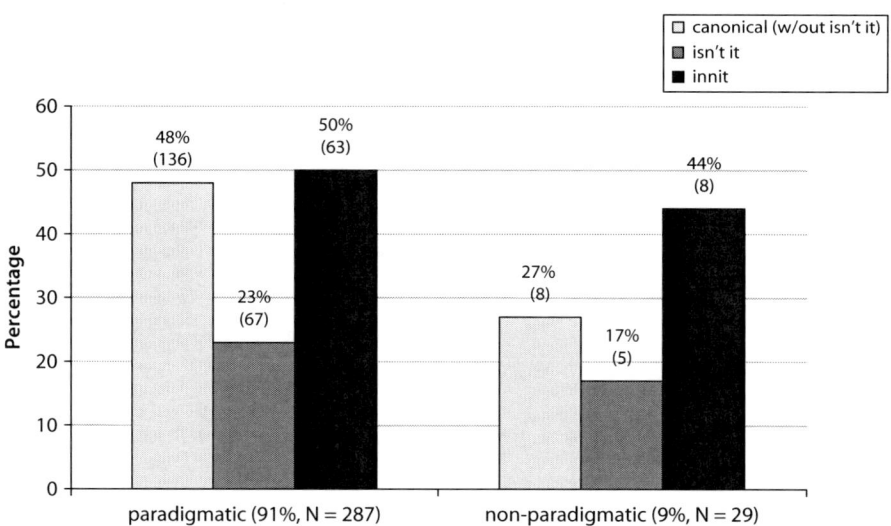

Figure 6.2 Distribution of NEG-TAG variants across syntactic-semantic contexts (Figures in round brackets indicate the raw token numbers, including infrequent variants. The results for *innit* are derived from data produced by *innit*-users only [N = 145].)

(11%, N = 8 out of 71) than for *isn't it* (7%, N = 5 out of 72). Taking into account the restricted data on which these figures are based, the results tentatively suggest two findings. Firstly, full and reduced variants of third person singular neuter tags with BE may not be spreading across the inflectional paradigm at the same speed. Secondly, the degree of *innit*'s spread across the inflectional paradigm in BwE lags far behind that reported for COLT (56%, N = 181 out of 323) (Andersen 2001: 108).

Comparison of the differently shaded bars along the y-axis in Figure 6.2 confirms that different NEG-TAG variants are differently distributed across syntactic-semantic contexts. While the aggregate of other canonical tags (light grey bars) manifest a strong propensity to occur in paradigmatic contexts, the distribution of *innit* (black bars) and *isn't it* (dark grey bars) is relatively unconstrained by the syntactic-semantic properties of the preceding anchor.[47] What *innit* and *isn't it*

---

47. Closer inspection of the canonical tag tokens that were coded as not matching the semantic-syntactic properties of their preceding anchors indicates that they cannot be construed as straightforward evidence of analogical levelling. In the example *We could go down to the beach all day, didn't we?*, the speaker's use of *did* instead of *could* in the tag may result from the fact that in spontaneous conversation speakers tend to repeat the general content rather than the exact words of propositions (Axelsson 2011: 36). The general idea expressed in the anchor is that when the speaker and her co-interviewee were young, they were able or allowed to visit the beach unsupervised. It may therefore be the case that in the tag, the speaker no longer focuses on the freedom she and her friend enjoyed in their youth but on the actions they performed as a result

also share is their tendency to replace canonical tags of the form *doesn't it* (e.g. *It depends,* innit? *That* kind of *puts* the span on the works, innit? *It* still *means* attractive, though, isn't it?). 50% of all environments in the data which, according to the rules of Standard English tag formation, require the tag form *doesn't it* are realised with *innit* or *isn't it*. No other canonical tag is substituted with *innit* or *isn't it* to the same extent. This result conforms to Andersen's (2001: 175) prediction that non-paradigmatic *innit* uses are favoured in environments with *it*-pronouns and present tense verbs.

Figure 6.3 examines the distribution of the variable and its variants across discourse-functional factors. The percentages provided below the x-axis reveal that almost half of all NEG-TAGs in the data serve to induce addressees' involvement in the interaction and more than a quarter function to signal an attitudinal stance. At 5–9%, the remaining tag functions, i.e., the signalling of epistemicity, alignment and mitigation, are comparatively infrequent.[48] The distribution of variants across the functional categories is shown by the bars along the y-axis. They demonstrate a tendency for canonical tags (light grey bars) to perform conducive functions, i.e., marking epistemicity and inducing involvement, and for *innit* (black bars) to perform non-conducive functions, i.e., signalling stance and alignment. *Isn't it* is more evenly distributed across function than other variants but hardly appears in the function most strongly associated with *innit*, i.e., attitudinal stance marking. Formal variation in NEG-TAG usage, then, is at least to some extent constrained by the function they perform in discourse.

Chapters 4 and 5 have shown how high degrees of inter-speaker and intra-group variation in the rate of use of discourse-pragmatic variables (and their variants) can distort the results of multiple regression analyses if their effect is not catered for through inclusion of individual speaker as a random effect in mixed-effects analyses. By plotting the frequency of NEG-TAG usage across the 18 male speakers (black bullets) and the 18 female speakers (grey squares) in the sample,

---

of this freedom. In *He* only *passed* away em this year, wasn't it?, it seems that when the speaker utters the filled pause *em* to signal her on-line presence, she mentally inserts *it was* in her utterance. The following tag matches this mental, though not verbal, insertion (*It was* this year, wasn't it?). Finally, in *He died* with cancer, wasn't it?, the tag matches the syntactically reanalysed clause *It was with cancer that he died*. In short, these anomalous tags seem to reflect (interactionally motivated) performance errors rather than speakers' indiscriminate use of selected tag forms across the inflectional paradigm.

48. Since the results in Figure 6.3 are based on NEG-TAGs only, we must not infer from them that they confirm the general marginality of epistemic tags and the overall persuasiveness of involvement inducing tags reported, for example, in Holmes (1982: 24) or Tottie & Hoffmann (2006: 301–302).

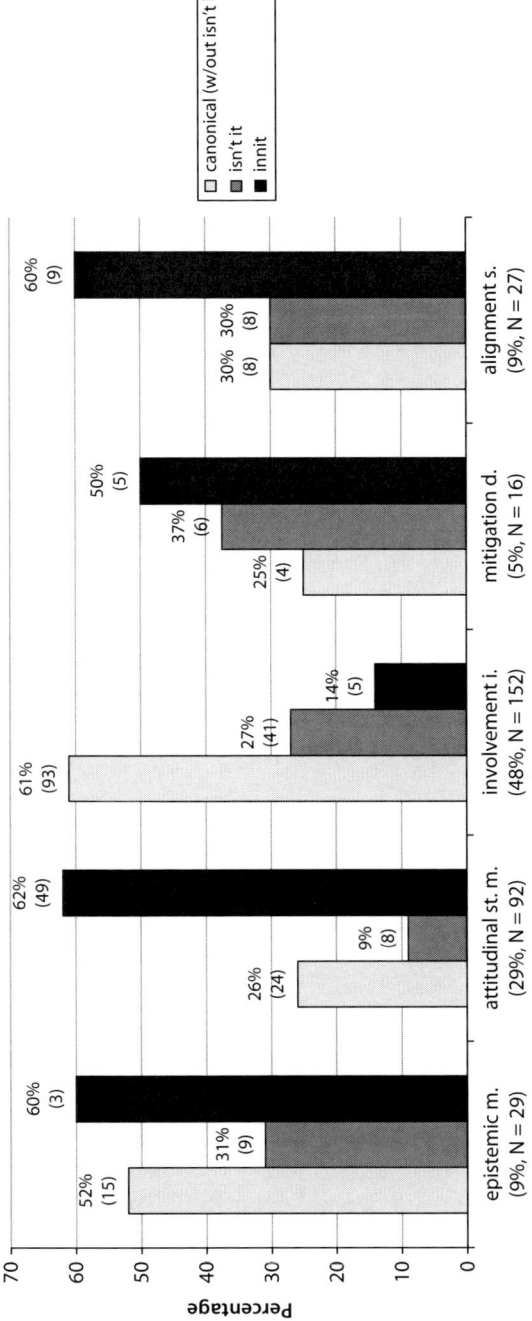

Figure 6.3 Distribution of NEG-TAG variants across functional categories (Figures in round brackets indicate raw token numbers, including all infrequent variants. The results for *innit* are derived from data produced by *innit*-users only [N = 145].)

Figure 6.4 establishes that mixed-effects analysis is also required to produce reliable results for NEG-TAG variation. The scatter plot shows that NEG-TAG frequencies range from zero to 38 tokens per 10,000 words in the youngest age group (on the left), from zero to 53 in the middle age group (in the centre), and from two to 46 in the oldest age group (on the right). However, most young and old speakers' rate of NEG-TAG usage is below 20 tokens per 10,000 words. In the middle age group, which has the most frequent and most excessive outliers, most speakers' rate is below 10 tokens per 10,000 words. To minimise the risk of providing inaccurate significance estimates of social factors, the following multivariate analysis is conducted with Rbrul.

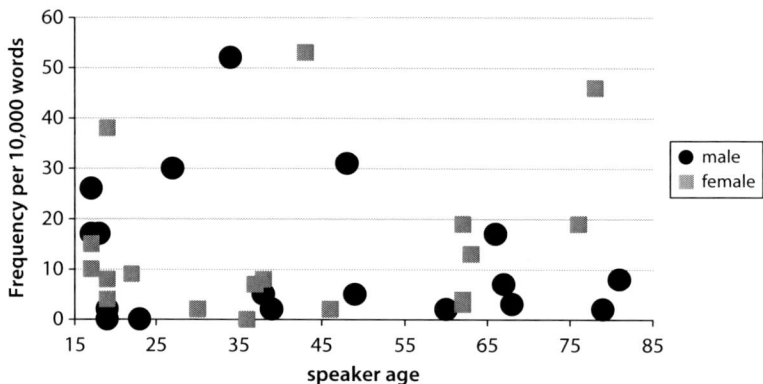

Figure 6.4 Normalised frequencies of NEG-TAGS across individuals

6.5.2 Multivariate analysis

The mixed-effects multivariate analyses reported in this section will establish the joint impact of the independent variables speaker sex, age, syntax and function to the probability of the most frequently instantiated NEG-TAG variants while consistently accounting for the high degrees of inter-speaker variation in NEG-TAG usage discussed immediately above (see further Chapter 2.3.3 for details on Rbrul analysis). Pitfalls associated with limited data are mitigated by recoding the five functional categories identified in Section 6.4 into two broader categories: conducive tags, i.e., those marking epistemicity and inducing involvement, and non-conducive tags, i.e., those signalling alignment or an attitudinal stance. Because they can be either conducive or non-conducive, tags initially categorised as mitigation devices were revisited to establish their conduciveness effect in their particular contexts of occurrence and ensure their accurate re-categorisation as either conducive or non-conducive tags. Also, for the purpose of the regression analysis, the variant *isn't it* is conflated with the aggregate of other non-localised canonical tags. While this re-configuration may conceal the differential patterning of *isn't it* and other canonical tags across syntax, it will not adversely affect the results but rather improve their reliability by increasing cell sizes (Guy 1980).

Table 6.5 displays the results of two independent multivariate analyses of the contribution of age, sex, syntax and function to the choice of *innit* and canonical tags in the BwE interview data. The variant listed at the top of a column is the one that was chosen as the application value for this particular run, with all other NEG-TAG variants included in the run as non-application values. Only the data from the thirteen speakers who use *innit* were included in the run for this variant; the data from all 33 NEG-TAG users in the sample were included in the run for canonical tags. (For further details on how to interpret the results in Table 6.5, see Chapter 2.3.3.)

The high input value for *innit* reveals that although this variant constitutes only a quarter of all NEG-TAGS in the data as a whole, it competes quite vigorously with other tag variants when only those speakers are considered who actively use *innit* in the data. Function is the only predictor included in the run that is selected as making a significant contribution to the occurrence of *innit*. It is strongly favoured for non-conducive tag uses such as marking an attitudinal stance and signalling alignment. Cross-tabulations (not shown here) reveal that this effect is consistent across the age groups represented in the data. Syntax does not exert a significant effect to the occurrence of *innit*. The variant is only weakly preferred in paradigmatic contexts.[49] The effect of age on variant selection does not reach statistical significance either, despite the constraint rankings and highly divergent factor weights creating the appearance of an apparent-time rise in the use of *innit*. The em-rule in Table 6.5 indicates that speaker sex was not included as a factor group in the multivariate analysis for *innit*. This decision was taken because of severely unbalanced data (see Section 6.5.1) and the fact that the token numbers for female speakers (N = 6) are well below the threshold for obtaining reliable results (Guy 1980). Nevertheless, several indicators suggest that speaker sex is the most important explanatory factor group for the occurrence of *innit* by far. Not only is *innit* used almost exclusively by male speakers in the sample but males also contribute all but 3 tokens of *innit* to the data.

---

49. The results for syntax are based on very low token numbers in non-paradigmatic contexts. However, since acceptable levels of accuracy can be obtained with numbers in excess of ten tokens per cell (Guy 1980), they must not be dismissed out of hand.

Table 6.5 Contribution of external and internal factors to the probability of *innit* and non-localised canonical tags (with infrequent variants included as non-application values)

	innit				non-localised canonical tags (including *isn't it*)			
	factor weights	%	N	log odds	factor weights	%	N	log odds
input prob.	0.417				0.754			
total N	145				316			
deviance	177.508				289.789			
sex					p = 0.0172			
male	–	–	139	–	.328	50.3	167	[−0.716]
female	–	–	6	–	.672	88.6	149	[0.716]
range					*.344*			
age	not significant				not significant			
young	[.642]	56.2	32	[0.586]	[.380]	37.0	73	[−0.488]
middle	[.573]	52.5	80	[0.294]	[.410]	38.1	113	[−0.365]
old	[.293]	33.3	33	[−0.880]	[.701]	56.9	130	[0.853]
range								
syntax	not significant				not significant			
paradigmatic	[.562]	49.6	127	[0.248]	[.624]	70.7	287	[0.508]
non-paradigmatic	[.438]	44.4	18	[−0.248]	[.376]	44.8	29	[−0.508]
range								
function	p = 1.96e-06				p = 7.12e-07			
non-conducive	.737	61.0	100	1.030	.292	42.3	130	−0.885
conducive	.263	22.2	45	−1.030	.708	86.6	186	0.885
range	*.474*				*.416*			
speaker	random st. dv 0.57				random st. dv 1.082			

As is the case with *innit*, function and speaker sex play an important role in affecting the occurrence of non-localised canonical tags. However, in stark contrast to *innit*, canonical tags are strongly favoured for conducive tag uses such as signalling epistemicity and inducing hearers' involvement in the interaction. This effect is consistent across age and speaker sex, as revealed by cross-tabulations not reproduced here. The range values show that speaker sex exerts the second most important effect to the occurrence of canonical tags. While *innit* is strongly associated with male speakers, canonical tags are favoured by the female speakers in the data, most noticeably by those in the middle and young age groups (as revealed by hidden cross-tabulations). Despite the divergent factor weights which associate canonical tags with older speakers and paradigmatic contexts, age and syntax are not selected as making a significant contribution to the occurrence of these tag variants. The appearance of an age effect is produced by unbalanced data in the middle age group. The non-significant effect of syntax is a result of conflating *isn't it* with the other non-localised canonical tag forms. As shown in Figure 6.2 above, the latter show a markedly stronger tendency than the former to occur in paradigmatic contexts. Also, the eight canonical tags (excluding *isn't it*) that do not match the syntactic-semantic properties of their preceding anchors may be construed as performance errors rather than non-paradigmatic tokens *sensu stricto* (see footnote 47 above). Despite the factor weights, then, there is strong reason to assume that canonical tags are generally favoured in paradigmatic contexts.

6.5.3 Summary of results

The preceding analysis into the formal variability of NEG-TAGS has yielded the following key findings:

– *The variable context is unevenly partitioned between variants*: The NEG-TAG system in BwE is largely split between non-localised canonical tag variants and the supra-local canonically-derived variant *innit*. The remaining supra-local variants with *din* and *in't* and the localised canonical tag variants with *divn't* and *no* occupy a trivial niche in the pool of available variants.
– *The most frequent variants in the data have complementary social and functional meanings*: The use of non-localised canonical tags in the BwE corpus is correlated with female speakers and conducive functions. Conversely, the use of *innit* is strongly associated with male speakers and non-conducive functions.
– *The BwE NEG-TAG system has not been affected by analogical levelling to any great extent*: The vast majority of NEG-TAGS in the data occur in contexts where they match the syntactic-semantic properties of their preceding anchor. The variant most likely to occur in non-paradigmatic contexts is *innit*, followed by *isn't it*.

Another important finding, generated through inspection of both the variable and its variants' distribution across individual speakers, is the following:

– *The data exhibit a considerable amount of inter- and intra-group variability in NEG-TAG usage*: Although the pragmatic meaning attached to the most frequent variants is consistent across the speaker sample, the frequency of NEG-TAGS and individual variants varies markedly across social cohorts and individual speakers. This is particularly true of the variant *innit* which is only used by a subsample of thirteen speakers, eleven of whom are male.

6.6 Discussion

This chapter set out to establish the rules governing the formal variability of NEG-TAGS and the entrenchment of innovating tag uses in BwE, a variety of British English remote from those varieties from which tag innovations are hypothesised to be diffusing. Qualitative and quantitative methods were combined to develop a functional taxonomy of NEG-TAGS in the BwE corpus and to model the choice process between NEG-TAG variants. This section discusses the key findings of the preceding analysis, situates them vis-á-vis previous studies of NEG-TAG variation in other varieties, and explores the origins of *innit* in BwE.

The detailed qualitative data analysis in Section 6.4 served to establish the functional inventory of NEG-TAGS in order to allow testing the effect of function on variant selection. It confirmed several findings obtained in previous functional analyses of tag usage. Firstly, NEG-TAGS are used by speakers to signal their attitudes towards propositions as well as hearers. Secondly, conduciveness is not a defining property of their use. In the BwE dataset, the tags that function subjectively to seek hearers' verification and confirmation of propositions or intersubjectively to draw co-conversationalists into the discourse tend to invoke a response from listeners. By contrast, the tags that function subjectively to emphasise speakers' attitudinal stance towards their propositions or intersubjectively to signal their alignment with prior talk do not solicit a response from listeners. Beyond confirming the strong link between the function tags perform and the conduciveness they entail (see in particular Kimps 2007: 274–280), these results show that non-conduciveness is not limited to those tags that signal hostility or aggression, as implied by Algeo (1988, 1990) and Cheshire (1981), but extends to those tags that signal a neutral or assertive stance as well as those that constitute a positive politeness device (e.g. when they signal approval of or involvement with prior speakers' talk). Moreover, the fact that some 40% of NEG-TAGS in the data analysed here are non-conducive calls into question previous functional accounts such as those by Cheshire (1981) and Holmes (1982) which imply that conducive tags are the unmarked and non-conducive tags the marked usage (see Andersen 1998 for a similar criticism).

The distinction between conducive and non-conducive tag functions has proved essential in accounting for the distribution of non-localised canonical tags and the supra-local tag variant *innit*. The former are strongly favoured for conducive functions, in particular for securing and maintaining listeners' involvement in the interaction; the latter are strongly favoured for non-conducive functions, in particular for emphasising speakers' attitudinal stance towards their propositions. The strong association of *innit* with non-conduciveness and subjectivity may be symptomatic of a more general pattern whereby reduced tag variants are not usually response-soliciting or hearer-oriented. The BwE data contain 14 tag tokens of the form *in't* + pronoun where *in't* is a reduced form of either *isn't* (e.g. *It's unbelievable, in't it?*) or *aren't* (e.g. *They're wise, in't they?*). Similar to *innit*, the majority of these tokens are non-conducive (71%, N = 10), half of them signalling an attitudinal stance (50%, N = 7). Cheshire's (1981) Reading data contain tags with the reduced form [eɪnt] + pronoun as well as tags with the even more reduced form [ɪnt] + pronoun. The latter are more strongly associated with lack of conduciveness than the former.

Assuming, with Hoffmann (2006) and Tottie & Hoffmann (2006), that the original meaning of question tags is interrogative, non-conducive tag uses can be construed as representing a more advanced stage in the grammaticalisation of tag meanings than conducive tag uses. Verification- and corroboration-seeking tags (Examples (22)–(23) and (27) above) constitute genuine questions by virtue of invoking listener response. Conversely, stance- and involvement-signalling tags (Examples (24)–(25) and (28)–(29) above) are devoid of interrogative qualities because they have undergone desemanticisation. In line with Traugott & Heine's (1991) implicational hierarchy of the type semantic > pragmatic > less semantic-pragmatic, the interrogative meaning associated with conducive question tags has faded away to the point that non-conducive tags do not have a response-elicitation effect. In the current dataset, the loss of interrogative qualities in advanced stages of the tags' semantic-pragmatic development is reflected in the form and structure of the variant most closely associated with non-conducive tag usage: *innit*. As a result of its structural reanalysis from three morphemes (*is, -n't, it*) into a single unit, *innit* is no longer easily identifiable as a reduced interrogative clause composed of an auxiliary, negator and pronoun. Evidence from analyses of *innit* in London English suggests that the variant's loss of analysability and compositionality leads to the gradual development in this variety of functions even more remote from tags' original verification- and corroboration-seeking meaning than the non-conducive stance- and involvement-signalling meanings discussed above. Andersen (2001: 139–156) reports instances of *innit* that constitute utterances in their own right, as in (30). Pichler & Torgersen (2012) report instances of *innit* that occur in non-clause final position, as in (31). Like the non-conducive NEG-TAGS described in Section 6.4.1, the *innit* tokens in (30) and (31) do not constitute genuine questions aimed at eliciting verbal contributions from listeners. Rather, they serve to mark the current speaker's agreement with the previous speaker's proposition (30), or to foreground new information (31). They thus differ phonologically, semantically and pragmatically from their source form, i.e., response-soliciting canonical tags of the type auxiliary + -n't + pronoun.

(30) Ken: They're about a year behind us in fashion.
     Selum: *Innit* man.   (Andersen 2001:149)
(31) Tina: I'm a lot smaller than all of them man and who were like, "whoa."
            I mean, the sister, *innit*, she's about five times bigger than you.
                                                              (Pichler & Torgersen 2012)

Returning to the functions identified for NEG-TAGS in the BwE data, the development of non-conducive tags from conducive tags sketched out above counterexemplifies widely attested hypotheses about the unidirectionality of semantic change: that subjective uses of constructions chronologically precede and give rise to intersubjective uses (Traugott 2003b, 2010; Traugott & Dasher 2002:40); and that a reverse order of development from intersubjective to subjective can be ruled out (Traugott & Dasher 2002:281). Although the conducive NEG-TAGS in the data are not categorically intersubjective (see Section 6.4.1 and Figure 6.3 in Section 6.5.1), it is clear that NEG-TAGS are intersubjective from the outset (see also Traugott 2012:10–11). By seeking listeners' support or corroboration of propositions (see Example (27) above), they signal speakers' attention to their hearers. At the same time, the data examined above demonstrate that in the process of desemanticisation NEG-TAGS develop new meanings which are primarily, though not exclusively, subjective (see Section 6.4.1 and Figure 6.3 in Section 6.5.1). By conveying an attitudinal stance and speaker commitment (see Examples (24) and (25) above), they signal speakers' orientation not towards their hearers but towards their propositions. The development of NEG-TAGS can therefore not be described as conforming to a strict unidirectionality between subjective and intersubjective meanings. It suggests that widely reported regularities of the type subjective > intersubjective are at best a weak hypothesis and that grammaticalising constructions do not by definition follow a single, rigid sequence of meaning changes.

In addition to the functional split discussed earlier, the preceding quantitative analysis has also uncovered a social split between non-localised canonical tags and the supra-local tag variant *innit*. Canonical tags are favoured by females; *innit* is used almost exclusively by males. A possible explanation for the strong association of *innit* with male speech is its functional compartmentalisation as an attitudinal stance marker noted in Section 6.5.2. There is ample evidence in the literature that women prefer a more addressee-oriented conversational style than men (see, for example, Coates 2004:85ff; Woods 1997:117). Question tags in particular tend to be used by women more than by men to signal politeness and involve addressees in the interaction (Cameron et al. 1988:85; Holmes 1984a:54, 1987:73, 1995:83–85). This trend is echoed in the current dataset. Women produced 66% (N = 101) of all 152 tags with a corroboration-seeking function but only 13% (N = 12) of all 92 tags with a stance-signalling function. The virtual non-existence of *innit* in female speech may therefore be due largely to its strong association with an assertive, speaker-oriented conversational style that is not generally embraced by women (or, if embraced, is achieved by means other than the use of question tags). More generally, these patterns demonstrate that not only do the women and men recorded for this project use different tag variants but they exploit the availability of these variants to pursue different interactional styles.

If we adopt, for now, the prevalent view that *innit* is innovating in and diffusing from varieties in southern England (Cheshire et al. 2005: 155–158; Krug 1998), its functional compartmentalisation as a stance marker in BwE might explain why it is adopted by men at a faster rate and/or to a greater extent than women. Several studies have pointed out that supra-local phonological variants are more likely to be adopted by women than men (see, *inter alia*, Foulkes & Docherty 1999: 16; Kerswill 2003: 226–227; Milroy et al. 1994: 26; Watt & Milroy 1999: 40, 43). The fact that the supra-local variant *innit* departs from this well-established sex pattern may be diagnostic of more general differences between the spread of discourse-pragmatic and phonological variants as well as the important role of function in discourse-pragmatic change. Because discourse-pragmatic variants are never void of pragmatic meaning, their adoption may be intrinsically tied up with their functionality and whether this functionality is compatible with the interactional style pursued by potential adopters. Whatever the precise role of function in the diffusion of *innit*, the fact that the male speakers in the BwE corpus are at the forefront of the use of *innit* is consistent with Andersen's (2001: 207) hypothesis that females are the innovators and males the leaders in changes affecting *innit* (see also Pichler & Torgersen 2012). (Alternatively, male Berwickers' favouring of *innit* over female Berwickers might be due to the fact that the variant carries covert prestige and is stigmatised. The OED (2010) describes *innit* as the "vulgar form of *isn't it*." As Stubbe & Holmes (1995: 81) point out, discourse-pragmatic innovations involving covert prestige are frequently adopted by men first.)

Several observations from the BwE data support the view that *innit* is diffusing from southern varieties of English, in particular London English. Firstly, *innit* is far less frequent in the northern variety of English investigated here than it is in varieties spoken in southern England. In the BwE corpus (collected in 2003–2005), *innit* accounts for 16% of all negative and positive polarity tags (N = 71 out of 432) and for 48% of all tags formed with or derived from *is* + *-n't* + *it* (N = 71 out of 149). Its average rate of occurrence in BwE is 2.7 tokens per 10,000 words. In COLT (collected in 1993), *innit* accounts for 27% (N = 323 out of 1205) of all negative and positive polarity tags in the data and for 52% of all tags formed with or derived from *is* + *-n't* + *it* (N = 323 out of 621). Its average rate of occurrence in COLT is 7.3 tokens per 10,000 words (Andersen 2001). The BNC (collected in 1991–1994) records the highest frequency of *innit* out of all tags formed with or derived from *is + -n't + it* for south-west England (Krug 1998: 193–194). Secondly, the spread of *innit* across the inflectional paradigm is by far not as advanced in the BwE data as it is in COLT. The rate of non-paradigmatic *innit* tokens in the BwE corpus is 11% (N = 8 out of 71) compared to 56% (N = 181 out of 323) in COLT. (This explains to some extent the cross-variety frequency differences described above. *Innit* is more frequent in London English because it occurs in a wider range of syntactic-semantic environments.) Cheshire et al. (2005: 156) also report low overall and low non-paradigmatic rates of *innit* in their adolescent data recorded in 1995–1999 in Reading, Milton Keynes and Hull (14%; N = 5 out of 36). They take these figures to suggest that *innit* has had a longer history and is more grammaticalised in London compared to the communities they studied.

Yet the results presented in the current investigation caution against assessing a form's degree of grammaticalisation solely on the basis of its syntactic-semantic distribution. As argued above, in BwE *innit* performs pragmatic functions that can be located towards the more advanced end of the cline of semantic-pragmatic change. This is not the case in COLT. Andersen (2001) does not describe *innit* as a speaker-oriented variable which signals an assertive stance but as a hearer-oriented variable which signals social rapport and aligned contextual assumptions (see also Cheshire et al. 2005). Comparison of the BwE and COLT data, then, suggests that *innit* is situated at opposite ends of the semantic-pragmatic and syntactic-semantic clines of change in these varieties. The only other variant in the BwE data that shows a propensity for use as an attitudinal stance marker is *in't* + pronoun which is only used by a small minority of speakers, mostly from the old and middle age groups. *Innit* may have been adopted in BwE to fill a niche in the system of NEG-TAG functions that has become vacant as a result of the decreasing use of *in't* + pronoun tags. In London English, on the other hand, *innit* may have developed as a marker of social or ethnic differentiation. As pointed out by Andersen (2001: 192), the actual form *innit* is not an ethnic minority feature because all ethnic groups in London use it. However, non-paradigmatic uses of the form definitely are ethnic identity markers because their frequency is vastly higher in ethnic minority speech.

The fact that *innit* has a different discourse-functional and syntactic-semantic profile in BwE than in COLT does not in and of itself preclude a diffusion view of the form's distribution in the UK. Britain (2002: 617–618) points out that supra-local innovations are not necessarily adopted wholesale but that they often interact with local structures to produce local outcomes. Buchstaller (2008) provides evidence for the outcome of such interaction on the level of discourse-pragmatics. She demonstrates that the innovative quotative variants BE *like* and *go* do not have the same distribution in British English as they do in American English from where they have diffused. She attributes these differences to the fact that not all properties of BE *like* and *go* were transferred in their spatial diffusion across the Atlantic but that some social, formal and functional attributes were created anew as the variants were adopted into British English dialects. It is at least possible that a similar process might have been at play in the adoption of *innit* into BwE. *Innit* might have been taken on as a linguistic form without its pragmatic envelope. Instead of putting *innit* to the same strategic use as their (mostly female) compatriots in the south, male Berwickers might have attributed a new function to *innit*, i.e., one that had been associated with a variant that has started to wane in BwE (see above), thus giving a supra-local form a local meaning.

However, we need to acknowledge the possibility of an alternative origin for *innit*. Rather than being the result of an outside adoption, *innit* might have developed through reduction from *isn't it* and/or *in't it* from within the dialect itself and irrespective of any developments in southern British English. There is no reason to assume that attrition and fusion, which are generally taken to be natural processes of linguistic change resulting from frequency of use and repetition (Bybee 2003), should only occur in one variety from which reduced forms spread rather than occur simultaneously and independently across varieties. Among those Berwickers who use the variant, *innit* is a well-established feature of BwE rather than a recent development that is only gradually gaining ground. This is evident from the results of the regression analysis in Section 6.5. The input value demonstrates *innit*'s high probability of occurrence amongst the 13 *innit*-users in the sample; the constraint hierarchy within the factor group age reveals only a non-significant rise in the use of *innit* in apparent time. However, non-paradigmatic tokens of *innit* are rare in the near-categorically mono-ethnic town of Berwick upon Tweed (99.6% of the population were white British at the time of data collection), especially when compared to multi-ethnic and multi-cultural London (see above). Because, according to Andersen (2001), non-paradigmatic uses of question tags thrive in multilingual communities and because ethnic minority speakers are the social forces driving tags' analogical levelling, we could argue that the form *innit per se* may be an independent development across varieties of UK English and that it may only be the form's non-paradigmatic uses that are diffusing from multi-ethnic London (and possibly other multi-ethnic cities such as Birmingham). The low rate of non-paradigmatic tokens of *innit* as opposed to paradigmatic tokens in the BwE data may then be attributable to the ethnic composition of Berwick upon Tweed and the lack of ethnic minority speakers who would generally lead the analogical levelling of *innit*. The non-existence of non-paradigmatic *innit* in Andersen's (2001) exclusively white British speaker sample from Hertfordshire tentatively supports this hypothesis.

6.7 Conclusion

The preceding analysis of NEG-TAGS has shown that variation in their realisation is not random but systematically constrained by extra- and intra-linguistic factors. The overarching finding to emerge from the analysis is the complementary functional and social distribution of non-localised canonical tags and the supra-local tag variant *innit*. Comparison of the results obtained in the present study with those obtained elsewhere, notably Andersen (2001), has demonstrated the complexity and function-dependency of discourse-pragmatic variation and change. It warns researchers against assuming that the occurrence of a discourse-pragmatic variant in different varieties is necessarily a result of its social and geographical diffusion, and that identical variants necessarily carry the same social and functional meanings across varieties. The results thus highlight the importance of closely investigating the sociolinguistic distribution of discourse-pragmatic variants before drawing any cross-variety comparisons about their use.

Without access to more data from across Britain any hypotheses about the origins, distribution and dissemination of *innit* must necessarily remain tentative. Accountable analyses of its extra- and intra-linguistic distribution across a range of British English varieties are needed to fully understand how and whether *innit* is diffusing across the UK. The study of question tag variation and change would also benefit from an increase in diachronic studies which closely investigate the semantic-pragmatic trajectory of tag usage over extended time periods.

PART III

## CHAPTER 7

Discussion & conclusion

7.1 Introduction

This project was devised to demonstrate the theoretical insights that can be gained into the structure of synchronic language variation and the interactional mechanisms creating it by subjecting discourse-pragmatic variables to systematic variationist analysis. To this end, the book has developed an innovative methodology which draws on the combined resources of variationist sociolinguistics, grammaticalisation studies and conversation analysis in order to uncover the complex organisation of discourse-pragmatic variation in synchronic dialect data. The method was applied to the analysis of the three variables I DON'T KNOW, I DON'T THINK and NEG-TAGS which were chosen for analysis on the basis of sharing the following properties: they function predominantly on the discourse-pragmatic level of the linguistic system where they perform multiple interpersonal and textual functions; they evince a high degree of formal variability which primarily affects their morphemic structure and/or the realisation of their negative auxiliaries; and, in the variety investigated here, they have variants which are differentiated by their geographical distribution within England and the English-speaking world. The analysis of these variables in a corpus of BwE, a peripheral variety of English spoken in the far north-east of England, has established the grammar underlying their formal variability in the data and demonstrated that they constitute formulaic discourse units whose synchronic distribution in the data is a product of changes associated with grammaticalisation. A key insight afforded by focusing the analysis on three variables which are composed of a similar string of components ((pronoun) + (auxiliary) + (negator) + (verb); (auxiliary) + (negator) + (pronoun)) is that the sociolinguistic organisation of formal discourse variation is not entirely uniform even across variables which are structurally related.

This chapter synthesises the results obtained in Chapters 4 to 6 with a view to illustrating more fully the important new insights into language variation and change which the rigorous and multi-faceted analyses in these chapters have produced. Following a short account of parallel distribution patterns in the data, Section 7.2 explores the mechanisms which give rise to the heterogeneous patterning of formal variants across the three variables investigated in this book. Section 7.3 discusses the far-reaching methodological and theoretical implications of the results obtained in this study for grammaticalisation studies, variationist sociolinguistics and linguistic theory more generally. It also examines why the patterns of variation and change uncovered here do not correspond fully to those reported for variables at other levels of the linguistic system, and outlines why formulation of general principles of discourse-pragmatic variation and change may be an objective that is not easily attained. Finally, Section 7.4 is the conclusion to this chapter.

7.2 Synthesis of the results

Investigation into the formal variability of I DON'T KNOW, I DON'T THINK and NEG-TAGS required identifying the whole inventory of variants for each variable, operationalising hypotheses about selection constraints as independent predictors and isolating the range of functions performed by the variables in the data, and, finally, quantifying the distribution of variants across the extra- and intra-linguistic predictors hypothesised to constrain variant distribution. This procedure yielded several important findings. Firstly, the speakers included in the sample have the option of encoding the selected variables with a range of variants which can be broadly divided into non-localised, supra-local and localised variants. Secondly, the targeted variables perform a wide range of functions which, for the purpose of quantification, can be divided into broad categories (e.g. referential vs. pragmatic; interpersonal vs. textual; conducive vs. non-conducive) or more narrow categories (e.g. hedge, booster, affiliator, mitigator, frame). Thirdly, the formal variability in the data is highly structured and systematically constrained by multiple contextual predictors. Comparison of the results obtained in Part II reveals that the structure of variation exhibits important similarities and dissimilarities across variables and variants.

One of the overarching parallelisms to emerge from the preceding analyses is the fact that the occurrence of non-localised and supra-local variants of I DON'T KNOW, I DON'T THINK and NEG-TAGS is consistently conditioned by discourse-functional constraints (see, however, *I dono*), with the result that: *I don't know* is favoured for referential meanings and *I dunno* for pragmatic meanings (see Tables 4.6 and 4.7 in Chapter 4.5); *I don't think* is associated with contexts where the negator is interactionally preferred and *I doØ think* with those where it is dispreferred (see Figure 5.5 in Chapter 5.5); canonical tags are favoured for conducive functions and *innit* for non-conducive functions (see Table 6.5 in Chapter 6.5). It follows from this that although the pool of formal variants available in BwE for encoding I DON'T KNOW, I DON'T THINK and NEG-TAGS is quite large, speakers' choice of variant is somewhat limited once functional constraints on variant usage are taken into account. I DON'T KNOW and NEG-TAGS were also found to resemble each other in that their full variants (*I don't know*, canonical tag forms) and their fused and reduced variants (*I dunno, innit*) encode distinct and complementary meanings which represent different stages of semantic-pragmatic change. Full variants are favoured for less semantically bleached meanings (referential, conducive); reduced variants are favoured for more semantically bleached meanings (pragmatic, non-conducive). The parallelisms highlighted here demonstrate that functionality plays a crucial role in constraining formal variability in discourse-pragmatics, and that formal reduction is strongly suggestive of desemanticisation (see, however, *I doØ think* discussed in Section 7.3 below).

Moreover, multivariate analyses of the non-localised and supra-local variants discussed above have shown that when social constraints are at all implicated in variant distribution, their effect is strongly linked with variants' functionality (canonical tags, *innit*) and/or is less important than that of function (*I don't know*, canonical tags) (see Table 4.6 in Chapter 4.5; Table 6.5 in Chapter 6.5). The weak or non-existent conditioning effect of the broad social factors age and speaker sex can be attributed to the remarkable constancy of variant meanings across the speaker sample. Cross-tabulations of the data have uncovered that although social groups and individuals vary in their frequency of use of non-localised and supra-local variants, they consistently use them with the same broad meanings. (Minor meaning fluctuations are observable within broad functional categories. However, they are neither significant nor symptomatic of apparent-time changes.) The social consistency in the strategic use of non-localised and supra-local variants suggests that the functional usage patterns described above have come to be fossilised in BwE. Their fossilisation may be motivated by the fact that consistent usage patterns of the type described above promote communicative efficiency.

This is not to say, however, that the formal variability of the targeted variables is completely void of social meanings. The regression analyses in Chapters 4 and 5 have uncovered important parallelisms relating to the localised variants of I DON'T KNOW and I DON'T THINK (*I divn't knaa, I divn't think*) which show that their occurrence is consistently affected by broad social factors (see Table 4.9 in Chapter 4.5; Table 5.3 in Chapter 5.5). In addition to confirming the social meaning-making potential of formal discourse variation previously documented in the literature (Cheshire 1981; Drager 2011; Moore & Podesva 2009), the analysis of localised variants has shown that *I divn't knaa* and *I divn't think* resemble each other in terms of their functional distribution. Both variants occur with roughly equal probability across the functional categories established for their respective variables.

The preceding outline of the similarities in the conditioning of formal variation patterns in the data could not avoid drawing attention to their dissimilarities. Due to the consistent conditioning effect of discourse-functional factors on non-localised and supra-local variants and the consistent effect of extra-linguistic factors on localised variants, the occurrence of variants with different geographical spreads is constrained by different parameters. As a result, their functional and social meanings are necessarily opposing. Non-localised variants (of I DON'T KNOW and I DON'T THINK) are functionally compartmentalised markers of social cohesion (see Tables 4.6 and 4.7 in Chapter 4.5; Table 5.3 and Figure 5.5 in Chapter 5.5); localised variants (of I DON'T KNOW and I DON'T THINK) are functionally versatile markers of social differentiation (see Table 4.8 in Chapter 4.5; Table 5.3 and Figure 5.5. in Chapter 5.5). (The distribution of NEG-TAG variants is asymmetrical in a different way and will be sketched out further below.)

Additional and more intricate disparities emerge when we examine in more detail the precise functional and social meanings attached to individual variants. As alluded to above, the painstaking qualitative and quantitative analyses of I DON'T KNOW and I DON'T THINK in Chapters 4 and 5 have revealed strong correlations between the variables' realisations and their functions. However, these correlations do not result in identical form-meaning correlations across the two variables. With I DON'T KNOW, formal variability tallies with broad functional categories at a macro-level of analysis. Full variants pattern with the variable's use as a referential expression of insufficient knowledge; reduced variants pattern with its use as a discourse-pragmatic feature that serves a wide range of interpersonal and textual functions (see Tables 4.6 and 4.7 in Chapter 4.5). With I DON'T THINK, formal variability reflects fine-grained functional differences at a micro-level of analysis. Full variants pattern with interactional contexts where the negator is the bearer of important focal information or where it is interactionally preferred; reduced variants pattern with contexts where the negator constitutes a potential face-threat (see Figure 5.5 in Chapter 5.5). These correlations demonstrate firstly that the pragmatic values of full and reduced variants of *don't* are not constant but are contingent on their collocational context of occurrence, and secondly that variation between reduction or lack of reduction is not random but is carefully monitored and controlled by speakers (see also Bybee & Hopper 2001: 11; Plug 2010). With I DON'T KNOW, speakers exploit the formal variation to mark the difference between referential and pragmatic meanings. With I DON'T THINK, speakers either allow or suppress reduction depending on the immediate interactional and social demands of the speech situation.

Another inconsistent pattern in the data involves the social indexicality of the localised variants *I divn't knaa* and *I divn't think*. The former is strongly favoured by young males (and, to a lesser extent, old females) (see Table 4.9 in Chapter 4.5); the latter is strongly favoured by females (see Table 5.3 in Chapter 5.5). In the aggregate of productive constructions in the data, social factors were found not to impact on the occurrence of *divn't* (see Table 3.4 in Chapter 3.4.2). The divergent social value of *divn't* across the two formulaic constructions, I DON'T KNOW and I DON'T THINK, and the aggregate of productive NP-negative DO-V constructions analysed in Chapter 3 may be a product of well-established gendered interactional styles. Men typically adopt a competitive, confrontational and dominant style; women characteristically adopt a tentative, involved and affective style (see, *inter alia*, Coates 1996, 2004; Holmes 1995; Tannen 1993). Young males are the most productive users of the variable I DON'T KNOW as well as the variant *I divn't knaa* (see Figure 4.5 and Table 4.9 in Chapter 4.5). Because I DON'T KNOW is used in the data predominantly for textual functions such as turn-regulation and topic-development (see Figure 4.3 in Chapter 4.5), young males' high use of *I divn't knaa* may be attributable to their pursuing an interactional style of control and dominance. Conversely, females are the more productive users of the variable I DON'T THINK as well as the variant *I divn't think* (see Figure 5.4 and Table 5.3 in Chapter 5.5). Because I DON'T THINK is used in the data predominantly for interpersonal functions such as epistemicity and mitigation (see Figure 5.5 in Chapter 5.5), females' high use of *I divn't think* may be attributable to their pursuing a tentative and hearer-oriented interactional style. In sum, *divn't*, which carries no social meaning in productive constructions (see Table 3.4 in Chapter 3.5), acquires social meanings in formulaic constructions as a result of these constructions' inherent functionality. Alternatively, the divergent social value of *divn't* in I DON'T KNOW and I DON'T THINK may be a product of the high variability and great instability in the formal implementation of pragmatic functions (see, *inter alia*, Barbieri 2008; Brinton 2001; Precht 2008). Social groups other than young males may rarely use *I divn't knaa* because they draw on features other than I DON'T KNOW to perform textual functions. Similarly, male speakers may rarely use *I divn't think* because they exploit features other than I DON'T THINK to signal interpersonal meanings. The hypotheses formulated above are necessarily speculative and require empirical verification. Also, they can be criticised for being essentialist and reductive because they are based on binary gender distinctions and ignore the potential diversity of gendered practices. Nevertheless, they demonstrate well that the social embedding of variation in discourse-pragmatics is highly complex, and that the social meaning of variants cannot easily be separated from variables' functionality.

   The analysis of NEG-TAGS in Chapter 6 provides additional and more conclusive evidence that discourse-pragmatic variants achieve their social meaning through their functionality. Multivariate analyses of the most frequent tag variants in the data revealed that unlike the occurrence of the majority of discourse-pragmatic variants investigated in this book, the occurrence of canonical tag variants and the variant *innit* is governed by both extra-linguistic and discourse-functional constraints. Canonical tags are favoured by females and for conducive functions such as inducing others' involvement in the interaction; *innit* is strongly associated with males and favoured for non-conducive functions such as signalling an assertive stance (see Table 6.5 in Chapter 6.5). As pointed out in Chapter 6.6, the association of canonical tags with women may be ascribed to women's preference for a facilitative, addressee-oriented interactional style; the association of *innit* with men may be ascribed to men's preference for an assertive, speaker-oriented interactional style. Because the social indexicality of NEG-TAG variants is parasitic on their functionality, their socio-pragmatic meaning differs from that sketched out above for non-localised and localised variants of I DON'T KNOW and I DON'T THINK. NEG-TAG variants are functionally compartmentalised markers of social differentiation.

7.3 Implications of the results

The results synthesised in Section 7.2 have important methodological and theoretical implications for grammaticalisation studies and variationist sociolinguistics. This section explores these implications with a view to illustrating the great importance of studying discourse-pragmatic variables for developing current theories of language.

Painstaking analyses in Chapters 4 and 5 have established that I DON'T KNOW and I DON'T THINK constitute formulaic discourse units whose synchronic distribution is a product of grammaticalisation changes operative prior to the timespan covered by the BwE corpus. The co-existence in the data of full and reduced variants of I DON'T KNOW and I DON'T THINK was therefore attributed to attrition, a grammaticalisation process reflecting changes to the cognitive representation of constructions (compositional > non-compositional) (Bybee 2006). In the BwE data as well as Bybee & Scheibman's (1999) American English data, the rate of *don't*-reduction was found to be higher in I DON'T KNOW than I DON'T THINK (67% vs. 37% in BwE; 74% vs. 35% in American English).[50] Bybee & Scheibman (1999) attribute the higher rate of formal reduction in I DON'T KNOW in their data to the fact that I DON'T KNOW has a higher discourse frequency than I DON'T THINK (N = 37 vs. N = 19). High-frequency words and constructions regularly undergo reduction and fusion at faster rates and to greater extents than low-frequency words and constructions (see, *inter alia*, Bybee 2001; Gregory et al. 1999; Jurafsky et al. 2001). The BwE data support Bybee & Scheibman's (1999) theory. The token frequency of I DON'T KNOW, which is at the forefront of the reduction of *don't*, is

---

50. The figures for BwE are based on consideration of non-localised variants only. For the purpose of generating these figures, the semi-reduced variant *I dono* was conflated with the full variant *I don't know.*

more than twice as high as that of I DON'T THINK (N = 600 vs. N = 270). Yet at the same time the results of the present investigation suggest that frequency may not be the sole or main determinant of the differential degree to which I DON'T KNOW and I DON'T THINK are affected by on-line reduction processes.

As pointed out in Section 7.2 above, reduction and lack of reduction have a different meaning in I DON'T KNOW and I DON'T THINK. In I DON'T KNOW, they mark the broad distinction between pragmatic and referential meaning; in I DON'T THINK, they signal fine-grained differences in pragmatic meaning which are inter-actionally motivated by referential weight and concerns about face. Moreover, it has been argued in Chapter 5.6 that the signalling of fine-grained nuances of mean-ing through prosody affects the realisation of *don't* in I DON'T THINK. Reduction is blocked when non-boosting tokens carry pitch prominence on *don't* to signal high degrees of doubt. The lack of consistent reduction in I DON'T THINK is therefore not exclusively due to its lower rate of occurrence compared to I DON'T KNOW, as argued by Bybee & Scheibman (1999). It is at least to some degree also conditioned by pragmatic factors and the way the variable is used in interaction as well as by prosodic factors and the way prosody is implemented to affect meaning.[51] These findings have important implications which I will discuss below.

Although it has not been possible to observe grammaticalisation changes un-fold in the time-span covered by the BwE corpus, the effects of these processes can be observed in the synchronic variation patterns uncovered by the multivariate analyses. With I DON'T KNOW, they demonstrate a strong link between semantic-pragmatic shift and formal attrition: desemanticised uses are near-consistently fused and reduced. The functional split between *I don't know* and *I dunno* in the BwE data can thus be conceptualised as the synchronic offshoot of form-meaning changes which either have unfolded concurrently throughout the evolution of I DON'T KNOW as a discourse-pragmatic variable or happen to coincide in the time-frame analysed here. (The fact that older male speakers were found to be more likely than other speakers to use *I don't know* for pragmatic uses weakly suggests that semantic-pragmatic changes may have preceded phonetic changes by one generation.) With I DON'T THINK, the patterns uncovered by the multi-variate analyses demonstrate only a weak link between semantic-pragmatic shift and formal attrition: desemanticised uses are mostly non-reduced. In light of the findings highlighted in the preceding paragraph, the functional distribution of *I don't think* and *I doØ think* can thus be conceptualised as the synchronic offshoot of form-meaning changes which, due to the strong interference of pragmatic and prosodic factors, have not progressed in lockstep. Beyond adding to the canon

---

51. The differential rates of reduction may also be affected by the differential phonemic struc-tures across word boundaries in I DON'T KNOW and I DON'T THINK.

of literature challenging Croft's (1990: 244) notion that the changes constituting grammaticalisation are strictly synchronised (see *inter alia* Bisang 2004; Romaine 1995), the divergent distribution patterns for I DON'T KNOW and I DON'T THINK highlighted above have the following implications for grammaticalisation studies. Firstly, they demonstrate that grammaticalisation does not affect constructions homogenously, even if they are composed of near-identical strings of components. Secondly, they show that the existence of non-concurrent grammaticalisation changes is not random but structured and interactionally motivated, thereby providing important hypotheses about why grammaticalisation changes do not by definition unfold concurrently.

Additional hypotheses about the asynchronous development of grammaticalisation changes were provided by the close analysis of the supra-local canonically-derived tag variant *innit* in Chapter 6. Close scrutiny of its synchronic distribution patterns revealed that although *innit* exhibits an advanced stage of formal reduction and semantic-pragmatic change, it has not been affected by analogical levelling to any great extent. Andersen (2001) argues that the spread of *innit* across the inflectional paradigm thrives in multilingual environments and that in London English it is driven by ethnic minority speakers. In view of Andersen's proposal, the near-categorical absence of non-paradigmatic tokens of *innit* in BwE was attributed to the virtual non-existence of ethnic minority speakers in Berwick upon Tweed. It follows that if different social groups activate and advance different changes constituting grammaticalisation (see Chapter 1.4) and if these groups are not universally present across communities, the set of changes constituting grammaticalisation may not co-evolve synchronously within, let alone across, varieties. As a result, the synchronic distribution of grammaticalising features may not be parallel even across closely related varieties. To fully illuminate the nature and progression of grammaticalisation changes, it is therefore necessary to closely examine their social dimension within and across varieties (see also Janda 2001).

Beyond grammaticalisation studies, the structured variability uncovered for the variables investigated in Part II has important implications for variationist sociolinguistics. As outlined at the beginning of this section and illustrated in more detail in Chapters 4.5 and 5.5, the conditioning effect of extra- and intra-linguistic predictors on patterns of formal variability is not homogeneous across the constructions I DON'T KNOW and I DON'T THINK. Non-localised variants have differential semantic-pragmatic meanings across the two constructions; their localised variants take on differential social meanings depending on the construction in which they occur. Additional comparisons of the two formulaic constructions with the aggregate of productive NP-negative DO-V constructions in the data (e.g. *they divn't like, you don't see, we divn't do, people don't bother*) show that the frequency of *don't*-reduction and *divn't*-usage varies dramatically not just across formulaic constructions but also across formulaic and productive constructions. At 12%, the aggregate of productive constructions have a much lower rate of *don't*-reduction than either I DON'T KNOW or I DON'T THINK (67% and 37% respectively), which may indicate that it is I DON'T KNOW and I DON'T THINK that advance *don't*-reduction.[52] Conversely, *divn't* has a markedly higher rate of occurrence in the aggregate of productive constructions than in I DON'T KNOW or I DON'T THINK (36% vs. 21% and 18% respectively), which may be linked to the internal fixation and holistic storage of these constructions in their non-localised forms. Moreover, the social distribution of *divn't* is more restricted in formulaic constructions than it is in productive constructions. In the former, its use is strongly associated with one or two social groups; in the latter, its use is largely unconstrained by the social factors sex and age. The frequency and constraint differences outlined above demonstrate the important role of formulaic constructions in shaping both the internal organisation as well as the social indexicality of linguistic variation, thus bolstering the arguments presented in Chapter 1.3 with regard to the non-peripheral and fully grammatical status of discourse-pragmatic variables in the linguistic system. They also demonstrate that provision of accurate accounts of linguistic variation crucially depends on studying grammatical morphemes in the constructions in which they occur and isolating formulaic constructions from each other and from productive constructions. Non-separation of formulaic or frequent constructions risks obscuring important constraints on variant choice and leaving unaccounted for their role in moulding linguistic variation and social meanings.

Equally important to the provision of accurate accounts of sociolinguistic variation in discourse-pragmatics is inclusion of function as an independent variable in the quantitative data analysis. As highlighted in Section 7.2 above, function is one of the key constraints on the formal variability of the discourse-pragmatic features analysed in Part II of the book. Crucially, consideration of function has shown that discourse-pragmatic variables do not achieve their social meanings in the same way as phonological or morpho-syntactic variables (see Cheshire [2005] and Cheshire et al. [2005] for similar arguments regarding higher-level syntactic variables). The frequency with which formal discourse variants occur across social groups is ultimately determined either by the function associated with the variant in question (if it is a single-purpose variant such as *innit*), or by the functional profile associated with its variable (if it is a multi-purpose variant such as *I divn't knaa* or *I divn't think*). Because of their dependency on discourse-functional conditioning and the fact that different social groups do not necessarily pursue identical discourse styles (see Section 7.2 above), the use of supra-local or

---

52. These figures are based on consideration of the variant *don't* only and do not include productive constructions with *divn't* or *dinnae*.

localised discourse variants cannot be ascribed definitively to one social group as is the case for example with supra-local or localised phonological variants which have been consistently associated with female and male speakers respectively (see, for example, Foulkes & Docherty 1999; Llamas 2007b; Milroy et al. 1994; Watt & Milroy 1999). It follows that the generalisations drawn by Labov (1998) and others regarding the social embedding of phonological variation and change are unlikely to apply without restrictions to discourse-pragmatic variables. What is more, it may prove unfeasible to formulate generalisations about the distinct social embedding of discourse-pragmatic variation and change. Which social group it is that drives semantic-pragmatic change will to a large part depend on the functions associated with evolving variables at different stages in their diachronic development.

This is not to imply that we should abandon the variationist analysis of discourse-pragmatic features. As demonstrated throughout this book, subjecting discourse-pragmatic variables to accountable quantitative analysis provides important new insights into the creation and organisation of synchronic language variation. Full investigation of every aspect of discourse-pragmatic variability is therefore imperative to testing and developing current theories of language which, by definition, must be based on systematic analyses of all levels of the linguistic system. One of the key offerings of this book is a robust body of empirical evidence for viewing discourse-pragmatic features as non-peripheral and fully grammatical elements of the linguistic system which interact with more productive constructions in shaping the structure of synchronic language variation.

7.4 Conclusion

In addition to advancing an analytical model for future investigations of discourse-pragmatic variables which accommodates their full complexity, this book has illustrated the descriptive, explanatory and theoretical potential of quantitative discourse variation studies. The corpus-based variationist analysis of three variables that are closely related by virtue of being constituted of similar components (I DON'T KNOW, I DON'T THINK and NEG-TAGS) has offered a number of previously undocumented findings. By way of summary, they include:

- *The occurrence of discourse-pragmatic variants with different geographical spreads is governed by different parameters*: Among the variables investigated in this book, the occurrence of non-localised variants is governed by discourse-functional constraints; that of localised variants by extra-linguistic constraints; and that of supra-local variants by both discourse-functional and extra-linguistic constraints.

- *The social indexicality of discourse-pragmatic variation is strongly dependent on variables' and/or variants' functional compartmentalisation in a variety*: Because their use is motivated by their functionality, discourse-pragmatic variants derive their social meanings either from the functions they encode in a given variety, or from the functional profiles associated with their variables in that variety.
- *Discourse-pragmatic variables play a key role in shaping linguistic variation and social meanings*: The frequency and sociolinguistic conditioning of linguistic variants is affected by whether they occur in productive constructions or in different formulaic constructions.
- *Grammaticalisation does not affect variables and variants homogeneously*: Interactional constraints bar processes of grammaticalisation from operating uniformly across closely related variables within a variety. Social constraints hamper the uniform progression of grammaticalisation changes across identical variants in different varieties.

The results summarised above demonstrate the range and depth of insights that can be gained from subjecting discourse-pragmatic features to rigorous qualitative and accountable quantitative analysis. As discussed in Section 7.3, these insights have far-reaching implications for current theories of language. Yet despite their indisputable theoretical value, the number of variationist analyses of discourse-pragmatic variables remains dwarfed compared to the number of variationist analyses of phonological and morpho-syntactic variables. To conclude this book, the next and last chapter explores some of the challenges scholars face in their attempts to advance the field of discourse variation analysis beyond its current rudimentary state and provide a more robust account of patterns of variation and change in discourse-pragmatics.

## CHAPTER 8

Challenges for the future

8.1 The state of the art and beyond

Just over a decade ago, Macaulay (2002a: 298) painted a rather bleak picture when he remarked of the state of discourse variation analysis at the time:

> [t]he study of discourse variation is still at an elementary stage. […] there are many different approaches to the sociolinguistic investigation of discourse, and it would take a braver person than I am to assert with confidence that we have much solid information on gender, age, or social class differences. What we have are a number of intriguing claims that need to be tested again and again, by the same or different methods, in similar or different settings, with similar or different samples […].

Although concerns remain about the robustness of the findings obtained in discourse variation research, considerable progress has been made since the turn of the century in the investigation of previously relatively unexplored aspects of discourse-pragmatic variation and change. Among others, these include:

- the social trajectories of discourse-pragmatic change (see *inter alia* Tagliamonte & D'Arcy 2009; Denis 2011);
- the role of youth in the creation and spread of new discourse-pragmatic variants (see *inter alia* Andersen 2001; Roth-Gordon 2007);
- social and geographical diffusion patterns of innovative and innovating discourse-pragmatic variants (see *inter alia* Andersen 2001; Buchstaller 2008; Buchstaller & D'Arcy 2009; Cheshire et al. 2005);
- mechanisms of discourse-pragmatic change in language contact situations (see *inter alia* Andersen 2001; Cheshire et al. 2011; Fuller 2001; Goss & Salmons 2000; Hllavac 2006; Levey et al. forthc.; Torres 2002);
- patterns of discourse-pragmatic variation across interactional, situational and technological settings (see *inter alia* Escalera 2009; Fuller 2003; Schleef 2008; Tagliamonte & Denis 2008; Verdonik et al. 2009);
- patterns of discourse-pragmatic variation and change in child and learner languages (see *inter alia* Furman & Özyürek 2007; Levey 2006, 2012; Liao 2009; Müller 2005; Terraschke 2007);

- the role of discourse-pragmatic variables in the construction and negotiation of social identities (see *inter alia* Bakht 2010; Drager 2011; Moore & Podesva 2009; Trester 2009); and
- social attitudes towards and perceptual loads of discourse-pragmatic variables (see *inter alia* Buchstaller 2006b; Parton et al. 2002; Russell et al. 2008).

The studies cited above address key questions about the nature and mechanisms of discourse-pragmatic variation and change. Together with the present investigation, they thus constitute an important step in the development of variationist discourse analysis and its expansion in new directions. However, for further advancement of the field, it will not be sufficient for scholars to gather more empirical and experimental evidence to substantiate or refute previous findings. They will also need to overcome a number of challenges which continue to obstruct progress.

This chapter explores some of these challenges, focusing specifically on: the low-frequency occurrence of many discourse-pragmatic features; the lack of a uniform set of reliable methods for discourse variation analysis; the focus on external and the insufficient attention paid to internal factors in accounting for discourse-pragmatic variation; the shallow time-depth of synchronic corpora; and the persistent trend to study a limited range of discourse-pragmatic variables while neglecting the wide expanse of other variables. In what follows I will identify the nature of these challenges and, where relevant, their origins; outline the reasons why they need to be overcome to allow progress to be made; and, where feasible, provide some suggestions as to how they might be overcome. What follows does not constitute an exhaustive list of all the challenges facing the field of discourse variation analysis. Rather, it represents a selective account of those challenges which seem particularly salient to me and which I believe need to be addressed most urgently if our ultimate aims are: firstly, to illuminate the sociolinguistic embedding of variation and change in discourse-pragmatics; and secondly, to progress towards a holistic theory of language variation and change which spans all levels of the linguistic system.

8.2 Dealing with low token frequency

By their very nature, phonological and some lower-level morpho-syntactic variables occur with high frequency even in relatively small corpora. Conversely, many discourse-pragmatic (and higher-level syntactic) variables tend to occur with far lower frequency even in corpora of moderate size. This is due to the fact that their use is strongly constrained by the operation of semantic-pragmatic and interactional-situational factors (e.g. details of the speech event and situation; topic and purpose of the interaction; speaker roles and relationships). Although understanding of these constraints has gradually improved (see Section 8.1 above for references), it is not feasible to increase token numbers by predicting typical contexts of occurrence of individual variables and concentrating data collection and analysis accordingly. Not only do the pragmatic functions performed by discourse-pragmatic features often overlap but they can be encoded by linguistic features from other levels of the linguistic system (see Chapter 1.3). Alas, what exactly it is that conditions the choice of one feature over another is, as yet, little understood.

As shown in Chapters 5 and 6 of this book, access to large token numbers need not be critical to yielding intriguing results and generating testable hypotheses about the mechanisms of discourse-pragmatic variation and change. Nevertheless, the typically low-frequency occurrence of many discourse-pragmatic features in dialect corpora may be problematic in at least two important ways. Firstly, the range of discourse-pragmatic features involved in sociolinguistic variation and change may remain hidden from observation if token numbers are severely limited. As a result, it may not be possible to produce accurate accounts of the full extent of discourse-pragmatic variation and change within and across varieties. Secondly, even where variables occur with sufficient frequency to make possible detection of variation, dialect corpora may not produce the amount of data required to uncover the grammar underlying the observed variation. Without detailed knowledge of how variables and their variants are distributed in the linguistic system and/or the speech community, understanding of the sociolinguistic embedding of discourse-pragmatic variation and change cannot advance. In short, the overall paucity of many discourse-pragmatic features may have descriptive as well as theoretical ramifications.

Studies of low-frequency morpho-syntactic variables have benefited from the increasing availability of public corpora such as the *British National Corpus* (Burnard 2000) or the *International Corpus of English* (Greenbaum 1992). Because they are much larger than private corpora, they are more likely to yield token files that are amenable to statistical analysis. However, D'Arcy (2011: 58–59) points out that despite their extraordinary size, public corpora are not necessarily suitable for the analysis of discourse-pragmatic variables: "the data are typically compiled from fragments rather than texts in their entirety [and some texts] may be systematically cropped to fit with the overall design of the corpus." This is alarming because discourse-pragmatic variables tend to occur in clusters rather than being evenly distributed throughout texts (Walker 2010: 74), and because the function of discourse-pragmatic variables cannot be determined independent of their larger context of occurrence, as demonstrated in Part II of this book. D'Arcy (2011: 59) also draws attention to Biber et al.'s (1999: 28) observation that the spoken components of publicly available corpora have tended to be collected in limited and artificial settings. This affects the representativeness and authenticity of the data, and the validity of any conclusions drawn from their analysis.

Fortunately, the low-frequency problem is not insoluble. Firstly, some publicly funded variationist projects have resulted in the construction of mega-corpora such as, for example, the 1.4-million-word *Linguistic Innovators Corpus* (Kerswill et al. 2007), the 1.2-million-word *Multicultural London English* corpus (Kerswill et al. 2011), the 3.5-million-word *Ottawa-Hull Corpus* (Poplack 1989), the 1.5-million-word *York English Corpus* (Tagliamonte 2002b), or the 1.8-million-word *Toronto English Archive* (Tagliamonte & D'Arcy 2007). These corpora constitute prolific resources for the investigation of discourse-pragmatic variables, as demonstrated in recent studies by Cheshire et al. (2011), D'Arcy (2007), Denis (2011), Ito & Tagliamonte (2003), Levey et al. (forthc.), Tagliamonte (2005, 2008), Tagliamonte & Denis (2010) and Waters (2013). Secondly, analyses of discourse-pragmatic variation and change in traditional sociolinguistic interviews can be supplemented, or even replaced, with analyses of other data sources. Notwithstanding obvious drawbacks such as their authenticity and comparability with corpus-based data of vernacular speech, internet newsgroups, instant messaging and popular television series provide valuable resources for investigating at least some discourse-pragmatic variables (e.g. Buchstaller et al. 2010; Tagliamonte & Denis 2008; Tagliamonte & Roberts 2005). In addition to boosting token numbers, web-based and media data may add a real-time dimension and wider geographical angle to apparent-time analyses, and capture short-lived innovations in discourse-pragmatics which may go undetected in analyses of synchronic private corpora (Buchstaller et al. 2010). These data thus have the potential not just to facilitate but also to enrich analyses of (sparse) discourse-pragmatic variables in traditional corpora.

8.3 Developing reliable analytical methods

Discourse-pragmatic features "are used by speakers in such complex and sophisticated ways [that] studying variation [and change] in their use is no straightforward task" (Stubbe & Holmes 1995:85). As previously discussed in this book, attempts to subject discourse-pragmatic features to accountable variationist investigation are complicated by two factors. Firstly, the Labovian framework is not easily applicable to the analysis of discourse-pragmatic variables (see Chapters 1.3 and 2.3). Secondly, the complexity of discourse-pragmatic features is not yet fully understood (Aijmer & Simon-Vandenbergen 2011). It would therefore be wrong to assume that the advances outlined in Section 8.1 result from scholars having fully surmounted the methodological difficulties they face in quantifying discourse-pragmatic variation and change.

In stark contrast to quantitative studies of lower-level phonological and morpho-syntactic variation and change which are relatively homogeneous and congruent in focus and methodology, studies of discourse-pragmatic variation and change lack a shared set of methodological and analytical principles. Macaulay (2002a: 284) neatly summarises the problems involved as follows:

> [t]here is no general agreement on methods of collecting or analyzing data, on what features are suitable for investigation, on how to identify possible discourse features, and what significance to attach to the use of a particular feature [...].

The persistent diversity of methods and the resultant lack of cross-corpora comparability impede significant progress. They make it difficult, if not altogether impossible, to synthesise the results of existing studies into a set of coherent findings, and thus, to formulate empirically grounded generalisations of discourse-pragmatic variation and change (see further Pichler 2010).

To address these problems, Pichler (2010) has advocated a uniform method for discourse variation analysis whose consistent application ensures reliability, intersubjectivity and comparability. The advocated method was elaborated and refined in Chapter 2 of this book, and its efficacy for uncovering the synchronic organisation of discourse-pragmatic variability was illustrated in Chapters 4 to 6. In addition to yielding accountable results and facilitating cross-corpora comparison, a great advantage of this methodology is that it can be tailored to the idiosyncrasies of a range of discourse-pragmatic variables, and that it can be developed and expanded to accommodate new theoretical insights into the complex nature of discourse-pragmatic features.

8.4 Exploring intra-linguistic constraints on discourse-pragmatic variation

In stark contrast to diachronic grammaticalisation studies which pay close attention to the morpho-syntactic and semantic-pragmatic properties of discourse-pragmatic features (e.g. Brinton 1996, 2008; van Bogaert 2010, 2011), synchronic variation studies have tended to focus most attention on these features' social meanings (e.g. Barbieri 2008; Crosby & Nyquist 1977; Dailey-O'Cain 2000; Macaulay 2002b, 2005; Stubbe & Holmes 1995; Woods 1991). The preoccupation with extra-linguistic factors at the expense of intra-linguistic factors is largely due to the methodological challenges outlined in Chapter 2.3, particularly those regarding the quantification of discourse-functionality and the circumscription of the variable context in linguistic-structural terms. Investigations focusing on social variation patterns in the overall frequency of discourse-pragmatic variables sidestep these difficulties because such patterns are identifiable without allocating tokens to functional categories or determining where in the linguistic system variables can but do not occur.

Consideration of social factors is, of course, a key concern of the variationist enterprise. Linguistic variation marks social differentiation, and linguistic changes are driven by social forces. However, the persistently narrow focus on social constraints in discourse variation studies to the near-exclusion of interactional-situational, discourse-functional and linguistic-structural constraints ignores the multi-dimensional nature of linguistic variation. As demonstrated in Part II of this book, the choice process in discourse-pragmatics is rarely constrained by social factors alone, and changes in discourse-pragmatics regularly manifest themselves in changes to variants' linguistic conditioning. It follows that studies which ignore the potential operation of non-social factors may yield incomplete, misleading or even inaccurate accounts of discourse-pragmatic variation. Moreover, they may fail to detect the mechanisms and trajectories of ongoing changes in discourse-pragmatics.

Successful resolution of the problems outlined at the beginning of this section depends on methodological advancements. Some progress in this direction has already been made. D'Arcy's (2005, 2007) study of discourse *like* in Toronto English has shown that the variable context for discourse-pragmatic variables can be circumscribed according to structural criteria. This makes possible linguistically based explanations for apparent-time frequency increases in variables' and/or variants' use. The present study has shown how multifunctionality can be incorporated as a parameter in the analysis to gauge reliable insights into the discourse-functional distribution of discourse-pragmatic variables. Recent studies of general extenders in contemporary varieties of British English have developed empirically accountable methods for operationalising the processes associated with grammaticalisation as independent variables for quantitative analysis (Cheshire 2007; Pichler & Levey 2011). Approaches such as these allow scholars to compare the linguistic distribution of variants across social cells and trace the linguistic trajectory of ongoing changes in apparent time. They thus yield important insights into the role of discourse-pragmatic features in the linguistic system.

8.5   Exploring patterns of discourse-pragmatic change

The variationist framework enables scholars to identify and trace ongoing linguistic changes by comparing patterns of synchronic variation across successive generations of speakers (see Chapters 2.3 and 4.5; Tagliamonte 2002a). Recent studies of intensifiers and quotatives demonstrate that the Labovian framework is well-suited to capturing the progression of rapidly changing discourse-pragmatic variables in synchronic dialect data (e.g. Buchstaller & D'Arcy 2009; Ito & Tagliamonte 2003; Tagliamonte 2005; Tagliamonte & D'Arcy 2004, 2007). Yet, as shown in Part II of this book and elsewhere (e.g. Pichler & Levey 2011; Raumolin-Brunberg & Nurmi 2001: 262), discourse-pragmatic change is not by definition quick and observable in the shallow time-span covered by synchronic corpora. The changes associated with grammaticalisation may take several decades, even centuries, to unfold and may involve long periods of stable variation (Bybee 2009: 350, 353; Traugott & Trousdale 2010: 28). A further complicating factor in the analysis of discourse-pragmatic change is the fact that the internal conditioning of discourse-pragmatic variation, which is key to observing grammaticalisation in cross-generational synchronic data, is under-researched (see Section 8.4 above). Without easy access to multiple stages in the diachronic development of discourse-pragmatic variables and without detailed knowledge of their linguistic conditioning, the existence, let alone the trajectory, of change cannot easily be inferred from synchronic data.

It comes as no surprise, then, that the body of variationist research into (ongoing) discourse-pragmatic change is negligible compared to the body of research into discourse-pragmatic variation, and that many questions surrounding the nature and mechanisms of (ongoing) discourse-pragmatic change remain virtually unexplored. Without access to a solid database of studies exploring diverse aspects of discourse-pragmatic change, we may not be able to provide satisfactory explanations of how synchronic structures of discourse-pragmatic variation emerge.

Information about the social embedding of discourse-pragmatic change cannot be gleaned from extant diachronic studies of language variation and change. Because they tend to assume that grammaticalisation changes are driven by language-internal factors, scholars of grammaticalisation are not generally concerned with examining the role of extra-linguistic factors when studying the diachronic development of discourse-pragmatic features (see, however, Beeching 2005, 2007; Bromhead 2009). Where extra-linguistic factors such as gender, socio-economic standing or speaker roles and relationships are considered in the investigation of diachronic data, these are generally correlated with usage patterns rather than usage changes (e.g. Culpeper & Kytö 2010; Jucker 2002; Lutzky 2008). Historical sociolinguistics, which is equipped to investigate the sociolinguistic embedding of changes at earlier stages of the language, has largely focused on analysing morpho-syntactic variables (see, however, Nevalainen 2008; Palander-Collin 1999). As a result, we lack comprehensive diachronic accounts of the social embedding of discourse-pragmatic change which could serve as a comparative baseline for synchronic variation studies.

Absent such data, discourse variationists may need to expand their synchronic databases into the past and exploit the increasing availability of diachronic corpora such as the *Corpus of Early English Correspondence* (Nevalainen & Raumolin-Brunberg 1996), the *Helsinki Corpus of English Texts* (Kytö 1996), the *Corpus of English Dialogues* (Kytö & Walker 2006), or the *Corpus of Late Modern English*

Texts (extended version) (De Smet 2005). These collections of written documents have obvious limitations for variationist analysis as regards their representativeness and authenticity, and they present methodological challenges as regards the reconstruction of social information and recovery of discourse functions (see Hernández-Campoy & Schilling-Estes 2012; Montgomery 2007 for comprehensive overviews of potential pitfalls). Nonetheless, if conducted with great care and acute awareness of these limitations (what Labov [1994: 11] calls "the art of making the best use of bad data"), variationist analyses of diachronic texts that represent language close to speech (e.g. trials, letters, conversations in novels, plays) will allow scholars to add historical depth to their synchronic analyses and probe the sociolinguistic dimension of discourse-pragmatic changes more extensively. In addition, the analysis of discourse-pragmatic change will benefit from the following: the construction of monitor corpora such as the *Diachronic Corpus of Tyneside English* (Buchstaller 2011), which consists of three corpora collected in three decades and at the time of writing spans five decades of speech recordings; and the availability of corpora such as the *Origins of New Zealand English Archive* (Gordon et al. 2007), a repository of longitudinal spoken language data that covers the history of New Zealand English from 1850 onwards. With their speakers born roughly a century apart, these corpora provide a fruitful resource for tracking slow or longer-term changes in discourse-pragmatics, as shown in recent work by Barnfield & Buchstaller (2010), Buchstaller (2011) and D'Arcy (2012). Exploring diachronic and real-time data has the added advantage that it allows scholars to verify hypotheses about discourse-pragmatic change which were formulated on the basis of synchronic analyses, as was the case in the present study.

8.6 Investigating the range of discourse-pragmatic variables

The gradual rise in the number of discourse variation studies produced in recent decades has not been accompanied by a meaningful broadening of the research focus to a wider and more diverse range of variables. Quotatives and intensifiers (and increasingly general extenders) continue to be the variables which feature most prominently on discourse variationists' all too narrow research agendas. To a great extent, the intense interest in quotatives and intensifiers is generated by their capacity to undergo rapid change and radical innovation within relatively short time-spans. The resultant co-existence of old and new usage patterns in synchronic cross-generational data makes it possible to study grammaticalisation in progress and investigate the often elusive actuation problem in language change (see, in particular, Tagliamonte & D'Arcy 2007, 2009). Other discourse-pragmatic variables have received far less quantitative attention and have been studied in far fewer varieties, not only because they may undergo change less quickly and are therefore less suitable to probing the mechanisms underlying discourse-pragmatic change in synchronic datasets (see Section 8.4 above) but also because they occur with lower frequency (see Section 8.2 above) and are less straightforward than quotatives and intensifiers to be conceptualised as discourse-pragmatic variables (see Chapter 2.3.2).

Variationist analyses of quotatives and intensifiers have addressed important questions about the nature and mechanisms of language variation and change. Yet they cannot in and of themselves constitute the basis for a theory of discourse-pragmatic variation and change. As uncovered by the comparable analyses in Part II of this book, the structure of discourse-pragmatic variation varies across variables, even those that are compositionally very similar, and is at least in part determined by variables' and variants' functional profiles. It is therefore unlikely that the female lead reported *inter alia* by Ferrara & Bell (1995), Ito & Tagliamonte (2003) and Tagliamonte & Hudson (1999) for changes in the quotative and intensifier systems extends without exception to all discourse-pragmatic variables, or that the morpho-syntactic expansion reported *inter alia* by Barnfield & Buchstaller (2010) and Ito & Tagliamonte (2003) for changes in intensification is a key diagnostic of increasing grammaticalisation across the board of variables (see Chapter 6 for counter-evidence to this hypothesis). In other words, we must not assume that findings produced by studies of quotatives and intensifiers will generalise to the range of discourse-pragmatic variables. A much wider range of functionally and syntactically diverse discourse-pragmatic features must be investigated before robust generalisations about discourse-pragmatic variation and change can be made.

A broadening of the field to include a more diverse range of discourse-pragmatic features in the quantitative analysis of linguistic variation and change is contingent on successful resolution of some of the problems highlighted in the preceding sections. The increasing construction and availability of mega-corpora and exploitation of web-based and media data will enable us to identify a more diverse set of discourse-pragmatic features that are highly variable, rapidly innovating or interesting in other ways. Also, easy access to diachronic and real-time data will allow us to explore the trajectories of variables which change less rapidly and rigorously than quotatives and intensifiers. The challenges we face are numerous but not insurmountable.

8.7 Conclusion

This chapter has by no means exhausted the challenges scholars need to over-come in order to advance the field of variationist discourse studies beyond its current state. The fact remains that we still have a long way to go before we can even contemplate formulating a general theory of discourse-pragmatic variation and change. Our journey to theoretically grounded analyses and to a fuller understanding of the labyrinthine intricacies of discourse-pragmatic variation and change may be less arduous if we collaborate more closely with scholars working in other research paradigms. Terkourafi's (2011) conceptualisation of higher-level variables in terms of stable inference processes shows how developments in pragmatics can provide a theoretical underpinning for variationist research tools (see Chapter 2.3.2). This study (and others before it) has benefited from the insights furnished by grammaticalisation studies in uncovering and explaining the structure of discourse-pragmatic variation. The current rudimentary state of discourse variation analysis can be overcome if we commit ourselves to increased cross-disciplinary dialogue.

References

Adger, David & Jennifer Smith. 2005. "Variation and the minimalist programme". *Syntax and Variation. Reconciling the Biological and the Social* ed. by Leonie Cornips & Karen Corrigan, 149–179. Amsterdam: John Benjamins.

Aijmer, Karin. 1997. "I think – an English modal particle". *Modality in Germanic Languages. Historical and Comparative Perspectives* ed. by Toril Swan & Olaf Jansen Westvik, 1–47. Berlin: Mouton de Gruyter.

Aijmer, Karin. 2002. *English Discourse Particles. Evidence from a Corpus.* Amsterdam: John Benjamins.

Aijmer, Karin. 2009. "'So er I just sort I dunno I think it's just because …': A corpus study of *I don't know* and *I dunno* in learners' spoken English". *Corpora. Pragmatics and Discourse* ed. by Andreas H. Jucker, Schreier Daniel & Marianne Hundt, 151–168. Amsterdam: Rodopi.

Aijmer, Karin & Anne-Marie Simon-Vandenbergen. 2011. "Pragmatic markers". *Discursive Pragmatics* ed. by Jan Zienkowski, Jan-Ola Östman & Jef Verschueren, 223–247. Amsterdam: John Benjamins.

Aitken, A. J. 1979. "Scottish speech: A historical view, with special reference to the Standard English of Scotland". *Languages of Scotland* ed. by A. J. Aitken & Tom McArthur, 85–118. Edinburgh: Chambers.

Aitken, A. J. 1984. "Scots and English in Scotland". *Language in the British Isles* ed. by Peter Trudgill, 517–532. Cambridge: Cambridge University Press.

Akatsuka, Noriko. 1985. "Conditionals and the epistemic scale". *Language* 61:3.625–639.

Algeo, John. 1988. "The tag question in British English: It's different, i'n'it?". *English World-Wide* 9:2.171–191.

Algeo, John. 1990. "It's a myth, innit? Politeness and the English tag question". *The State of the Language* ed. by Christopher Ricks & Leonard Michaels, 443–450. London: Faber & Faber.

Andersen, Elaine S., Maquea Briznela, Beatrice Du Puy & Laura Gonnerman. 1999. "Cross-linguistic evidence for the early acquisition of discourse markers as register variables". *Journal of Pragmatics* 31:11.1339–1357.

Andersen, Gisle. 1998. Are tag questions questions? Evidence from spoken data. Paper presented at the 19th ICAME Conference, May, Belfast.

Andersen, Gisle. 2001. *Pragmatic Markers and Sociolinguistic Variation. A Relevance-Theoretic Approach to the Language of Adolescents.* Amsterdam: John Benjamins.

Anderwald, Lieselotte. 2002. *Negation in Non-Standard British English. Gaps, Regularizations and Asymmetries.* London: Routledge.

Axelsson, Karin. 2011. Tag questions in fiction dialogue. PhD diss., University of Gothenburg.

Baayen, R. H. 2008. *Analysing Linguistic Data. A Practical Introduction to Statistics Using R.* Cambridge: Cambridge University Press.

Bailey, Guy. 2002. "Real and apparent time". *The Handbook of Language Variation and Change* ed. by J. K. Chambers, Peter Trudgill & Natalie Schilling-Estes, 312–332. Oxford: Blackwell.

Bakht, Maryam M. 2010. Lexical variation and the negotiation of linguistic style in a Long Island middle school. PhD diss., New York University.

Barbieri, Federica. 2008. "Patterns of age-based linguistic variation in American English". *Journal of Sociolinguistics* 12: 1.58–88.

Barnfield, Kate & Isabelle Buchstaller. 2010. "Intensifiers in Tyneside: Longitudinal developments and new trends". *English World-Wide* 31: 3.252–287.

Barron, Anne. 2008. "Contrasting requests in Inner Circle Englishes: A study in variational pragmatics". *Developing Contrastive Pragmatics. Interlanguage and Cross-Cultural Perspectives* ed. by Martin Pütz & JoAnne Neff-van Aertselaer, 355–402. Berlin: Mouton de Gruyter.

Baumgarten, Nicole & Juliane House. 2010. "*I think* and *I don't know* in English as lingua franca and native English discourse". *Journal of Pragmatics* 42: 4.1184–1200.

Bayley, Robert. 2002. "The quantitative paradigm". *The Handbook of Language Variation and Change* ed. by J. K. Chambers, Peter Trudgill & Natalie Schilling-Estes, 117–141. Oxford: Blackwell.

Bazzanella, Carla. 2006. "Discourse markers in Italian: Towards a 'compositional' meaning". *Approaches to Discourse Particles* ed. by Kerstin Fischer, 449–464. Amsterdam: Elsevier.

Beach, Wayne A. & Terri R. Metzger. 1997. "Claiming insufficient knowledge". *Human Communication Research* 23: 4.562–588.

Beal, Joan. 1993. "The grammar of Tyneside and Northumbrian English". *Real English. The Grammar of British English Dialects* ed. by James Milroy & Lesley Milroy, 187–213. London: Longman.

Beal, Joan. 1997. "Syntax and morphology". *The Edinburgh History of the Scots Language* ed. by Charles Jones, 335–377. Edinburgh: Edinburgh University Press.

Beal, Joan. 2004. "English dialects in the North of England: Morphology and syntax". *A Handbook of Varieties of English. A Multimedia Reference Tool. Vol. 2: Morphology and Syntax* ed. by Bernd Kortmann, Kate Burridge, Rajend Mesthrie, Edgar W. Schneider & Clive Upton, 114–141. Berlin: Mouton de Gruyter.

Beal, Joan C. & Karen P. Corrigan. 2005. "*No, nay, never*: Negation in Tyneside English". *Aspects of English Negation* ed. by Yoko Iyeiri, 139–156. Amsterdam: John Benjamins.

Beeching, Kate. 2005. "Politeness-induced semantic change". *Language Variation and Change* 17: 2.155–180.

Beeching, Kate. 2007. "A politeness-theoretic approach to pragmatico-semantic change". *Journal of Historical Pragmatics* 8: 1.69–108.

Bell, Allan & Gary Johnson. 1997. "Towards a sociolinguistics of style". *University of Pennsylvania Working Papers in Linguistics* 4: 1.1–21.

Berkley, Susan. 2002. "How to cure the 'verbal virus': A five-step treatment plan", <http://www.school-for-champions.com/speaking/verbalvirus.htm> (01 March 2011).

Biber, Douglas, Stig Johansson, Geoffrey Leech, Edward Finnegan & Susan Conrad. 1999. *The Longman Grammar of Spoken and Written English*. London: Longman.

Bisang, Walter. 2004. "Grammaticalization without co-evolution of form and meaning: The case of tense-aspect-modality in East and Mainland Southeast Asia". *What Makes Grammaticalization? A Look from Its Fringes and Components* ed. by Walter Bisang, Nikolaus Himmelmann & Bjoern Wiemer, 109–138. Berlin: Mouton de Gruyter.

Blakemore, Diane. 1987. *Semantic Constraints on Relevance*. Oxford: Blackwell.

Blakemore, Diane. 1988. "*So* as a constraint on relevance". *Mental Representations. The Interface between Language and Reality* ed. by Ruth M. Kempson, 183–195. Cambridge: Cambridge University Press.

Boye, Kasper & Peter Harder. 2007. "Complement-taking predicates: Usage and linguistic structure". *Studies in Language* 31:3.569–606.

Brinton, Laurel J. 1996. *Pragmatic Markers in English. Grammaticalization and Discourse Function*. Berlin: Mouton de Gruyter.

Brinton, Laurel J. 2001. "Historical discourse analysis". *The Handbook of Discourse Analysis* ed. by Deborah Schiffrin, Deborah Tannen & Heidi E. Hamilton, 138–160. Oxford: Blackwell.

Brinton, Laurel J. 2005. "Processes underlying the development of pragmatic markers: The case of *(I) say*". *Opening Windows on Texts and Discourses of the Past* ed. by Janne Skaffari, 279–299. Amsterdam: John Benjamins.

Brinton, Laurel J. 2006. "Pathways in the development of pragmatic markers in English". *The Handbook of the History of English* ed. by Ans van Kemenade & Bettelou Los, 307–334. London: Blackwell.

Brinton, Laurel J. 2007. "The development of *I mean*: Implications for the study of historical pragmatics". *Methods in Historical Pragmatics* ed. by Susan Fitzmaurice & Irma Taavitsainen, 37–79. Berlin: Mouton de Gruyter.

Brinton, Laurel J. 2008. *The Comment Clause in English. Syntactic Origins and Pragmatic Development*. Cambridge: Cambridge University Press.

Britain, David. 2002. "Space and spatial diffusion". *The Handbook of Language Variation and Change* ed. by J. K. Chambers, Peter Trudgill & Natalie Schilling-Estes, 603–637. Oxford: Blackwell.

Britain, David, ed. 2007. *Language in the British Isles*. Cambridge: Cambridge University Press.

Britton, Derek. 2002. Northern fronting and the north Lincolnshire merger of the reflexes of ME /u:/ and ME /o:/. *Language Sciences* 24:3-4.221–229.

Bromhead, Helen. 2009. *The Reign of Truth and Faith. Epistemic Expressions in 16th and 17th Century English*. Berlin: Mouton de Gruyter.

Brown, Gillian. 1977. *Listening to Spoken English*. London: Longman.

Brown, Gillian & George Yule. 1983. *Discourse Analysis*. Cambridge: Cambridge University Press.

Brown, Keith & Martin Millar. 1980. "Auxiliary verbs in Edinburgh speech". *Transactions of the Philological Society* 78:1.81–133.

Brown, Penelope & Stephen C. Levinson. 1987. *Politeness. Some Universals in Language Usage*. Cambridge: Cambridge University Press.

Bublitz, Wolfram. 1992. "Transferred negation and modality". *Journal of Pragmatics* 18:5-6.551–577.

Buchstaller, Isabelle. 2004. The sociolinguistic constraints on the quotative system – British English and US English compared. PhD diss., University of Edinburgh.

Buchstaller, Isabelle. 2006a. "Diagnostics of age-graded linguistic behaviour: The case of the quotative system". *Journal of Sociolinguistics* 10:1.3–30.

Buchstaller, Isabelle. 2006b. "Social stereotypes, personality traits and regional perception displaced: Attitudes towards the 'new' quotatives in the U.K.". *Journal of Sociolinguistics* 10:3.362–381.

Buchstaller, Isabelle. 2008. "The localization of global linguistic variants". *English World-Wide* 29:1.15–44.

Buchstaller, Isabelle. 2011. "Quotations across the generations: A multivariate analysis of speech and thought introducers across 5 decades of Tyneside speech". *Corpus Linguistics and Linguistic Theory* 7:1.59–92.

Buchstaller, Isabelle & Alexandra D'Arcy. 2009. "Localised globalization: A multi-local, multi-variate investigation of quotative *be like*". *Journal of Sociolinguistics* 13:3.291–331.

Buchstaller, Isabelle, John R. Rickford, Elizabeth Closs Traugott, Thomas Wasow & Arnold Zwicky. 2010. "The sociolinguistics of a short-lived innovation: Tracking the development of quotative *all* across spoken and internet corpora". *Language Variation and Change* 22:2.191–219.

Burnard, Lou, ed. 2000. "The British National Corpus users reference guide", http://www.natcorp.ox.ac.uk/docs/userManual (21 January 2010).

Bybee, Joan. 2001. *Phonology and Language Use*. Cambridge: Cambridge University Press.

Bybee, Joan. 2003. "Mechanisms of change in grammaticization: The role of frequency". *The Handbook of Historical Linguistics* ed. by Brian D. Joseph & Richard D. Janda, 602–623. London: Blackwell.

Bybee, Joan. 2006. "From usage to grammar: The mind's response to repetition". *Language* 82:4.711–733.

Bybee, Joan. 2009. "Grammaticization: Implications for a theory of language". *Crosslinguistic Approaches to the Psychology of Language. Research in the Tradition of Isaac Slobin* ed. by Jiansheng Guo, Eelena Lieven, Nanchy Budwig, Susan Ervin-Tripp, Keiko Nakamura & Seyda Özçaliskan, 345–355. Hove: Psychology Press.

Bybee, Joan. 2010. *Language, Usage and Cognition*. Cambridge: Cambridge University Press.

Bybee, Joan. 2011. "Usage-based theory and grammaticalization". *The Oxford Handbook of Grammaticalization* ed. by Heiko Narrog & Bernd Heine, 69–78. Oxford: Oxford University Press.

Bybee, Joan & Paul Hopper. 2001. "Introduction to frequency and the emergence of linguistic structure". *Frequency and the Emergence of Linguistic Structure* ed. by Joan Bybee & Paul Hopper, 1–24. Amsterdam: John Benjamins.

Bybee, Joan & Joanne Scheibman. 1999. "The effect of usage on degrees of constituency: The reduction of *don't* in English". *Linguistics* 37:4.575–596.

Cameron, Deborah. 2001. *Working with Spoken Discourse*. London: Sage.

Cameron, Deborah. 2005. "Language, gender, and sexuality: Current issues and new directions". *Applied Linguistics* 26:4.482–502.

Cameron, Deborah, Fiona McAlinden & Kathy O'Leary. 1988. "Lakoff in context: The social and linguistic functions of tag questions". *Women in Their Speech Communities* ed. by Jennifer Coates & Deborah Cameron, 74–93. London: Longman.

Campbell, Lyle. 2001. "What's wrong with grammaticalization?". *Language Sciences* 23:2-3.113–161.

Cattell, Ray. 1973. "Negative transportation and tag questions". *Language* 49:3.612–639.

Cheshire, Jenny. 1981. "Variation in the use of *ain't* in an urban British English dialect". *Language in Society* 10:2.365–381.

Cheshire, Jenny. 1982. *Variation in an English Dialect. A Sociolinguistic Study*. Cambridge: Cambridge University Press.

Cheshire, Jenny. 1987. "Syntactic variation, the linguistic variable, and sociolinguistic theory". *Linguistics* 25:2.257–282.

Cheshire, Jenny. 1997. "Involvement in 'standard' and 'nonstandard' English". *Taming the Vernacular. From Dialect to Written Standard Language* ed. by Jenny Cheshire & Dieter Stein, 68–82. Harlow: Longman.

Cheshire, Jenny. 1998. "English negation from an interactional perspective". *Negation in the History of English* ed. by Ingrid Tieken-Boon van Ostade, Gunnel Tottie & Wim van der Wurff, 29–53. Berlin: Mouton de Gruyter.

Cheshire, Jenny. 2005. "Syntactic variation and beyond: Gender and social class variation in the use of discourse-new markers". *Journal of Sociolinguistics* 9:4.479–508.

Cheshire, Jenny. 2007. "Discourse variation, grammaticalisation and stuff like that". *Journal of Sociolinguistics* 11:2.155–193.

Cheshire, Jenny, Paul Kerswill, Sue Fox & Eivind Torgersen. 2011. "Contact, the feature pool and the speech community: The emergence of Multicultural London English". *Journal of Sociolinguistics* 15:2.151–196.

Cheshire, Jenny, Paul Kerswill & Ann Williams. 2005. "Phonology, grammar, and discourse in dialect convergence". *Dialect Change. Convergence and Divergence in European Languages* ed. by Peter Auer, Frans Hinskens & Paul Kerswill, 135–167. Cambridge: Cambridge University Press.

Coates, Jennifer. 1987. "Epistemic modality and spoken discourse". *Transactions of the Philological Society* 85:1.110–131.

Coates, Jennifer. 1996. *Women Talk. Conversations between Women Friends*. Oxford: Blackwell.

Coates, Jennifer. 2004. *Women, Men and Language. A Sociolinguistic Account of Gender Differences in Language*. 3rd ed. London: Pearson.

Corbett, John, J. Derrick McClure & Jane Stuart-Smith. 2003. "A brief history of Scots". *The Edinburgh Companion to Scots* ed. by John Corbett, J. Derrick McClure & Jane Stuart-Smith, 1–16. Edinburgh: Edinburgh University Press.

Couper-Kuhlen, Elizabeth & Margret Selting. 1996. "Towards an interactional perspective on prosody and a prosodic perspective on interaction". *Prosody in Conversation* ed. by Elizabeth Couper-Kuhlen & Margret Selting, 11–56. Cambridge: Cambridge University Press.

Coupland, Nikolas. 1983. "Patterns of encounter management: Further arguments for discourse variables". *Language in Society* 12:3.459–476.

Craigie, William, Adam J. Aitken, James A. C. Stevenson, Harry D. Watson, Margaret G. Dareau & K. Lorna Pike, eds. 1937–2002. *A Dictionary of the Older Scottish Tongue*. Aberdeen: Aberdeen University Press.

Croft, William. 1990. *Typology and Universals*. Cambridge: Cambridge University Press.

Crosby, Faye & Linda Nyquist. 1977. "The female register: An empirical study of Lakoff's hypotheses". *Language in Society* 6:3.313–322.

Culpeper, Jonathan & Merja Kytö. 2010. *Early Modern English Dialogues. Spoken Interaction as Writing*. Cambridge: Cambridge University Press.

Dailey-O'Cain, Jennifer. 2000. "The sociolinguistic distribution of and attitudes toward focuser *like* and quotative *like*". *Journal of Sociolinguistics* 4:1.60–80.

D'Arcy, Alexandra. 2005. *Like*: Syntax and development. PhD diss., University of Toronto.

D'Arcy, Alexandra. 2007. "*Like* and language ideology: Disentangling fact from fiction". *American Speech* 82:4.386–419.

D'Arcy, Alexandra. 2011. "Corpora: Capturing language in use". *Analysing Variation in English* ed. by Warren Maguire & April McMahon, 49–71. Cambridge: Cambridge University Press.

D'Arcy, Alexandra. 2012. "The diachrony of quotation: Evidence from New Zealand English". *Language Variation and Change* 24:3.343–369.

Degand, Liesbeth & Anne-Marie Simon-Vandenbergen, eds. 2011. Grammaticalization, Pragmaticalization and/or (Inter)Subjectification: Methodological Issues for the Study of Discourse Markers. Thematic issue: *Linguistics* 49:2.

Dehé, Nicole & Anne Wichmann. 2010. "The multifunctionality of epistemic parentheticals in discourse: Prosodic cues to the semantic-pragmatic boundary". *Functions of Language* 17:1.1–25.

Denis, Derek. 2011. "Innovators & innovation: Tracking the innovators of *and stuff* in York English". *University of Pennsylvania Working Papers in Linguistics* 17:2.60–70.

Denis, Derek. MS. Grammaticalization of general extenders in York English. Unpublished manuscript, University of Toronto.

De Smet, Henrik. 2005. "A corpus of Late Modern English texts". *International Computer Archive of Modern and Medieval English* 29.69–82.

Diani, Giuliana. 2004. "The discourse functions of *I don't know* in English conversation". *Discourse Patterns in Spoken and Written Corpora* ed. by Karin Aijmer & Anna-Brita Stenström, 157–171. Amsterdam: John Benjamins.

Diewald, Gabriele. 2006. "Discourse particles and modal particles as grammatical elements". *Approaches to Discourse Particles* ed. by Kerstin Fischer, 403–425. Amsterdam: Elsevier.

Dines, Elizabeth R. 1980. "Variation in discourse – 'and stuff like that'". *Language in Society* 9: 1.13–31.

Douglas, Fiona M. 2003. "Scottish Corpus of Text and Speech: Problems of corpus design". *Literary and Linguistic Computing* 18: 1.23–37.

Douglas-Cowie, Ellen. 1978. "Linguistic code-switching in a Northern Irish village: Social interaction and social ambition". *Sociolinguistic Patterns in British English* ed. by Peter Trudgill, 37–51. London: Edward Arnold.

Drager, Katie. 2011. "Sociophonetic variation and the lemma". *Journal of Phonetics* 39: 4.694–707.

Drew, Paul. 1992. "Contested evidence in courtroom cross-examination: The case of a trial for rape". *Talk at Work. Interaction in Institutional Settings* ed. by Paul Drew & John Heritage, 470–520. Cambridge: Cambridge University Press.

Dubois, Betty Lou & Isabel Crouch. 1975. "The question of tag questions in women's speech: They don't really use more of them, do they?". *Language in Society* 4: 3.289–294.

Du Bois, John W., Stephan Schuetze-Coburn, Susanna Cumming & Danae Paolino. 1993. "Outline of discourse transcription". *Talking Data. Transcription and Coding in Discourse Research* ed. by Jane A. Edwards & Martin D. Lampert, 45–89. Hillsdale: Lawrence Erlbaum.

Eckardt, Regine. 2012. "Grammaticalization and semantic reanalysis". *Semantics. An International Handbook of Natural Language Meaning. Vol. 3.* ed. by Claudia Maienborn, Klaus von Heusinger & Paul Portner, 2675–2702. Berlin: Mouton de Gruyter.

Eckert, Penelope. 1997. "Age as a sociolinguistic variable". *The Handbook of Sociolinguistics* ed. by Florian Coulmas, 151–167. Oxford: Blackwell.

Eckert, Penelope & Sally McConnell-Ginet. 1992. "Think practically and look locally: Language and gender as community-based practice". *Annual Review of Anthropology* 21.461–490.

Edelsky, Carole. 1993. "Who's got the floor?". *Gender and Conversational Interaction* ed. by Deborah Tannen, 189–227. Oxford: Oxford University Press.

Erman, Britt. 1987. *Pragmatic Expressions in English. A Study of* you know, you see *and* I mean *in Face-to-Face Conversation*. Stockholm: Minab/Gotab.

Erman, Britt. 1992. "Female and male usage of pragmatic expressions in same-gender and mixed-gender interaction". *Language Variation and Change* 4: 2.217–234.

Erman, Britt. 1998. "'Just wear the wig innit!' From identifying and proposition-oriented to intensifying and speaker-oriented: Grammaticalization in progress". *Papers from the 16th Scandinavian Conference of Linguistics* ed. by Timo Hankioja, 87–100. University of Turku: Department of Finnish and General Linguistics.

Erman, Britt. 2001. "Pragmatic markers revisited with a focus on *you know* in adult and adolescent talk". *Journal of Pragmatics* 32: 9.1337–1359.

Erman, Britt & Ulla-Britt Kotsinas. 1993. "Pragmaticalization: The case of *ba'* and *you know*". *Acta Universitatis Stockholmiensis*, 76–93. Stockholm: Almqvist and Wiksell.

Escalera, Elena Andrea. 2009. "Gender differences in children's use of discourse markers: Separate worlds or different contexts?". *Journal of Pragmatics* 41: 12.2479–2495.

Ferrara, Kathleen W. 1997. "Form and function of the discourse marker *anyway*: Implications for discourse analysis". *Linguistics* 35: 2.343–378.

Ferrara, Kathleen W. & Barbara Bell. 1995. "Sociolinguistic variation and discourse function of constructed dialogue introducers: The case of *be* + *like*". *American Speech* 70: 3.265–289.

Fetzer, Anita. 2011. "'I think this is I mean perhaps this is too erm too tough a view of the world but I often think …': Redundancy as a contextualization device". *Language Sciences* 33: 2.255–267.

Fillmore, Charles J. 1963. "The position of embedding transformation in a grammar". *Word* 19.208–231.

Fischer, Kerstin. 2000. "Discourse particles, turn-taking, and the semantics-pragmatics interface". *Revue de Sémantique et Pragmatique* 8.111–137.

Fischer, Kerstin. 2006. "Towards an understanding of the spectrum of approaches to discourse particles: Introduction to the volume". *Approaches to Discourse Particles* ed. by Kerstin Fischer, 1–20. Amsterdam: Elsevier.

Fischer, Olga. 1998. "On negative raising in the history of English". *Negation in the History of English* ed. by Ingrid Tieken-Boon von Ostade, Gunnel Tottie & Wim van der Wurff, 55–100. Berlin: Mouton de Gruyter.

Fishman, Pamela. 1983. "Interaction: The work women do". *Language, Gender and Society* ed. by Barrie Thorne, Cheris Kramarae & Nancy Henley, 89–101. Cambridge: Newbury House.

Fleischman, Suzanne. 1999. Pragmatic markers in comparative and historical perspective: Theoretical implications of a case study. Paper presented at the 14th International Conference on Historical Linguistics, August, Vancouver.

Ford, Cecilia E. 2001. "At the intersection of turn and sequence: Negation and what comes next". *Studies in Interactional Linguistics* ed. by Margret Selting, 51–79. Amsterdam: John Benjamins.

Ford, Cecilia E. & Sandra A. Thompson. 1996. "Interactional units in conversation: Syntactic, intonational, and pragmatic resources for the management of turns". *Interaction and Grammar* ed. by Elinor Ochs, Emanuel A. Schegloff & Sandra A. Thompson, 134–184. Cambridge: Cambridge University Press.

Foulkes, Paul & Gerard J. Docherty. 1999. "Urban voices – overview". *Urban Voices. Accent Studies in the British Isles* ed. by Paul Foulkes & Gerard J. Docherty, 1–24. London: Arnold.

Fox, Barbara A., Makoto Hayashi & Robert Jasperson. 1996. "Resources and repair: A cross-linguistic study of syntax and repair". *Interaction and Grammar* ed. by Elinor Ochs, Emanuel A. Schegloff & Sandra A. Thompson, 185–237. Cambridge: Cambridge University Press.

Fox Tree, Jean E. 2007. "Folk notions of *um* and *uh*, *you know*, and *like*". *Text & Talk* 27: 3.297–314.

Fox Tree, Jean E. 2010. "Discourse markers across speakers and settings". *Language and Linguistics Compass* 4: 5.269–281.

Frank-Job, Barbara. 2006. "A dynamic-interactional approach to discourse markers". *Approaches to Discourse Particles* ed. by Kerstin Fischer, 359–374. Amsterdam: Elsevier.

Fraser, Bruce. 1980. "Conversational mitigation". *Journal of Pragmatics* 4: 4.341–350.

Fraser, Bruce. 1990. "An approach to discourse markers". *Journal of Pragmatics* 14: 3.383–395.

Fraser, Bruce. 1999. "What are discourse markers?". *Journal of Pragmatics* 31: 7.931–952.

Fuller, Janet M. 2001. "The principle of pragmatic detachability in borrowing: English-origin discourse markers in Pennsylvania German". *Linguistics* 39: 2.351–369.

Fuller, Janet M. 2003. "The influence of speaker roles on discourse marker use". *Journal of Pragmatics* 35:1.23–45.

Furman, Reyhan & Asli Özyürek. 2007. "Development of interactional discourse markers: Insights from Turkish children's and adults' oral narratives". *Journal of Pragmatics* 39:10.1742–1757.

Geluykens, Ronald. 1993. "Topic introduction in English conversation". *Transactions of the Philological Society* 91:2.181–214.

Gisborne, Nikolas & Graeme Trousdale. 2008. "Constructional approaches to language-particular description". *Constructional Approaches to English Grammar* ed. by Graeme Trousdale & Nikolas Gisborne, 1–4. Berlin: Mouton de Gruyter.

Givón, Talmy. 1993. *English Grammar. A Function-Based Introduction.* Amsterdam: John Benjamins.

Glauser, Beat. 1974. *The Scottish-English Linguistic Border. Lexical Aspects.* Bern: Francke.

Goffman, Erving. 1967. *Interaction Ritual. Essays on Face to Face Behavior.* Garden City, New York: Doubleday.

Goldberg, Adele E. 1995. *A Construction Grammar Approach to Argument Structure.* Chicago: University of Chicago Press.

Goldberg, Julia Anna. 1980. Discourse particles: An analysis of the role of *y'know, I mean, well* and *actually* in conversation. PhD diss., University of Cambridge.

Gordon, Elizabeth, Jennifer Hay & Margaret Maclagan. 2007. "The ONZE corpus". *Creating and Digitizing Language Corpora* ed. by Joan C. Beal, Karen P. Corrigan & Herman L. Moisl, 82–104. New York: Palgrave Macmillan.

Goss, Emily L. & Joseph C. Salmons. 2000. "The evolution of bilingual discourse marking: Modal particles and English markers in 19th century German-American dialects". *International Journal of Bilingualism* 4:4.469–494.

Grant, Lynn E. 2010. "A corpus comparison of the use of *I don't know* by British and New Zealand speakers". *Journal of Pragmatics* 42:9.2282–2296.

Grant, William & James M. Dixon. 1921. *Manual of Modern Scots.* Cambridge: Cambridge University Press.

Grant, William & David D. Murison. 1931. *The Scottish National Dictionary.* Aberdeen: Aberdeen University Press.

Gregory, Michelle, William D. Raymond, Alan Bell, E. Fosler-Lussier & Daniel Jurafsky. 1999. "The effects of collocational strength and contextual predictability in lexical production". *Chicago Linguistic Society* 35.151–166.

Greenbaum, Sidney. 1992. "A new corpus of English: ICE". *Directions in Corpus Linguistics. Proceedings of Nobel Symposium 82, Stockholm 4–8 August 1991* ed. by Jan Svartvik, 171–183. Berlin: Mouton de Gruyter.

Griffiths, Bill. 2005. *A Dictionary of North-East Dialect.* 2nd ed. Newcastle: Northumbria University Press.

Günthner, Susanne. 2000. "From concessive connector to discourse marker: The use of *obwohl* in everyday German interaction". *Cause, Condition, Concession, Contrast* ed. by Elizabeth Couper-Kuhlen & Bernd Kortmann, 439–468. Berlin: Mouton de Gruyter.

Guy, Gregory R. 1980. "Variation in the group and the individual: The case of final stop deletion". *Locating Language in Time and Space* ed. by William Labov, 1–36. New York: Academic Press.

Guy, Gregory G. 1993. "The quantitative analysis of linguistic variation". *American Dialect Research* ed. by Dennis Preston, 223–249. Amsterdam: John Benjamins.

Halliday, M. A. K. 1979. "Modes of meaning and modes of expression: Types of grammatical structures and their determination by different semantic functions". *Function and Context in Linguistic Analysis. A Festschrift for William Haas* ed. by D. J. Allerton, Edward Carney & David Holdcroft, 57–79. Cambridge: Cambridge University Press.

Halliday, M. A. K. 1985. *Introduction to Functional Grammar*. London: Arnold.

Halliday, M. A. K. & Ruqaiya Hasan. 1976. *Cohesion in English*. London: Longman.

Hansen, Maj-Britt Mosegaard. 2006. "A dynamic polysemy approach to the lexical semantics of discourse markers (with an exemplary analysis of *toujours*)". *Approaches to Discourse Particles* ed. by Kerstin Fischer, 21–41. Amsterdam: Elsevier.

Harris, Sandra. 1984. "Questions as a mode of control in the magistrates' courts". *International Journal of the Sociology of Language* 49:1.5–27.

Haspelmath, Martin. 2004. "On directionality in language change with a particular reference to grammaticalization". *Up and Down the Cline. The Nature of Grammaticalization* ed. by Olga Fischer, Muriel Norde & Harry Perridon, 17–44. Amsterdam: John Benjamins.

Hazen, Kirk. 2000. "The role of researcher identity in conducting sociolinguistic research: A reflective case study". *Southern Journal of Linguistics* 24.103–120.

He, Agnes Weiyun. 1993. "Exploring modality in institutional interaction: Cases from academic counselling encounters". *Text* 13:4.503–528.

Heine, Bernd. 1993. *Auxiliaries. Cognitive Forces and Grammaticalization*. Oxford: Oxford University Press.

Heine, Bernd. 2003. "Grammaticalization". *The Handbook of Historical Linguistics* ed. by Brian D. Joseph & Richard D. Janda, 575–601. London: Blackwell.

Heinemann, Trine. 2005. "Where grammar and interaction meet: The preference for matched polarity in responsive turns in Danish". *Syntax and Lexis in Conversation. Studies on the Use of Linguistic Resources in Talk-in-Interaction* ed. by Auli Hakulinen & Margret Selting, 375–402. Amsterdam: John Benjamins.

Heritage, John. 1984. *Garfinkel and Ethnomethodology*. Cambridge: Polity Press.

Heritage, John & J. Maxwell Atkinson. 1984. "Introduction". *Structures of Social Action. Studies in Conversation Analysis* ed. by J. Maxwell Atkinson & John Heritage, 1–15. Cambridge: Cambridge University Press.

Hernández-Campoy, Juan Manuel & Natalie Schilling-Estes. 2012. "The application of the quantitative paradigm to historical sociolinguistics: Problems with the generalisability principle". *The Handbook of Historical Sociolinguistics* ed. by Juan Manuel Hernández-Campoy & J. Camilo Conde-Silvestre, 63–79. Oxford: Wiley-Blackwell.

Hewitt, Roger. 1986. *White Talk Black Talk. Inter-Racial Friendship and Communication amongst Adolescents*. Cambridge: Cambridge University Press.

Himmelmann, Nikolaus P. 2004. "Lexicalization and grammaticization: Opposite or orthogonal?" *What Makes Grammaticalization? A Look from Its Fringes and Its Components* ed. by Walter Bisang, Nikolaus P. Himmelmann & Björn Wiener, 21–42. Berlin: Mouton de Gruyter.

Hirschberg, Julia & Diane Litman. 1993. "Empirical studies on the disambiguation of cue phrases". *Computational Linguistics* 19:3.501–531.

Hllavac, Jim. 2006. "Bilingual discourse markers: Evidence from Croatian-English code-switching". *Journal of Pragmatics* 38:11.1870–1900.

Hoffmann, Sebastian. 2006. "Tag questions in Early and Late Modern English: Historical description and theoretical implications". *Anglistik* 17:2.35–55.

Hoffmann, Sebastian, Anne-Katrin Blass & Joybrato Mukherjee. forthc. "Canonical tag questions in Asian Englishes: Forms, functions and frequencies in Hong Kong English, Indian English and Singapore English". *The Oxford Handbook of World Englishes* ed. by Markku Filppula, Juhani Klemola & Devyani Sharma. Oxford: Oxford University Press.

Holmes, Janet. 1982. "The functions of tag questions". *English Language Research Journal* 4.40–65.

Holmes, Janet. 1984a. "Hedging your bets and sitting on the fence: Some evidence for hedges as support structures". *Te Reo* 27.47–62.

Holmes, Janet. 1984b. "Modifying illocutionary force". *Journal of Pragmatics* 8:3.345–365.

Holmes, Janet. 1986. "Functions of *you know* in women's and men's speech". *Language in Society* 15:1.1–22.

Holmes, Janet. 1987. "Hedging, fencing and other conversational gambits: An analysis of gender differences in New Zealand speech". *Women and Language in Australian and New Zealand Society* ed. by Anne Pauwels, 47–62. Sydney: Australian Professional Publications.

Holmes, Janet. 1990. "Hedges and boosters in women's and men's speech". *Language and Communication* 10:3.185–205.

Holmes, Janet. 1995. *Women, Men and Politeness.* London: Longman.

Hooper, Joan B. 1975. "On assertive predicates". *Syntax and Semantics* ed. by John P. Kimball, 91–124. London: Academic Press.

Hopper, Paul J. 1991. "On some principles of grammaticization". *Approaches to Grammaticalization. Vol. 1: Focus on Theoretical and Methodological Issues* ed. by Elizabeth Closs Traugott & Bernd Heine, 17–35. Amsterdam: John Benjamins.

Hopper, Paul J. & Elizabeth Closs Traugott. 2003. *Grammaticalization.* 2nd ed. Cambridge: Cambridge University Press.

Horn, Laurence R. 1978. "Remarks on neg-raising". *Syntax and Semantics. Pragmatics* ed. by Peter Cole, 129–220. London: Academic Press.

Horn, Laurence R. 2001. *A Natural History of Negation.* Stanford: CSLI Publications.

Huddleston, Rodney. 2002. "The verb". *The Cambridge Grammar of the English Language* ed. by Rodney Huddleston & Geoffrey K. Pullum, 71–212. Cambridge: Cambridge University Press.

Hudson, Richard A. 1975. "The meaning of questions". *Language* 51:1.1–31.

Hughes, Arthur, Peter Trudgill & Dominic Watt. 2012. *English Accents and Dialects. An Introduction to the Social and Regional Varieties of English in the British Isles.* 5th ed. London: Arnold.

Hutchby, Ian. 2002. "Resisting the incitement to talk in child counselling: Aspects of the utterance 'I don't know'". *Discourse Studies* 4:2.147–168.

Hutchby, Ian & Robin Wooffitt. 1998. *Conversation Analysis. Principles, Practices and Applications.* Cambridge: Polity.

Ito, Rika & Sali Tagliamonte. 2003. "*Well* weird, *right* dodgy, *very* strange, *really* cool: Layering and recycling in English intensifiers". *Language in Society* 32:2.257–279.

Janda, Richard. 2001. "Beyond 'pathways' and 'unidirectionality': On the discontinuity of language transmission and the counterability of grammaticalization". *Language Sciences* 23:2-3.265–340.

Jefferson, Gail. 2002. "Is 'no' an acknowledgment token? Comparing American and British uses of (+)/(−) tokens". *Journal of Pragmatics* 34:10–11.1345–1383.

Jespersen, Otto. 1917. *Negation in English and Other Languages.* Copenhagen: Bianco Lunos Bogtrykkeri.

Johnson, Daniel Ezra. 2009. "Getting off the GoldVarb standard: Introducing Rbrul for mixed-effects variable rule analysis". *Language and Linguistics Compass* 3:1.359–383.

Johnstone, Barbara. 1990. "Variation in discourse: Midwestern narrative style". *American Speech* 65:3.195–214.

Jucker, Andreas H. 1993. "The discourse marker *well*: A relevance-theoretical account". *Journal of Pragmatics* 19:5.435–452.

Jucker, Andreas H. 2002. "Discourse markers in Early Modern English". *Alternative Histories of English* ed. by Peter Trudgill & Richard J. Watts, 210–230. London: Routledge.

Jucker, Andreas H. & Sara W. Smith. 1998. "And people just you know like 'wow': Discourse markers as negotiating strategies". *Discourse Markers. Descriptions and Theory* ed. by Andreas H. Jucker & Yael Ziv, 171–201. Amsterdam: John Benjamin.

Jucker, Andreas H. & Irma Taavitsainen. 2012. "Pragmatic variables". *The Handbook of Historical Sociolinguistics* ed. by Juan Manuel Hernández-Campoy & J. Camilo Condes-Silvestre, 293–306. Oxford: Wiley-Blackwell

Jucker, Andreas H. & Yael Ziv. 1998. "Discourse markers: Introduction". *Discourse Markers. Descriptions and Theory* ed. by Andreas H. Jucker & Yael Ziv, 1–12. Amsterdam: John Benjamins.

Jurafsky, Daniel, Alan Bell, Michelle Gregory & William D. Raymond. 2001. "Probabilistic relations between words: Evidence from reduction in lexical production". *Frequency and the Emergence of Linguistic Structure* ed. by Joan Bybee & Paul Hopper, 229–254. Amsterdam: John Benjamins.

Kaltenböck, Gunther. 2005. "Charting boundaries of syntax: A taxonomy of spoken parenthetical clauses". *Vienna English Working Papers* 14:1.21–53.

Kaltenböck, Gunther, Bernd Heine & Tania Kuteva. 2011. "On thetical grammar". *Studies in Language* 35:4.852–897.

Kärkkäinen, Elise. 2003. *Epistemic Stance in English Conversation. A Description of Its Interactional Functions with a Focus on* I think. Amsterdam: John Benjamins.

Kärkkäinen, Elise. 2007. "The role of *I guess* in conversational stancetaking". *Stancetaking in Discourse* ed. by Robert Englebretson, 183–219. Amsterdam: John Benjamins.

Kay, Paul & Charles J. Fillmore. 1999. "Grammatical constructions and linguistic generalizations: The *What's X doing Y* construction". *Language* 75:1.1–33.

Kearns, Kate. 2007. "Epistemic verbs and zero complementizer". *English Language and Linguistics* 11:3.475–505.

Keevallik, Leelo. 2006. "From discourse pattern to epistemic marker: Estonian *(ei) tea* 'don't know'". *Nordic Journal of Linguistics* 29:2.173–200.

Kerswill, Paul. 2003. "Dialect levelling and geographical diffusion in British English". *Social Dialectology. In Honour of Peter Trudgill* ed. by David Britain & Jenny Cheshire, 223–243. Amsterdam: John Benjamins.

Kerswill, Paul, Jenny Cheshire, Sue Fox & Eivind Torgersen. 2007. Linguistic Innovators: The English of Adolescents in London: Full Research Report. ESRC End of Award Report, RES-000-23-0680. Swindon: ESRC.

Kerswill, Paul, Jenny Cheshire, Sue Fox & Eivind Torgersen. 2011. Multicultural London English: The Emergence, Acquisition and Diffusion of a New Variety. ESRC End of Award Report, RES-062-23-0814. Swindon: ESRC.

Kimps, Ditte. 2007. "Declarative constant polarity tag questions: A data-driven analysis of their form, meaning and attitudinal use". *Journal of Pragmatics* 39:2.270–291.

Kjellmer, Göran. 2003. "Hesitation. In defence of *er* and *erm*". *English Studies* 2:2.170–198.

Kortmann, Bernd, Kate Burridge, Rajend Mesthrie, Edgar W. Schneider & Clive Upton, eds. 2004. *A Handbook of Varieties of English. A Multimedia Reference Tool. Vol. 2: Morphology and Syntax.* Berlin: Mouton de Gruyter.

Kotthoff, Helga. 1993. "Disagreement and concession in disputes: On the context sensitivity of preference structures". *Language in Society* 22:2.193–216.

Kristiansen, Tore. 2011. "Attitudes, ideology and awareness". *The SAGE Handbook of Sociolinguistics* ed. by Ruth Wodak, Barbara Johnstone & Paul Kerswill, 265–278. Los Angeles: Sage.

Krug, Manfred. 1998. "British English is developing a new discourse marker, innit? A study in lexicalisation based on social, regional and stylistic variation". *Arbeiten aus Anglistik und Amerikanistik* 23:2.146–197.

Kytö, Merja. 1996. *Manual to the Diachronic Part of the Helsinki Corpus of English Texts. Coding Conventions and Lists of Sources.* University of Helsinki: English Department.

Kytö, Merja & Terry Walker. 2006. *Guide to* A Corpus of English Dialogues 1560–1760 (Studia Anglistica Upsaliensia 130). Uppsala: Acta Universitatis Upsaliensis.

Labov, William. 1963. "The social motivation of a sound change". *Word* 19.273–309.

Labov, William. 1966. *The Social Stratification of English in New York City.* Washington, DC: Center for Applied Linguistics.

Labov, William. 1972. *Sociolinguistic Patterns.* Oxford: Blackwell.

Labov, William. 1982. "Building on empirical foundations". *Perspectives on Historical Linguistics* ed. by Winfred P. Lehmann & Yakov Malkiel, 17–92. Amsterdam: John Benjamins.

Labov, William. 1994. *Principles of Linguistic Change. Vol. 1: Internal Factors.* Oxford: Blackwell.

Labov, William. 1998. "The intersection of sex and social class in the course of linguistic change". *The Sociolinguistics Reader. Vol. 2: Gender and Discourse* ed. by Jenny Cheshire & Peter Trudgill, 7–52. Oxford: Oxford University Press.

Labov, William. 2001. *Principles of Linguistic Change. Vol. 2: Social Factors.* Oxford: Blackwell.

Lakoff, Robin. 1973. "Language and woman's place". *Language in Society* 2:1.45–81.

Lam, Phoenix W. Y. 2009. "The effect of text type on the use of *so* as a discourse particle". *Discourse Studies* 11:3.353–372.

Lavandera, Beatriz R. 1978. "Where does the sociolinguistic variable stop?". *Language in Society* 7:2.171–182.

Leech, Geoffrey. 1983. *Principles of Pragmatics.* London: Longman.

Lehmann, Christian. 1995 [1982]. *Thoughts on Grammaticalization.* Munich: Lincom Europa.

Lenk, Ute. 1998. *Marking Discourse Coherence. Functions of Discourse Markers in Spoken English.* Tübingen: Gunter Narr.

Levey, Stephen. 2003. "He's like 'Do it now!' and I'm like 'No!'". *English Today* 19:1.24–32.

Levey, Stephen. 2006. "The sociolinguistic distribution of discourse marker *like* in preadolescent speech". *Multilingua* 25:4.413–441.

Levey, Stephen. 2012. "General extenders and grammaticalization: Insights from London preadolescents". *Applied Linguistics* 33:3.257–281.

Levey, Stephen, Karine Groulx & Joseph Roy. forthc. "A variationist perspective on discourse-pragmatic change in a contact setting". *Language Variation and Change.*

Levinson, Stephen C. 1988. "Conceptual problems in the study of regional and cultural style". *The Sociolinguistics of Urban Vernaculars* ed. by Norbert Dittmar & P. Schlobinski, 161–190. Berlin: Mouton de Gruyter.

Liao, Silvie. 2009. "Variation in the use of discourse markers by Chinese teaching assistants in the US". *Journal of Pragmatics* 41:7.1313–1328.

Lindemann, Stephanie & Anna Mauranen. 2001. "'It's just real messy': The occurrence and function of *just* in a corpus of academic speech". *English for Specific Purposes* 20.459–475.

Llamas, Carmen. 2001. Language variation and innovation in Teesside English. PhD diss., University of Leeds.

Llamas, Carmen. 2007a. "A new methodology: Data elicitation for regional and social language variation studies". *York Papers in Linguistics* 8.138–163.

Llamas, Carmen. 2007b. "'A place between places': Language and identities in a border town". *Language in Society* 36:4.579–604.

Llamas, Carmen, Dominic Watt & Daniel Ezra Johnson. 2009. "Linguistic accommodation and the salience of national identity markers in a border town". *Journal of Language and Social Psychology* 28:4.381–407.

Lutzky, Ursula. 2008. "The discourse marker *marry* – a sociopragmatic analysis". *Vienna English Working Papers* 17:2.3–20.

Macafee, Caroline. 1992. "Characteristics of non-standard grammar in Scotland". <http://www.abdn.ac.uk/~enl038/grammar.htm> (08 September 2007).

Macaulay, Ronald K. S. 1991. *Locating Dialect in Discourse. The Language of Honest Men and Bonnie Lasses in Ayr*. Oxford: Oxford University Press.

Macaulay, Ronald K. S. 1995. "The adverbs of authority". *English World-Wide* 16:1.37–60.

Macaulay, Ronald. 2001. "*You're like 'why not?*': The quotative expressions of Glasgow adolescents". *Journal of Sociolinguistics* 5:1.3–21.

Macaulay, Ronald. 2002a. "Discourse variation". *The Handbook of Language Variation and Change* ed. by J. K. Chambers, Peter Trudgill & Natalie Schilling-Estes, 283–305. London: Blackwell.

Macaulay, Ronald. 2002b. "*Extremely* interesting, *very* interesting, or only *quite* interesting? Adverbs and social class". *Journal of Sociolinguistics* 6:3.398–417.

Macaulay, Ronald. 2002c. "You know, it depends". *Journal of Pragmatics* 34:6.749–767.

Macaulay, Ronald K. S. 2005. *Talk That Counts. Age, Gender, and Social Class Differences in Discourse*. Oxford: Oxford University Press.

Macaulay, Ronald. 2006. "Pure grammaticalization: The development of a teenage intensifier". *Language Variation and Change* 18:3.267–283.

Macaulay, Ronald K. S. 2009. "Adolescents and identity". *Intercultural Pragmatics* 6:4.597–612.

McGregor, William. 1995. "The English 'tag question': A new analysis, is(n't) it?". *On Subject and Theme. A Discourse Functional Perspective* ed. by Ruqaiya Hasan, 91–121. Amsterdam: John Benjamins.

Meehan, Teresa. 1991. "It's like, 'What's happening in the evolution of *like*?': A theory of grammaticalization". *Kansas Working Papers in Linguistics* 16.37–51.

Meillet, Antoine. 1912. "L'évolution des formes grammaticales". *Scientia* 26:6.130–148.

Meyerhoff, Miriam. 1994. "Sounds pretty ethnic, *eh*?: A pragmatic particle in New Zealand English". *Language in Society* 23:3.367–388.

Millar, Martin & Keith Brown. 1979. "Tag questions in Edinburgh speech". *Linguistische Berichte* 60.24–45.

Millar, Robert McColl. 2007. *Northern and Insular Scots*. Edinburgh: Edinburgh University Press.

Miller, Jim. 1993. "The grammar of Scottish English". *Real English. The Grammar of English Dialects in the British Isles* ed. by James Milroy & Lesley Milroy, 99–138. London: Longman.

Miller, Jim. 2003. "Syntax and discourse in Modern Scots". *The Edinburgh Companion to Scots* ed. by John Corbett, J. Derrick McClure & Jane Stuart-Smith, 72–109. Edinburgh: Edinburgh University Press.

Miller, Jim. 2004. "Scottish English: Morphology and syntax". *A Handbook of Varieties of English. A Multimedia Reference Tool. Vol. 2: Morphology and Syntax* ed. by Bernd Kortmann, Kate Burridge, Rajend Mesthrie, Edgar W. Schneider, & Clive Upton, 47–72. Berlin: Mouton de Gruyter.

Miller, Jim & Keith Brown. 1982. "Aspects of Scottish English syntax". *English World-Wide* 3:1.3–17.

Miller, Jim & Regina Weinert. 1995. "The function of LIKE in dialogue". *Journal of Pragmatics* 23:4.365–393.

Milroy, James & Lesley Milroy. 1997. "Varieties and variation". *The Handbook of Sociolinguistics* ed. by Florian Coulmas, 47–64. Oxford: Blackwell.

Milroy, James & Lesley Milroy. 1998. "Mechanisms of change in urban dialects: The role of class, social network and gender". *The Sociolinguistics Reader. Vol. 1: Variation and Multilingualism* ed. by Peter Trudgill & Jenny Cheshire, 179–195. London: Arnold.

Milroy, James, Lesley Milroy & Sue Hartley. 1994. "Local and supra-local change in British English: The case of glottalisation". *English World-Wide* 15:1.1–33.

Montgomery, Michael. 2007. "Variation and historical linguistics". *Sociolinguistic Variation. Theories, Methods, and Applications* ed. by Robert Bayley & Ceil Lucas, 110–132. Cambridge: Cambridge University Press.

Moore, Emma & Robert Podesva. 2009. "Style, indexicality, and the social meaning of tag questions". *Language in Society* 38:4.447–485.

Müller, Simone. 2005. *Discourse Markers in Native and Non-Native English Discourse*. Amsterdam: John Benjamins.

Murray, James A. H. 1873. *The Dialect of the Southern Counties of Scotland. Its Pronunciation, Grammar, and Historical Relations*. London: Philological Society.

Narrog, Heiko. 2012. "Beyond intersubjectification: Textual uses of modality and mood in subordinate clauses as part of speech-act orientation". *English Text Construction* 5:1.29–52.

Nevalainen, Terttu. 2008. "Social variation in intensifier use: Constraint on *-ly* adverbialization in the past?". *English Language and Linguistics* 12:2.289–315.

Nevalainen, Terttu & Helena Raumolin-Brunberg, eds. 1996. *Sociolinguistics and Language History. Studies Based on the Corpus of Early English Correspondence*. Amsterdam: Rodopi.

Newmeyer, Frederick J. 1998. *Language Form and Language Function*. Cambridge, MA: MIT Press.

Norrick, Neal R. 1995. "*Hunh*-tags and evidentiality in conversation". *Journal of Pragmatics* 23:6.687–692.

Nuyts, Jan. 1990. "Negative-raising reconsidered: Arguments for a cognitive-pragmatic approach". *Journal of Pragmatics* 14:4.559–588.

Orton, H. & W. J. Halliday. 1963. *Survey of English Dialects*. Leeds: E. J. Arnold.

Östman, Jan-Ola. 1981. *You know. A Discourse Functional Approach*. Amsterdam: John Benjamins.

Oxford English Dictionary. 2010. 3rd ed. online. Oxford: Oxford University Press. <http://www.oed.com>

Palander-Collin, Minna. 1999. *Grammaticalization and Social Embedding. I THINK and METHINKS in Middle and Early Modern English*. Helsinki: Société Néophilologique.

Parton, Sabrena R., Susan A. Siltanen, Lawrence A. Hosman & Jeff Langenderfer. 2002. "Employment interview outcomes and speech style effects". *Journal of Language and Social Psychology* 21:2.144–161.

Peitsara, Kirist & Anna-Liisa Vasko. 2002. "The *Helsinki Dialect Corpus*: Characteristics of speech and aspects of variation". *Helsinki English Studies* 2. http://blogs.helsinki.fi/hes-eng/files/2011/03/HES_Vol2_Peitsara_Vasko.pdf (24 January 2013).

Persson, Gunnar. 1993. "*Think* in panchronic perspective". *Studia Neophilologica* 65: 1.3–18.

Petersen, Andrew. 2004. "The campaign against 'like'". *The Wall Street Journal* 3 February.

Petyt, K. M. 1978. "Secondary contractions in West Yorkshire negatives". *Sociolinguistic Patterns in British English* ed. by Peter Trudgill, 91–100. London: Edward Arnold.

Pichler, Heike. 2009. "The functional and social reality of discourse variants in a northern English dialect: I DON'T KNOW and I DON'T THINK compared". *Intercultural Pragmatics* 6: 4.561–596.

Pichler, Heike. 2010. "Methods in discourse variation analysis: Reflections on the way forward". *Journal of Sociolinguistics* 14: 5.581–608.

Pichler, Heike & Stephen Levey. 2011. "In search of grammaticalization in synchronic dialect data: General extenders in north-east England". *English Language and Linguistics* 15: 3.441–471.

Pichler, Heike & Eivind Torgersen. 2012. Tag questions in contemporary London English: Current trends in invariabilisation. Paper presented at the 33rd ICAME conference, June, Leuven.

Plug, Leendert. 2010. "Pragmatic constraints in usage-based phonology, with reference to some Dutch phrases". *Journal of Pragmatics* 42: 7.2014–2035.

Pomerantz, Anita. 1984. "Agreeing and disagreeing with assessments: Some features of preferred/dispreferred turn shapes". *Structures of Social Action. Studies in Conversation Analysis* ed. by J. Maxwell Atkinson & John Heritage, 57–101. Cambridge: Cambridge University Press.

Pope, Jennifer, Miriam Meyerhoff & D. Robert Ladd. 2007. "Forty years of language change on Martha's Vineyard". *Language* 83: 3.615–627.

Poplack, Shana. 1989. "The care and handling of a mega-corpus: The Ottawa-Hull French Project". *Language Change and Variation* ed. by Ralph W. Fasold & Deborah Schiffrin, 411–451. Amsterdam: John Benjamins.

Poplack, Shana. 2011. "A variationist perspective on grammaticalization". *The Oxford Handbook of Grammaticalization* ed. by Heiko Narrog & Bernd Heine, 209–224. Oxford: Oxford University Press.

Poplack, Shana & Sali Tagliamonte. 2001. *African American English in the Diaspora*. Oxford: Blackwell.

Potter, Jonathan. 2004. "Discourse analysis as a way of analysing naturally occurring talk". *Qualitative Research: Theory, Method and Practice* ed. by David Silverman, 200–221. London: Sage.

Precht, Kristen. 2008. "Sex similarities and differences in stance in informal American conversation". *Journal of Sociolinguistics* 12: 1.89–111.

Psathas, George & Timothy Anderson. 1990. "The 'practices' of transcription in conversation analysis". *Semiotica* 78: 1-2.75–99.

Quirk, Randolph, Sidney Greenbaum, Geoffrey Leech & Jan Svartvik. 1985. *A Comprehensive Grammar of the English Language*. London: Longman.

Raumolin-Brunberg, Helena & Arja Nurmi. 2011. "Grammaticalization and language change in the individual". *The Oxford Handbook of Grammaticalization* ed. by Heike Narrog & Bernd Heine, 251–262. Oxford: Oxford University Press.

Redeker, Gisela. 1990. "Ideational and pragmatic markers of discourse structure". *Journal of Pragmatics* 14: 3.367–381.

Redeker, Gisela. 1991. "Linguistic markers of discourse structure". *Linguistics* 29: 4.1139–1172.

Richards, Hazel. 2008. Mechanisms, motivations and outcomes of change in Morley (Leeds) English. PhD diss., University of York.

Rickford, John, Isabelle Buchstaller, Thomas Wasow, Arnold Zwicky & Elizabeth Traugott. 2007. "Intensive and quotative *all*: Something old, something new". *American Speech* 82: 1.3–31.

Romaine, Suzanne. 1984. "On the problem of syntactic variation and pragmatic meaning in sociolinguistic theory". *Folia Linguistica* 18: 3-4.409–437.

Romaine, Suzanne. 1995. "The grammaticalization of irrealis in Tok Pisin". *Modality in Grammar and Discourse* ed. by Joan Bybee & Suzanne Fleischman, 389–428. Amsterdam: John Benjamins.

Romaine, Suzanne & Deborah Lange. 1991. "The use of *like* as a marker of reported speech and thought: A case of grammaticalization in progress". *American Speech* 66: 3.227–279.

Roth-Gordon, Jennifer. 2007. "Youth, slang, and pragmatic expressions: Examples from Brazilian Portuguese". *Journal of Sociolinguistics* 11: 3.322–345.

Rudolph, Elisabeth. 1991. "Relationship between particle occurrence and text type". *Multilingua* 10: 1-2.203–223.

Russell, Brenda, Jenna Perkins & Heather Grinnel. 2008. "Interviewees' overuse of the word 'like' and hesitations: Effects in simulated hiring decisions". *Psychological Reports* 102: 1.111–118.

Sacks, Harvey, Emanuel A. Schegloff & Gail Jefferson. 1974. "A simplest systematics for the organisation of turn-taking for conversation". *Language* 50: 4.696–735.

Sankoff, David. 1988. "Variable rules". *Sociolinguistics. An International Handbook of the Science of Language and Society* ed. by Ulrich Ammon, Norbert Dittmar & Klaus J. Mattheier, 984–997. Berlin: Mouton de Gruyter.

Sankoff, David, Sali Tagliamonte & E. Smith. 2005. Goldvarb X. A multivariate analysis application. Department of Linguistics, University of Toronto, and Department of Mathematics, University of Ottawa.

Sankoff, David & Pierrette Thibault. 1981. "Weak complementarity: Tense and aspect in Montreal French". *Syntactic Change* ed. by B. Johns & D. Strong, 206–216. Ann Arbor: University of Michigan.

Sankoff, Gillian. 1973. "Above and beyond phonology in variable rules". *New Ways of Analysing Variation in English* ed. by Charles-James N. Bailey & Roger W. Shuy, 44–61. Washington: Georgetown University Press.

Sankoff, Gillian & Hélène Blondeau. 2007. "Language change across the lifespan: /r/ in Montreal French". *Language* 83: 3.560–588.

Schegloff, Emanuel A. & Harvey Sacks. 1973. "Opening up closings". *Semiotica* 7: 4.289–327.

Schegloff, Emanuel A. 1982. "Discourse as an interactional achievement: Some uses of 'uh huh' and other things that come between sentences". *Analyzing Discourse. Text and Talk* ed. by Deborah Tannen, 71–93. Washington, D.C.: Georgetown University Press.

Schegloff, Emanuel A. 1996. "Turn organisation: One intersection of grammar and interaction". *Interaction and Grammar* ed. by Elinor Ochs, Emanuel A. Schegloff & Sandra A. Thompson, 52–133. Cambridge: Cambridge University Press.

Schegloff, Emanuel A. 2007. *Sequence Organisation in Interaction. A Primer in Conversation Analysis.* Cambridge: Cambridge University Press.

Scheibman, Joanne. 2000. "*I dunno*: A usage-based account of the phonological reduction of *don't* in American English conversation". *Journal of Pragmatics* 32: 1.105–124.

Scheibman, Joanne. 2001. "Local patterns of subjectivity in person and verb type in American English conversation". *Frequency and the Emergence of Linguistic Structure* ed. by Joan Bybee & Paul Hopper, 61–97. Amsterdam: John Benjamins.

Schiffrin, Deborah. 1980. "Meta-talk: Organisational and evaluative brackets in discourse". *Sociological Inquiry* 50: 3-4.199–236.

Schiffrin, Deborah. 1987. *Discourse Markers*. Cambridge: Cambridge University Press.

Schiffrin, Deborah. 2001. "Discourse markers: Language, meaning and context". *The Handbook of Discourse Analysis* ed. by Deborah Schiffrin, Deborah Tannen & Heidi E. Hamilton, 54–75. Oxford: Blackwell.

Schleef, Erik. 2008. "The 'lecturer's ok' revisited: Changing discourse conventions and the influence of academic division". *American Speech* 83: 1.62–84.

Schneider, Klaus P. & Anne Barron. 2008. "Where pragmatics and dialectology meet: Introducing variational pragmatics". *Variational Pragmatics. A Focus on Regional Varieties in Pluricentric Languages* ed. by Klaus P. Schneider & Anne Barron, 1–32. Amsterdam: John Benjamins.

Schourup, Lawrence. 1985. *Common Discourse Particles in English Conversation*. New York: Garland.

Schourup, Lawrence. 1999. "Discourse markers: Tutorial overview". *Lingua* 107: 3-4.227–265.

Simon-Vandenbergen, Anne-Marie. 1998. "The modal metaphor *I don't think*: System and text". *English as a Human Language. To Honour Louis Goossens* ed. by Johan van der Auwera, Louis Goosens, Frank Durieux & Ludo Lejeune, 312–324. München: Lincom Europa.

Simon-Vandenbergen, Anne-Marie. 2000. "The functions of *I think* in political discourse". *International Journal of Applied Linguistics* 10: 1.41–63.

Smith, Jennifer. 2000. "'You Ø Na Hear O' That Kind O' Things': Negative *do* in Buckie Scots". *English World-Wide* 21: 2.231–259.

Smith, Jennifer. 2009. Obsolescence vs. stability in a Shetland dialect: Evidence from three generations of speakers: Full Research Report. ESRC End of Award Report, RES-000-22-2052. Swindon: ESRC.

Smith, Jennifer, Mercedes Durham & Hazel Richards. forthc. "The social and linguistic in the acquisition of sociolinguistic norms: Caregivers, children and variation". *Linguistics*.

Sowa, Joseph. 2009. "'Sweet as!': The intensifier *as* in New Zealand and Australian English". *English Today* 25: 2.58–61.

Sperber, Dan & Deirdre Wilson. 1995. *Relevance*. 2nd ed. Oxford: Blackwell.

Starks, Donna, Laura Thompson & James Christie. 2008. "Whose discourse particles?: New Zealand *eh* in the Niuean migrant community". *Journal of Pragmatics* 40: 7.1279–1295.

Steele, Hazel. 2003. Caregiver and child in the transmission and acquisition of variable dialect features. MA diss., University of York.

Stein, Dieter. 1985. "Discourse markers in Early Modern English". *Papers from the 4th International Conference on English Historical Linguistics* ed. by R. Eaton, 283–302. Amsterdam: John Benjamins.

Stenström, Anna-Brita. 1990. "Pauses in monologue and dialogue". *The London-Lund Corpus of Spoken English. Description and Research* ed. by Jan Svartvik, 211–252. Lund: Lund University Press.

Stenström, Anna-Brita. 1998. "From sentence to discourse: Cos (because) in teenage talk". *Discourse Markers. Descriptions and Theory* ed. by Andreas H. Jucker & Yael Ziv, 127–146. Amsterdam: John Benjamins.

Stenström, Anna-Brita, Gisle Andersen & Ingrid Kristine Hasund. 2002. *Trends in Teenage Talk. Corpus Compilation, Analysis and Findings*. Amsterdam: John Benjamins.

Stubbe, Maria & Janet Holmes. 1995. "*You know, eh* and other exasperating expressions: An analysis of social and stylistic variation in the use of pragmatic particles in a sample of New Zealand English". *Language and Communication* 15: 1.63–88.

Stubbs, Michael. 1983. *Discourse Analysis. The Sociolinguistic Analysis of Natural Language.* Chicago: The University of Chicago Press.

Stubbs, Michael. 1986. "'A matter of prolonged fieldwork': Notes towards a modal grammar of English". *Applied Linguistics* 7:1.1–25.

Svartvik, Jan, ed. 1990. *The London-Lund Corpus of Spoken English. Description and Research.* Lund: Lund University Press.

Tagliamonte, Sali. 2002a. "Comparative sociolinguistics". *The Handbook of Language Variation and Change* ed. by J. K. Chambers, Peter Trudgill & Natalie Schilling-Estes, 729–763. Oxford: Blackwell.

Tagliamonte, Sali. 2002b. Grammatical Variation and Change in British English: Perspectives from York: Full Research Report. ESRC End of Award Report, R-000-23-8287. Swindon: ESRC.

Tagliamonte, Sali. 2005. "*So* who? *Like* how? *Just* what? Discourse markers in the conversations of young Canadians". *Journal of Pragmatics* 37:11.1896–1915.

Tagliamonte, Sali. 2008. "So different and pretty cool! Recycling intensifiers in Toronto, Canada". *English Language and Linguistics* 12:2.361–394.

Tagliamonte, Sali & Alexandra D'Arcy. 2004. "*He's like, she's like*: The quotative system in Canadian youth". *Journal of Sociolinguistics* 8:4.493–514.

Tagliamonte, Sali & Alexandra D'Arcy. 2007. "Frequency and variation in the community grammar: Tracking a new change through the generations". *Language Variation and Change* 19:2.199–217.

Tagliamonte, Sali & Alexandra D'Arcy. 2009. "Peaks beyond phonology: Adolescence, incrementation, and language change". *Language* 85:1.58–108.

Tagliamonte, Sali & Derek Denis. 2008. "Linguistic ruin? LOL! Instant messaging and teen language". *American Speech* 83:1.3–34.

Tagliamonte, Sali & Derek Denis. 2010. "The stuff of change: General extenders in Toronto, Canada". *Journal of English Linguistics* 38:4.335–368.

Tagliamonte, Sali & Rachel Hudson. 1999. "*Be like* et al. beyond America: The quotative system in British and Canadian youth". *Journal of Sociolinguistics* 3:2.147–172.

Tagliamonte, Sali & Chris Roberts. 2005. "So weird; so cool; so innovative: The use of intensifiers in the television series *Friends*". *American Speech* 80:3.280–300.

Tagliamonte, Sali & Jennifer Smith. 2002. "'Either it isn't or it's not': NEG/AUX contraction in British dialects". *English World-Wide* 23:2.251–281.

Tannen, Deborah. 1993. *Gender and Conversational Interaction.* Oxford: Oxford University Press.

Terkourafi, Marina. 2011. "The pragmatic variable: Toward a procedural interpretation". *Language in Society* 40:3.343–372.

Terraschke, Agnes. 2007. "Use of general extenders by German non-native speakers of English". *International Review of Applied Linguistics* 45:2.141–160.

Thompson, Sandra A. 2002. "'Object complements' and conversation". *Studies in Language* 26:1.125–164.

Thompson, Sandra A. & Paul J. Hopper. 2001. "Transitivity, clause structure, and argument structure: Evidence from conversation". *Frequency and the Emergence of Linguistic Structure* ed. by Joan L. Bybee & Paul Hopper, 27–60. Amsterdam: John Benjamins.

Thompson, Sandra A. & Anthony Mulac. 1991a. "The discourse conditions for the use of the complementizer *that* in conversational English". *Journal of Pragmatics* 15:3.237–251.

Thompson, Sandra A. & Anthony Mulac. 1991b. "A quantitative perspective on the grammaticization of epistemic parentheticals in English". *Approaches to Grammaticalization. Vol. 2: Types of Grammatical Markers* ed. by Elizabeth Closs Traugott & Bernd Heine, 313–329. Amsterdam: John Benjamins.

Todd, Loreto & Ian Hancock. 1986. *International English Usage*. London: Croom Helm.

Torgersen, Eivind, Costas Gabrielatos, Sebastian Hoffmann & Susan Fox. 2011. "A corpus-based study of pragmatic markers in London English". *Corpus Linguistics and Linguistic Theory* 7:1.93–118.

Torres Cacoullos, Rena. 2011. "Variation and grammaticalization". *The Handbook of Hispanic Sociolinguistics* ed. by Juan Manuel Hernández-Campoy & J. Camilo Condes-Silvestre, 148–167. Oxford: Wiley-Blackwell.

Torres Cacoullos, Rena & James Walker. 2009. "The present of the English future: Grammatical variation and collocations in discourse". *Language* 85:2.321–354.

Torres Cacoullos, Rena & James Walker. 2011. "Collocations in grammaticalization and variation". *The Oxford Handbook of Grammaticalization* ed. by Bernd Heine & Heiko Narrog, 225–238. Oxford: Oxford University Press.

Torres, Lourdes. 2002. "Bilingual discourse markers in Puerto Rican Spanish". *Language in Society* 31:1.65–83.

Tottie, Gunnel. 1992. "Introduction: Seven types of continuity in discourse". *Language Variation and Change* 4:2.121–123.

Tottie, Gunnel & Sebastian Hoffmann. 2006. "Tag questions in British and American English". *Journal of English Linguistics* 34:4.283–311.

Tovena, L. M. 2001. "Neg-raising: Negation as failure". *Perspectives on Negation and Polarity Items* ed. by Jack Hoeksema, Hotze Rullmann, Victor Sanchez-Valencia & Ton van der Wonden, 331–356. Amsterdam: John Benjamins.

Traugott, Elizabeth Closs. 1982. "From propositional to textual to expressive meanings: Some semantic-pragmatic aspects of grammaticalization". *Perspectives on Historical Linguistics* ed. by Winnfried P. Lehmann & Yakov Malkiel, 245–271. Amsterdam: John Benjamins.

Traugott, Elizabeth Closs. 1995. "Subjectification in grammaticalization". *Subjectivity and Subjectivisation* ed. by Dieter Stein & Susan Wright, 31–54. Cambridge: Cambridge University Press.

Traugott, Elizabeth Closs. 2003a. "Constructions in grammaticalization". *The Handbook of Historical Linguistics* ed. by Brian D. Joseph & Richard D. Janda, 624–647. Oxford: Blackwell.

Traugott, Elizabeth Closs. 2003b. "From subjectification to intersubjectification". *Motives for Language Change* ed. by Raymond Hickey, 124–139. Cambridge: Cambridge University Press.

Traugott, Elizabeth Closs. 2010. "Grammaticalization". *Continuum Companion to Historical Linguistics* ed. Silvia Luraghi & Vit Bubenik, 269–283. London: Continuum Press.

Traugott, Elizabeth Closs. 2012. "Intersubjectification and clause periphery". *English Text Construction* 5:1.7–28.

Traugott, Elizabeth Closs & Richard B. Dasher. 2002. *Regularity in Semantic Change*. Cambridge: Cambridge University Press.

Traugott, Elizabeth Closs & Bernd Heine. 1991. "Introduction". *Approaches to Grammaticalization. Vol. 2: Focus on Types of Grammatical Markers* ed. by Elizabeth Closs Traugott & Bernd Heine, 1–14. Amsterdam: John Benjamins.

Traugott, Elizabeth Closs & Ekkehard König. 1991. "The semantics-pragmatics of grammaticalization revisited". *Approaches to Grammaticalization. Vol. 1: Theoretical and Methodological Issues,* ed. by Elizabeth Closs Traugott & Bernd Heine, 189–218. Amsterdam: John Benjamins.

Traugott, Elizabeth Closs & Graeme Trousdale. 2010. "Gradience, gradualness and grammaticalization. How do they intersect?". *Gradience, Gradualness and Grammaticalization* ed. by Elizabeth Closs Traugott & Graeme Trousdale, 19–44. Amsterdam: John Benjamins.

Trester, Anna Marie. 2009. "Discourse marker 'oh' as a means for realizing the identity potential of constructed dialogue in interaction". *Journal of Sociolinguistics* 13:2.147–168.

Trudgill, Peter & Jean Hannah. 1982. *International English. A Guide to Varieties of Standard English.* London: Edward Arnold.

Tsui, Amy B. M. 1991. "The pragmatic functions of *I don't know*". *Text* 11:4.607–622.

Upton, Clive, David Parry & J. D. A. Widdowson. 1994. *Survey of English Dialects. The Dictionary and Grammar.* London: Routledge.

Urmson, J. O. 1952. "Parenthetical verbs". *Mind* 61.480–496.

van Bogaert, Julie. 2010. "A constructional taxonomy of *I think* and related expressions: Accounting for the variability in complement-taking mental predicates". *English Language and Linguistics* 14:3.399–427.

van Bogaert, Julie. 2011. "*I think* and other complement-taking mental predicates: A case of and for constructional grammaticalization". *Linguistics* 49:2.295–332.

van der Auwera, Johan. 2009. "The Jespersen Cycles". *Cyclical Change* ed. by Elly van Gelderen, 35–71. Amsterdam: John Benjamins.

Verdonik, Darinka, Andrej Žgank & Agnes Pisanski Peterlin. 2009. "The impact of context on discourse marker use in two conversational genres". *Discourse Studies* 10:6.759–775.

Wales, Katie. 2006. *Northern English. A Social and Cultural History.* Cambridge: Cambridge University Press.

Walker, James A. 2010. *Variation in the Linguistic System.* London: Routledge.

Wallage, Phillip. 2008. "Jespersen's Cyle in Middle English: Parametric variation and grammatical competition". *Lingua* 118:5.643–674.

Waters, Cathleen. 2013. "Transatlantic variation in English adverb placement". *Language Variation and Change* 25:2.

Watt, Dominic & Catherine Ingham. 2000. "Durational evidence of the Scottish Vowel Length Rule in Berwick English". *Leeds Working Papers in Linguistics and Phonetics* 8.205–228.

Watt, Dominic & Lesley Milroy. 1999. "Patterns of variation and change in three Newcastle vowels: Is this dialect levelling?". *Urban Voices. Accent Studies in the British Isles* ed. by Paul Foulkes & Gerard J. Docherty, 25–46. London: Arnold.

Watt, Dominic, Carmen Llamas & Gerard J. Docherty. 2012. Linguistic Variation and National Identities on the Scottish/English Border: Full Research Report. ESRC End of Award Report, RES-062-23-0525. Swindon: ESRC.

Watts, Richard J. 1984. "An analysis of epistemic possibility and probability". *English Studies* 65:2.129–140.

Watts, Richard J. 1989. "Taking the pitcher to the 'well': Native speakers' perception of their use of discourse markers in conversation". *Journal of Pragmatics* 13:3.203–237.

Wauchope, Mary Michele. 1993. "Discourse functions of *just*". *Lacus Forum* 19.181–189.

Weatherall, Ann. 2011. "*I don't know* as a prepositioned epistemic hedge". *Research on Language and Social Interaction* 44:4.317–337.

Weinreich, Uriel, William Labov & Marvin Herzog. 1968. "Empirical foundations for a theory of language change". *Directions for Historical Linguistics* ed. by Winfried Lehmann & Yakov Malkiel, 95–188. Austin: University of Texas Press.

Whisker, Kate. 2007. Secondary contraction of clitic negatives in urban North Yorkshire. MA diss., University of York.

Whisker-Taylor, Kate. in prep. A century of language variation and change in Huddersfield. PhD diss. in progress, Lancaster University.

Wichmann, Anne. 2011. "Grammaticalization and prosody". *The Oxford Handbook of Grammaticalization* ed. by Heiko Narrog & Bernd Heine, 331–341. Oxford: Oxford University Press.

Wilson, Deirdre & Dan Sperber. 1993. "Linguistic form and relevance". *Lingua* 90: 1.1–25.

Wilson, James. 1915. *Lowland Scotch as Spoken in the Lower Strathrearn District of Perthshire.* Oxford: Oxford University Press.

Winford, Donald. 1984. "The linguistic variable and syntactic variation in creole continua". *Lingua* 62: 4.267–288.

Winford, Donald. 1996. "The problem of syntactic variation". *Sociolinguistic Variation. Selected Papers from NWAV 23 at Stanford* ed. by Jennifer Arnold, Renée Blake, Brad Davidson, Scott Schwenter & Julie Solomon, 177–192. Stanford, CA: CSLI Publications.

Wolfson, Nessa. 1976. "Speech events and natural speech: Some implications for sociolinguistic methodology". *Language in Society* 5: 2.189–209.

Woods, Howard B. 1991. "Social differentiation in Ottawa". *English around the World. Sociolinguistic Perspectives* ed. by Jenny Cheshire, 134–149. Cambridge: Cambridge University Press.

Woods, Nicola. 1997. "The formation and development of New Zealand English: Interaction of gender-related variation and linguistic change". *Journal of Sociolinguistics* 1: 1.95–126.

Wooffitt, Robin. 2005. *Conversation Analysis and Discourse Analysis. A Comparative and Critical Introduction.* London: Sage.

Wray, Alison. 2002. *Formulaic Language and the Lexicon.* Cambridge: Cambridge University Press.

Wray, Alison & Michael R. Perkins. 2000. "The functions of formulaic language: An integrated model". *Language & Communication* 20: 1.1–28.

Wright, Joseph. 1902. *The English Dialect Dictionary.* London: Henry Frowde.

Yaeger-Dror, Malcah. 1985. "Intonational prominence on negatives in English". *Language and Speech* 28: 3.197–230.

Yaeger-Dror, Malcah. 1997. "Contraction of negatives as evidence of variance in register-specific interactive rules". *Language Variation and Change* 9: 1.1–36.

Yang, Li-chiung. 2006. "Integrating prosodic and contextual cues in the interpretation of discourse markers". *Approaches to Discourse Particles* ed. by Kerstin Fischer, 265–297. Amsterdam: Elsevier.

Young, Richard & Robert Bayley. 1996. "VARBRUL analysis for second language acquisition research". *Second Language Acquisition and Linguistic Variation* ed. by Robert Bayley & Dennis R. Preston, 253–306. Amsterdam: John Benjamins.

Zilles, Ana M. S. 2005. "The development of a new pronoun: The linguistic and social embedding of *a gente* in Brazilian Portuguese". *Language Variation and Change* 17: 1.19–53.

APPENDICES

Appendix 1. Inventory of functions of unbound I DON'T KNOW in the BwE corpus

function	description	accompanying features	(turn-)position	example in Chapter 4
INTERPERSONAL MODE				
# subjective uses: epistemic marker	– signals speakers' uncertainty vis-à-vis the validity of propositions (global scope)	+ rising/fall-rising intonation + usually co-occurs with other expressions of epistemicity	~ any ~ external to syntactic structures	(3)
	– signals that the following lexical material is in some way problematic (local scope)	+ rising intonation + lexical material in its scope set off prosodically from surrounding discourse	~ turn-medially before modified lexical material ~ utterance-medially between obligatory constituents of a clause	(4)
# intersubjective uses: mitigation device	– mitigates potentially controversial propositions	+ rising intonation	~ any (turn-initial pre-positioning preferred)	(5a)
	– softens disagreements	+ high pitch and/or rising intonation	~ turn-initially	(5b)
	– avoids unwelcome assessments	+ falling intonation	~ turn-initially or constituting sole turn-component	(6)
TEXTUAL MODE				
# repair device	– bridges transitions between repaired and repairing elements	+ after cut-offs, abandoned utterances, false starts + usually level intonation + with discourse-pragmatic features, (un)filled pauses & higher pitch to signal hesitant repair	~ turn-medially between repaired and repairing elements ~ near-turn-initially after false starts	(7a) (7b)
# topic-development device	– declines proffered topics	+ usually no pitch movement + occasionally descending intonation contour	~ sole turn-component ~ after topic-proffers	(8)

function	description	accompanying features	(turn-)position	example in Chapter 4
	– curtails topical sequences	+ usually no pitch movement + occasionally with descending intonation contour	~ sole turn component or near-turn-finally ~ after topic-proffer was briefly embraced	(9)
	– dismisses successful disruptions from hearers to pursue original topic	+ often (moderately) rising intonation	~ turn-initially ~ after disruptions of speakers' hold on the floor	(10)
# turn-taking device	– launches contributions whilst planning is still underway (sometimes but not necessarily in competition for the floor)	+ often with increased speech rate + co-occurs with unfilled pauses and other hesitation signals + following elements sometimes produced with reduced speech rate + not usually with rising intonation	~ turn-initially	(11a)
	– non-hesitantly launches pre-planned turns	+ usually no noticeable pitch movement + when in overlap position, sometimes with syllable lengthening	~ turn-initially	(11b)
# turn-holding device	– links (thematically unrelated) TCUs to maintain speakers' hold on floor	+ no noticeable pitch movement + increased speech rate (when produced in competition for the floor)	~ turn-medially	(12a)
	– signals speakers' communicative presence in hesitation and planning areas of turns	+ often after transition-marking discourse-pragmatic features + usually co-occurs with hesitation signals (discourse-pragmatic features, filled and unfilled pauses) + moderately rising pitch or no prosodic variation	~ turn medially or near-turn-initially after discourse-pragmatic features or filled pauses	(12b)

function	description	accompanying features	(turn-)position	example in Chapter 4
# turn-yielding/-closing device	– yields turns	+ falling tone (to signal finality and completion) or rising tone (to appeal for cooperation) + often softly spoken	~ (near-)turn-finally	(13)
	– closes turns to signal intention to yield the floor and/or desire to terminate topics	+ usually descending intonation to indicate finality/completeness + occasionally with high rising pitch to signal appeal for co-operation	~ turn-finally ~ at CTRPs and non-CTRPs	(14a) (14b)
INTERPERSONAL-TEXTUAL MODE				
# epistemic turn-taking device	– launches turns and marks following propositions as uncertain	+ rising intonation	~ turn-initially	(15)
# epistemic repair or turn-holding device	– marks transitions between repaired and repairing elements and qualifies upcoming propositions OR functions as turn-holder while qualifying preceding or following propositions	+ between repairing and repaired elements with rising intonation OR after transition-markers with hesitation signals and high-rising pitch	~ turn-medially	(16a) (16b)
# epistemic turn-closing device	– qualifies preceding propositions and closes turns	+ rising or falling intonation	~ turn-finally	(17)
IDEATIONAL MODE				
# referential uses	– communicates insufficient knowledge	+ *know* carries primary stress + not usually co-occurring with other discourse-pragmatic features or pauses + not usually produced with prosodic variation + frequently with *really*	~ any	(18a) (18b)

Appendix 2. Inventory of functions of bound I DON'T KNOW in the BwE corpus
[Shading indicates functions performed by utterances containing I DON'T KNOW rather than by the construction I DON'T KNOW *per se.*]

function	description	accompanying features	(turn-)position	example in Chapter 4
IDEATIONAL MODE				
# referential uses	– communicates lack of knowledge of or familiarity with referents in complements	+ accented + sometimes strong emphatic stress on (almost) all elements of utterance + falling intonation contour + not usually co-occurs with other discourse-pragmatic features or pauses + often with *really*	~ any turn-position	(19a) (19b) (19c)
INTERPERSONAL MODE				
# epistemic marker	– signals speakers' uncertainty vis-à-vis validity of propositions in following complements (local scope)	+ soft volume + rising pitch on *know* or (last element of) complements	~ any turn-position	(20) (21) (22)
	– signals speakers' uncertainty vis-à-vis validity or relevance of (a) surrounding utterance(s) (global scope)	+ usually co-occurs with other epistemic markers + usually with rising intonation contour or high pitch	~ any turn-position ~ usually before the modified utterance, but occasionally after it	(23a) (23b) (24)
TEXTUAL MODE				
# topic-development device	– declines proffered topics	+ no pitch movement or descending intonation contour + often softly spoken with slightly raised pitch	~ (near) sole turn-component	(25a)
	– curtails topical sequences	+ any intonation contour	~ sole turn component after lengthy discussion of topics	(25b)
# turn-yielding/-closing device	– yields turns	+ high pitch on the I DON'T KNOW with final falling tone on complement	~ turn-finally	(25c)

Appendix 3. Inventory of functions of I DON'T KNOW + WH-word in the BwE corpus
[Shading indicates functions performed by utterances containing I DON'T KNOW rather than by the construction I DON'T KNOW *per se.*]

function	description	accompanying features	(turn-)position	example in Chapter 4
INTERPERSONAL MODE				
# (local or global) epistemic marker	– signals low reliability	+ high pitch or rising intonation	~ any	(26a) (26b)
TEXTUAL MODE				
# topic-development device	– declines proffered topics	+ falling intonation contour	~ (near-)sole turn-component ~ in response to topic-proffers	(27a)
# turn-yielding/ -closing device	– yields turns	+ at CTRPs or non-CTRPs + descending intonation to indicate finality & completeness	~ turn-finally	(27b)

Appendix 4. Inventory of functions of I DON'T THINK in the BwE corpus

function	description	accompanying features	sequential positioning	example in Chapter 5
INTERPERSONAL MODE				
# subjective uses: subjective epistemic modality marker	− signals speakers' uncertainty vis-à-vis validity of propositions	+ with high pitch, low volume, decreased tempo (and moderate rise on *think*, *don't* or the end of the utterance) (high degree of uncertainty) + without prosodic variation and mostly with level or falling intonation (low degree of uncertainty) + sometimes with other low modality items + usually no stress; only occasionally stress on *I* to emphasise subjectivity, or on *think* if followed by *so*	~ any turn-position ~ mostly in response to opinion questions: mostly (near-)sole turn-component or (near-)turn-initial positioning occasionally followed by validation often preceded or followed by tentative *no* after polar questions often with pro-form *so* ~ in response to prior assessments ~ as part of extended opinion sequences involving one or more speakers	(7) (8)
	− signals speakers' certainty vis-à-vis validity of propositions	+ stress on *don't* (*think*) (and other negative polarity items in the utterance) + falling or final intonation contour + sometimes decreased speech rate and/or increased loudness + sometimes accompanied by assertiveness devices	~ any turn-position ~ mostly (near-)turn-initially in second-pair parts of question-answer or assessment-assessment adjacency pairs ~ also in opinion sequences to emphasise a point	(9) (10) (11)

function	description	accompanying features	sequential positioning	example in Chapter 5
# intersubjective uses (1): mitigation device	– mitigates potentially controversial or face-threatening propositions	+ level or falling intonation contour + sometimes contrastive pitch, speed and volume + unaccented	~ any turn-position	(12)
	– softens presentation of disaligning turns	+ frequently with high pitch and/or reduced tempo + sometimes preceded by filled and/or unfilled pauses + unaccented	~ (near-)turn-initially ~ usually followed by resolution of rejection (explication for denial or provision of alternative assessment)	(13)
	– avoids or reduces bluntness of overt denials and rejections	+ flat or falling intonation + always without noticeable variation in tempo and loudness + unaccented + often co-occurs with definitive-sounding *no*	~ (near-)turn-initially ~ in response to polar questions ~ sometimes followed by explication of denial	(14)
# intersubjective uses (2): affiliation marker	– signals current speakers' agreement with or corroboration of previous speakers' propositions or inferences	+ with level or falling intonation (boosts agreement) + with (moderately) rising intonation (hedges agreement)	~ usually (near-)sole turn component (including complementation) or with *no* ~ not usually followed by further talk	(15)
INTERPERSONAL-TEXTUAL FUNCTIONS				
# information- & discourse-structuring device: frame	– marks transitions from provisions of factual information to provisions of personal assessments of facts	+ usually without prosodic variation + falling intonation contour + often with *but*	~ turn-medially between provision of facts and provision of personal stance ~ usually in extended turns	(16)

function	description	accompanying features	sequential positioning	example in Chapter 5
	– marks transitions between explications and provisions of final assessments/ conclusions	+ mostly with no marked prosodic variation + sometimes with increased speech rate (neutral to assertive conclusion) + infrequently with high pitch, slow speed, low volume (tentative conclusion) + often with *so* or *but*	~ usually (near-)turn-finally after extended validation sequences	(17)
	– marks onsets of opinion sequences after turn-initial hesitation, or elaborations after turn-initial minimally coherent responses	+ usually with neutral prosody + sometimes produced with increased speed (meaning of un/certainty is bleached) + sometimes with reduced tempo and variation in pitch (tentative explication)	~ mostly near-turn-initially ~ after *yes/no* or hesitation ~ points backwards and forwards	(18)
	– marks shifts in the topical development of interactions	+ mostly falling but also level intonation + not usually accompanied by variation in prosodic marking	~ turn-medially when providing additional unsolicited information ~ very occasionally turn-initially after taking the floor and providing new, unsolicited information	(19)
	– structures longer opinion sequences	+ mostly neutral to assertive tone + sometimes bleached of epistemic content + mostly with *I think* in extended turns	~ any position	(20)

Appendix 5. Inventory of functions of NEG-TAGS in the BwE corpus

function	description	accompanying features	(turn-)position	example in Chapter 6
SUBJECTIVE USES				
# epistemic marker	– signals speakers' uncertainty vis-à-vis validity of preceding propositions – seeks verification of propositions from addressees – conducive	+ usually rising intonation and/or high pitch + often co-occurs with other expressions of epistemicity and/or signals of hesitancy in the anchor clause	~ turn-finally ~ followed by turn-exchange: addressees provide minimal or elaborate responses to verify previous speakers' propositions	(22) (23)
# attitudinal stance marker	– foregrounds and emphasises preceding propositions – signals speaker commitment – non-conducive	+ usually level intonation contour	~ turn-medially: followed by brief pause whilst addressee signals continued attention and interest, or amidst flow of rapid speech ~ turn-finally: generally followed by topic-change initiated by addressees	(24)
	– underlines obviousness of preceding statements – non-conducive	+ level or falling intonation + neutral tone	~ usually turn-finally at the end of longer topic sequences ~ generally followed by topic-shifts	(25)
INTERSUBJECTIVE USES				
# mitigation device	– mitigates face-threat of dismissals, disagreements and ironic/sarcastic remarks – conducive and non-conducive	+ rising or falling intonation	~ usually turn-finally ~ usually followed by turn-exchange and further elaboration of topic	(26)

function	description	accompanying features	(turn-)position	example in Chapter 6
# involvement inducer	– draws listeners into discourse – seeks corroboration of propositions – secures addressees' involvement in discourse – conducive	+ falling intonation	~ turn-medially followed by brief pause to allow room for minimal agreement tokens ~ turn-finally to yield the floor to interlocutors	(27)
# alignment signal	– signals alignment with previous speakers and involvement in interaction – non-conducive	+ rising tone to signal enthusiasm + level and falling intonation to signal confidence and emphasis	~ usually turn-finally ~ generally not followed by further talk to allow interlocutors to continue	(28) (29)

Index